Henry Morley

Ireland Under Elizabeth and James the First
Described by Edmund Spenser

ISBN/EAN: 9783337322342

Printed in Europe, USA, Canada, Australia, Japan

Cover: Foto ©ninafisch / pixelio.de

More available books at **www.hansebooks.com**

IRELAND
UNDER ELIZABETH AND JAMES I.

CONTENTS.

	PAGES
INTRODUCTION	1–32
A VIEW OF THE STATE OF IRELAND: WRITTEN DIALOGUE-WISE BETWEEN EUDOXUS AND IRENEUS. By EDMUND SPENSER. MDXCVII. . . .	33–212
A DISCOVERY OF THE TRUE CAUSES WHY IRELAND WAS NEVER ENTIRELY SUBDUED NOR BROUGHT UNDER OBEDIENCE OF THE CROWN OF ENGLAND UNTIL THE BEGINNING OF HIS MAJESTY'S HAPPY REIGN. BY SIR JOHN DAVIES, His Majesty's Attorney-General for Ireland. MDCXII. . .	213–342
A LETTER FROM SIR JOHN DAVIES, KNIGHT, ATTORNEY-GENERAL OF IRELAND, TO ROBERT EARL OF SALISBURY, TOUCHING THE STATE OF MONAGHAN, FERMANAGH, AND CAVAN, wherein is a Discourse concerning the Corbes and Irenahs of Ireland. MDCVII.	343–380
PLANTATION OF ULSTER: A LETTER FROM SIR JOHN DAVIES CONCERNING THE STATE OF IRELAND. MDCX.	381–390
THE IRISH PARLIAMENT: SIR JOHN DAVIES'S SPEECH TO THE LORD DEPUTY OF IRELAND when he approved of him as Speaker of the Commons. MDCXIII.	391–409

CONTENTS.

PAGES

A DESCRIPTION OF IRELAND by FYNES MORYSON,
Secretary to the Lord Mountjoy, Lord Deputy.
MDXCIX to MDCIII. 411–430

APPENDIX—

The Geraldines 431–435
The O'Neills 436–440
Lord Mountjoy, from Fynes Moryson's " History of
England from 1599 to 1603" . . . 441–445

INTRODUCTION.

IRELAND under Elizabeth and James will be found in this volume not only described in words of contemporaries, but in great measure accounted for by them. A reader chiefly interested in the sequence and significance of those events in history which best illustrate the relations between England and Ireland down to the time of the Plantation of Ulster, might find it convenient not to begin with Spenser's View of the State of Ireland. Taking first, from the end of this collection, Fynes Moryson's Description of the country and the people as they were regarded by the English gentlemen who went to Ireland and served the Lord Deputy, in the last years of Elizabeth's reign, the reader would obtain in small compass a matter-of-fact view of the state of Ireland as then seen with English eyes. Spenser, long resident in Ireland, was a sage and serious poet, who, when he wrote on the condition of the country, sought, in his own way, to get at the heart of a great question.

Sir John Davies, poet also, was a lawyer and a statesman, for whom the present grew out of the past, and who sought light from experience of the past for action in the present.

Fynes Moryson was a gentleman who remembered the built pastry and the daintinesses of a polite English table, who resented ill-cooked meat, did not regard bad butter as a trifle, chronicled ill-swept lodgings, dirty beds, was one of those for whom especially soap and starch were carried to the field of battle, and delights to tell how the poor Irish, having captured such a store, mistook the soap and starch for delicacies of the dinner-table, fell to them greedily, and cursed English daintiness between the teeth in which the soap was sticking. Spenser does not report for us this chatter of the day. He tells that he saw at Limerick, when Murrough O'Brian was executed there, how "an old woman, which was his fostermother, took up his head whilst he was quartered, and sucked up all the blood running thereout, saying that the earth was not worthy to drink it, and therewith also steeped her face and breast, and tore her hair, crying and shrieking out most terribly." He tells what he saw of the starvation of the Irish "in those late wars in Munster," so that "any stony heart would have rued the same. Out of every corner of the wood and glens they came creeping forth upon their hands, for their legs could not bear them; they looked anatomies of death, they spake like ghosts crying out of their graves; they did eat of the carrions, happy when they could find them, yea, and one another soon after, insomuch as the very carcasses they spared not to scrape out of their graves; and if they found a plot of watercresses or shamrocks, there they flocked as to a feast for the time, yet not able long to continue therewithal; that in short space there were none almost left, and a most populous and plentiful country suddenly left void of man or beast." But the eye for small things, the ear for gossip in the English camp, which, near truth or far from it, was still the gossip of the hour, the troubled soul's desire for a clean sheet of nights, help to bring home to us a clearer knowledge of the time. The long sleeve of the Irishwoman's smock suggests to Spenser the fashion of the manche in Armoury, and sleeves of ladies worn by knights of old upon their arms; and on the uses of the Irish mantle Spenser has a memorable passage; but he does not tell like Fynes Moryson how in a poor house of clay, where there are no "feather beds or sheets," Irish and English-Irish "make a fire in the midst of the

INTRODUCTION.   13

room, and round about it they sleep upon the ground, without straw or other thing under them, lying all in a circle about the fire with their feet towards it. And their bodies being naked, they cover their heads and upper parts with their mantles, which they first make very wet, steeping them in water of purpose, for they find that when their bodies have once warmed the wet mantles, the smoke of them keeps their bodies in temperate heat all the night following."

Having crossed with Fynes Moryson into Ireland near the close of Elizabeth's reign, and read his general description of what he found there, if he wish to take the contents of this volume in historical order, the student might turn next to Sir John Davies, and follow his careful tracing of the causes of confusion from the time of Strongbow till the time of that great conflict at the close of the reign of Elizabeth. Then he might turn from Sir John Davies (on page 330 in this book), when Sir John has finished his political retrospect and is about to tell what was done by King James after the crushing of Tyrone's rebellion.

Spenser's "View," here interpolated, would add breadth and depth to the record of the great struggle under Elizabeth, and join to it a good man's endeavour to interpret its significance and show the way on to a happier future. Having read Spenser's argument, the student might return to Sir John Davies, where he writes, "Now I am come to the happy reign of my Most Gracious Lord and Master, King James," and follow his interpretation of King James's policy, supplemented by his letters. These describe from the scene of action the endeavours to work out a policy of peace in his account of the Visitations of Monaghan, Fermanagh, and Cavan by the Lord Deputy; of the Plantation of Ulster; and in his sketch of the history of Irish Parliaments up to the date of his being chosen Speaker of the Irish House of Commons on the 2nd of May 1613. There ends the story which this volume tells.

INTRODUCTION.

As the story is here told, one or two points come out very distinctly. Spenser advocates unpitying severity in the suppression of rebellion, and does not shut his eyes to what that means. His Ireneus, the peacemaker, says to his Eudoxus, "Where you think that good and sound laws might amend and reform things amiss there, you think surely amiss. For it is vain to prescribe laws where no man careth for the keeping of them, nor feareth the danger for breaking of them. But all the realm is first to be reformed, and laws afterwards to be made for keeping and continuing it in that reformed estate." "How then," Eudoxus asks, "do you think is the reformation thereof to begin, if not by laws and ordinances?" Says Ireneus, "Even by the sword." Thereby he hoped "to settle an eternal peace," which "must be brought in by a strong hand, and so continued until it grow into a steadfast course of government." The strong hand had prevailed. In Fynes Moryson's "History of Ireland from the Year 1599 to 1603," the book to which he appended the Description of Ireland which is here reprinted, we read of horrors seen by Sir Arthur Chichester, Sir Richard Moryson, and the other commanders of the forces sent against Brian MacArt, in their return homeward at the end of March 1603: "Three children (whereof the eldest was not above ten years old), all eating and gnawing with their teeth the entrails of their dead mother, upon whose flesh they had fed twenty days past, and having eaten all from the feet upward to the bare bones, roasting it continually by a slow fire, were now come to the eating of her said entrails in like sort roasted, yet not divided from the body, being as yet raw. Former mention hath been made in the Lord Deputy's letters of carcasses scattered in every place, dead of famine. And no doubt the famine was so great as the rebel soldiers taking all the common people had to feed upon."—[not to recall preceding notes of "the Army's cutting down the Rebels' corn for these last two years," and such record as Sir Henry

Dockwra's, "Then through the country, spoiling and burning such a quantity of corn and number of houses as I should hardly have believed so small a circuit of ground could have afforded, if I had not seen it"]—"the common sort of the rebels were driven to unspeakable extremities, beyond the record of most histories, that ever I did read in that kind, the ample relating whereof were an infinite task, yet will I not pass it over without adding a few instances. Capt. Trevor and many honest gentlemen lying in the Newry can witness, that some old women of those parts used to make a fire in the fields, and divers little children driving out the cattle in the cold mornings, and coming thither to warm them, were by them surprised, killed and eaten; which at last was discovered by a great girl breaking from them by strength of her body, and Capt. Trevor sending out soldiers to know the truth, they found the children's skulls and bones, and apprehended the old women, who were executed for the fact. The captains of Carrickfergus and the adjacent garrisons of the northern parts can witness, that upon the making of peace and receiving the rebels to mercy, it was a common practice among the common sort of them (I mean such as were not sword-men) to thrust long needles into the horses of our English troops, and they dying thereupon, to be ready to tear out one another's throat for a share of them. And no spectacle was more frequent in the ditches of towns, and especially in wasted countries, than to see multitudes of these poor people dead, with their mouths all coloured green by eating nettles, docks, and all things they could rend up above ground."

Tyrone made his submission to Queen Elizabeth at a time when it was not yet known in Ireland that she was dead; for she died on the 24th of March. A messenger from London brought the news as private information to Mountjoy, the Lord Deputy, at night on the 27th, and the information was kept secret. Tyrone made his submission formally on the 30th of March, and on the 5th of April came the public and official information of Elizabeth's death and the accession of King James the First.

Here Sir John Davies takes up the tale, holds that the cruelty of force has done its work, and that King James has in Ireland the one purpose before him of uniting England and Ireland by community of laws and interests and national goodwill. In his retrospect of the past causes of failure to attain this end, he finds, as Spenser and others did, one cause of failure in community of blood. From the days of Strongbow downward, English settled in Ireland had become more Irish than the Irish. They had added lands to lands by the strong hand; had thrown off allegiance to English law and fastened on the Brehon laws of which they could make profit for themselves; they intermarried with their neighbours, put their children to the breasts of Irish foster-mothers, changed English for Irish names, and became oppressors of the Irish people upon their estates by their exactions of coin and livery. English armies in Ireland had been usually too weak to enforce submission; or, if strong at any time, were too soon broken up. They were always ill-paid, and therefore ill-governed, whereby they added to the general confusion. The kings and the great lords of England seldom visited the neighbour land. "Touching the absence of our kings," said Sir John Davies, "three of them only since the Norman Conquest have made royal journies into this land, namely, King Henry the Second, King John, and King Richard the Second. And yet they no sooner arrived here but all the Irish (as if they had been but one man) submitted themselves, took oaths of fidelity, and gave pledges and hostages to continue loyal; and if any of those kings had continued here in person a competent time till they had settled both English and Irish in their several possessions, and had set the law in a due course throughout the kingdom, these times wherein we live had not gained the honour of the first conquest and reducing of Ireland." And Sir John Davies laid all stress upon the past neglect, which those times were to repair, of equal laws for the inhabitants of England and Ireland. English law had been current only in the English Pale. It had not even been accounted felony to slay a man of Irish blood. Even Sir Edward Poynings' Act, passed in the time of Henry the Seventh, whereby all statutes made in England were enacted, established, and made of force in Ireland, though wisely intended to be general for the whole kingdom, was not in force beyond the English Pale. "These good laws and provisions made by Sir Edward Poynings were like good lessons set for a lute that is broken and out of tune ; of which lessons little use can be made, till the lute be made fit to be played on."

Within the English Pale we have strong evidence from Spenser of the equal greed with which men preyed upon the government they served and on the people among whom they were planted. He asks in aid of reform, "that no offices should be sold by the Lord Deputy for money, nor no pardon nor no protections bought for reward, nor no beeves taken for captaincies of countries, nor no shares of bishoprics for nominating their bishops, nor no forfeitures nor dispensations with penal statutes given to their servants or friends, nor no selling of licences for exportation of prohibited wares, and specially corn and flesh, with many the like, which need some manner of restraint, or else very great trust in the honourable disposition of the Lord Deputy." Where the Lord Deputy himself misused his opportunities, what could be looked for from the captain, colonel, or man-at-arms? Richard Boyle, who was knighted at the beginning of King James's reign, was sworn in 1606 a privy councillor for the province of Munster, was created Lord Boyle, baron of Youghall, in 1616, and Earl of Cork in 1620. He tells us himself, that when he first landed at Dublin in June 1588, "all my wealth then was twenty-seven pounds three shillings in money, and two tokens which my mother had given me, viz., a diamond ring, which I have ever since and still do wear, and a bracelet of gold worth ten pounds; a taffety doublet cut with and upon taffety, a pair of black velvet breeches laced, a new Milan fustian suit laced and cut upon taffety, two cloaks, competent linen and necessaries, with my rapier and dagger." He had seven sons, of whom five survived him, and eight daughters, of whom seven married noblemen; and to each of his children he was able to leave, when he died, a fine estate in Ireland. But he died after the year 1613, and his name reminds us that we have in this volume no more than a chapter of the story which the generous sketch by Sir John Davies and his faith in James the First have made to look like a completed tale.

I will add only one more of the general impressions left after a reading of these records. There is recognition in each of the courage of the Irish. They depended much upon their cattle, and so especially upon food made from the milk of their cows, that extremes of famine would not drive them to the killing of a milch cow. In the horrible story of the killing and eating of children by old women in the fields, the children were in charge of cows whose daily milk made their lives precious. From oldest time there had been cattle plunder; it was in some sense the theme of a great cycle of ancient Irish poems, the *Tain Bo*, the Cattle Plunder of Chuailgne. But Fynes Moryson, when he tells of precautions against cattle plunder, adds note of "the Irish using almost no other kind of theft;" and Sir John Davies is found making special note of a fact that has been observed in our own day of the wildest seasons of political offence:—" I dare affirm," he says of the circuits of judges in Ireland upon the end of the war, "that for the space of five years last past there have not been found so many malefactors worthy of death in all the six circuits of this realm (which is now divided into thirty-two shires at large) as in one circuit of six shires, namely, the western circuit, in England. For the truth is," he adds, "that in time of peace the Irish are more fearful to offend the law than the English, or any other nation whatsoever."

Let us turn now to the writers of these sketches.

EDMUND SPENSER, one of the four greatest English poets,—for he is to be named with Milton, as Chaucer with Shakespeare,—was born in East Smithfield, London, about the year 1552, son probably of a John Spenser who was a clothmaker, and whose family connections were about Hurstwood and Pendle, in the hill country of North-East Lancashire. Born, as he says, in—

> "Merry London, my most kindly nurse,
> That to me gave this life's first native source,
> Though from another place I take my name,
> A house of ancient fame,"

Spenser was sent to Merchant Taylors' School immediately, or almost immediately, after its foundation in 1561, with Dr. Mulcaster for its head-master. Spenser was at school there in 1568; and in the next year, when he was leaving for Cambridge, he contributed translations of Visions from Petrarch and from Bellay to a miscellany by John van der Noodt, a Flemish physician, who had taken refuge in England from the persecutions of the Duke of Alva. Such work in such fellowship show Spenser's strong religious feeling when, as a youth of about seventeen, he was on his way from school to College. The miscellany was called "A Theatre, wherein be represented as well the Miseries and Calamities that follow the Voluptuous Worldlings, as also the great Joys and Pleasures which the Faithful do enjoy. An Argument both Profitable and Delectable to all that sincerely love the Word of God."

Spenser went to Cambridge, and there matriculated as a sizar at Pembroke Hall on the 20th of May 1569. Having graduated as B.A. in 1573, and as M.A. in 1576, he left Cambridge, after

INTRODUCTION.

seven years' study, aged about twenty-four, and went home into Lancashire, where he perhaps earned for a short time as a tutor, and fell in love with the daughter of a "widow of the glen," the Rosalind of early verses, who did not favour his suit. It does not at all matter who she was; Spenser's real love went to the wife he found years afterwards in Ireland.

Gabriel Harvey, a good Cambridge friend of Spenser's, whom the Earl of Leicester sometimes employed on missions, and who was to have been sent abroad in 1577, had ambitions of his own at Cambridge—he was aiming at the post of Public Orator—and did not go; but he brought his friend Spenser from the north into the service of Leicester, and Spenser seems to have been sent to Ireland on some mission in the days when Sir Henry Sidney was Lord Deputy. For Spenser twice says that he saw the incident of the old foster-mother's drinking of the blood from the head of Murrough O'Brian at his execution; and that execution took place in the first week of July 1577, when Spenser's age was about five-and-twenty.

In 1579 Spenser published his first volume of poems, *The Shepheards Calendar*, to which he did not set his name. Its various music represented love and loyalty, and above all, his strong interest in the religious questions of the day. He drew some inspiration from the French pastorals of Clement Marot, which figured good and bad pastors of congregations in the Church, under the good and bad pastors of flocks in the field. With all his loyalty to Elizabeth, Spenser boldly took his stand by Archbishop Grindal, who was in disgrace with her for opening the door to diversities of doctrine, by his strenuous encouragement of preaching based on independent searching of the Scriptures.

In 1580, on the 12th of July, Arthur Lord Grey of Wilton landed in Dublin as Lord Deputy, having brought with him Edmund Spenser as his Secretary. On the 12th of September following, a merchant of Dingle, Garrat Trante, wrote information "that there came a Sunday last past over, foure shippes of the Pope's army, in which the Pope's nuncio is. There was in their company other foure shippes and a galley, which they suppose will be with them or it be long."

On the next day, the 13th of September, Captain Andrew Marten wrote to Sir Warham St. Leger, Lord President of Munster, how he had that day heard from the Knight of Kerry that there were "four sail of Spaniards landed at Smerwick, also that a great fleet is to descend on the west." The landing in Smerwick Bay was at a fort called "del Ore," which had been used before as a point of foreign support for the conflict against England. On the 7th of November, Admiral Winter and Lord Grey, with Spenser as his secretary, arrived at the fort with a besieging force, and landed their artillery. On the 9th the besieged craved a parley. What followed was thus told in the despatch written on the 12th of November by Lord Grey himself to the Queen:—

"Presently was sent one Alexandro, the camp master, who said that they were there on false speeches and great promises. I said I found two nations, and willed a Spanish captain to be by, who came. I said I marvelled, their nation at peace with your Majesty, they should come. The Spaniard said the King had not sent them, but one John Martines di Ricaldi, Governor for the King at Bilboa. The other avouched that they were all sent by the Pope for the defence of the *Catholica Fide*. I answered, I marvelled that men of that account as some of them made show of, should be carried into unjust, wicked, and desperate action by one that neither from God or man could claim any princely power or empire, but indeed a desperate shaveling, the right Antichrist, and general ambitious tyrant over all right principalities, and patron of the *diabolico fide*, I could not rest but greatly wonder. Their fault, therefore, I saw to be greatly aggravated by the malice of their commander, and at my hands no condition, no composition, were they to expect, other than they should simply render me the fort, and yield themselves to my will for life or death: with this answer they departed. There were but one or two that came to and fro to have gotten a certainty for some of their lives, but finding that it would not be, the Colonel came forth to ask respite; but finding it a gaining time, I would not grant it.

"He then embraced my knees, simply putting himself to my mercy; only he prayed that for that night he might abide in the fort. I asked hostages, and they were given.

"Morning came: I presented my forces in battle before the fort: the Colonel came with ten or eleven of his chief gentlemen, trailing their ensigns rolled up, and presented them to me, with their lives and the fort. I sent straight certain gentlemen in to see their weapons and armours laid down, and to guard the munition and victual then left from spoil. Then I put in certain bands, who straight fell to execution. There were six hundred slain; ammunition and victual great store, though much wasted through the disorder of the soldiers, which in the fusion could not be helped."

One of the two captains of the day sent in to carry out this order of execution was Walter Raleigh, then, like Spenser, about twenty-six years old. Twenty of the chief men were spared, chiefly for the prize money to be got by their ransom; but two of them, one Plunkett, a friar born near Drogheda, and an Englishman who was chief man to Dr. Sanders, the Pope's nuncio allied with Spain, were saved only for a more cruel death. They had their arms and legs broken before they were hanged on a gibbet on the walls of the fort, as traitors to their country.

With this policy Edmund Spenser was in full accord. He justifies it in his "View of the State of Ireland," and justifies Lord Grey against those in England who saw cruelty in an uncompromising zeal which complained to the authorities at home of the pernicious practice of granting pardons to the rebels, "whereby the soldiers were letted from the destruction of their corn." The recall Grey had often asked for came in 1582, and he left Ireland on the 31st of August in that year. Spenser's justification of him will be found in this volume, on pages 145–148. If war be necessary, it must be sharp to be short; relentings in its course can only make it a long misery. That was his view. For the effectual and lasting triumph over wrong, and prompt establishment of right, he thought it mercy to be merciless. Sweet as its music is, the same austerity runs through Spenser's "Faerie Queene," in which also he is one with his patron Arthur, Lord Grey of Wilton, in looking on Catholicism as the diabolical faith.

Spenser had begun his "Faerie Queene" before he went to Ireland with Lord Grey, who was his best friend and patron there. On the 22nd of March 1581 Spenser obtained, by purchase from his friend Lodowick Bryskett, the office of Clerk of Decrees and Recognizances in the Court of Chancery, or Registrar of Chancery for the Faculties. In the same year he received a lease of the Abbey and Castle and Manor of Enniscorthy, in the County of Wexford, which he sold to a Richard Synot, who sold it again to Sir Henry Wallop. He then bought, and sold again at profit, another Abbey in New Ross. In January 1582 Lord Grey thus included Edmund Spenser in a list of persons to whom he had given benefit from forfeited estates: "The lease of a house in Dublin belonging to Baltinglas, for six years to come unto Edmund Spenser, one of the Lord Deputy's Secretaries, valued at £5; and of a custodian of John Eustace's land of the Newland to Edmund Spenser, one of the Lord Deputy's Secretaries." Later in 1582, on the 24th of August, letters patent were passed to Spenser of the dissolved Franciscan house of New Abbey in Kildare, with its possession for twenty-one years at a rent of sixty shillings. This lease became forfeited seven or eight years later because no rent had been paid. Also in the year 1582 Spenser received £162 for "rewards"—secret service money—paid by him as Secretary. On the 22nd of June 1588, about the time when his six years' lease of Lord Baltinglasse's house in Dublin would expire, Spenser resigned his office of Clerk or Registrar in Chancery, and he probably removed then to Kilcolman. On the 27th of June 1586, he had been set down as an "undertaker" for the occupation of 3028 acres, and in 1589 he reported that he had so far satisfied the conditions upon which, as undertaker, he received the land, as to have six English householders settled under him. He had obtained also in 1588, by purchase again from his friend Lodowick Bryskett, the succession to the office of Clerk of the Government Council of Munster. This would give him business in Cork, while living at his castle of Kilcolman, about three miles from Doneraile. He had a sister, Sarah, who seems to have kept house for him before her marriage with a Lancashire man settled in Ireland.

Sir Walter Raleigh, who had large grants of land in Ireland, was resident in 1589 at Youghal, visited Spenser, heard him read what he had written of the "Faerie Queene," persuaded the poet to be his companion to London, and introduced him to Elizabeth. Thus the first three books of the "Faerie Queene" were published in 1590. He was rewarded by Elizabeth with a pension of £50; and it is to be remembered that a pound in Elizabeth's time had about ten times its present buying power. Spenser published also many of his minor poems as "Complaints of the World's Vanity," which were entered at Stationer's Hall on the 29th of December 1590. In 1591 he was back at Kilcolman, where he wrote a poetical account of his visit to Court, under the title "Colin Clout's Come Home Again."

Then there were Sonnets addressed to a lady whom Spenser made his wife on Barnabas Day, 1594, and for whom he wrote the finest Marriage-song in all our literature. The Rev. Dr.

INTRODUCTION. 25

Grosart has made it appear most probable that Spenser's wife was an Elizabeth Boyle who lived at Kilcoran, that looks out upon the Bay of Youghal, and who was a kinswoman of Richard Boyle, afterwards Earl of Cork, then only at the beginning of his prosperous career. It was in the following year, 1595, that Richard Boyle married at Limerick his first wife, Joan Ansley, who died in 1599, and left him an estate of £500 a year in lands.

Spenser's marriage, on the 11th of June 1594, was followed by the birth of a child in each of the four succeeding years. The names of the children were Sylvanus, Lawrence, Peregrine, and Catherine. His "Amoretti" and "Epithalamium" were sent to London and published in 1595. At the close of that year he went to London with the MS. of three more books of the "Faerie Queene." These were published as a second part of the poem in 1596. Among other pieces published in this latter time were the four "Hymns to Earthly and Heavenly Love and Beauty." It was at this time that Spenser wrote that "View of the State of Ireland" which is the first piece in the present volume. The publication of it in Spenser's lifetime was stayed by the course of events; but he had meant to publish it, and in the books of the Stationers' Company it was entered on the 13th of April 1598 for publication by Matthew Lownes "upon condicion that hee gett further aucthoritie before yt be prynted." It was not printed until 1633, when it was published at Dublin by Sir James Ware.

In 1597 Spenser had returned to his wife and three little ones, of three, two, and one year old, at Kilcolman. In the next year, 1598, the fourth child was born; and on the 30th of September 1598 Spenser was appointed Sheriff of Cork by the Queen's letters, which described him as "a gentleman dwelling in the County of Cork, who is so well known unto you all for his good and commendable parts, being a man endowed with good knowledge in learning, and not unskilful or without experience in the wars."

Spenser had not been Sheriff of Cork for a month when all Munster had risen at the call of Tyrone. Fire was set to Kilcolman Castle, and Spenser fled with his family to Cork. There was tradition—only tradition—that a fifth child, an infant, perished in the flames. On the 9th of December 1598, Sir Thomas Norreys, President of Munster, wrote a despatch containing details of the rising, and in another, written on the 21st of the same month, he said that his despatch of the 9th had been "sent by Mr. Spenser." It reached Whitehall on the 24th of December; and Spenser, who had written a paper of his own upon the state of Munster, and the need of a strong force to quell rebellion, died within the next four weeks. John Chamberlain, writing on Sunday, January 17, 1599 (new style), a letter to Sir Dudley Carleton, said in it—"Lady Cope is dead, and Spenser the Poet, who lately came from Ireland, died at Westminster last Saturday."

SIR JOHN DAVIES was of a Welsh family, of which one member came to England with Sir William Herbert, who was created Earl of Pembroke by Edward the Sixth, and settling near the Earl at Wilton, established a Wiltshire branch, of which came John Davies of Chisgrove, in the parish of Tisbury, father of Sir John. John Davies of Tisbury had been of New Inn. He practised law in Wiltshire, throve, and died when his three boys were young. John, the eldest of the three, was born in April 1569—that is to say, he was sixteen or seventeen years younger than Edmund Spenser. His mother—who before her marriage had been Mary Bennett, daughter of John Bennett, of Pitt House, Wiltshire,—took charge of the education of her boys, sent John to Winchester, and thence to Oxford, where he matriculated at Queen's College in October 1585. In February 1588 (new style) John Davies

INTRODUCTION.

was admitted a member of the Middle Temple. In 1590 he took at Oxford his B.A. degree. In 1594 he had already written an ingenious poem that has wisdom in its wit, "Orchestra, or a Poem of Dancing."

"Dancing, bright lady, then began to be
  When the first seeds whereof the world did spring,—
  The Fire, Air, Earth, and Water,—did agree
  By Love's persuasion, Nature's mighty king,
  To leave their first disordered combating,
    And in a Dance such measures to observe
    As all the World their motion should preserve."

The poem was left unfinished, but the hundred and thirty-one stanzas, which were first printed in 1596, a year after Davies had been called to the Bar, he wrote in fifteen days, while the humour of it lasted. In 1596 "Orchestra" was dedicated to a witty friend who was also of the Middle Temple, Richard Martin; but in February 1597 Davies was disbarred for breaking a cudgel over his friend Martin's head while dining in hall at the barristers' table. Expelled from the Middle Temple, Davies went back to Oxford as a sojourner, and, called by adversity to reckon up his wasted time, wrote his best poem, "Know Thyself, *Nosce Teipsum.*"

"If aught can teach us aught, Affliction's looks—
  Making us pry into ourselves so near—
  Teach us to know ourselves beyond all books,
  Or all the learned schools that ever were.

This mistress lately plucked me by the ear,
  And many a golden lesson hath me taught;
  Hath made my senses quick, and reason clear,
  Reformed my will and rectified my thought."

The poem reasoned faith in the immortal part within a man, and thenceforth John Davies weighed his life by a new scale. "*Nosce Teipsum*" was published in 1599, the year of Spenser's death, and dedicated to Queen Elizabeth at the suggestion of Charles Blount,

28 INTRODUCTION.

Lord Mountjoy, then Lord-Deputy in Ireland. Queen Elizabeth liked his poem, and had him sworn her servant-in-ordinary. In November 1601 he was readmitted to the Middle Temple, and returned to Parliament as member for Corfe Castle. In 1602 he wrote "A Contention betwixt a Wife, a Widow, and a Maid," which was presented before Queen Elizabeth at Sir Robert Cecil's house in the Strand. After the Queen's death, in March 1603, Lord Hunsdon took John Davies northward to King James, who asked him whether he was "*Nosce Teipsum;*" and when he said he was, embraced him graciously, and took him into favour. In September 1603 James the First wrote to the Lord-Deputy Mountjoy that Davies should have the office, which Mountjoy had asked for him, of Solicitor-General for Ireland. He reached Dublin in November. At once he began to write to Cecil a series of most valuable letters upon the condition of the country and the remedies he wished to see applied. On the 29th of May 1606 John Davies succeeded Sir Charles Calthorpe as Attorney-General for Ireland; directly afterwards he was made Sergeant-at-Law—at the same time with Sir Edward Coke—and knighted on the 11th of February 1607. His services were continuous. His letters of information and counsel were most welcome to Robert Cecil, who, in May 1605, had been created Earl of Salisbury, and whose confidence in John Davies was great. In March 1608 Sir John Davies married Eleanor Touchet, third daughter of George, Baron Audley; and in the same year he was sent to England with the Chief-Justice of Ireland to represent to King James the good effects of measures taken for the establishment, by equal laws, of peace and order. The Earl of Salisbury and Lord Chancellor Ellesmere, his two best friends in England, received him with new kindness, and took counsel with him upon those measures which were to be carried out for the plantation of Ulster. The manner of carrying them out he reported to Lord Salisbury in a letter written in 1610, which will be found in the

INTRODUCTION.

present volume. In 1612 Sir John Davies published, with a dedication to the King, his "Discovery of the True Causes why Ireland was never entirely subdued till the beginning of His Majesty's Reign," a masterpiece in English political literature, which here follows Spenser's "View of the State of Ireland."

In June 1612 Sir John Davies was appointed the King's Serjeant, and when, after seven-and-twenty years without the calling of an Irish Parliament, a Parliament at last was called, Sir John Davies was returned, in the same year 1612, as the first member who ever sat for Fermanagh. When the Parliament met there were returned to it 121 of the Protestant party and 101 of the Catholic, and there was hot conflict over the election of a Speaker. The nominee of the Crown was Sir John Davies. The Roman Catholics supported Sir John Everard, who had been an Irish judge, but resigned because he could not take the oath of supremacy. The result was a disputed election and political deadlock. The Lord-Deputy prorogued Parliament. The disputed question was argued in London. Bacon told King James that it was always safe to keep in the middle way between extremes. The King used his influence, and when the Parliament in Dublin met again in May 1613, Sir John Davies, as Speaker, delivered the speech that will be found in this volume, setting forth the early history of Parliamentary government in Ireland. That Parliament, after its stormy opening, did much good work before its dissolution in October 1615.

Sir John Davies returned to London in 1616; was active in the revival of the Society of Antiquaries; entered the English Parliament in 1620 as member for Newcastle-under-Lyne; and when he was known to be on the way to the office of Chief-Justice of England, he died of apoplexy, on the 7th of December 1626, the year of the death of his friend, Francis Bacon. He had only one son, an idiot, who was drowned in Ireland, and one daughter, who married the sixth Earl of Huntingdon.

INTRODUCTION.

FYNES MORYSON, born in Lincolnshire in 1566, obtained a fellowship at Cambridge and studied Civil Law. His fellowship was at Peterhouse, where they gave him in 1589 leave of absence for travel until July 1600. In 1600, after ten years of foreign travel, he went to Ireland. His brother, Sir Richard Moryson, Vice-President of Munster, who was very intimate with Lord Mountjoy, had obtained for Fynes the promise of appointment as his secretary; but this was not applied for until three secretaries had been already appointed. Fynes Moryson was invited by Lord Mountjoy to proceed to Ireland nevertheless, and something should be found for him. He resigned his fellowship at Peterhouse, of which the income (£20) was continued to him for the next two years. Mountjoy's chief secretary, George Cranmer, was killed in the fight at Carlingford. Fynes Moryson was then put in his place. Fynes Moryson died about three years before the appearance, in 1617, of the "Itinerary of his Travels," which he wrote first in Latin, and afterwards himself translated into English.

THE OPENING OF SIR JOHN DAVIES'S
"NOSCE TEIPSUM."

THE lights of heaven (which are the world's fair eyes)
  Look down into the world, the world to see,
And as they turn, or wander in the skies,
  Survey all things that on the centre be.

And yet the lights which in my tower do shine,
  Mine eyes, which view all objects nigh and far,
Look not into this little world of mine,
  Nor see my face, wherein they fixéd are.

Since Nature fails us in no needful thing,
  Why want I means my inward self to see?
Which sight the knowledge of myself might bring,
  Which to true wisdom is the first degree.

That Power which gave me eyes the world to view,
  To view myself infus'd an inward light,
Whereby my soul, as by a mirror true,
  Of her own form may take a perfect sight.

But as the sharpest eye discerneth nought,
  Except the sunbeams in the air do shine;
So the best soul, with her reflecting thought,
  Sees not herself, without some light divine.

O Light which mak'st the light which makes the day,
    Which sett'st the eye without and mind within,
Lighten my spirit with one clear heavenly ray,
    Which now to view itself doth first begin.

For her true form, how can my spark discern,
    Which, dim by nature, art did never clear;
When the great wits, from whom all skill we learn,
    Are ignorant both what she is, and where?

One thinks the soul is air, another fire,
    Another blood diffused about the heart,
Another saith, the elements conspire
    And to her essence each doth give a part.

Musicians think our souls are harmonies;
    Physicians hold that they complexions be;
Epicures make them swarms of atomies,
    Which do by chance into our bodies flee.

Some think one general soul fills ev'ry brain,
    As the bright sun sheds light in ev'ry star;
And others think the name of soul is vain,
    And that we only well-mixed bodies are.

In judgment of her substance thus they vary,
    And vary thus in judgment of her seat;
For some her chair up to the brain do carry,
    Some sink it down into the stomach's heat.

Some place it in the root of life, the heart;
    Some in the liver, fountain of the veins;
Some say she's all in all, and all in ev'ry part;
    Some say she's not contained, but all contains.

A VIEW

OF

THE STATE OF IRELAND.

WRITTEN DIALOGUE-WISE BETWEEN
EUDOXUS AND IRENEUS.

MDXCV.

A VIEW

OF

THE STATE OF IRELAND.

Eudox. But if that country of Ireland, whence you lately came, be of so goodly and commodious a soil, as you report, I wonder that no course is taken for the turning thereof to good uses, and reducing that nation to better government and civility.

Iren. Marry, so there have been divers good plots devised, and wise counsels cast already about reformation of that realm; but they say it is the fatal destiny of that land, that no purposes whatsoever which are meant for her good will prosper or take good effect; which, whether it proceed from the very genius of the soil, or influence of the stars, or that Almighty God hath not yet appointed the time of her reformation, or that He reserveth her in this unquiet state still for some secret scourge, which shall by her come unto England, it is hard to be known, but yet much to be feared.

Eudox. Surely I suppose this but a vain conceit of simple men, which judge things by their effects, and not by their causes; for I would rather think the cause of this evil, which hangeth upon that country, to proceed rather of the unsoundness of the counsels and plots[1] which you say have been oftentimes laid for

---

[1] *Plots,* ground-plans. Not in a bad sense, from the French *complot,* but from English plot or plat, as in grass-plots or political platforms.

the reformation, or of faintness in following and effecting the same, than of any such fatal course appointed of God, as you misdeem: but it is the manner of men, that when they are fallen into any absurdity, or their actions succeed not as they would, they are always ready to impute the blame thereof unto the heavens, so to excuse their own follies and imperfections. So have I heard it often wished also, even of some whose great wisdoms in opinion should seem to judge more soundly of so weighty a consideration, that all that land were a sea-pool: which kind of speech is the manner rather of desperate men far driven, to wish the utter ruin of that which they cannot redress, than of grave counsellors, which ought to think nothing so hard but that through wisdom it may be mastered and subdued; since the poet saith that "the wise man shall rule over the stars," much more over the earth: for were it not the part of a desperate physician to wish his diseased patient dead, rather than to apply the best endeavour of his skill for his recovery? But since we are so far entered, let us, I pray you, a little devise of those evils by which that country is held in this wretched case, that it cannot, as you say, be recured.[1] And if it be not painful to you, tell us what things, during your late continuance there, you observed to be most offensive, and greatest impeachment[2] to the good rule and government thereof.

Iren. Surely, Eudoxus, the evils which you desire to be recounted are very many, and almost countable with those which were hidden in the basket of Pandora. But since you please, I will, out of that infinite number, reckon but some that are most capital, and commonly occurrent both in the life and conditions of private men, as also in the managing of public affairs and policy; the which you shall understand to be of divers natures, as I observed them. For some of them are of great antiquity and continuance; others more late and of less endurance; others daily

---

[1] *Recured*, recovered.   [2] *Impeachment*, French *empêchement*, hindrance.

growing and increasing continually by their evil occasions, which are every day offered.

Eudox. Tell me then, I pray you, in the same order that you have now rehearsed them; for there can be no better method than this which the very matter itself offereth. And when you have reckoned all the evils, let us hear your opinion for the redressing of them. After which, there will perhaps of itself appear some reasonable way to settle a sound and perfect rule of government, by shunning the former evils, and following the offered good. The which method we may learn of the wise physicians, which first require that the malady be known thoroughly, and discovered; afterwards to reach how to cure and redress it; and lastly, do prescribe a diet, with straight[1] rule and orders to be daily observed, for fear of relapse into the former disease, or falling into some other more dangerous than it.

Iren. I will then, according to your advisement, begin to declare the evils which seem to me most hurtful to the common weal of that land; and first those, I say, which were most ancient and long grown; and they also are of three sorts: the first in the laws, the second in customs, and the last in religion.

Eudox. Why, Ireneus, can there be any evil in the laws? Can things which are ordained for the good and safety of all turn to the evil and hurt of them? This well I wot both in that state and in all other, that were they not contained in duty with fear of law, which restraineth offences and inflicteth sharp punishment to misdoers, no man should enjoy anything; every man's hand would be against another. Therefore, in finding fault with the laws, I doubt me you shall much overshoot yourself, and make me the more dislike your other dislikes of that government.

Iren. The laws, Eudoxus, I do not blame for themselves, knowing right well that all laws are ordained for the good of the common weal, and for repressing of licentiousness and vice; but

[1] *Straight*, strict.

it falleth out in laws, no otherwise than it doth in physic,—which was at first devised, and is yet daily meant, and ministered for the health of the patient, but nevertheless we often see that, either through ignorance of the disease, or through unseasonableness of the time, or other accidents coming between, instead of good, it worketh hurt, and out of one evil throweth the patient into many miseries. So the laws were at first intended for the reformation of abuses and peaceable continuance of the subject, but are sithence [1] either disannulled or quite prevaricated [2] through change and alteration of times; yet are they good still in themselves, but in that commonwealth which is ruled by them they work not that good which they should, and sometimes also that evil which they would not.

Eudox. Whether do you mean this by the Common Laws of that realm, or by the Statute Laws and Acts of Parliament?

Iren. Surely by them both; for even the Common Law being that which William of Normandy brought in with his Conquest and laid upon the neck of England, though perhaps it fitted well with the state of England then being, and was readily obeyed through the power of the commander, which had before subdued the people unto him and made easy way to the settling of his will; yet with the state of Ireland, peradventure, it doth not so well agree, being a people very stubborn and untamed,—or if it were ever tamed, yet now lately having quite shaken off their yoke and broken the bonds of their obedience. For England before the entrance of the Conqueror was a peaceable kingdom, and but lately inured to the mild and goodly government of Edward surnamed the Confessor; besides now lately grown into a loathing and detestation of the unjust and tyrannous rule of Harold, an usurper, which made them the more willing to accept of any reasonable conditions and order of the new victor, thinking surely that it could be no worse than the latter, and hoping well it

[1] *Sithence*, since.   [2] *Prevaricated*, bent and stretched.

would be as good as the former. Yet what the proof of first bringing in and establishing of those laws was, was to many full bitterly made known. But with Ireland it is far otherwise; for it is a nation ever acquainted with wars, though but amongst themselves, and in their own kind of military discipline trained up ever from their youths; which they have never yet been taught to lay aside, nor made to learn obedience unto laws, scarcely to know the name of law, but instead thereof have always preserved and kept their own law, which is the Brehon law.

Eudox. What is that which you call the Brehon law? It is a word unto us altogether unknown.

Iren. It is a rule of right unwritten, but delivered by tradition from one to another, in which oftentimes there appeareth great show of equity, in determining the right between party and party, but in many things repugning quite both to God's law and man's; as, for example, in the case of murder, the Brehon—that is, their judge—will compound between the murderer and the friends of the party murdered, which prosecute the action, that the malefactor shall give unto them, or to the child or wife of him that is slain, a recompense, which they call an eriach. By which vile law of theirs many murders amongst them are made up and smothered. And this judge being (as he is called) the lord's Brehon, adjudgeth for the most part a better share unto his lord—that is, the lord of the soil or the head of that sept— and also unto himself for his judgment a greater portion, than unto the plaintiffs or parties aggrieved.[1]

[1] *The Brehon Law.*—Spenser was wrong in thinking that the Brehon Laws were not committed to writing. They were so called from a late English corruption of the Irish name for the old hereditary judges, "Broitheamhuin," pronounced brei-hoo-in, brehon. Traditions of St. Patrick say that the old laws were revised by him at the command of King Laeghaire for the omission of everything inconsistent with Christianity. No MS. now known is older than the end of the thirteenth century, but there are quotations made from the collection in the Glossary of Cormac MacCullinan, made in the ninth century. There are collections of these Laws in MS. in the libraries of the Royal Irish Academy, Trinity College, Dublin, the British Museum, the Bodleian, and elsewhere, written in the

Eudox. This is a most wicked law indeed; but I trust it is not now used in Ireland, since the kings of England have had the absolute dominion thereof, and establish their own laws there.

Iren. Yes, truly; for there be many wide countries in Ireland which the laws of England were never established in, nor any acknowledgment of subjection made; and also even in those which are subdued and seem to acknowledge subjection, yet the same Brehon law is practised among themselves, by reason that, dwelling as they do, whole nations and septs of the Irish together, without any Englishman among them, they may do what they list, and compound or altogether conceal amongst themselves their own crimes, of which no notice can be had by them which would and might amend the same by the rule of the laws of England.

Eudox. What is this which you say? And is there any part of that realm or any nation therein which have not yet been subdued to the crown of England? Did not the whole realm universally accept and acknowledge our late Prince of famous memory, Henry VIII., for their only king and liege lord?

Iren. Yes, verily. In a Parliament held in the time of Sir Anthony Saint-Leger, then Lord-Deputy, all the Irish lords and principal men came in, and being by fair means wrought thereunto, acknowledged King Henry for their sovereign lord, reserving yet, as some say, unto themselves all their own former privileges and seigniories inviolate.[1]

fourteenth, fifteenth, and sixteenth centuries, and they contain records of old usages, like that of compensation for the taking of life, that belong to the early civilisation of both Teuton and Celt. The old collection was called the Sanchas Mor (pronounced Shanchus môr), the Great Law Compilation, and it was treasured by the people of Ireland in Spenser's time as the written code of their old National Law. A Royal Commission was appointed in 1852 to secure the accurate transcription and translation of the Brehon Laws, and four volumes have accordingly been published, the last in 1885, of Ancient Laws and Institutes of Ireland, giving the Irish text, with translations, dissertations, and indexes.

[1] It was in 1541 that Henry VIII. elevated Ireland from a lordship into a kingdom, gratifying at the same time the great Irish chiefs by giving them rank as earls. Ulliac de Burgh was made Earl of Clanricarde, Murrough O'Brien Earl of Thomond, O'Neill Earl of Tyrone.

Eudox. Then by that acceptance of his sovereignty they also accepted of his laws. Why then should any other laws be now used amongst them?

Iren. True it is that thereby they bound themselves to his laws and obedience, and in case it had been followed upon them, as it should have been, and a government thereupon settled among them agreeable thereunto, they should have been reduced to perpetual civility and contained in continual duty. But what boots it to break a colt and to let him straight run loose at random? So were these people at first well handled, and wisely brought to acknowledge allegiance to the kings of England. But being straight left unto themselves and their own inordinate life and manners, they eftsoons forgot what before they were taught, and so soon as they were out of sight, by themselves shook off their bridles and began to colt anew, more licentiously than before.

Eudox. It is a great pity that so good an opportunity was omitted, and so happy an occasion fore-slacked, that might have been the eternal good of the land. But do they not still acknowledge that submission?

Iren. No, they do not; for now the heirs and posterity of them which yielded the same are, as they say, either ignorant thereof, or do wilfully deny or steadfastly disavow it.

Eudox. How can they so do justly? Doth not the act of the parent, in any lawful grant or conveyance, bind their heirs for ever thereunto? Sith then the ancestors of those that now live yielded themselves then subjects and liegemen, shall it not tie their children to the same subjection?

Iren. They say no; for their ancestors had no estate in any their lands, seigniories, or hereditaments longer than during their own lives, as they allege; for all the Irish do hold their land by tanistry, which is, say they, no more but a personal estate for his lifetime—that is, tanist—by reason that he is admitted thereunto by election of the country.

Eudox. What is this which you call Tanist and Tanistry? They be names and terms never heard of nor known to us.

Iren. It is a custom amongst all the Irish, that presently after the death of any of their chief lords or captains they do presently assemble themselves to a place generally appointed and known unto them to choose another in his stead, where they do nominate and elect for the most part, not the eldest son, nor any of the children of the lord deceased, but the next to him of blood, that is the eldest and worthiest; as commonly the next brother unto him, if he have any, or the next cousin, or so forth, as any is elder in that kindred or sept: and then next to him do they choose the next of the blood to be tanist, who shall next succeed him in the said captainry, if he live thereunto.

Eudox. Do they not use any ceremony in this election? For all barbarous nations are commonly great observers of ceremonies and superstitious rites.

Iren. They used to place him that shall be their captain upon a stone always reserved for that purpose, and placed commonly upon a hill; in some of which I have seen formed and engraven a foot, which they say was the measure of their first captain's foot, whereon he, standing, received an oath to preserve all the ancient former customs of the country inviolable, and to deliver up the succession peaceably to his tanist; and then hath a wand delivered unto him by some whose proper office that is; after which, descending from the stone, he turneth himself round, thrice forward and thrice backward.

Eudox. But how is the tanist chosen?

Iren. They say he setteth but one foot upon the stone, and receiveth the like oath that the captain did.

Eudox. Have you ever heard what was the occasion and first beginning of this custom? For it is good to know the same, and may perhaps discover some secret meaning and intent therein very material to the state of that government.

VIEW OF THE STATE OF IRELAND. 43

Iren. I have heard that the beginning and cause of this ordinance amongst the Irish was specially for the defence and maintenance of their lands in their posterity, and for excluding all innovation or alienation thereof unto strangers, and specially to the English. For when their captain dieth, if the seigniory should descend to his child, and he perhaps an infant, another peradventure would step in between, or thrust him out by strong hand, being then unable to defend his right or to withstand the force of a foreigner; and therefore they do appoint the eldest of the kin to have the seigniory, for that he commonly is a man of stronger years and better experience to maintain the inheritance and to defend the country, either against the next bordering lords, which used commonly to encroach one upon another, as one is stronger, or against the English, which they think lie still in wait to wipe them out of their lands and territories. And to this end, the tanist is always ready known, if it should happen the captain suddenly to die or to be slain in battle, or to be out of the country, to defend and keep it from all such doubts and dangers. For which cause the tanist hath also a share of the country allotted unto him, and certain cuttings and spendings upon all the inhabitants under the lord.

Eudox. When I hear this word tanist, it bringeth to my remembrance what I have read of Tania, that it should signify a province or seigniory, as Aquitania, Lusitania, and Britania, the which some think to be derived of Dania, that is, from the Danes; but, I think, amiss. But sure it seemeth that it came anciently from those barbarous nations that overran the world, which possessed those dominions, whereof they are now so called. And so it may well be, that from thence the first original of this word tanist and tanistry came, and the custom thereof hath sithence, as many others else, been continued.[1] But to that general subject

[1] *Tanistry* and *Tanist*, to represent the custom of appointing an able-bodied heir to the government, and the name of such an heir, who becomes thereby the

of the land, whereof we formerly spake, meseems that this custom or tenure can be no bar nor impeachment, seeing that in open Parliament by their said acknowledgment they waived the benefit thereof, and submitted themselves to the benefit of their new sovereign.

Iren. Yea, but they say, as I erst told you, that they reserved their titles, tenures, and seigniories whole and sound to themselves; and for proof, allege that they have ever sithence remained to them untouched, so as now to alter them should, say they, be a great wrong.

Eudox. What remedy is there, then, or means to avoid this inconveniency? For without first cutting off this dangerous custom, it seemeth hard to plant any sound ordinance or reduce them to a civil government, since all their ill customs are permitted unto them.

Iren. Surely nothing hard; for by this Act of Parliament whereof we speak, nothing was given to King Henry which he had not before from his ancestors, but only the bare name of a king; for all other absolute power of principality he had in himself before derived from many former kings, his famous progenitors and worthy conquerors of that land. The which sithence [2]

---

second person in the land, are names derived from the Irish ordinal number *tánise* meaning second; and that ordinal was formed from the root of the numeral two (*masc.* dá, *fem.* dí, *neuter* dán). The Irish cardinal numbers one, two, three, four, five, six, for example, were *óin, dá, trí, cethir, cóic, sé*, and their ordinals were *cétne, tánise, tris, cethramad, cóiced, sessed*. Thus *tánise* or *tánaise*, meaning simply second, *tanise ríg* (second king), was the name given to the appointed heir. With addition of the final *t*,—as it is used to represent an abstract conception, as in theft, thrift,—such heir came to be called the tanist, and tanistry, by help of another suffix, became the name for the old national custom.

[2] *Sithence*, the preceding form of the word since, originally two words, a preposition governing a pronoun in the dative, *sith thám*, after that. *Sith thám* then became the one word *sithen*, commonly used in the reign of Henry VIII. Taken adverbially it then came to receive a genitive suffix in further suggestion of its adverbial character, and grew to be sithenes. The *es* came to be spelt with *ce*, and as *ones, twies* became *once, twice*, so *sithenes* became *sithence*. The last change was by the speaker's common elision of *th* in the middle of a word of two short syllables, and as *other* became *o'r*, or, *sithence* became *sin'ce*, *since*.

they first conquered and by force subdued unto them, what needed afterwards to enter into any such idle terms with them to be called their king, when it is in the power of the conqueror to take upon himself what title he will over his dominions conquered? For all is the conqueror's, as Tully to Brutus saith. Therefore, meseems, instead of so great and meritorious a service as they boast they performed to the king, in bringing all the Irish to acknowledge him for their liege, they did great hurt unto his title, and have left a perpetual gall in the mind of the people; who before being absolutely bound to his obedience, are now tied but with terms; whereas else both their lives, their lands, and their liberties were in his free power to appoint what tenures, what laws, what conditions, he would over them which were all his; against which there could be no rightful resistance, or if there were, he might, when he would, establish them with a stronger hand.

Eudox. Yea; but perhaps it seemed better unto that noble king to bring them by their own accord to his obedience, and to plant a peaceable government amongst them, than by such violent means to pluck them under. Neither yet hath he thereby lost anything that he formerly had; for, having all before absolutely in his own power, it remaineth so still unto him, he having thereby neither forgiven nor foregone anything thereby unto them, but having received something from them—that is, a more voluntary and loyal subjection. So as Her Majesty may yet, when it shall please her, alter anything of those former ordinances or appoint other laws that may be more both for her own behoof and for the good of that people.

Iren. Not so; for it is not so easy, now that things are grown into an habit and have their certain course, to change the channel and turn their streams another way; for they have now a colourable pretence to withstand innovations, having accepted of other laws and rules already.

Eudox. But you say they do not accept of them, but delight rather to lean to their old customs and Brehon laws, though they be more unjust and also more inconvenient for the common people, as by your late relation of them I have gathered. As for the laws of England, they are surely most just and most agreeable both with the government and with the nature of the people. How falls it, then, that you seem to dislike of them, as not so meet for that realm of Ireland, and not only the Common Law, but also the Statutes and Acts of Parliament, which were specially provided and intended for the only benefit thereof?

Iren. I was about to have told you my reason therein, but that yourself drew me away with other questions; for I was showing you by what means and by what sort the Positive Laws were first brought in and established by the Norman Conqueror, which were not by him devised, nor applied to the state of the realm then being,—nor as yet might best be, as should by lawgivers principally be regarded,—but were indeed the very laws of his own country of Normandy; the condition whereof, how far it differeth from this of England, is apparent to every least judgment. But to transfer the same laws for the governing of the realm of Ireland was much more inconvenient and unmeet; for he found a better advantage of the time than was in the planting of them in Ireland, and followed the execution of them with more severity, and was also present in person to overlook the magistrates and to overawe these subjects with the terror of his sword and countenance of his majesty. But not so in Ireland, for they were otherwise affected, and yet do so remain; so as the same laws, meseems, can ill fit with their disposition or work that reformation that is wished; for laws ought to be fashioned unto the manners and conditions of the people to whom they are meant, and not to be imposed upon them according to the simple rule of right; for then, as I said, instead of good they may work ill, and pervert justice to extreme injustice. For he that transfers the laws of the Lacedemonians to the people of Athens should find a great absurdity and inconvenience. For those laws of Lacedemon were devised by Lycurgus, as most proper and best agreeing with that people, whom he knew to be inclined altogether to wars, and therefore wholly trained them up even from their cradles in arms and military exercises, clean contrary to the institution of Solon, who in his laws to the Athenians laboured by all means to temper their warlike courages with sweet delights of learning and sciences; so that as much as the one excelled in arms the other exceeded in knowledge. The like regard and moderation ought to be had in tempering and managing this stubborn nation of the Irish, to bring them from their delight of licentious barbarism unto the love of goodness and civility.

Eudox. I cannot see how that may better be than by the discipline of the laws of England; for the English were at first as stout and warlike a people as ever the Irish, and yet, you see, are now brought unto that civility, that no nation in the world excelleth them in all goodly conversation and all the studies of knowledge and humanity.

Iren. What they now be both you and I see very well; but by how many thorny and hard ways they are come thereunto, by how many civil broils, by how many tumultuous rebellions, that even hazarded oftentimes the whole safety of the kingdom, may easily be considered; all which they nevertheless fairly overcame, by reason of the continual presence of their king, whose only person is oftentimes instead of an army, to contain the unruly people from a thousand evil occasions, which this wretched kingdom for want thereof is daily carried into. The which, whensoever they make head, no laws, no penalties, can restrain, but that they do, in the violence of that fury, tread down and trample under foot all, both divine and human, things, and the laws themselves they do specially rage at and rend in pieces, as most repugnant to their liberty and natural freedom, which in their madness they effect.

Eudox. It is then a very unseasonable time to plead law when swords are in the hands of the vulgar, or to think to retain them with fear of punishment when they look after liberty and shake off all government.

— *Iren.* Then so it is with Ireland continually, Eudoxus; for the sword was never yet out of their hand; but when they are weary of wars and brought down to extreme wretchedness, then they creep a little perhaps, and sue for grace, till they have gotten new breath and recovered their strength again. So as it is in vain to speak of planting laws and plotting policy till they be altogether subdued.

— *Eudox.* Were they not so at the first conquering of them by Strongbow, in the time of King Henry the Second? Was there not a thorough way then made by the sword for the imposing of the laws upon them? and were they not then executed with such a mighty hand as you said was used by the Norman Conqueror? What odds is there then in this case? Why should not the same laws take as good effect on that people as they did here, being in like sort prepared by the sword and brought under by extremity? And why should they not continue in as good force and vigour for the containing of the people?

Iren. The case yet is not like, but there appeareth great odds between them; for by the conquest of Henry II. true it is that the Irish were utterly vanquished and subdued, so as no enemy was able to hold up head against his power: in which their weakness he brought in his laws, and settled them as now they there remain, like as William the Conqueror did; so as in thus much they agree, but in the rest, that is, the chiefest, they vary. For to whom did King Henry II. impose those laws? Not to the Irish, for the most part of them fled from his power into deserts and mountains, leaving the wide country to the Conqueror; who in their stead eftsoons placed Englishmen, who possessed all their lands, and did quite shut out the Irish, or the most part of them. And to those new inhabitants and colonies he gave his laws, to wit, the same law under which they were born and bred; the which it was no difficulty to place amongst them, being formerly well inured thereunto, unto whom afterwards there repaired divers of the poor distressed people of the Irish for succour and relief; of whom, such as they thought fit for labour and industriously disposed, as the most part of their baser sort are, they received unto them as their vassals, but scarcely vouchsafed to impart unto them the benefit of those laws under which themselves lived, but every one made his will and commandment a law unto his own vassal. Thus was not the law of England ever properly applied unto the Irish nation, as by a purposed plot of government, but as they could insinuate and steal themselves under the same, by their humble carriage and submission.

Eudox. How comes it then to pass that, having been once so low brought and thoroughly subjected, they afterwards lifted up themselves so strongly again, and sithence do stand so stiffly against all rule and government?

Iren. They say that they continued in that lowliness until the time that the division between the two Houses of Lancaster and York arose for the crown of England; at which time all the great English lords and gentlemen which had great possessions in Ireland repaired over hither into England, some to succour their friends here and to strengthen their party for to obtain the crown; others to defend their lands and possessions here against such as hovered after the same, upon hope of the alteration of the kingdom, and success of that side which they favoured and affected. Then the Irish, whom before they had banished into the mountains, where they lived only upon whit meats,[1] as it is

---

[1] In the *Promptorium Parvulorum*, the ancient English Latin Dictionary—it was made about the year 1440—many old English words, of course, occur, and have

D

recorded, seeing now their lands so dispeopled and weakened, came down into all the plains adjoining, and thence expelling those few English that remained, repossessed them again; since which they have remained in them, and growing greater, have brought under them many of the English which were before their lords. This was one of the occasions by which all those countries which, lying near unto any mountains or Irish deserts, had been planted with English were shortly displanted and lost; as, namely, in Munster, all the lands adjoining unto Slieve Logher, Arlo, and the Bog of Allen; in Connaught, all the countries bordering upon the Connors, MacDiermods, and O'Rourke's country; in Leinster, all the lands bordering unto the mountains of Glenmalure, unto Shillelah, unto the Brackenah, and Polmont; in Ulster, all the countries near unto Tyrconnel, Tyrone, and Fermanagh, and the Scots.

Eudox. Surely this was a great violence; but yet by your speech it seemeth that only the countries and valleys near adjoining unto those mountains and deserts were thus recovered by the Irish. But how comes it now that we see almost all that realm repossessed of them? Were there any more such evil occasions growing by the troubles of England? Or did the Irish, out of those places so by them gotten, break further, and stretch themselves out through the whole land? For now, for aught that I can understand, there is no part but the bare English Pale, in which the Irish have not the greatest footing.

Iren. But out of these small beginnings by them gotten near to the mountains did they spread themselves into the inland, and also, to their further advantage, there did other like unhappy accidents happen out of England, which gave heart and good opportunity to them to regain their old possessions. For in the

_{their meanings added in Latin. The Promptorium has "Whytmete, Lacticinium." *Lacticinium* is a word used by Apicius for *cibus ex lacte*, preparation of food in which milk has the chief place. The "meats" is used in "whitmeats" as in "sweetmeats."}

reign of King Edward the Fourth things remained yet in the same state that they were after the late breaking out of the Irish which I spake of; and that noble Prince began to cast an eye unto Ireland, and to mind the reformation of things there run amiss. For he sent over his brother, the worthy Duke of Clarence, who, having married the heir of the Earl of Ulster, and by her having all the earldom of Ulster, and much in Meath and in Munster, very carefully went about the redressing of all those late evils; and though he could not beat out the Irish again, by reason of his short continuance, yet he did shut them up within those narrow corners and glens under the mountain's foot, in which they lurked, and so kept them from breaking any further by building strongholds upon every border and fortifying all passages. Amongst the which, he repaired the castle of Clare in Thomond, of which country he had the inheritance, and of Mortimer's lands adjoining, which is now by the Irish called Killaloe. But the times of that good king growing also troublesome did let the thorough reformation of all things; and thereunto, soon after, was added another fatal mischief, which wrought a greater calamity than all the former. For the said Duke of Clarence, then Lord-Lieutenant of Ireland, was by practice of evil persons about the King, his brother, called thence away; and soon after, by sinister means, was clean made away. Presently after whose death, all the north revolting, did set up O'Neill for their captain, being before that of small power and regard; and there arose in that part of Thomond one of the O'Briens, called Murrogh en Ranagh—that is, Morrice of the Fern, or waste wild places—who, gathering unto him all the relics of the discontented Irish, eftsoons surprised the said castle of Clare, burnt and spoiled all the English there dwelling, and in short space possessed all that country beyond the river of Shannon and near adjoining. Whence shortly breaking forth like a sudden tempest, he overran all Munster and Connaught, breaking down all the holds and fortresses of the English, defacing and utterly subverting all corporate towns that were not strongly walled. For those he had no means nor engines to overthrow, neither indeed would he stay at all about them, but speedily ran forward, counting his suddenness his most advantage, that he might overtake the English before they could fortify or gather themselves together. So in short space he clean wiped out many great towns, as first Inchiquin, then Killaloe, before called Clariford; also Thurles, Mourne, Buttevant, and many others whose names I cannot remember, and of some of which there is now no memory or sign remaining. Upon report whereof there flocked unto him all the scum of the Irish out of all places, that ere long he had a mighty army, and thence marched forth into Leinster, where he wrought great outrages, wasting all the country where he went; for it was his policy to leave no hold behind him, but to make all plain and waste. In the which he soon after created himself king, and was called king of all Ireland, which before him I do not read that any did so generally, but only Edward le Bruce.

Eudox. What? Was there ever any general king of all Ireland? I never heard it before, but that it was always, whilst it was under the Irish, divided into four, and sometimes into five kingdoms or dominions. But this Edward le Bruce, what was he that could make himself king of all Ireland?

Iren. I would tell you, in case you would not challenge me anon for forgetting the matter which I had in hand; that is, the inconvenience and unfitness which I supposed to be in the laws of the land.

Eudox. No, surely, I have no cause, for neither is this impertinent thereunto; for sithence you did set your course (as I remember in your first part) to treat of the evils which hindered the peace and good-ordering of that land; amongst which, that of the inconvenience in the laws was the first which you had in hand; this discourse of the overrunning and wasting of the realm is very material thereunto, for that it was the beginning of all the other evils which sithence have afflicted that land, and opened a way unto the Irish to recover their possession and to beat out the English which had formerly won the same. And, besides, it will give a great light both unto the second and third part, which is the redressing of those evils, and planting of some good form or policy therein, by renewing the remembrance of these occasions and accidents by which those ruins happened, and laying before us the ensamples of those times to be compared to ours, and to be warned by those which shall have to do in the like. Therefore, I pray you, tell them unto us; and as for the point where you left, I will not forget afterwards to call you back again thereunto.

Iren. This Edward le Bruce was brother of Robert le Bruce, who was king of Scotland at such time as King Edward the Second reigned here in England, and bare a most malicious and spiteful mind against King Edward, doing him all the scathe that he could, and annoying his territories of England, whilst he was troubled with civil wars of his barons at home. He also, to work him the more mischief, sent over his said brother Edward with a power of Scots and Redshanks into Ireland, where by means of the Lacys, and of the Irish, with whom they combined, they got footing; and gathering unto him all the scatterlings and outlaws out of all the woods and mountains in which they long had lurked, marched forth into the English Pale; which then was chiefly in the north from the Point of Donluce, and beyond unto Dublin, having in the midst of her Knockfergus, Belfast, Armagh, and Carlingford, which are now the most outbounds and abandoned places in the English Pale, and indeed not counted of the English Pale at all; for it stretcheth now no farther than Dundalk towards the north. There the said Edward le Bruce spoiled and burned all the old English Pale inhabitants, and sacked and rased all cities and corporate towns, no less than

Murrough en Ranagh, of whom I erst told you. For he wasted Belfast, Greencastle, Kells, Belturbut, Castletown, Newton, and many other very good towns and strongholds. He rooted out the noble families of the Audleys, Talbots, Tuchets, Chamberlains, Mandevilles, and the Savages out of Ardes; though of the Lord Savage there remaineth yet an heir, that is now a poor gentleman of very mean condition, yet dwelling in the Ardes. And coming lastly to Dundalk, he there made himself king, and reigned the space of one whole year, until that Edward, king of England, having some quiet in his affairs at home, sent over the Lord John Birmingham to be General of the wars against him, who, encountering him near to Dundalk, overthrew his army and slew him. Also he presently followed the victory so hotly upon the Scots, that he suffered them not to breathe or gather themselves together again until they came to the sea-coast. Notwithstanding all the way that they fled, for very rancour and despite, in their return they utterly consumed and wasted whatsoever they had before left unspoiled; so as of all towns, castles, forts, bridges, and habitations they left not any stick standing nor any people remaining; for those few which yet survived fled from their fury farther into the English Pale that now is. Thus was all that goodly country utterly wasted. And sure it is yet a most beautiful and sweet country as any is under heaven, being stored throughout with many goodly rivers, replenished with all sorts of fish most abundantly, sprinkled with many very sweet islands and goodly lakes, like little inland seas, that will carry even ships upon their waters; adorned with goodly woods, even fit for building of houses and ships, so commodiously, as that, if some princes in the world had them, they would soon hope to be lords of all the seas, and ere long of all the world. Also full of very good ports and havens opening upon England, as inviting us to come unto them, to see what excellent commodities that country can afford; besides the soil itself, most fertile, fit to yield all kind of fruit that shall be committed thereunto. And lastly, the heavens most mild and temperate, though somewhat more moist than the parts towards the west.

Eudox. Truly Ireneus, what with your praises of the country, and what with your discourse of the lamentable desolation thereof made by those Scots, you have filled me with a great compassion of their calamities, that I do much pity that sweet land, to be subject to so many evils, as I see more and more to be laid upon her, and do half begin to think, that it is, as you said at the beginning, her fatal misfortune, above all other countries that I know, to be thus miserably tossed and turmoiled with these variable storms of affliction. But since we are thus far entered into the consideration of her mishaps, tell me, have there been any more such tempests, as you term them, wherein she hath thus wretchedly been wrecked?

Iren. Many more, God wot, have there been; in which principal parts have been rent and torn asunder, but none, as I can remember, so universal as this. And yet the rebellion of Thomas Fitz-Garret did well-nigh stretch itself into all parts of Ireland. But that which was in the time of the government of the Lord Grey was surely no less general than all those, for there was no part free from the contagion, but all conspired in one to cast off their subjection to the crown of England. Nevertheless, through the most wise and valiant handling of that right noble Lord, it got not the head which the former evils found, for in them the realm was left like a ship in a storm, amidst all the raging surges, unruled and undirected of any; for they to whom she was committed either fainted in their labour or forsook their charge. But he, like a most wise pilot, kept her course carefully, and held her most strongly even against those roaring billows, that he safely brought her out of all; so as long after, even by the space of twelve or thirteen whole years, she rode at peace, through his only pains and excellent endurance, however envy list to blatter[1]

---

[1] *Blatter*, patter, babble (from the noise of rain).

against him. But of this we shall have occasion to speak in another place. Now, if you please, let us return again unto our first course.

Eudox. Truly I am very glad to hear your judgment of the government of that honourable man so soundly; for I have heard it oftentimes maligned, and his doings depraved of some, who, I perceive, did rather of malicious mind or private grievance seek to detract from the honour of his deeds and counsels than of any just cause; but he was nevertheless, in the judgments of all good and wise men, defended and maintained. And now that he is dead, his immortal fame surviveth and flourisheth in the mouths of all people, that even those which did backbite him are checked with their own venom and break their galls to hear his so honourable report. But let him rest in peace, and turn we to our more troublesome matters of discourse, of which I am right sorry that you make so short an end, and covet to pass over to your former purposes; for there be many other parts of Ireland which I have heard have been no less vexed with the like storms than these which you have treated of; as the countries of the Byrnes and Tooles near Dublin, with the insolent outrages and spoils of Feagh mac Hugh; the countries of Catherlagh, Wexford, and Waterford, by the Cavenaghs; the countries of Leix, Kilkenny, and Kildare, by the O'Moores; the countries of Ofaly and Longford, by the Connors; the countries of Westmeath, Cavan, and Lowth, by the O'Reillys, the Kellys, and many others. So as the discoursing of them, besides the pleasure which would redound out of their history, be also very profitable for matters of policy.

Iren. All this which you have named, and many more besides, oftentimes have I right well known, and yet often do kindle great fires of tumultuous broils in the countries bordering upon them. All which to rehearse should rather be to chronicle times than to search into reformation of abuses in that realm; and yet very needful it will be to consider them, and the evils which they have often stirred up, that some redress thereof, and prevention of the evils to come, may thereby rather be devised. But I suppose we shall have a fitter opportunity for the same when we shall speak of the particular abuses and enormities of the government, which will be next after these general defects and inconveniences which I said were in the laws, customs, and religion.

Eudox. Go to them, a God's name, and follow the course which you have promised to yourself; for it fitteth best, I must confess, with the purpose of our discourse. Declare your opinion, as you began, about the Laws of the Realm, what incommodity you have conceived to be in them, chiefly in the Common Law, which I would have thought most free from all such dislike.

Iren. The Common Law is, as I said before, of itself most rightful and very convenient, I suppose, for the kingdom for which it was first devised. For this, I think, as it seems reasonable, that out of your manners of your people and abuses of your country, for which they were invented, they take their first beginning, or else they should be most unjust; for no laws of man, according to the straight rule of right, are just but as in regard of the evils which they prevent and the safety of the commonweal which they provide for. As, for example, in your true balancing of justice, it is a flat wrong to punish the thought or purpose of any before it be enacted; for true justice punisheth nothing but the evil act or wicked word. That by the laws of all kingdoms it is a capital crime to devise or purpose the death of your king, the reason is, for that when such a purpose is effected it should then be too late to devise thereof, and should turn the commonwealth to more loss by the death of their prince than such punishment of the malefactors. And therefore the law in that case punisheth the thought; for better is a mischief than an inconvenience. So that *jus politicum*, though it be not of itself just, yet by application, or rather necessity, it is made just, and this only respect maketh all laws just. Now then, if these laws of Ireland be not likewise applied and fitted for that realm, they are sure very inconvenient.

Eudox. You reason strongly; but what unfitness do you find in them for that realm? Show us some particulars.

Iren. The Common Law appointeth that all trials, as well of crimes as titles and right, shall be made by verdict of a jury, chosen out of the honest and most substantial freeholders. Now, most of the freeholders of that realm are Irish, which when the cause shall fall betwixt an Englishman and an Irish, or between the Queen and any freeholder of that country, they make no more scruple to pass against an Englishman and the Queen, though it be to strain their oaths, than to drink milk unstrained. So that before the jury go together it is all to nothing what the verdict shall be. The trial have I so often seen that I dare confidently avouch the abuse thereof. Yet is the law of itself, as I said, good, and the first institution thereof, being given to all Englishmen very rightfully; but now that the Irish have stepped into the very rooms of our English, we are now to become heedful and provident in juries.

Eudox. In sooth, Ireneus, you have discovered a point worthy consideration; for hereby not only the English subject findeth no indifferency in deciding of his cause, be it never so just, but the Queen, as well in all pleas of the crown as also in inquiries for escheats, lands attainted, wardships, concealments, and all such-like, is abused and exceedingly damaged.

Iren. You say very true; for I dare undertake that at this day there are more attainted lands concealed from Her Majesty than she hath now possessions in all Ireland. And it is no small inconvenience; for, besides that she loseth so much land as should turn to her great profit, she besides loseth so many good subjects, which might be assured unto her, as those lands would yield inhabitants and living unto.

VIEW OF THE STATE OF IRELAND. 59

Eudox. But doth many of that people, say you, make no more conscience to perjure themselves in their verdicts and damn their souls?

Iren. Not only so in their verdicts, but also in all other their dealings, especially with the English, they are most wilfully bent; for though they will not seem manifestly to do it, yet will some one or other subtle-headed fellow amongst them put some quirk or devise some evasion, whereof the rest will likely take hold, and suffer themselves easily to be led by him to that themselves desired. For in the most apparent matter that may be, the least question or doubt that may be moved will make a stop unto them, and put them quite out of the way. Besides that, of themselves, for the most part, they are so cautelous and wily-headed, especially being men of so small experience and practice in law-matters, that you would wonder whence they borrow such subtleties and sly shifts.

Eudox. But methinks this inconvenience might be much helped in the judges and chief magistrates, which have the choosing and nominating of those jurors, if they would have dared to appoint either most Englishmen, or such Irishmen as were of the soundest judgment and disposition, for no doubt but some there be incorruptible.

Iren. Some there be indeed, as you say; but then would the Irish party cry out of partiality, and complain he hath no justice, he is not used as a subject, he is not suffered to have the free benefit of the law, and these outcries the magistrates there do much shun, as they have cause, since they are readily hearkened unto here; neither can it be indeed, although the Irish party would be so contented to be so compassed, that such English freeholders, which are but few, and such faithful Irishmen, which are indeed as few, shall always be chosen for trials; for, being so few, they should be made weary of their freeholds. And therefore a good care is to be had, by all good occasions, to increase their number and to plant more by them. But were it so that the jurors could be picked out of such choice men as you desire, this would nevertheless be as bad a corruption in the trial; for the evidence being brought in by the baser Irish people will be as deceitful as the verdict; for they care much less than the others what they swear, and sure their lords may compel them to say anything, for I myself have heard, when one of the baser sort, which they call churls, being challenged and reproved for his false oath, hath answered confidently that his lord commanded him, and it was the least thing that he could do for his lord to swear for him. So unconscionable are these common people, and so little feeling have they of God or their own soul's good.

Eudox. It is a most miserable case; but what help can there be in this? For though the manner of their trials should be altered, yet the proof of everything must needs be by the testimony of such persons as the parties shall produce; which if they shall be corrupt, how can there ever any light of the truth appear? What remedy is there for this evil but to make heavy laws and penalties against jurors?

Iren. I think sure that will do small good, for when a people be inclined to any vice, or have no touch of conscience, nor sense of their evil doings, it is bootless to think to restrain them by any penalties or fear of punishment, but either the occasion is to be taken away, or a more understanding of the right and shame of the fault to be imprinted. For if that Lycurgus should have made it death for the Lacedæmonians to steal, they being a people which naturally delighted in stealth, or if it should be made a capital crime for the Flemings to be taken in drunkenness, there should have been few Lacedæmonians then left, and few Flemings now. So impossible it is to remove any fault so general in a people with terror of laws or most sharp restraints.

Eudox. What means may there be then to avoid this inconvenience? for the case seems very hard.

VIEW OF THE STATE OF IRELAND. 61

Iren. We are not yet come to the point to devise remedies for the evils, but only have now to recount them, of the which this which I have told you is one defect in the Common Law.

Eudox. Tell us then, I pray you, further, have you any more of this sort in the Common Law?

Iren. By rehearsal of this I remember also of another like, which I have often observed in trials to have wrought great hurt and hindrance, and that is, the exceptions which the Common Law alloweth a felon in his trial; for he may have, as you know, fifty-six exceptions peremptory against the jurors, of which he shall show no cause. By which shift there being, as I have showed you, so small store of honest jurymen, he will either put off his trial, or drive it to such men as, perhaps, are not of the soundest sort; by whose means, if he can acquit himself of the crime, as he is likely, then will he plague such as were brought first to be of his jury, and all such as made any party against him, and when he comes forth he will make their cows and garrons[1] to walk, if he do no other harm to their persons.

Eudox. This is a sly device, but I think might soon be remedied; but we must leave it a while to the rest. In the meanwhile do you go forwards with others.

Iren. There is another no less inconvenience than this, which is, the trial of accessories to felony; for by the common law the accessories cannot be proceeded against till the principal have received his trial. Now to the case, how it often falleth out in Ireland that, a stealth being made by a rebel or an outlaw, the stolen goods are conveyed to some husbandman or gentleman, which hath well to take to, and yet liveth most by the receipt of such stealths, where they are found by the owner and handled. Whereupon the party is perhaps apprehended and committed to jail, or put upon sureties till the sessions; at which time the owner, preferring a bill of indictment, proveth sufficiently the

[1] *Garrons*, working horses; old Irish *gerrán*, a work-horse, a hack.

stealth to have been committed upon him by such an outlaw, and to have been found in the possession of the prisoner: against whom, nevertheless, no course of law can proceed nor trial can be had, for that the principal thief is not to be gotten; notwithstanding that he likewise standing perhaps indicted at once with the receiver, being in rebellion or in the woods, where peradventure he is slain before he can be gotten, and so the receiver clean acquitted and discharged of the crime. By which means the thieves are greatly encouraged to steal, and their maintainers emboldened to receive their stealths, knowing how hardly they can be brought to any trial of law.

Eudox. Truly this is a great inconvenience, and a great cause, as you say, of the maintenance of thieves, knowing their receivers always ready; for were there no receivers there would be no thieves. But this, meseems, might easily be provided for by some Act of Parliament, that the receiver, being convicted by good proofs, might receive his trial without the principal.

Iren. You say very well, Eudox, but that is almost impossible to be compassed; and herein also you discover another imperfection in the course of the Common Law and first ordinance of the realm; for you know that the said Parliament must consist of the peers, gentlemen, freeholders, and burgesses of that realm itself. Now, these being perhaps themselves, or the most part of them (as may seem by their stiff withstanding of this Act) culpable of this crime, or favourers of their friends which are such, by whom their kitchens are sometimes amended, will not suffer any such statute to pass. Yet hath it oftentimes been attempted, and in the time of Sir John Parrot very earnestly, I remember, laboured, but could by no means be effected. And not only this, but many other like which are as needful for the reformation of that realm.

Eudox. This also is surely a great defect; but we may not talk, you say, of the redressing of this until our second part come, which is purposely appointed thereunto. Therefore proceed to the recounting of more such evils, if at least you have any more.

Iren. There is also a great inconvenience, which hath wrought great damage both to Her Majesty and to that commonwealth, through close and colourable conveyances of the lands and goods of traitors, felons, and fugitives. As when one of them mindeth to go into rebellion, he will convey away all his lands and lordships to feoffees in trust, whereby he reserveth to himself but a state for term of life; which being determined either by the sword or by the halter, their lands straight cometh to their heir, and the Queen is defrauded of the intent of the law, which laid that grievous punishment upon traitors, to forfeit all their lands to the Prince, to the end that men might the rather be terrified from committing treasons; for many which would little esteem of their own lives, yet for remorse of their wives and children would be withheld from that heinous crime. This appeared plainly in the late Earl of Desmond; for before his breaking forth into open rebellion he had conveyed secretly all his lands to feoffees in trust, in hope to have cut off Her Majesty from the escheat of his lands.

Eudox. Yea; but that was well enough avoided, for the Act of Parliament which gave all his lands to the Queen did, as I have heard, cut off and frustrate all such conveyances as had at any time by the space of twelve years before his rebellion been made; within the compass whereof the fraudulent feoffment and many the like of others his accomplices and fellow-traitors were contained.

Iren. Very true; but how hardly that Act of Parliament was wrought out of them I can witness; and were it to be passed again I dare undertake it would never be compassed. But were it also that such Acts might be easily brought to pass against traitors and felons, yet were it not an endless trouble that no traitor or felon should be attainted but a Parliament must be called for bringing of his lands to the Queen which the Common Law giveth her?

Eudox. Then this is no fault of the Common Law, but of the persons which work this fraud to Her Majesty.

Iren. Yes, marry; for the Common Law hath left them this benefit, whereof they make advantage and wrest it to their bad purposes; so as thereby they are the bolder to enter into evil actions, knowing that, if the worst befall them, they shall lose nothing but themselves; whereof they seem surely very careless.

Eudox. But what meant you of fugitives herein? Or how doth this concern them?

Iren. Yes, very greatly; for you shall understand that there be many ill-disposed and undutiful persons of that realm, like as in this point there are also in this realm of England too many which, being men of good inheritance, are for dislike of religion or danger of the law into which they are run, or discontent of the present government, fled beyond the seas, where they live under princes which are Her Majesty's professed enemies, and converse and are confederates with other traitors and fugitives which are there abiding. The which nevertheless have the benefits and profits of their lands here, by pretence of such colourable conveyances thereof, formerly made by them unto their privy friends here in trust, who privily do send over unto them the said revenues, wherewith they are there maintained and enabled against Her Majesty.

Eudox. I do not think that there be any such fugitives which are relieved by the profit of their lands in England, for there is a straighter order taken. And if there be any such in Ireland, it were good it were likewise looked unto, for this evil may easily be remedied. But proceed.

Iren. It is also inconvenient in the realm of Ireland that the wards and marriages of gentlemen's children should be in the disposition of any of those Irish lords, as now they are, by reason

VIEW OF THE STATE OF IRELAND. 65

that their lands be held by knight's service of those lords. By which means it comes to pass that those gentlemen, being thus in the ward of those lords, are not only thereby brought up lewdly and Irish-like, but also for ever after so bound to their services that they will run with them into any disloyal action.

Eudox. This grievance, Ireneus, is also complained of in England, but how can it be remedied, since the service must follow the tenure of the lands, and the lands were given away by the kings of England to those lords when they first conquered that realm? And to say truth, this also would be some prejudice to the Prince in her wardships.

Iren. I do not mean this by the Prince's wards, but by such as fall into the hands of Irish lords; for I could wish, and this I could enforce, that all those wardships were in the Prince's disposition; for then it might be hoped that she, for the universal reformation of that realm, would take better order for bringing up those wards in good nurture, and not suffer them to come into so bad hands. And although these things be already passed away, by her progenitors' former grants unto those said lords, yet I could find a way to remedy a great part thereof, as hereafter, when fit time serves, shall appear. And since we are entered into speech of such grants of former princes to sundry persons of this realm of Ireland, I will mention unto you some other, of like nature to this, and of like inconvenience, by which the former kings of England passed unto them a great part of their prerogatives; which, though then it was well intended, and perhaps well deserved of them which received the same, yet now such a gap of mischief lies open thereby that I could wish it were well stopped. Of this sort are the grants of Counties Palatines in Ireland, which though at first were granted upon good consideration when they were first conquered, for that those lands lay then as a very border to the wild Irish, subject to continual invasion, so as it was needful to give them great privileges for the defence of the inhabitants

E

thereof; yet now that it is no more a border nor frontiered with enemies, why should such privileges be any more continued?

Eudox. I would gladly know what you call a County Palatine, and whence it is so called.

Iren. It was, I suppose, first named Palatine of a pale, as it were a pale and defence to their inward lands, so as it is called the English Pale; and therefore is a Palsgrave named an Earl Palatine. Others think of the Latin *palare;* that is, to forage or outrun, because those marchers and borderers used commonly so to do. So as to have a County Palatine is, in effect, to have a privilege to spoil the enemies' borders adjoining. And surely so it is used at this day, as a privilege place of spoils and stealths; for the county of Tipperary, which is now the only County Palatine in Ireland, is by abuse of some bad ones made a receptacle to rob the rest of the counties about it, by means of whose privileges none will follow their stealths: so as it, being situate in the very lap of all the land, is made now a border; which how inconvenient it is let every man judge. And though that right noble man—that is, the lord of the liberty—do pain himself all he may to yield equal justice unto all, yet can there not but great abuses lurk in so inward and absolute a privilege, the consideration whereof is to be respected carefully for the next succession. And much like unto this grant, there are other privileges granted unto most of the corporations there; that they shall not be bound to any other government than their own; that they shall not be charged with garrisons; that they shall not be travailed forth of their own franchises; that they may buy and sell with thieves and rebels; that all amercements and fines that shall be imposed upon them shall come unto themselves. All which, though at the time of their first grant they were tolerable, and perhaps reasonable, yet now are most unreasonable and inconvenient; but all these will easily be cut off with the superior power of Her

Majesty's prerogative, against which her own grants are not to be pleaded or enforced.

Eudox. Now, truly, Ireneus, you have, meseems, very well handled this point, touching inconveniences in the Common Law there by you observed; and it seemeth that you have had a mindful regard unto the things that may concern the good of that realm. And if you can as well go through with the Statute Laws of that land, I will think you have not lost all your time there. Therefore, I pray you, now take them in hand, and tell us what you think to be amiss in them.

Iren. The Statutes of that realm are not many, and therefore we shall the sooner run through them; and yet of those few, there are impertinent and unnecessary: the which, though perhaps at the time of the making of them were very needful, yet now, through change of time, are clean antiquated and altogether idle; as that which forbiddeth any to wear their beards all on the upper lip, and none under the chin; and that which putteth away saffron shirts and smocks; and that which restraineth the use of gilt bridles and petronels;[1] and that which is appointed for the recorders and clerks of Dublin and Drogheda to take but twopence for the copy of a plaint; and that which commands bows and arrows; and that which makes that all Irishmen which shall converse among the English shall be taken for spies, and so punished; and that which forbids persons amenable to law to enter and distrain in the lands in which they have title; and many other the like I could rehearse.

Eudox. These, truly, which ye have repeated seem very frivolous and fruitless; for by the breach of them little damage or

---
[1] *Petronels*, horse-pistols, from Spanish *petrina*, a belt round the breast, in which they were carried.

inconvenience can come to the commonwealth; neither, indeed, if any transgress them, shall he seem worthy of punishment, scarce of blame, saving but for that they abide by that name of Laws. But laws ought to be such as that the keeping of them should be greatly for the behoof of the commonweal, and the violating of them should be very heinous, and sharply punishable. But tell us of some more weighty dislikes in the statutes than these, and that may more behooffully[2] import the reformation of them.

Iren. There are one or two Statutes which make the wrongful distraining of any man's goods against the form of Common Law to be felony; the which Statutes seem surely to have been at first meant for the good of that realm and for restraining of a foul abuse which then reigned commonly amongst that people, and yet is not altogether laid aside, that when any one was indebted to another, he would first demand his debt; and if he were not paid, he would straight go and take a distress of his goods or cattle, where he could find them, to the value; which he would keep till he were satisfied. And this the simple churl, as they call him, doth commonly use to do; yet through ignorance of his misdoing, or evil use that hath long settled amongst them. But this, though it be sure most unlawful, yet surely, meseems, too hard to make it death, since there is no purpose in the party to steal the other's goods or to conceal the distress; but he doth it openly, for the most part, before witnesses. And again, the same Statutes are so slackly penned (besides the latter of them is so unsensibly contrived, that it scarce carrieth any reason in it) that they are often and very easily wrested to the fraud of the subject; as if one going to distrain upon his own land or tenement, where lawfully he may, if yet in doing thereof he transgress the least point of the Common Law, he straight committeth felony; or if one, by any other occasion, take anything from another, as boys

[2] *Behooffully*, advantageously, from First-English *behóf*, behoof, advantage.

use sometimes to cap one another, the same is straight felony. This is a very hard law.

Eudox. Nevertheless, that evil use of distraining of another man's goods, ye will not deny but it is to be abolished and taken away.

Iren. It is so, but not by taking away the subject withal, for that is too violent a medicine; especially this use being permitted and made lawful to some, and to other some death. As to most of the corporate towns there it is granted by their charter that they may, every man by himself, without an officer (for that were more tolerable), for any debt, to distrain the goods of any Irish being found within their liberty or but passing through their towns. And the first permission of this was for that in those times when that grant was made the Irish were not amenable to law, so as it was not safety for the townsman to go to him forth to demand his debt, nor possible to draw him into law; so that he had leave to be his own bailiff, to arrest his said debtor's goods within his own franchise. The which the Irish seeing, thought it as lawful for them to distrain the townsman's goods in the country where they found it; and so, by ensample of that grant to townsmen, they thought it lawful and made it a use to distrain one another's goods for small debts. And to say truth, methinks it is hard for every trifling debt of two or three shillings to be driven to law, which is so far from them sometimes to be sought; for which methinketh it too heavy an ordinance to give death, especially to a rude man that is ignorant of law, and thinketh that a common use or grant to other men is a law for himself.

Eudox. Yea; but the judge, when it cometh before him to trial, may easily decide this doubt, and lay open the intent of the law by his better discretion.

Iren. Yea; but it is dangerous to leave the sense of the law unto the reason or will of the judges, who are men, and may be miscarried by affections and many other means. But the laws ought to be like stony tables, plain, steadfast, and unmovable. There is also such another statute or two, which made coigny and livery[1] to be treason, no less inconvenient than the former, being as it is penned, however the first purport thereof were expedient. For thereby now no man can go into another man's house for lodging, nor to his own tenant's house to take victualling by the way, notwithstanding that there is no other means for him to have lodging, nor horse-meat, nor man's meat, there being no inns, nor none otherwise to be bought for money, but that he is endangered by that statute for treason, whensoever he shall happen to fall out with his tenant or that his said host list to complain of grievance, as oftentimes I have seen them very maliciously to do through the least provocation.

Eudox. I do not well know, but by guess, what you do mean by these terms of coigny and livery; therefore, I pray you, explain them.

Iren. I know not whether the words be English or Irish, but I suppose them to be rather ancient English, for the Irishmen can make no derivation of them. What livery is we by common use in England know well enough, namely, that it is an allowance of horse-meat, as they commonly use the word in stabling, as to keep horses at livery, the which word, I guess, is derived of livering or delivering forth their nightly food. So in great houses the livery is said to be served up for all night; that is, their evening's allowance for drink. And livery is also called the upper weed which a serving-man weareth, so called, as I suppose, for that it was delivered and taken from him at pleasure. So it is apparent that by the word livery is there meant horse-meat, like as by the word coigny is understood man's meat; but whence the word is derived is hard to tell. Some say of coin, for that they

---

[1] *Coigny and livery.* "Coigny" for man's meat is probably from the Irish *coic*, a cook, derivative from "coquus," with the flexional *n*, or *cucenn*, a kitchen, from "coquina." Livery, fully and rightly explained by Spenser, is *livrée*, a delivery.

used commonly in their coignies not only to take meat, but coin also, and that taking of money was specially meant to be prohibited by that Statute. But I think, rather, this word coigny is derived of the Irish. The which is a common use amongst landlords of the Irish to have a common spending upon their tenants; for all their tenants, being commonly but tenants at will, they used to take of them what victuals they list, for of victuals they were wont to make small reckoning. Neither in this was the tenant wronged, for it was an ordinary and known custom, and his lord used commonly so to covenant with him, which if at any time the tenant disliked, he might freely depart at his pleasure. But now by this Statute the said Irish lord is wronged, for that he is cut off from his customary services, of the which this was one, besides many other of the like—as cuddy, coshery, bonnaght, shrah, sorehin, and such others, the which, I think, were customs at first brought in by the English upon the Irish; for they were never wont, and yet are loth, to yield any certain rent, but only spendings; for their common saying is, "Spend me and defend me."

Eudox. Surely I take it, as you say, that therein the Irish lord hath wrong, since it was an ancient custom, and nothing contrary to law; for to the willing there is no wrong done. And this right well I wot, that even here in England there are in many places as large customs and privileges as that of coigny and livery. But I suppose by your speech that it was the first meaning of the Statute to forbid the violent taking of victuals upon other men's tenants against their wills, which surely is a great outrage; and yet not so great, meseems, as that it should be made treason. For, considering that the nature of treason is concerning the royal estate or person of the Prince, or practising with his enemies, to the derogation and danger of his crown and dignity, it is hardly wrested to make this treason. But, as you said, "Better a mischief than an inconvenience."

Iren. Another Statute I remember, which, having been an ancient Irish custom, is now, upon advisement, made a law, and that is called the custom of kin-cogish;[1] which is, that every head of every sept[2] and every chief of every kindred or family should be answerable, and bound to bring forth every one of that sept and kindred under it, at all times to be justified, when he should be required or charged with any treason, felony, or other heinous crime.

Eudox. Why, surely this seems a very necessary law. For considering that many of them be such losels and scatterlings as that they cannot easily, by any sheriff, constable, bailiff, or other ordinary officer, be gotten when they are challenged for any such fact, this is a very good means to get them to be brought in by him that is the head of that sept or chief of that house; wherefore I wonder what just exception you can make against the same.

Iren. Truly, Eudoxus, in the pretence of the good of this Statute you have nothing erred, for it seemed very expedient and necessary; but the hurt which cometh thereby is greater than the good. For whilst every chief of a sept standeth so bound to the law for every man of his blood or sept that is under him, he is made great by the commanding of them all. For if he may not command them, then that law doth wrong that bindeth him to bring them forth to be justified. And if he may command them, then he may command them as well to ill as to good. Hereby the lords and captains of countries, the principals and heads of septs, are made stronger, whom it should be a most special care in policy to weaken, and to set up and strengthen divers of his underlings against him; which, whensoever he shall swerve from duty, may be able to beard him. For it is dangerous to leave the command of so many as some septs are, being five or six

---

[1] *Kin-cogish*, perhaps the Irish word here is cocrich, a boundary or bounded district, and "kin-cogish" is the district of men of one kinship or blood alliance.
[2] *Sept*, clan; equivalent to sect, or division.

VIEW OF THE STATE OF IRELAND. 73

thousand persons, to the will of one man, who may lead them to what he will, as he himself shall be inclined.

Eudox. In very deed, Ireneus, it is very dangerous, seeing the disposition of those people is not always inclinable to the best; and, therefore, I hold it no wisdom to leave unto them too much command over their kindred, but rather to withdraw their followers from them as much as may be, and to gather them under the command of law by some better means than this custom of kincogish, the which word I would be glad to know what it namely signifieth, for the meaning thereof I seem to understand reasonably well.

Iren. It is a word mingled of English and Irish together, so as I am partly led to think that the custom thereof was first English and afterwards made Irish; for such another law they had here in England, as I remember, made by King Alfred, that every gentleman should bring forth his kindred and followers to the law. So kin is English, and cogish affinity in Irish.

Eudox. Sith, then, we have thus reasonably handled the inconveniences in the law, let us now pass unto the Second Part, which was, I remember, of the Abuses of the Customs, in which, meseems, you have a fair champain laid open unto you, in which you may at large stretch out your discourse into many sweet remembrances of antiquities, from whence it seemeth that the customs of that nation proceeded.

Iren. Indeed, Eudoxus, you say very true; for all the Customs of the Irish, which I have often noted and compared with that I have read, would minister occasion of a most ample discourse of the original of them, and the antiquity of that people. Which, in truth, I think to be more ancient than most that I know in this end of the world, so as if it were in the handling of some man of sound judgment and plentiful reading, it would be most pleasant and profitable. But, it may be, we may, at some other time of meeting, take occasion to treat thereof more at large. Here only it shall suffice to touch such Customs of the Irish as seem offensive and repugnant to the good government of the realm.

Eudox. Follow then your own course, for I shall the better content myself to forbear my desire now, in hope that you will, as you say, some other time, more abundantly satisfy it.

Iren. Before we enter into the treaty of their Customs, it is first needful to consider from whence they first sprang; for from the sundry manners of the nations from whence that people which now is called Irish were derived some of the customs which now remain amongst them have been first fetched, and sithence there continued amongst them; for not of one nation was it peopled as it is, but of sundry people of different conditions and manners. But the chiefest which have first possessed and inhabited it I suppose to be Scythians.

Eudox. How cometh it then to pass that the Irish do derive themselves from Gathelus, the Spaniard?[1]

Iren. They do indeed, but, I conceive, without any good ground. For if there were any such notable transmission of a colony hither out of Spain, or any such famous conquest of this kingdom by Gathelus, a Spaniard, as they would fain believe, it is not unlikely but the very chronicles of Spain (had Spain then been in so high regard as they now have it) would not have omitted so memorable a thing as the subduing of so noble a realm to the Spaniard, no more than they do now neglect to

---

[1] *Gathelus* or Gadelas, or Gædhal, was said to have lived in the time of Moses. His father Niul had married a daughter of the Pharaoh who, in pursuit of the Israelites, was drowned in the Red Sea. He called her Scota, because he was himself a Scythian; they had a son called Gaodhal, as being a lover of learning, from *gaoith*, which is learning, and *dil*, which is love. So the old Irish clergy invented men to account for names of tribes, and gave a founder to the Gaedhels, or Gaels.

memorise their conquest of the Indians; especially in those times in which the same was supposed, being nearer unto the flourishing age of learning and writers under the Romans. But the Irish do herein no otherwise than our vain Englishmen do in the tale of Brutus, whom they devise to have first conquered and inhabited this land; it being as impossible to prove that there was ever any such Brutus of Albion, or England, as it is that there was any such Gathelus of Spain. But surely the Scythians, of whom I erst spoke, at such time as the northern nations overflowed all Christendom came down to the sea-coast; where inquiring for other countries abroad, and getting intelligence of this country of Ireland, finding shipping convenient, passed thither, and arrived in the north part thereof, which is now called Ulster; which first inhabiting, and afterwards stretching themselves forth into the land, as their numbers increased, named it all of themselves Scuttenland, which more briefly is called Scutland, or Scotland.

Eudox. I wonder, Ireneus, whither you run so far astray; for whilst we talk of Ireland, methinks you rip up the original of Scotland; but what is that to this?

Iren. Surely very much, for Scotland and Ireland are all one and the same.

Eudox. That seemeth more strange; for we all know right well they are distinguished by a great sea running between them; or else there are two Scotlands.

Iren. Never the more are there two Scotlands; but two kinds of Scots were indeed, as you may gather out of Buchanan; the one Iren, or Irish Scots, the other Albine-Scots; for those Scots are Scythians, arrived, as I said, in the north parts of Ireland; where some of them after passed into the next coast of Albine, now called Scotland, which, after much trouble, they possessed, and of themselves named Scotland. But in process of time, as it is commonly seen, the denomination of the part prevaileth in the whole; for the Irish Scots, putting away the name of Scots, were called only Irish, and the Albine-Scots, leaving the name of Albine, were called only Scots. Therefore it cometh thence, that of some writers Ireland is called Scotia Major, and that which now is called Scotland, Scotia Minor.

Eudox. I do now well understand your distinguishing of the two sorts of Scots and two Scotlands; how that this which now is called Ireland was anciently called Erin, and afterwards of some written Scotland; and that which now is called Scotland was formerly called Albine, before the coming of the Scyths thither.[1] But what other nation inhabited the other parts of Ireland?

Iren. After this people thus planted in the north, or before (for the certainty of things in times so far from all knowledge cannot be justly avouched), another nation, coming out of Spain, arrived in the west part of Ireland, and finding it waste, or weakly inhabited, possessed it; who whether they were native Spaniards, or Gauls, or Africans, or Goths, or some other of those northern nations which did overspread all Christendom, it is impossible to affirm; only some naked conjectures may be gathered: but that out of Spain certainly they came, that do all the Irish chronicles agree.

Eudox. You do very boldly, Ireneus, adventure upon the histories of ancient times, and lean too confidently on those Irish chronicles which are most fabulous and forged, in that out of them you dare take in hand to lay open the original of such a nation so

[1] The two branches of the Celtic stock, the Gaels and Cymry, are supposed to have occupied of old the lands north of the Black Sea, the Cymry on that side of the Don occupied by the Κιμμέριοι of Æschylus, where the Crimea retains signs of their name, the Gaels on the other side, known in Europe afterwards as Gauls. Canon George Rawlinson, in his edition of Herodotus, supports the belief in an original identity of the words Scyth and Scot. There are no subjects of study upon which men are so positive as those in which it is impossible to obtain certain knowledge. Nearly every antiquary makes religion either of his personal opinion or of the last new theory out, and disdains the heresy of all who differ from him. Spenser's theory of the origin of the Irish accords with the best knowledge of his time. Scotland was called Albine—Shakespeare's Albany in "Lear"—from its mountain heights, by those who approached it on the north, the word being akin to Alp.

antique as that no monument remains of her beginning and first inhabiting; especially having been in those times without letters, but only bare traditions of times and remembrances of bards, which used to forge and falsify everything as they list, to please or displease any man.

Iren. Truly I must confess I do so, but yet not so absolutely as you suppose. I do herein rely upon those bards or Irish chronicles, though the Irish themselves, through their ignorance in matters of learning and deep judgment, do most constantly believe and avouch them: but unto them besides I add mine own reading; and out of them both together, with comparison of times, likewise of manners and customs, affinity of words and names, properties of natures and uses, resemblances of rites and ceremonies, monuments of churches and tombs, and many other like circumstances, I do gather a likelihood of truth, not certainly affirming anything, but by conferring of times, language, monuments, and such like, I do hunt out a probability of things, which I leave to your judgment to believe or refuse. Nevertheless there be some very ancient authors that make mention of these things, and some modern; which by comparing them with present times, experience, and their own reason, do open a window of great light unto the rest that is yet unseen; as, namely, of the elder times, Cæsar, Strabo, Tacitus, Ptolemy, Pliny, Pomponius Mela, and Berosus; of the later, Vincentius, Æneas Sylvius, Ludus, Buchanan; for that he himself being an Irish Scot, or Pict, by nation, and being very excellently learned, and industrious to seek out the truth of all things concerning the original of his own people, hath both set down the testimony of the ancients truly and his own opinion together, withal very reasonably, though in some things he doth somewhat flatter. Besides, the bards and Irish chroniclers themselves, though, through desire of pleasing too much, and ignorances of arts and purer learning, they have clouded the truth of those lines, yet there appear among them some relics of the true antiquity, though disguised, which a well-eyed man may happily discover and find out.

Eudox. How can there be any truth in them at all, since the ancient nations which first inhabited Ireland were altogether destitute of letters, much more of learning, by which they might leave the verity of things written? And those bards, coming also so many hundred years after, could not know what was done in former ages, nor deliver certainty of anything, but what they feigned out of their unlearned heads.

Iren. Those bards indeed, Cæsar writeth, delivered no certain truth of anything: neither is there any certain hold to be taken of any antiquity which is received by tradition, since all men be liars, and many lie when they will; yet for the antiquities of the written chronicles of Ireland, give me leave to say something, not to justify them, but to show that some of them might say truth. For where you say the Irish have always been without letters, you are therein much deceived; for it is certain that Ireland hath had the use of letters very anciently, and long before England.

Eudox. Is it possible? How comes it, then, that they are so unlearned still, being so old scholars? For learning, as the poet saith, *Emollit mores, nec sinit esse feros.* Whence then, I pray you, could they have those letters?

Iren. It is hard to say; for whether they at their first coming into the land, or afterwards by trading with other nations which had letters, learned them of them, or devised them amongst themselves, is very doubtful; but that they had letters anciently is nothing doubtful, for the Saxons of England are said to have their letters and learning and learned men from the Irish; and that also appeareth by the likeness of the character, for the Saxons' character is the same with the Irish. Now, the Scythians never, as I can read, of old had letters amongst them; therefore it seemeth that they had them from the nation which came out of Spain; for in Spain there were, as Strabo writeth, letters anciently used, whether brought unto them by the Phœnicians or the Persians, which, as it appeareth by him, had some footing there, or from Marsellis, which is said to have been inhabited by the Greeks, and from them to have had the Greek character: of which Marsellians it is said that the Gauls learned them first, and used them only for the furtherance of their trades and private business. For the Gauls, as is strongly to be proved by many ancient and authentical writers, did first inhabit all the sea-coast of Spain, even unto Cales and the mouth of the Straits, and peopled also a great part of Italy; which appeareth by sundry havens and cities in Spain called from them, as Portugallia, Gallecia, Galdunum, and also by sundry nations therein dwelling, which yet have received their own names of the Gauls; as the Regni, Presamarci, Tamari, Cineri, and divers others. All which Pomponius Mela, being himself a Spaniard, yet said to have descended from the Celts of France; whereby it is to be gathered that that nation which came out of Spain into Ireland were anciently Gauls, and that they brought with them those letters which they had anciently learned in Spain, first into Ireland, which some also say do much resemble the old Phœnician character, being likewise distinguished with prick and accent, as theirs anciently: but the further inquiry hereof needeth a place of longer discourse than this our short conference.

Eudox. Surely you have showed a great probability of that which I had thought impossible to have been proved; but that which you now say, that Ireland should have been peopled with the Gauls, seemeth much more strange; for all the chronicles do say that the west and south were possessed and inhabited of Spaniards, and Cornelius Tacitus doth also strongly affirm the same; all which you must overthrow and falsify, or else renounce your opinion.

Iren. Neither so nor so, for the Irish chronicles, as I showed you, being made by unlearned men, and writing things according to the appearance of the truth which they conceived, do err in the circumstances, not in the matter. For all that came out of Spain, they, being no diligent searchers into the differences of the nations, supposed to be Spaniards, and so called them; but the groundwork thereof is nevertheless true and certain, however they through ignorance disguise the same; or through vanity, whilst they would not seem to be ignorant, do thereupon build and enlarge many forged histories of their own antiquity, which they deliver to fools, and make them believe for true. As, for example, that first of one Gathelus, the son of Cecrops or Argos, who, having married the King of Egypt his daughter, thence sailed with her into Spain, and there inhabited. Then that of Nemedus and his sons, who, coming out of Scythia, peopled Ireland, and inhabited it with his sons 250 years, until he was overcome of the giants dwelling then in Ireland, and at the last quite banished and rooted out. After whom 200 years, the sons of one Dela, being Scythians, arrived there again and possessed the whole land, of which the youngest, called Slanius, in the end made himself monarch. Lastly, of the four sons of Milesius, king of Spain, which conquered the land from the Scythians and inhabited it with Spaniards, and called it of the name of the youngest, Hiberus, Hibernia. All which are in truth fables and very Milesian lies, as the Latin proverb is; for never was there such a king of Spain called Milesius, nor any such colony seated with his sons, as they feign, that can ever be proved; but yet under these tales you may in a manner see the truth lurk. For Scythians here inhabiting they name and put Spaniards, whereby appeareth that both these nations here inhabited, but whether very Spaniards, as the Irish greatly affect, is no ways to be proved.

Eudox. Whence cometh it, then, that the Irish do so greatly covet to fetch themselves from the Spaniards, since the old Gauls are a more ancient and much more honourable nation?

Iren. Even of a very desire of newfangledness and vanity; for they derive themselves from the Spaniards, as seeing them to be a very honourable people, and near bordering unto them. But all that is most vain; for from the Spaniards that now are, or that people that now inhabit Spain, they no ways can prove themselves to descend; neither should it be greatly glorious unto them, for the Spaniard that now is, is come from as rude and savage nations as they, there being, as there may be gathered by course of ages and view of their own history, though they therein labour much to ennoble themselves, scarce any drop of the old Spanish blood left in them; for all Spain was first conquered by the Romans, and filled with colonies from them, which were still increased, and the native Spaniard still cut off. Afterwards the Carthaginians, in all the long Punic wars having spoiled all Spain, and in the end subdued it wholly unto themselves, did, as it is likely, root out all that were affected to the Romans. And lastly, the Romans, having again recovered that country and beat out Hannibal, did doubtless cut off all that favoured the Carthaginians, so that betwixt them both, to and fro, there was scarce a native Spaniard left, but all inhabited of Romans. All which tempests of troubles being overblown, there long after arose a new storm, more dreadful than all the former, which overran all Spain, and made an infinite confusion of all things; that was, the coming down of the Goths, the Huns, and the Vandals; and lastly, all the nations of Scythia, which, like a mountain flood, did overflow all Spain, and quite drowned and washed away whatsoever relics there were left of the land-bred people; yea, and of all the Romans too. The which northern nations, finding the nature of the soil and the vehement heat thereof far differing from their constitutions, took no felicity in that country, but from thence passed over and did spread themselves into all countries of Christendom, of all which there is none but hath some mixture or sprinkling, if not thoroughly peopling of them. And yet, after all these, the Moors and the Barbarians, breaking over out of Africa, did finally possess all

Spain, or the most part thereof, and did tread under their heathenish feet whatever little they found yet there standing. The which though after they were beaten out by Ferdinand of Aragon and Isabella his wife, yet they were not so cleansed but that, through the marriages which they had made and mixture with the people of the land during their long continuance there, they had left no pure drop of Spanish blood, no more than of Roman or Scythian. So that, of all nations under heaven, I suppose the Spaniard is the most mingled and most uncertain. Wherefore most foolishly do the Irish think to ennoble themselves by wresting their ancientry from the Spaniard, who is unable to derive himself from any in certain.

Eudox. You speak very sharply, Ireneus, in dispraise of the Spaniard, whom some others boast to be the only brave nation under the sky.

Iren. So surely he is a very brave man; neither is that anything which I speak to his derogation; for in that I said he is a mingled people it is no dispraise, for I think there is no nation now in Christendom nor much further but is mingled and compounded with others. For it was a singular providence of God, and a most admirable purpose of His wisdom, to draw those northern heathen nations down into those Christian parts where they might receive Christianity, and to mingle nations so remote, miraculously to make, as it were, one blood and kindred of all people, and each to have knowledge of Him.

Eudox. Neither have you, sure, any more dishonoured the Irish, for you have brought them from very great and ancient nations as any were in the world, however fondly they affect the Spanish; for both Scythians and Gauls were two as mighty nations as ever the world brought forth. But is there any token, denomination or monument of the Gauls yet remaining in Ireland, as there is of the Scythians?

Iren. Yes, surely, very many words of the Gauls remaining, and yet daily used in common speech.

Eudox. What was the Gaulish speech? Is there any part of it still used among any nation?

Iren. The Gaulish speech is the very British, the which was very generally used here in all Britain before the coming of the Saxons, and yet is retained of the Welshmen, Cornishmen, and the Bretons of France; though time working the alteration of all things, and the trading and interdeal with other nations round about, have changed and greatly altered the dialect thereof; but yet the original words appear to be the same, as who hath list to read in Camden and Buchanan may see at large. Besides, there be many places, as havens, hills, towns, and castles, which yet bear the names from the Gauls, of the which Buchanan rehearseth above five hundred in Scotland; and I can, I think, recount near as many in Ireland which retain the old denomination of the Gauls, as the Menapii, Cauci, Venti, and others. By all which, and many other reasonable probabilities, which this short course will not suffer to be laid forth, it appeareth that the chief inhabitants in Ireland were Gauls, coming thither first out of Spain, and after from besides Tanais,[1] where the Goths, the Huns, and the Getes sat down; they also being, as it is said of some, ancient Gauls. And, lastly, passing out of Gallia itself, from all the seacoast of Belgia and Getica into all the southern coasts of Ireland, which they possessed and inhabited; whereupon it is at this day amongst the Irish a common use to call any stranger inhabitant there amongst them Gald; that is, descended from the Gauls.

Eudox. This is very likely, for even so did those Gauls anciently possess all the southern coasts of our Britain, which yet retain their old names; as the Belgæ in Somersetshire, Wiltshire, and part of Hampshire; Atrebatii in Berkshire; Regni in Sussex and Surrey; and many others. Now, thus far then I understand your opinion, that the Scythians planted in the north part of Ireland, the Spaniards (for so we call them, whatever they were that came

---

[1] *Tanais*, the River Don.

from Spain) in the west, the Gauls in the south; so that there now remain the east parts towards England, which I would be glad to understand from whence you do think them to be peopled.

Iren. Marry, I think of the Britons themselves, of which, though there be little footing now remaining, by reason that the Saxons afterwards, and lastly the English, driving out the inhabitants thereof, did possess and people it themselves; yet amongst the Tooles, the Byrnes or Briens, the Cavenaghs, and other nations in Leinster there is some memory of the Britons remaining, as the Tooles are called of the old British word *tol,* that is, a hill-country; the Briens of the British word *brin,* that is, woods; and the Cavenaghs of the word *caune,* that is, strong; so that in these three people the very denomination of the old Britons do still remain. Besides, when any flieth under the succour and protection of any against an enemy, he crieth unto him, "Comericke," that is, in the British, help, for the Briton is called in their own language Cymery. Furthermore, to prove the same, Ireland is, by Diodorus Siculus and by Strabo called Britannia, and a part of Great Britain. Finally, it appeareth by good record yet extant, that King Arthur, and before him Gurgunt, had all that island under their allegiance and subjection. Hereunto I could add many probabilities of the names of places, persons, and speeches, as I did in the former; but they should be too long for this, and I reserve them for another. And thus you have had my opinion how all that realm of Ireland was first peopled, and by what nations. After all which the Saxons succeeding, subdued it wholly to themselves. For, first, Egfrid, king of Northumberland, did utterly waste and subdue it, as appeareth out of Beda's complaint against him; and after him King Edgar brought it under his obedience, as appeareth by an ancient record, in which it is found written that he subdued all the islands of the north even unto Norway, and brought them into his subjection.

Eudox. This ripping of ancestors is very pleasing unto me, and indeed savoureth of good conceit and some reading withal. I see hereby how profitable travel and experience of foreign nations is to him that will apply them to good purpose. Neither, indeed, would I have thought that any such antiquities could have been avouched for the Irish, that maketh me the more to long to see some other of your observations which you have gathered out of that country, and have erst half promised to put forth. And sure in this mingling of nations appeareth (as you erst well noted) a wonderful providence and purpose of Almighty God, that stirred up the people in the farther parts of the world to seek out the regions so remote from them, and by that means both to restore their decayed habitations and to make Himself known to the heathen. But was there, I pray you, no more general employing of that island than first by the Scythians, which you say were the Scots, and afterwards by the Spaniards, besides the Gauls, Britons, and Saxons?

Iren. Yes, there was another, and that last and greatest, which was by the English, when the Earl Strongbow, having conquered that land, delivered up the same into the hands of Henry the Second, then king, who sent over thither a great store of gentlemen and other warlike people, amongst whom he distributed the land, and settled such a strong colony therein as never since could, with all the subtle practices of the Irish, be rooted out, but abide still a mighty people of so many as remain English of them.

Eudox. What is this that you say, of so many as remain English of them? Why, are not they that were once English English still?

Iren. No; for some of them are degenerated and grown mere Irish; yea, and more malicious to the English than the Irish themselves.

Eudox. What heard I? And is it possible that an Englishman, brought up in such sweet civility as England affords, should find such liking in that barbarous rudeness that he should forget his own nature and forego his own nation? How may this be, or what, I pray you, may be the cause thereof?

Iren. Surely nothing but the first evil ordinance and institution of that commonwealth. But thereof here is no fit place to speak, lest by the occasion thereof offering matter of a long discourse we might be drawn from this that we have in hand, namely, the handling of Abuses in the Customs of Ireland.

Eudox. In truth, Ireneus, you do well remember the plot of your first purpose; but yet from that, meseems, ye have much swerved in all this long discourse of the first inhabiting of Ireland, for what is that to your purpose?

Iren. Truly, very material; for if you marked the course of all that speech well, it was to show by what means the customs that now are in Ireland, being some of them indeed very strange and almost heathenish, were first brought in, and that was, as I said, by those nations from whom that country was first peopled; for the difference in manners and customs doth follow the difference of nations and people. The which I have declared to you to have been three especially which seated themselves here; to wit, first the Scythian, then the Gauls, and lastly the English. Notwithstanding that, I am not ignorant that there were sundry nations which got footing in that land, of the which there yet remain divers great families and septs, of whom I will also in their proper places make mention.

Eudox. You bring yourself, Ireneus, very well into the way again, notwithstanding that it seemeth that you were never out of the way; but now that you have passed through those antiquities, which I could have wished not so soon ended, begin when you please to declare what customs and manners have been derived from those nations to the Irish, and which of them you find fault withal.

VIEW OF THE STATE OF IRELAND. 87

Iren. I will begin, then, to count their customs in the same order that I counted their nations, and first with the Scythian or Scottish manners, of the which there is one use amongst them, to keep their cattle and to live themselves the most part of the year in boolies,[1] pasturing upon the mountain and waste wild places, and removing still to fresh land as they have depastured the former. The which appeareth plain to be the manner of the Scythians, as you may read in Olaus Magnus and Joh. Boemus, and yet is used amongst all the Tartarians and the people about the Caspian Sea, which are naturally Scythians, to live in herds, as they call them, being the very same that the Irish boolies are, driving their cattle continually with them and feeding only on their milk and white meats.

Eudox. What fault can you find with this custom? For though it be an old Scythian use, yet it is very behooveful in this country of Ireland, where there are great mountains and waste deserts full of grass, that the same should be eaten down and nourish many thousands of cattle for the good of the whole realm, which cannot, methinks, well be any other way than by keeping those boolies there, as ye have showed.

Iren. But by this custom of boolying there grow in the meantime many great enormities unto that commonwealth. For, first, if there be any outlaws or loose people, as they are never without some, which live upon stealths and spoils, they are evermore succoured and find relief only in these boolies, being upon the waste places; whereas else they should be driven shortly to starve, or to come down to the towns to seek relief, where by one means or other they should soon be caught. Besides, such stealths of cattle as they make they bring commonly to those boolies, being upon those waste places, where they are readily received, and the thief harboured from danger of law or such

---

[1] *Boolies*, herdsmen's huts in the hill pastures ; old Irish bó, a cow or ox, bóchaill or búachaijl, a herdsman.

officers as might light upon him. Moreover, the people that thus live in those boolies grow thereby the more barbarous and live more licentiously than they could in towns, using what manners they list and practising what mischiefs and villanies they will, either against the government there by their combinations, or against private men, whom they malign[1] by stealing their goods or murdering themselves; for there they think themselves half-exempted from law and obedience, and having once tasted freedom, do, like a steer that hath been long out of his yoke, grudge and repine ever after to come under rule again.

Eudox. By your speech, Ireneus, I perceive more evil comes by this use of boolies than good by their grazing, and therefore it may well be reformed; but that must be in his due course. Do you proceed to the next.

Iren. They have another custom from the Scythians; that is, the wearing of mantles and long glibbs,[2] which is a thick curled bush of hair hanging down over their eyes, and monstrously disguising them; which are both very bad and hurtful.

Eudox. Do you think that the mantle cometh from the Scythians? I would surely think otherwise; for by that which I have read, it appeareth that most nations of the world anciently used the mantle. For the Jews used it, as you may read of Elias's mantle, &c.; the Chaldees also used it, as ye may read in Diodorus; the Egyptians likewise used it, as ye may read in Herodotus, and may be gathered by the description of Berenice, in the Greek commentary upon Callimachus. The Greeks also used it anciently, as appeareth by Venus's mantle lined with stars, though afterwards they changed the form thereof into their cloaks, called *pallia*, as some of the Irish also use. And the ancient Latins and Romans used it; as you may read in Virgil, who was

[1] *Malign*, now limited in sense to speaking ill, when used as a verb, was applied first to malicious action. The "gn" in malign representing geno, gigno; malignity, ill nature.

[2] *Glibbs.* "Glib" is the old Irish word for a lock of hair.

a very great antiquary, that Evander, when Æneas came to him at his feast, did entertain and feast him, sitting on the ground and lying on mantles; insomuch as he useth the very word *mantile* for a mantle :—

———"*Humi mantilia sternunt.*"

So that it seemeth that the mantle was a general habit to most nations, and not proper to the Scythians only, as you suppose.

Iren. I cannot deny but that anciently it was common to most; and yet sithence disused and laid away. But in this latter age of the world, since the decay of the Roman Empire, it was renewed and brought in again by those northern nations, when, breaking out of their cold caves and frozen habitations, into the sweet soil of Europe, they brought with them their usual weeds, fit to shield the cold and that continual frost to which they had at home been inured. The which yet they left not off, by reason that they were in perpetual wars with the nations whom they had invaded, but still removing from place to place, carried always with them that weed, as their house, their bed, and their garment; and coming lastly into Ireland, they found there more special use thereof, by reason of the raw, cold climate, from whom it is now grown into that general use in which that people now have it. After whom the Gauls succeeding, yet finding the like necessity of that garment, continued the like use thereof.

Eudox. Since, then, the necessity thereof is so commodious, as you allege, that it is instead of housing, bedding, and clothing, what reason have you then to wish so necessary a thing cast off?

Iren. Because the commodity doth not countervail the discommodity, for the inconveniences which thereby do arise are much more many; for it is a fit house for an outlaw, a meet bed for a rebel, and an apt cloak for a thief. First, the outlaw, being for his many crimes and villanies banished from the towns and houses of honest men, and wandering in waste places, far from danger of law, maketh his mantle his house, and under it covereth himself from the wrath of Heaven, from the offence of the earth, and from the sight of men. When it raineth, it is his pent-house; when it bloweth, it is his tent; when it freezeth, it is his tabernacle. In summer he can wear it loose; in winter he can wrap it close; at all times he can use it, never heavy, never cumbersome. Likewise for a rebel it is as serviceable; for in this war that he maketh — if at least it deserve the name of war, when he still flieth from his foe, and lurketh in the thick woods and strait passages, waiting for advantages—it is his bed, yea, and almost his household stuff. For the wood is his house against all weathers, and his mantle is his couch to sleep in; therein he wrappeth himself round, and coucheth himself strongly against the gnats, which in that country do more annoy the naked rebels whilst they keep the woods, and do more sharply wound them, than all their enemies' swords or spears, which can seldom come nigh them. Yea, and oftentimes their mantle serveth them when they are near driven, being wrapped above their left arm, instead of a target; for it is hard to cut through with a sword. Besides, it is light to bear, light to throw away, and being, as they commonly are, naked, it is to them all in all. Lastly, for a thief it is so handsome,[1] as it may seem it was first invented for him, for under it he may cleanly convey any fit pillage that cometh handsomely in his way. And when he goeth abroad in the night in freebooting, it is his best and surest friend; for, lying, as they often do, two or three nights together abroad to watch for their booty, with that they can prettily shroud themselves under a bush or a bankside till they can conveniently do their errand; and when all is over, he can, in his mantle, pass through any town or company, being close hooded over his head, as he useth, from knowledge of any to whom he is endangered. Besides this, he or any man else that is disposed to mischief or villainy may, under his mantle, go privily armed;

[1] *Handsome*, handy, serviceable.

VIEW OF THE STATE OF IRELAND. 91

without suspicion of any, carry his headpiece, his skean,[1] or pistol if he please, to be always in readiness. Thus necessary and fitting is a mantle for a bad man, and surely for a bad housewife it is no less convenient; for some of them that be wandering women, called of them mona-shull, it is half a wardrobe; for in summer you shall find her arrayed commonly but in her smock and mantle, to be more ready for her light services: in winter, and in her travail, it is her cloak and safeguard, and also a coverlet for her lewd exercise; and when she hath filled her vessel, under it she can hide both her burden and her blame; yea, and when her bastard is born it serves instead of swaddling-clouts. And as for all other good women which love to do but little work, how handsome it is to lie in and sleep, or to louse[2] themselves in the sunshine, they that have been but a while in Ireland can well witness. Sure I am that you will think it very unfit for a good housewife to stir in, or to busy herself about her housewifery in such sort as she should. These be some of the abuses for which I would think it meet to forbid all mantles.

Eudox. O evil-minded man, that, having reckoned up so many uses of a mantle, will yet wish it to be abandoned! Sure I think Diogenes's dish did never serve his master for more turns, notwithstanding that he made it his dish, his cup, his cap, his measure, his water-pot, than a mantle doth an Irishman. But I see they be most to bad intents, and therefore I will join with you in abolishing it. But what blame lay you to the glibb? Take heed, I pray you, that you be not too busy therewith, for fear of your own blame; seeing our Englishmen take it up in such a general fashion to wear their hair so immeasurably long that some of them exceed the longest Irish glibbs.

Iren. I fear not the blame of any undeserved dislikes; but for the Irish glibbs, they are as fit masks as a mantle is for a thief.

---

[1] *Skean*, knife, dagger, old Irish *scian*.
[2] *Louse*, be free from encumbrance or employment; old French leisir, later loysir.

For whensoever he hath run himself into that peril of law that he will not be known, he either cutteth off his glibb quite, by which he becometh nothing like himself, or pulleth it so low down over his eyes that it is very hard to discern his thievish countenance, and therefore fit to be trussed up with the mantle.

Eudox. Truly these three Scythian abuses I hold most fit to be taken away with sharp penalties, and sure I wonder how they have been kept thus long, notwithstanding so many good provisions and orders as have been devised for that people.

Iren. The cause thereof shall appear to you hereafter; but let us now go forward with our Scythian customs. Of which the next that I have to treat of is the manner of raising their cry in their conflicts, and at other troublesome times of uproar; the which is very natural Scythian, as you may read in Diodorus Siculus and in Herodotus, describing the manner of the Scythians and Parthians coming to give the charge at battles; at which it is said that they came running with a terrible yell, as if heaven and earth would have gone together; which is the very image of the Irish hubbub which their kern[1] use at their first encounter. Besides, the same Herodotus writeth, that they used in their battles to call upon the names of their captains or generals, and sometimes upon their greatest kings deceased, as in that battle of Thomyris against Cyrus; which custom to this day manifestly appeareth amongst the Irish. For at their joining of battle they likewise call upon their captain's name, or the word of his ancestors; as they under O'Neil cry "Laundarg-abo," that is, the bloody hand, which is O'Neil's badge; they under O'Brien call "Launlaider," that is, the strong hand. And to their ensample, the old English also, which there remaineth, have gotten up their cries Scythian-like, as "Crom-abo" and "Butler-abo."[2] And here also lieth open

[1] *Kern*, the light-armed Irish foot soldier, carrying dart and skean; *cearn*, a man; *cern*, victory.

[2] The old Irish battle shout, "abo," is in our word "bugaboo," where bug is the old word for a cause of terror, a spectre, as bugbear, a spectre in form of a bear. This word "bug" and the cry "abo" may be akin.

VIEW OF THE STATE OF IRELAND. 93

another manifest proof that the Irish be Scyths or Scots, for in all their encounters they use one very common word, crying " Ferragh, Ferragh," which is a Scottish word; to wit, the name of one of the first kings of Scotland, called Feragus, or Fergus, which fought against the Picts, as you may read in Buchanan, *De Rebus Scoticis ;* but, as others write, it was long before that the name of their chief captain, under whom they fought against the Africans; the which was then so fortunate unto them, that ever sithence they have used to call upon his name in their battles.

Eudox. Believe me, this observation of yours, Ireneus, is very good and delightful; far beyond the blind conceit of some who, I remember, have upon the same word Ferragh made a very blunt conjecture; as, namely, Mr. Stanihurst,[1] who, though he be the same countryman born, that should search more nearly into the secret of these things, yet hath strayed from the truth all the heavens wide, as they say; for he thereupon grounded a very gross imagination that the Irish should descend from the Egyptians which came into that island, first under the leading of one Scota, the daughter of Pharaoh; whereupon they use, saith he, in all their battles, to call upon the name of Pharaoh, crying " Ferragh, Ferragh." Surely he shoots wide on the bowhand and very far from the mark. For I would first know of him what ancient ground of authority he hath for such a senseless fable, and if he have any of the rude Irish books, as it may be he hath; yet meseems that a man of his learning should not so lightly have been carried away with old wives' tales from approvance of his own reason; for whether it be a smack of any learned judgment to say that Scota is like an Egyptian word, let the learned judge. But his Scota rather comes of the Greek σκότος,

---

[1] Richard Stanihurst, the translator of Virgil, published at Antwerp in 1584 a book, *De Rebus in Hibernia Gestis.* He had been at work on it since the close of his college days. Though born in Dublin, he was bred in England, and held the opinions prevalent in England upon Irish policy. Afterwards he became a Roman Catholic, and is said to have wished to recant the errors in his Irish Chronicle.

that is, darkness, which hath not let him see the light of the truth.

Iren. You know not, Eudoxus, how well Mr. Stanihurst could see in the dark; perhaps he hath owls' or cats' eyes; but well I wot he seeth not well the very light in matters of more weight. But as for Ferragh, I have told my conjecture only; and yet thus much I have more to prove a likelihood, that there be yet at this day in Ireland many Irishmen, chiefly in the northern parts, called by the name of Ferragh. But let that now be; this only for this place sufficeth, that it is a word used in their common hubbubs, the which, with all the rest, is to be abolished, for that it discovereth an affectation to Irish captainry, which in this platform [1] I endeavour specially to beat down. There be other sorts of cries also used amongst the Irish which savour greatly of the Scythian barbarism; as their lamentations at their burials with despairful outcries and immoderate wailings, the which Mr. Stanihurst might also have used for an argument to prove them Egyptians; for so in Scripture it is mentioned that the Egyptians lamented for the death of Joseph. Others think this custom to come from the Spaniards, for that they do immeasurably likewise bewail their dead. But the same is not proper Spanish, but altogether heathenish, brought in thither first either by the Scythians, or the Moors that were Africans, and long possessed that country. For it is the manner of all pagans and infidels to be intemperate in their wailings of their dead, for that they had no faith nor hope of salvation. And this ill custom also is specially noted by Diodorus Siculus to have been in the Scythians, and is yet amongst the northern Scots at this day, as you may read in their chronicles.

---

[1] *Platform*, used here as, "plot," for scheme or plan. So the Maid of Orleans in *Henry VI.*, Part I., Act ii. scene 1, counsels against the English—

"To gather our soldiers, scattered and dispersed,
And lay new platforms to endamage them."

Eudox. This is sure an ill custom also, but yet doth not so much concern civil reformation as abuse in religion.

Iren. I did not rehearse it as one of the abuses which I thought most worthy of reformation; but having made mention of Irish cries, I thought this manner of lewd crying and howling not impertinent to be noted, as uncivil and Scythian-like; for by these old customs and other like conjectural circumstances the descents of nations can only be proved where other monuments of writings are not remaining.

Eudox. Then, I pray you, whensoever in your discourse you meet with them by the way, do not shun, but boldly touch them; for, besides their great pleasure and delight for their antiquity, they bring also great profit and help unto civility.

Iren. Then sith you will have it so, I will here take occasion, since I lately spake of their manner of cries in joining of battle, to speak also somewhat of the manner of their arms and array in battle, with other customs perhaps worthy the noting. And first of their arms and weapons, amongst which their broadswords are proper Scythian; for such the Scyths used commonly, as you may read in Olaus Magnus; and the same also the old Scots used, as you may read in Buchanan and in Solinus, where the pictures of them are in the same form expressed. Also their short bows and little quivers with short-bearded arrows are very Scythian, as you may read in the same Olaus. And the same sort both of bows, quivers, and arrows are at this day to be seen commonly amongst the northern Irish-Scots, whose Scottish bows are not past three-quarters of a yard long, with a string of wreathed hemp slackly bent, and whose arrows are not much above half-an-ell long, tipped with steel heads, made like common broad arrow-heads, but much more sharp and slender, that they enter into a man or horse most cruelly, notwithstanding that they are shot forth weakly. Moreover, their long broad shields, made up with wicker rods, which are commonly used amongst the said northern Irish, but especially of the Scots, are brought from the Scythians, as you may read in Olaus Magnus, Solinus, and others; likewise their going to battle without armour on their bodies or heads, but trusting to the thickness of their glibbs, the which, they say, will sometimes bear off a good stroke, is mere Scythian, as you may see in the said images of the old Scyths or Scots set forth by Herodianus and others. Besides, their confused kind of march in heaps without any order or array, their clashing of swords together, their fierce running upon their enemies, and their manner of fight resembleth altogether that which is read in histories to have been used of the Scythians. By which it may almost infallibly be gathered, together with other circumstances, that the Irish are very Scots or Scyths originally, though sithence intermingled with many other nations repairing and joining unto them. And to these I may also add another strong conjecture which cometh to my mind that I have often observed there amongst them; that is, certain religious ceremonies which are very superstitiously yet used amongst them, the which are also written by sundry authors to have been observed amongst the Scythians, by which it may very vehemently be presumed that the nations were anciently all one. For Plutarch, as I remember, in his treatise of Homer, endeavouring to search out the truth what countryman Homer was, proveth it most strongly, as he thinketh, that he was an Æolian born, for that, in describing a sacrifice of the Greeks, he omitted the loin, the which all the other Grecians, saving the Æolians, used to burn in their sacrifices; also for that he makes the entrails to be roasted on five spits, which was the proper manner of the Æolians, who only, of all the nations of Grecia, used to sacrifice in that sort. By which he inferreth, necessarily, that Homer was an Æolian. And by the same reason may I as reasonably conclude that the Irish are descended from the Scythians, for that they use, even to this day, some of the same ceremonies which the Scythians anciently used. As, for example,

VIEW OF THE STATE OF IRELAND. 97

you may read in Lucian, in that sweet dialogue which is entitled *Toxaris*, or of Friendship, that the common oath of the Scythian was by the sword and by the fire, for that they accounted those two special divine powers which should work vengeance on the perjurers. So do the Irish at this day, when they go to battle, say certain prayers or charms to their swords, making a cross therewith upon the earth and thrusting the points of their blades into the ground, thinking thereby to have the better success in fight. Also they use commonly to swear by their swords. Also the Scythians used, when they would bind any solemn vow or combination amongst them, to drink a bowl of blood together, vowing thereby to spend their last blood in that quarrel; and even so do the wild Scots, as you may read in Buchanan, and some of the northern Irish. Likewise at the kindling of the fire and lighting of candles they say certain prayers and use some other superstitious rites, which show that they honour the fire and the light; for all those northern nations, having been used to be annoyed with much cold and darkness, are wont, therefore, to have the fire and sun in great veneration; like as, contrariwise, the Moors and Egyptians, which are much offended and grieved with extreme heat of the sun, do every morning when the sun ariseth fall to cursing and banning of him as their plague. You may also read in the same book, in the tale of Anacharsis, that it was the manner of the Scythians, when any one of them was heavily wronged, and would assemble unto him any forces of people to join with him in his revenge, to sit in some public place for certain days upon an ox-hide, to which there would resort all such persons as, being disposed to take arms, would enter into his pay or join with him in his quarrel. And the same you may likewise read to have been the ancient manner of the wild Scots, which are indeed the very natural Irish. Moreover, the Scythians used to swear by their king's hand, as Olaus showeth. And so do the Irish use now to swear by their lord's hand; and to forswear it, hold it more

G

criminal than to swear by God. Also, the Scythians said that they were once a year turned into wolves, and so is it written of the Irish; though Master Camden, in a better sense, doth suppose it was a disease called lycanthropia, so named of the wolf. And yet some of the Irish do use to make the wolf their gossip. The Scythians used also to seethe the flesh in the hide, and so do the northern Irish. The Scythians used to draw the blood of the beast living, and to make meat thereof, and so do the Irish in the north still. Many such customs I could recount unto you, as of their old manner of marrying, of burying, of dancing, of singing, of feasting, of cursing, though Christians have wiped out the most part of them; by resemblance whereof it might plainly appear to you that the nations are the same, but that by the reckoning of these few which I have told unto you I find my speech drawn out to a greater length than I purposed. Thus much only for this time, I hope, shall suffice you, to think that the Irish are anciently deduced from the Scythians.

Eudox. Surely, Ireneus, I have heard, in these few words, that from you which I would have thought had been impossible to have been spoken of times so remote and customs so ancient; with delight whereof I was all that while, as it were, entranced, and carried so far from myself as that I am now right sorry that you ended so soon. But I marvel much how it cometh to pass that in so long continuance of time, and so many ages come between, yet any jot of those old rites and superstitious customs should remain amongst them.

Iren. It is no cause of wonder at all, for it is the manner of many nations to be very superstitious and diligent observers of old customs and antiquities, which they receive by continual tradition from their parents, by recording of their bards and chronicles, in their songs, and by daily use and ensample of their elders.

Eudox. But have you, I pray you, observed any such customs amongst them, brought likewise from the Spaniards or Gauls, as these from the Scythians, that may sure be very material to your first purpose?

Iren. Some perhaps I have, and who that will by this occasion more diligently mark and compare their customs shall find many more. But there are fewer remaining of the Gauls or Spaniards than of the Scythians, by reason that the parts which they then possessed, lying upon the coast of the western and southern sea, were sithence visited with strangers and foreign people, repairing thither for traffic and for fishing, which is very plentiful upon those coasts, for the trade and interdeal of sea-coast nations one with another worketh more civility and good fashions, all seamen being naturally desirous of new fashions, than amongst the inland folk, which are seldom seen of foreigners; yet some of such as I have noted I will recount unto you. And first I will, for the better credit of the rest, show you one out of their statutes, among which it is enacted that no man shall wear his beard, only on the upper lip, shaving all his chin. And this was the ancient manner of the Spaniards, as yet it is of all the Mahometans to cut off all their beards close, save only their moustaches, which they wear long. And the cause of this use was, for that they, being bred in a hot country, found much hair on their faces and other parts to be noyous unto them, for which cause they did cut it most away; like as, contrarily, all other nations brought up in cold countries do use to nourish their hair to keep them the warmer, which was the cause that the Scythians and Scots wore glibbs, as I showed you, to keep their heads warm, and long beards to defend their faces from cold. From them also, I think, came saffron shirts and smocks, which were devised by them in those hot countries where saffron is very common and rife, for avoiding that evil which cometh by much sweating and long wearing of linen. Also the women amongst the old Spaniards had the charge of all household affairs, both at home and abroad, as Boemus writeth, though now the Spaniards use it quite otherwise. And so have the Irish women the trust and care of all things, both at home and in the field. Likewise round leather targets in the Spanish fashion, who used it, for the most part, painted, which in Ireland they use also in many places, coloured after their rude fashion. Moreover, the manner of their women riding on the wrong side of the horse, I mean with their faces toward the right side, as the Irish use, is, as they say, old Spanish, and some say African, for amongst them the women, they say, used so to ride. Also the deep smock-sleeve which the Irish women use, they say, was old Spanish, and is used yet in Barbary; and yet that should seem rather to be an old English fashion, for in armoury the fashion of the Manche, which is given in arms by many, being indeed nothing else but a sleeve, is fashioned much like to that sleeve; and that knights in ancient times used to wear their mistress's or love's sleeve upon their arms, as appeareth by that which is written of Sir Launcelot, that he wore the sleeve of the fair maid of Asteloth in a tourney, whereat Queen Guinivere was much displeased.

Eudox. Your conceit is good and well fitting for things so far grown from certainty of knowledge and learning, only upon likelihoods and conjectures. But have you any customs remaining from the Gauls or Britons?

Iren. I have observed a few of either, and who will better search into them may find more; and first, the profession of their bards was, as Cæsar writeth, usual amongst the Gauls, and the same was also common amongst the Britons, and is not yet altogether left off with the Welsh, which are their posterity. For all the fashions of the Gauls and Britons, as he testifieth, were much like. The long darts came also from the Gauls, as you may read in the same Cæsar and in Joh. Boemus. Likewise the said Joh. Boemus writeth that the Gauls used swords a handful broad, and so do the Irish now; also they used long wicker shields in battle, that should cover their whole bodies; and so do the

VIEW OF THE STATE OF IRELAND.

northern Irish. But I have not seen such fashioned targets used in the southern parts, but only amongst the northern people and Irish-Scots; I do think that they were brought in rather by the Scythians than by the Gauls. Also the Gauls used to drink their enemies' blood and paint themselves therewith. So also they write that the old Irish were wont; and so have I seen some of the Irish do, but not their enemies' but friends' blood, as, namely, at the execution of a notable traitor at Limerick, called Murrogh O'Brien, I saw an old woman, which was his foster-mother, take up his head whilst he was quartered and suck up all the blood that ran thereout, saying that the earth was not worthy to drink it, and therewith also steeped her face and breast and tore her hair, crying out and shrieking most terribly.

Eudox. You have very well run through such customs as the Irish have derived from the first old nations which inhabited the land; namely, the Scythians, the Spaniards, the Gauls, and Britons. It now remaineth that you take in hand the customs of the old English which are amongst the Irish; of which I do not think that you shall have much cause to find fault with, considering that by the English most of the old bad Irish customs were abolished, and more civil fashions brought in their stead.

Iren. You think otherwise, Eudox, than I do; for the chiefest abuses which are now in that realm are grown from the English, and some of them are now much more lawless and licentious than the very wild Irish; so that as much care as was by them had to reform the Irish, so and much more must now be used to reform them; so much time doth alter the manners of men.

Eudox. That seemeth very strange which you say, that men should so much degenerate from their first natures as to grow wild.

Iren. So much can liberty and ill examples do.

Eudox. What liberty had the English there, more than they had here at home? Were not the laws planted amongst them at the first, and had they not governors to curb and keep them still in awe and obedience?

Iren. They had, but it was for the most part such as did more hurt than good; for they had governors for the most part of themselves, and commonly out of the two families of the Geraldines and Butlers, both adversaries and co-rivals one against the other; who, though for the most part they were but deputies under some of the kings of England's sons, brethren, or other near kinsmen, who were the king's lieutenants, yet they swayed so much, as they had all the rule and the others but the title. Of which Butlers and Geraldines, albeit, I must confess, they were very brave and worthy men, as also of others the peers of that realm, made lord-deputies and lord-justices at sundry times; yet through greatness of their late conquests and seigniories they grew insolent, and bent both the regal authority and also their private powers one against another, to the utter subversion of themselves and strengthening of the Irish again. This you may read plainly discovered by a letter written from the citizens of Cork out of Ireland to the Earl of Shrewsbury, then in England, and remaining yet upon record, both in the Tower of London and also among the chronicles of Ireland; wherein it is by them complained that the English lords and gentlemen who then had great possessions in Ireland began, through pride and insolency, to make private wars one against another; and when either party was weak, they would wage and draw in the Irish to take their part; by which means they both greatly encouraged and enabled the Irish, which till that time had been shut up within the mountains of Slewlogher, and weakened and disabled themselves: insomuch that their revenues were wonderfully impaired, and some of them which are there reckoned to have been able to have spent £1200 or £1300 per annum of old rent (that I may say no more), besides their commodities of creeks and havens, were now scarce able to dispend the third part. From which disorder, and through other huge calamities which have come upon them thereby, they are almost now grown like the Irish—I mean of such English as were planted above towards the west; for the English Pale hath preserved itself through nearness of the state in reasonable civility; but the rest which dwelt in Connaught and in Munster, which is the sweetest soil of Ireland, and some in Leinster and Ulster, are degenerate; yea, and some of them have quite shaken off their English names and put on Irish, that they might be altogether Irish.

Eudox. Is it possible that any should so far grow out of frame that they should, in so short space, quite forget their country and their own name? That is a most dangerous lethargy, much worse than that of Messala Corvinus,[1] who, being a most learned man, through sickness forgat his own name. But can you count us any of this kind?

Iren. I cannot, but by the report of the Irish themselves, who report that the Macmahons in the north were anciently English; to wit, descended from the Fitz-Ursulas, which was a noble family in England; and that the same appeareth by the signification of their Irish names. Likewise that the Macswynes, now in Ulster, were anciently of the Veres in England; but that they themselves, for hatred of the English, so disguised their names.

Eudox. Could they ever conceive any such dislike of their own natural countries as that they would be ashamed of their name, and bite at the dug from which they sucked life?

Iren. I wot well there should be none; but proud hearts do oftentimes (like wanton colts) kick at their mothers; as we read Alcibiades and Themistocles did, who, being banished out of Athens, fled unto the kings of Asia, and there stirred them up to war against their country, in which wars they themselves were chieftains. So, they say, did these Macswynes and Macmahons, or rather Veres and Fitz-Ursulas, for private despite, turn themselves

---

[1] *Messala Corvinus*, who died B.C. 3, was a soldier and scholar who had the favour of Antony and Augustus, and was a friend of Horace, Ovid, and Tibullus.

against England. For at such time as Robert Vere, Earl of Oxford, was in the Barons' wars against King Richard the Second, through the malice of the peers, banished the realm and proscribed, he with his kinsman Fitz-Ursula fled into Ireland; where being prosecuted, and afterwards in England put to death, his kinsman there remaining behind in Ireland rebelled, and conspiring with the Irish, did quite cast off both their English name and allegiance; since which time they have so remained still, and have since been counted mere Irish. The very like is also reported of the Macswynes, Macmahons, and Macshehies of Munster, how they likewise were anciently English, and old followers to the Earl of Desmond, until the reign of King Edward the Fourth; at which time the Earl of Desmond that then was, called Thomas, being through false subornation, as they say, of the Queen, for some offence by her against him conceived, brought to his death at Tredagh most unjustly, notwithstanding that he was a very good and sound subject to the King; thereupon all his kinsmen of the Geraldines, which then was a mighty family in Munster, in revenge of that huge wrong, rose into arms against the King, and utterly renounced and forsook all obedience to the Crown of England; to whom the said Macswynes, Macshehies, and Macmahons, being then servants and followers, did the like, and have ever sithence so continued. And with them, they say, all the people of Munster went out, and many other of them which were mere English thenceforth joined with the Irish against the King, and termed themselves very Irish, taking on them Irish habits and customs, which could never since be clean wiped away; but the contagion hath remained still amongst their posterities. Of which sort, they say, be most of their surnames which end in *an*, as Hernan, Shinan, Mungan, &c., the which now account themselves natural Irish. Other great houses there be of the English in Ireland, which, through licentious conversing with the Irish, or marrying, or fostering with them or lack of meet nurture, or other such unhappy occasions, have degenerated from their ancient dignities, and are now grown as Irish as O'Hanlon's breech, as the proverb there is.

Eudox. In truth, this which you tell is a most shameful hearing, and to be reformed with most sharp censures in so great personages, to the terror of the meaner; for if the lords and chief men degenerate, what shall be hoped of the peasants and baser people? And hereby sure you have made a fair way unto yourself to lay open the Abuses of their evil Customs, which you have now next to declare; the which no doubt but are very bad, being borrowed from the Irish, as their apparel, their language, their riding, and many other the like.

Iren. You cannot but hold them sure to be very uncivil; for were they at the best that they were of old, when they were brought in, they should in so long an alteration of time seem very uncouth and strange. For it is to be thought that the use of all England was in the reign of Henry the Second, when Ireland was planted with English, very rude and barbarous; so as, if the same should be now used in England by any, it would seem worthy of sharp correction and of new laws for reformation, for it is but even the other day since England grew civil. Therefore, in counting the evil Customs of the English there, I will not have regard whether the beginning thereof were English or Irish, but will have respect only to the inconvenience thereof. And first I have to find fault with the abuse of language; that is, for the speaking of Irish among the English, which as it is unnatural that any people should love another's language more than their own, so it is very inconvenient and the cause of many other evils.

Eudox. It seemeth strange to me that the English should take more delight to speak that language than their own, whereas they should, methinks, rather take scorn to inure their tongues thereto. For it hath ever been the use of the conqueror to despise the language of the conquered and to force him by all means to learn his. So did the Romans always use, insomuch that there is almost no nation in the world but is sprinkled with their language. It were good therefore, meseems, to search out the original cause of this evil, for the same being discovered, a redress thereof will the more easily be provided; for I think it very strange that, the English being so many and the Irish so few as they then were left, the fewer should draw the more unto their use.

Iren. I suppose that the chief cause of bringing in the Irish language amongst them was specially their fostering and marrying with the Irish, the which are two most dangerous infections. For, first, the child that sucketh the milk of the nurse must of necessity learn his first speech of her, the which being the first inured to his tongue, is ever after most pleasing unto him; insomuch as, though he afterwards be taught English, yet the smack of the first will always abide with him; and not only of the speech, but also of the manners and conditions.[1] For, besides that young children be like apes, which will affect and imitate what they see done before them, especially by their nurses whom they love so well, they moreover draw into themselves together with their suck even the nature and disposition of their nurses; for the mind followeth much the temperature of the body, and also the words are the image of the mind; so as they proceeding from the mind, the mind must needs be affected with the words; so that, the speech being Irish, the heart must needs be Irish, for out of the abundance of the heart the tongue speaketh. The next is the marrying with the Irish, which how dangerous a thing it is in all commonwealths appeareth to every simplest sense; and though some great ones have perhaps used such matches with their vassals, and have of them nevertheless raised worthy issue, as Telamon did with Tecmessa, Alexander the Great with Roxana,

---

[1] In like manner the Northmen, who came with Rollo into France, lost, after a generation or two, their original language, their children learning the language of French-speaking nurses and mothers.

and Julius Cæsar with Cleopatra, yet the example is so perilous as it is not to be adventured; for instead of those few good I could count unto them infinite many evil. And, indeed, how can such matching succeed well, seeing that commonly the child taketh most of his nature of the mother, besides speech, manners, and inclination, which are, for the most part, agreeable to the conditions of their mothers? For by them they are first framed and fashioned, so as what they receive once from them they will hardly ever after forego. Therefore are these evil customs of fostering and marrying with Irish most carefully to be restrained, for of these two the third evil, that is, the custom of language, which I spake of, chiefly proceedeth.

Eudox. But are there not laws already provided for avoiding of this evil?

Iren. Yes, I think there be, but as good never a whit as never the better; for what do statutes avail without penalties, or laws without charge of execution? For so there is another like law enacted against wearing of the Irish apparel, but neverthemore is it observed by any, or executed by them that have the charge; for they in their private discretions think it not fit to be forced upon the poor wretches of that country, which are not worth the price of English apparel, nor expedient to be practised against the abler sort, by reason that the country, say they, doth yield no better; and were there better to be had, yet these were fitter to be used; as, namely, the mantle in travelling, because there be no inns where meet bedding may be had, so that his mantle serves him then for a bed; the leather-quilted jack[1] in journeying and in camping, for that it is fittest to be under his shirt of mail and for any occasion of sudden service, as there happen many, to cover his trouse on horseback; the great linen roll which the

---

[1] The old jack, as a coat worn with a coat of mail, has its name ascribed by Ducange to the revolt of the peasantry known as the *Jacquerie* in 1358. Our word jacket, Fr. jaquette, is its diminutive.

women wear to keep their heads warm after cutting their hair, which they use in any sickness; besides their thick-folded linen shirts, their long-sleeved smocks, their half-sleeved coats, their silken fillets, and all the rest, they will devise some colour for, either of necessity, or of antiquity, or of comeliness.

Eudox. But what colour soever they allege, methinks it not expedient that the execution of a law once ordained should be left to the discretion of the judge or officer, but that, without partiality or regard, it should be fulfilled as well on English as Irish.

Iren. But they think this preciseness in reformation of apparel not to be so material or greatly pertinent.

Eudox. Yes, surely, but it is; for men's apparel is commonly made according to their conditions, and their conditions are oftentimes governed by their garments; for the person that is gowned is by his gown put in mind of gravity, and also restrained from lightness, by the very unaptness of his weed. Therefore it is written by Aristotle, that when Cyrus had overcome the Lydians, that were a warlike nation, and devised to bring them to a more peaceable life, he changed their apparel and music, and instead of their short warlike coat, clothed them in long garments like women; and instead of their warlike music, appointed to them certain lascivious lays and loose jigs, by which, in short space, their minds were so mollified and abated that they forgot their former fierceness and became most tender and effeminate. Whereby it appeareth that there is not a little in the garment to the fashioning of the mind and conditions. But be these which you have described the fashions of the Irish weeds?

Iren. No; all these which I have rehearsed to you be not Irish garments, but English, for the quilted-leather jack is old English; for it was the proper weed of the horseman, as you may read in Chaucer, when he describeth Sir Thopas's apparel and armour, as he went to fight against the giant in his robe of shecklaton,[1] which is that kind of gilded leather with which they used to embroider their Irish jackets. And there likewise by all that description you may see the very fashion and manner of the Irish horseman most truly set forth in his long hose, his riding-shoes of costly cordwain, his hacqueton and his haberjeon,[2] with all the rest thereunto belonging.

Eudox. I surely thought that the manner had been Irish, for it is far differing from that we have now; as also all the furniture of his horse, his strong brass bit, his sliding-reins, his shank-pillion without stirrups, his manner of mounting, his fashion of riding, his charging of his spear aloft above head, the form of his spear.

Iren. No, sure, they be native English, and brought in by the Englishmen first into Ireland. Neither is the same accounted an uncomely manner of riding; for I have heard some great warriors say that, in all the services which they had seen abroad in foreign countries, they never saw a more comely man than the Irishman, nor that cometh on more bravely in his charge; neither is his manner of mounting unseemly, though he lack stirrups, but more ready than with stirrups, for in his getting up his horse is still going, whereby he gaineth way. And therefore the stirrup was called so in scorn, as it were a stay to get up, being derived of the old English word *sty*, which is, to get up or mount.[3]

Eudox. It seemeth, then, that you find no fault with this manner of riding; why, then, would you have the quilted jack laid away?

[1] *Shecklaton*, also *siclatoun*—
"His robé was of sickladoun
That costé many a jane."

Spenser's explanation of the sort of material represented by this word is probably wrong. The old French *ciclaton*, whatever its origin, was a costly material, named in company with silks and satins, and, as Mr. Skeat observes, it is worn by Sir Thopas before he puts on his raiment of war.

[2] *Cordwain*, Cordovan leather. Hacqueton, a sleeveless jacket of plate for the war; habergeon, French, from the German *hals*, neck, and *bergan*, to protect, neck armour of chain-mail, hauberk.

[3] Stirrup, from stigan to mount, is sty-rope, rope to mount by.

Iren. I do not wish it to be laid away, but the abuse thereof to be put away; for being used to the end that it was framed, that is, to be worn in war under a shirt of mail, it is allowable; as also the shirt of mail and all his other furniture; but to be worn daily at home, and in towns and civil places, is a rude habit, and most uncomely, seeming like a player's painted coat.

Eudox. But it is worn, they say, likewise of Irish footmen. How do you allow of that? for I should think it very unseemly.

Iren. No, not as it is used in war; for it is worn then likewise of footmen under their shirts of mail, the which footmen they call gallowglasses; the which name doth discover them also to be ancient English, for gallogla signifies an English servitor or yeoman.[1] And he being so armed in a long shirt of mail down to the calf of his leg, with a long broad axe in his hand, was then *pedes gravis armaturæ*, and was instead of the footman that now weareth a corselet, before the corselet was used or almost invented.

Eudox. Then him belike you likewise allow in your strait reformation of old customs.

Iren. Both him and the kern also, whom only I take to be the proper Irish soldier, can I allow, so that they use that habit and custom of theirs in the wars only, when they are led forth to the service of their prince, and not usually at home and in civil places; and, besides, do lay aside the evil and wild uses which the galloglasse and kern do use in their common trade of life.

Eudox. What be those?

Iren. Marry, those be the most barbarous and loathly conditions of any people, I think, under heaven; for from the time that they enter into that course they do use all the beastly behaviour that

[1] *Gallowglas*, "galloglach," the heavy-armed Irish foot soldiers. Old Irish *géillius*, service, *giallaim*, I obey;—whence *gilla*, a servant (Highland *gillie*), a young man in the third of the six ages into which life was divided;—and perhaps *gleic*, wrestling, or *gluaisim*, I pass, move. But more probably the original division is gallog-lach, where lach is the common nominal ending, as in *lucht*, a part or division, *lucht-lach*, a party of people; *tegdas*, a house, *teglach*, the people of the house.

may be; they oppress all men; they spoil as well the subject as the enemy; they steal, they are cruel and bloody, full of revenge, and delighting in deadly execution, licentious, swearers and blasphemers, common ravishers of women, and murderers of children.

Eudox. These be most villainous conditions. I marvel, then, that they be ever used or employed, or almost suffered to live: what good can there then be in them?

Iren. Yet sure they are very valiant and hardy, for the most part great endurers of cold, labour, hunger, and all hardiness, very active and strong of hand, very swift of foot, very vigilant and circumspect in their enterprises, very present in perils, very great scorners of death.

Eudox. Truly, by this that you say, it seems that the Irishman is a very brave soldier.

Iren. Yea, surely, in that rude kind of service he beareth himself very courageously. But when he cometh to experience of service abroad, or is put to a piece or a pike, he maketh as worthy a soldier as any nation he meeteth with. But let us, I pray you, turn again to our discourse of evil Customs amongst the Irish.

Eudox. Methinks all this which you speak of concerneth the customs of the Irish very materially; for their uses in war are of no small importance to be considered, as well to reform those which are evil as to confirm and continue those which are good. But follow you your own course, and show what other their customs you have to dislike of.

Iren. There is amongst the Irish a certain kind of people called bards, which are to them instead of poets, whose profession is to set forth the praises or dispraises of men in their poems or rhymes; the which are had in so high regard and estimation amongst them, that none dare displease them for fear to run into reproach through their offence, and to be made infamous in the mouths of all men. For their verses are taken up with a general applause, and usually sung at all feasts and meetings by certain other persons, whose proper function that is, who also receive for the same great rewards and reputation amongst them.

Eudox. Do you blame this in them, which I would otherwise have thought to have been worthy of good account, and rather to have been maintained and augmented amongst them than to have been disliked; for I have read that in all ages poets have been had in special reputation, and that methinks not without great cause; for, besides their sweet inventions and most witty lays, they have always used to set forth the praises of the good and virtuous, and to beat down and disgrace the bad and vicious. So that many brave young minds have oftentimes, through hearing the praises and famous eulogies of worthy men sung and reported unto them, been stirred up to affect the like commendations, and so to strive to the like deserts. So they say that the Lacedæmonians were more excited to desire of honour with the excellent verses of the poet Tyrtæus than with all the exhortations of their captains, or authority of their rulers and magistrates.

Iren. It is most true that such poets as in their writings do labour to better the manners of men, and through the sweet bait of their numbers to steal into the young spirits a desire of honour and virtue, are worthy to be had in great respect. But these Irish bards are for the most part of another mind, and so far from instructing young men in moral discipline, that they themselves do more deserve to be sharply disciplined; for they seldom use to choose unto themselves the doings of good men for the arguments of their poems, but whomsoever they find to be most licentious of life, most bold and lawless in his doings, most dangerous and desperate in all parts of disobedience and rebellious disposition, him they set up and glorify in their rhymes, him they praise to the people, and to young men make an example to follow.

Eudox. I marvel what kind of speeches they can find or what faces they can put on to praise such bad persons as live so lawlessly and licentiously upon stealths and spoils, as most of them do; or how can they think that any good mind will applaud or approve the same?

Iren. There is none so bad, Eudoxus, but shall find some to favour his doings; but such licentious parts as these, tending for the most part to the hurt of the English or maintenance of their own lewd liberty, they themselves being most desirous thereof, do most allow. Besides this, evil things, being decked and attired with the gay attire of goodly words, may easily deceive and carry away the affection of a young mind that is not well stayed, but desirous by some bold adventures to make proof of himself. For being, as they all be, brought up idly, without awe of parents, without precepts of masters, and without fear of offence, not being directed nor employed in any course of life which may carry them to virtue, will easily be drawn to follow such as any shall set before them: for a young mind cannot rest; if he be not still busied in some goodness, he will find himself such business as shall soon busy all about him. In which, if he shall find any to praise him and to give him encouragement, as those bards and rhymers do for little reward, or a share of a stolen cow, then waxeth he most insolent and half-mad with the love of himself and his own lewd deeds. And as for words to set forth such lewdness, it is not hard for them to give a goodly and painted show thereunto, borrowed even from the praises which are proper to virtue itself. As of a most notorious thief and wicked outlaw, which had lived all his lifetime of spoils and robberies, one of their bards in his praise will say that he was none of the idle milksops that was brought up by the fireside, but that most of his days he spent in arms and valiant enterprises; that he did never eat his meat before he had won it with his sword; that he lay not all night slugging in a cabin under his mantle, but used commonly to keep others waking to defend their lives; and did light his candle at the flames of their houses to lead him in the darkness; that the day was his night, and the night his day; that he loved not to be long wooing of wenches to yield to him, but where he came he took by force the spoil of other men's love, and left but lamentation to their lovers; that his music was not the harp nor lays of love, but the cries of people and clashing of armour; and finally, that he died not bewailed of many, but made many wail when he died that dearly bought his death. Do you not think, Eudoxus, that many of these praises might be applied to men of best deserts? Yet are they all yielded to a most notable traitor, and amongst some of the Irish not smally accounted of. For the song, when it was first made and sung to a person of high degree there, was bought, as their manner is, for forty crowns.

Eudox. And well worthy, sure. But tell me, I pray you, have they any art in their compositions? Or be they anything witty or well-favoured, as poems should be?

Iren. Yea, truly. I have caused divers of them to be translated unto me, that I might understand them; and surely they savoured of sweet wit and good invention, but skilled not of the goodly ornaments of poetry; yet were they sprinkled with some pretty flowers of their natural device which gave good grace and comeliness unto them; the which it is great pity to see so abused, to the gracing of wickedness and vice, which with good usage would serve to adorn and beautify virtue. This evil custom therefore needeth reformation. And now next after the Irish kern, methinks the Irish horse-boys would come well in order; the use of which, though necessity, as times now be, do enforce, yet in the thorough reformation of that realm they should be cut off. For the cause why they are now to be permitted is want of convenient inns for lodging of travellers on horseback, and of hostlers to tend their horses by the way. But when things shall be reduced to a better pass, this needeth specially to be reformed. For out of the fry of these rake-hell horse-boys, growing up in knavery and villainy, are their kern continually supplied and maintained. For, having been once brought up an idle horse-boy, he will never

VIEW OF THE STATE OF IRELAND. 115

after fall to labour, but is only made fit for the halter. And these also, the which is one foul oversight, are, for the most part, bred up amongst the Englishmen; of whom learning to shoot in a piece, and being made acquainted with all the trades of the English, they are afterwards, when they become kern, made more fit to cut their throats. Next to this, there is another much like, but much more lewd and dishonest, and that is, of their carrows;[1] which is a kind of people that wander up and down to gentlemen's houses, living only upon cards and dice; the which, though they have little or nothing of their own, yet will they play for much money; which if they win, they waste most lightly; and if they lose, they pay as slenderly, but make recompense with one stealth or another; whose only hurt is, not that they themselves are idle losses, but that, through gaming, they draw others to like lewdness and idleness. And to these may be added another sort of like loose fellows, which do pass up and down amongst gentlemen by the name of jesters, but are, indeed, notable rogues, and partakers not only of many stealths, by setting forth other men's goods to be stolen, but also privy to many traitorous practices, and common carriers of news; with desire whereof you would wonder how much the Irish are fed, for they send commonly up and down to know news; and if any meet with another, his second word is, "What news?" Insomuch that hereof is told a pretty jest of a Frenchman, who, having been sometimes in Ireland, where he marked their great inquiry for news, and meeting afterwards in France an Irishman whom he knew in Ireland, first saluted him, and afterwards said thus merrily, "O sir, I pray you tell me of courtesy, have you heard anything of the news that you so much inquired for in your country?"

Eudox. This argueth sure in them a great desire of innovation, and therefore these occasions which nourish the same must be

---

[1] *Carrows. Cor* in old Irish was a throw, as of dice, or a curved movement, as in dealing round of cards.

taken away; as, namely, those jesters, carrows, morashites,[1] and all such stragglers; for whom, methinks, the short riddance of a marshal were meeter than an ordinance or prohibition to restrain them. Therefore, I pray you, leave all this rabblement of runagates, and pass to other customs.

Iren. There is a great use amongst the Irish to make great Assemblies together upon a rath or hill, there to parley, as they say, about matters and wrongs between township and township, or one private person and another. But well I wot, and true it hath been oftentimes proved, that in their meetings many mischiefs have been both practised and wrought; for to them do commonly resort all the scum of the people, where they may meet and confer of what they list, which else they could not do without suspicion or knowledge of others. Besides, at these meetings I have known divers times that many Englishmen and good Irish subjects have been villainously murdered, by moving one quarrel or another against them. For the Irish never come to those raths but armed, whether on horse or on foot, which the English nothing suspecting, are then commonly taken at advantage like sheep in the penfold.

Eudox. It may be, Ireneus, that abuse may be in those meetings. But these round hills and square bawns [2] which you see so strongly trenched and thrown up were, they say, at first ordained for the same purpose, that people might assemble themselves therein; and therefore anciently they were called folkmotes, that is, a place of people to meet or talk of anything that concerned any difference between parties and townships, which seemeth yet to me very requisite.

Iren. You say very true, Eudoxus; the first making of these high hills was at first indeed to very good purpose for people

---

[1] *Morashites,* men of the morasses or bogs, bog-trotters.
[2] *Bawns,* high places. "Ban" as in Ban-gor, the high choir; Pan Down, near Carisbrooke.

to meet; but howsoever the times when they were first made might well serve to good occasions, as perhaps they did then in England, yet things being since altered, and now Ireland much differing from the state of England, the good use that then was of them is now turned to abuse; for those hills whereof you speak were, as you may gather by reading, appointed for two special uses and built by two several nations. The one is that which you call folkmotes, which were built by the Saxons, as the word bewrayeth, for it signifieth in Saxon a meeting of folk; and these are, for the most part, in form four-square, well intrenched; the others that were round were cast up by the Danes, as the name of them doth betoken; for they are called Danes-raths, that is, hills of the Danes; the which were by them devised, not for treaties and parleys, but appointed as forts for them to gather unto in troublesome time, when any trouble arose. For the Danes, being but a few in comparison of the Saxons in England, used this for their safety; they made those small round hills so strongly fenced in every quarter of the hundred, to the end that if in the night, or any other time, any troublous cry or uproar should happen, they might repair with all speed unto their own fort which was appointed for their quarter, and there remain safe till they could assemble themselves in greater strength. For they were made so strong, with one small entrance, that whosoever came thither first, were he one or two, or like few, he or they might there rest safe, and defend themselves against many, till more succour came unto them; and when they were gathered to a sufficient number they marched to the next fort, and so forward till they met with the peril or knew the occasions thereof. But besides these two sorts of hills, there were anciently divers others. For some were raised where there had been a great battle fought, as a memory or trophy thereof; others as monuments of burials of the carcasses of all those that were slain in any field, upon whom they did throw such round mounts as memorials of them;

and sometimes did cast up great heaps of stones, as you may read the like in many places of the Scripture. And other whiles they did throw up many round heaps of earth in a circle like a garland, or pitch many long stones on end in compass, every of which, they say, betokened some person of note there slain and buried; for this was their ancient custom before Christianity came in amongst them, that churchyards were enclosed.

Eudox. You have very well declared the original of their mounts and great stones encompassed, which some vainly term the old giants' trevetts,[1] and think that those huge stones would not else be brought into order or reared up without the strength of giants. And others vainly think they were never placed there by man's hand or art, but only remained there so since the beginning, and were afterwards discovered by the Deluge, and laid open as then by the washing of the waters or other like casualty. But let them dream their own imaginations to please themselves; you have satisfied me much better, both for that I see some confirmation thereof in the Holy Writ, and also remember that I have read in many histories and chronicles the like mounts and stones oftentimes mentioned.

Iren. There be many great authorities, I assure you, to prove the same; but as for these meetings on hills whereof we were speaking, it is very inconvenient that any such should be permitted.

Eudox. But yet it is very needful, methinks, for many other purposes, as for the countries to gather together when there is any imposition to be laid upon them, to the which they then may all agree at such meetings to divide upon themselves, according to their holdings and abilities. So as if at these assemblies there be any officers, as constables, bailiffs, or such-like, amongst them, there can be no peril or doubt of such bad practices.

---

[1] *Trevett*, trivet, a three-legged support; alike with tripod, but the *p* has undergone the same change that turned *pod* into *foot*.

Iren. Nevertheless, dangerous are such assemblies, whether for cess or aught else, the constables and officers being also of the Irish; and if any of the English happen to be there, even to them they may prove perilous. Therefore, for avoiding of all such evil occasions, they were best to be abolished.

Eudox. But what is that which you call cess? It is a word, sure, unused amongst us here; therefore, I pray you, expound the same.

Iren. Cess[1] is none other than that which you yourself called imposition, but is in a kind unacquainted perhaps unto you, for there are cesses of sundry sorts. One is the cessing of soldiers upon the country. For Ireland being a country of war, as it is handled, and always full of soldiers, they which have the government, whether they find it the most ease to the Queen's purse, or the most ready means at hand for victualling of the soldier, or that necessity enforceth them thereunto, do scatter the army abroad in the country, and place them in villages to take their victuals of them, at such vacant times as they lie not in camp nor are otherwise employed in service. Another kind of cess is the imposing of provision for the governor's housekeeping, which, though it be most necessary, and be also, for avoiding of all the evils formerly therein used, lately brought to a composition, yet it is not without great inconveniences, no less than here in England, or rather much more. The like cess is also charged upon the country sometimes for victualling of the soldiers when they lie in garrison, at such times as there is none remaining in the Queen's store, or that the same cannot be conveniently conveyed to their place of garrison. But these two are not easily to be redressed when necessity thereto compelleth; but as for the former, as it is not necessary, so it is most hurtful and offensive to the poor country, and nothing convenient for the soldiers themselves, who during their lying at cess use all kind of outrageous disorder and

[1] *Cess*, assessment, with *c* written for *s* in "sess."

villainy, both towards the poor men which victual and lodge them, as also to all the country round about them, whom they abuse, oppress, spoil, and afflict by all the means they can invent; for they will not only not content themselves with such victuals as their host, nor yet as the place perhaps affords, but they will have other meat provided for them, and *aqua vitæ* sent for; yea, and money besides laid at their trenchers, which if they want, then about the house they walk with the wretched poor man and his silly wife, who are glad to purchase their peace with anything. By which vile manner of abuse the country-people, yea, and the very English which dwell abroad and see and sometimes feel this outrage, grow into great detestation of the soldiers, and thereby into hatred of the very government which draweth upon them such evils; and therefore this you may also join unto the former evil customs which we have to reprove in Ireland.

Eudox. Truly this is one not the least; and though the persons by whom it is used be of better note than the former roguish sort which you reckoned, yet the fault, methinks, is no less worthy of a marshal.

Iren. That were a harder course, Euxodus, to redress every abuse by a marshal. It would seem to you very evil surgery to cut off every unsound or sick part of the body, which being by other due means recovered, might afterwards do very good service to the body again, and haply help to save the whole; therefore I think better that some good salve for the redress of the evil be sought forth than the least part suffered to perish; but hereof we have to speak in another place. Now we will proceed to other like defects, amongst which there is one general inconvenience which reigneth almost throughout all Ireland; that is, the lords of land and freeholders do not there use to set out their land in farm or for term of years to their tenants, but only from year to year, and some during pleasure; neither, indeed, will the Irish tenant or husbandman otherwise take his land than so long as he list himself. The reason hereof in the tenant is, for that the landlords there use most shamefully to rack their tenants, laying upon them coigny and livery at pleasure, and exacting of them, besides his covenants, what he pleaseth. So that the poor husbandman either dare not bind himself to him for longer term, or thinketh by his continual liberty of change to keep his landlord the rather in awe from wronging of him. And the reason why the landlord will no longer covenant with him is, for that he daily looketh after change and alteration, and hovereth in expectation of new worlds.

Eudox. But what evil cometh hereby to the commonwealth, or what reason is it that any landlord should not set nor any tenant take his land as himself list?

Iren. Marry, the evils which come hereby are great, for by this means both the landlord thinketh that he hath his tenant more at command to follow him into what action soever he shall enter, and also the tenant, being left at his liberty, is fit for every occasion of change that shall be offered by time, and so much also the more ready and willing is he to run into the same; for that he hath no such state in any his holding, no such building upon any farm, no such cost employed in fencing or husbanding the same, as might withhold him from any such wilful course as his lord's cause or his own lewd disposition may carry him unto. All which he hath forborne and spared so much expense, for that he had no firm estate in his tenement, but was only a tenant-at-will or little more, and so at will may leave it. And this inconvenience may be reason enough to ground any ordinance for the good of the commonwealth against the private behoof or will of any landlord that shall refuse to grant any such term or estate unto his tenant as may tend to the good of the whole realm.

Eudox. Indeed, methinks it is a great wilfulness in any such landlord to refuse to make any longer farms unto their tenants as may, besides the general good of the realm, be also greatly for their own profit and avail. For what reasonable man will not think that the tenement shall be made much better for the lord's behoof if the tenant may by such good means be drawn to build himself some handsome[1] habitation thereon, to ditch and enclose his ground, to manure and husband it, as good farmers use? For when his tenant's term shall be expired, it will yield him in the renewing his lease both a good fine and also a better rent. And also it shall be for the good of the tenant likewise, who by such buildings and enclosures shall receive many benefits: first, by the handsomeness of his house he shall take more comfort of his life, more safe dwelling, and a delight to keep his said house neat and cleanly; which now being, as they commonly are, rather swine-sties than houses, is the chiefest cause of his so beastly manner of life and savage condition, lying and living together with his beast in one house, in one room, in one bed; that is, clean straw, or rather a foul dunghill. And to all these other commodities he shall in short time find a greater added; that is, his own wealth and riches increased and wonderfully enlarged by keeping his cattle in enclosures, where they shall always have fresh pasture, that now is all trampled and overrun; warm covert, that now lieth open to all weather; safe being, that now are continually filched and stolen.

Iren. You have, Eudoxus, well accompted the commodities of this one good ordinance, amongst which this that you named last is not the least; for all the other being most beneficial to the landlord and tenant, this chiefly redoundeth to the good of the commonwealth, to have the land thus enclosed and well fenced. For it is both a principal bar and impeachment[2] unto thieves from stealing of cattle in the night, and also a gall against all rebels and outlaws that shall rise up in any numbers against the government; for the thief thereby shall have much ado, first to bring forth, and afterwards to drive away, his stolen prey, but

---

[1] *Handsome*, handy, convenient.
[2] *Impeachment*, hindrance.

VIEW OF THE STATE OF IRELAND. 123

through the common highways, where he shall soon be descried and met withal. And the rebel or open enemy, if any such shall happen, either at home or from abroad, shall easily be found when he cometh forth, and also be well encountered withal by a few in so strait passages and strong enclosures. This, therefore, when we come to the reforming of all those evil Customs before mentioned, is needful to be remembered; but now by this time methinks I have well run through the evil uses which I have observed in Ireland. Nevertheless, I well note that there be many more, and infinitely many more, in the private abuses of men. But these that are most general, and tending to the hurt of the commonweal, as they have come to my remembrance, I have, as briefly as I could, rehearsed unto you. And therefore now I think best that we pass unto our third part, in which we noted the inconveniences that are in Religion.

Eudox. Surely you have very well handled these two former; and if ye shall as well go through the third likewise, you shall merit a very good meed.

Iren. Little have I to say of Religion, both because the parts thereof be not many, itself being but one, and myself have not much been conversant in that calling, but as, lightly passing by, I have seen or heard. Therefore, the fault which I find in Religion is but one, but the same is universal throughout all that country; that is, that they be all Papists by their profession, but in the same so blindly and brutishly informed, for the most part, that not one amongst a hundred knoweth any ground of Religion or any article of his faith, but can perhaps say his *Paternoster* or his *Ave-Maria*, without any knowledge or understanding what one word thereof meaneth.

Eudox. Is it not, then, a little blot to them that now hold the place of government, that they which now are in the light themselves suffer a people under their charge to wallow in such deadly darkness?

Iren. That which you blame, Eudoxus, is not, I suppose, any fault of will in those godly fathers which have charge thereof, but the inconvenience of the time and troublous occasions wherewith that wretched realm hath continually been turmoiled. For instruction in Religion needeth quiet times; and ere we seek to settle a sound discipline in the clergy we must purchase peace unto the laity. For it is ill time to preach among swords, and most hard, or rather impossible, it is to settle a good opinion in the minds of men for matters of religion doubtful, which have doubtless an evil opinion of us. For ere a new be brought in the old must be removed.

Eudox. Then belike it is meet that some fitter time be attended, that God send peace and quietness there in civil matters before it be attempted in ecclesiastical. I would rather have thought that, as it is said, correction must first begin at the House of God, and that the care of the soul should have been preferred before the care of the body.

Iren. Most true, Eudoxus; the care of the soul and soul matters is to be preferred before the care of the body, in consideration of the worthiness thereof; but not till the time of reformation. For if you should know a wicked person dangerously sick, having now both soul and body greatly diseased, yet both recoverable, would you not think it evil advertisement to bring the preacher before the physician? For if his body were neglected, it is like that his languishing soul, being disquieted by his diseaseful body, would utterly refuse and loathe all spiritual comfort; but if his body were first recured[1] and brought to good frame, should there not then be found best time to re-

---
[1] *Recured*, recovered.

cover the soul also? So it is in the state of a realm. Therefore, as I said, it is expedient first to settle such a course of government there as thereby both civil disorders and ecclesiastical abuses may be reformed and amended; whereto needeth not any such great distance of times as you suppose; I require but one joint resolution for both, that each might second and confirm the other.

Eudox. That we shall see when we come thereunto; in the meantime I conceive thus much, as you have delivered, touching the general fault which you suppose in Religion, to wit, that it is Popish; but do you find no particular abuses therein, nor in the ministers thereof?

Iren. Yes, verily; for whatever disorders you see in the Church of England you may find there, and many more; namely, gross simony, greedy covetousness, fleshly incontinency, careless sloth, and generally all disordered life in the common clergymen. And besides all these, they have their particular enormities. For all Irish priests which now enjoy the Church livings, they are in a manner mere laymen, saving that they have taken holy ordérs; but otherwise they do go and live like laymen, follow all kind of husbandry and other worldly affairs, as other Irishmen do. They neither read Scriptures, nor preach to the people, nor administer the Communion; but baptism they do, for they christen yet after the Popish fashion; only they take the tithes and offerings, and gather what fruit else they may of their livings, the which they convert as badly; and some of them, they say, pay as due tributes and shares of their livings to their bishops (I speak of those which are Irish) as they receive them duly.

Eudox. But is that suffered amongst them? It is wonder but that the governors do redress such shameful abuses.

Iren. How can they, since they know them not? For the Irish bishops have their clergy in such awe and subjection under them, that they dare not complain of them; so as they may do to them what they please. For they, knowing their own unworthiness and incapacity, and that they are therefore still removable at their bishop's will, yield what pleaseth him, and he taketh what he listeth; yea, and some of them whose dioceses are in remote parts, somewhat out of the world's eye, do not at all bestow the benefices which are in their own donation upon any, but keep them in their own hands, and set their own servants and horse boys to take up the tithes and fruits of them, with the which some of them purchase great lands and build fair castles upon the same. Of which abuse, if any question be moved, they have a very seemly colour and excuse, that they have no worthy ministers to bestow them upon, but keep them so bestowed for any such sufficient person as any shall bring unto them.

Eudox. But is there no law nor ordinance to meet with this mischief? Nor hath it never before been looked into?

Iren. Yes, it seems it hath; for there is a statute there enacted in Ireland which seems to have been grounded upon a good meaning; that whatsoever Englishman, of good conversation and sufficiency, shall be brought unto any of the bishops, and nominated unto any living within their diocese that is presently void, that he shall, without contradiction, be admitted thereunto before any Irish.

Eudox. This is surely a very good law, and well provided for this evil whereof you speak; but why is not the same observed?

Iren. I think it is well observed, and that none of the bishops transgress the same; but yet it worketh no reformation thereof, for many defects. First, there are no such sufficient English ministers sent over as might be presented to any bishop for any living; but the most part of such English as come over thither of themselves are either unlearned or men of some bad note, for which they have forsaken England; so as the bishop to whom they shall be presented may justly reject them as incapable and insufficient. Secondly, the bishop himself is perhaps an Irishman, who, being made judge by that law of the sufficiency of the ministers, may at his own will dislike of the Englishman as unworthy in his opinion, and admit of any Irish whom he shall think more for his turn. And if he shall, at the instance of any Englishman of countenance there, whom he will not displease, accept of any such English minister as shall be tendered unto him, yet he will underhand carry such a hard hand over him, or by his officers wring him so sore, that he will soon make him weary of his poor living. Lastly, the benefices themselves are so mean and of so small profit in those Irish countries, through the ill husbandry of the Irish people which do inhabit them, that they will not yield any competent maintenance for any honest minister to live upon, scarcely to buy him a gown. And were all this redressed, as haply it might be, yet what good should any English minister do amongst them by teaching or preaching to them, which either cannot understand him or will not hear him? Or what comfort of life shall he have where his parishioners are so insatiable, so intractable, so ill-affected to him, as they usually be to all the English? Or, finally, how dare almost any honest minister, that are peaceable civil men, commit his safety to the hands of such neighbours as the boldest captains dare scarcely dwell by?

Eudox. Little good then, I see, was by that statute wrought, however well intended; but the reformation thereof must grow higher, and be brought from a stronger ordinance than the commandment or penalty of a law which none dare inform or complain of when it is broken. But have you any more of those abuses in the clergy?

Iren. I could, perhaps, reckon more, but I perceive my speech to grow too long, and these may suffice to judge of the general disorders which reign amongst them. As for the particulars, they are too many to be reckoned. For the clergy there, excepting the grave fathers which are in high place about the State and some few others which are lately planted in their new college,[1] are generally bad, licentious, and most disordered.

Eudox. You have then, as I suppose, gone through these three first parts which you proposed unto yourself; to wit, the inconveniences which you observed in the Laws, in the Customs, and in the Religion of that land. The which, methinks, you have so thoroughly touched as that nothing more remaineth to be spoken thereof.

Iren. Not so thoroughly as you suppose, that nothing can remain, but so generally as I purposed; that is, to lay open the general evils of that realm which do hinder the good reformation thereof. For to count the particular faults of private men should be a work too infinite; yet some there be of that nature, that though they be in private men, yet their evil reacheth to a general hurt; as the extortion of sheriffs and their sub-sheriffs and bailiffs; the corruption of victuallers, cessors, and purveyors; the disorders of seneschals, captains, and their soldiers, and many such like. All which I will only name here, that their reformation may be mended in place where it most concerneth. But there is one very foul abuse which, by the way, I may not omit, and that is in captains, who, notwithstanding that they are specially employed to make peace through strong execution of war, yet they do so dawdle their doings and dally in the service to them committed, as if they would not have the enemy subdued or utterly beaten down, for fear lest afterwards they should need employment, and so be discharged of pay. For which cause some

[1] Trinity College, Dublin, was just founded when Spenser wrote this View of Ireland. Its origin was a grant made by Elizabeth, in 1591, of the Augustine Monastery of All Saints for a Church of England College. Its first stone was laid on the first of January 1593, and it began work in the same year.

of them that are laid in garrison do so handle the matter that they will do no great hurt to the enemies; yet for colour sake some men they will kill, even half with the consent of the enemy, being persons either of base regard or enemies to the enemy, whose heads eftsoons they send to the governor for a commendation of their great endeavour, telling how weighty a service they performed by cutting off such-and-such dangerous rebels.

Eudox. Truly this is a pretty mockery, and not to be permitted by the governors.

Iren. But how can the governor know readily what persons those were, and what the purpose of their killing was? Yea, and what will you say if the captains do justify this their course by ensample of some of their governors, which (under *Benedicite* I do tell it to you) do practise the like sleight in their governments?

Eudox. Is it possible? Take heed what you say, Ireneus.

Iren. To you only, Eudoxus, I do tell it, and that even with great heart's grief and inward trouble of mind, to see Her Majesty so much abused by some who are put in special trust of those great affairs, of which, some being martial men, will not do always what they may for quieting of things, but will rather wink at some faults and will suffer them unpunished, lest that, having put all things in that assurance of peace that they might, they should seem afterwards not to be needed, nor continued in their governments, with so great a charge to Her Majesty. And, therefore, they do cunningly carry their course of government, and from one hand to another do bandy the service like a tennis-ball, which they will never strike quite away, for fear lest afterwards they should want.

Eudox. Do you speak of under-magistrates, Ireneus, or principal governors?

Iren. I do speak of no particulars, but the truth may be found out by trial and reasonable insight into some of their doings. And if I should say there is some blame thereof in the principal

I

governors, I think I might also show some reasonable proof of my speech. As, for example, some of them, seeing the end of their government to draw nigh, and some mischiefs and troublous practice growing up, which afterwards may work trouble to the next succeeding governor, will not attempt the redress or cutting-off thereof, either for fear they should leave the realm unquiet at the end of their government, or that the next that cometh should receive the same too quiet, and so haply win more praise thereof than they before. And therefore they will not, as I said, seek at all to repress that evil, but will, either by granting protection for a time, or holding some emparlance with the rebel, or by treaty of commissioners, or by other like devices, only smother and keep down the flame of the mischief, so as it may not break out in their time of government. What comes afterwards they care not, or rather wish the worst. This course hath been noted in some governors.

Eudox. Surely, Ireneus, this, if it were true, should be worthy of an heavy judgment; but it is hardly to be thought that any governor should so much either envy the good of that realm which is put into his hand, or defraud Her Majesty who trusteth him so much, or malign his successor which shall possess his place, as to suffer an evil to grow up which he might timely have kept under, or perhaps to nourish it with coloured countenance or such sinister means.

Iren. I do not certainly avouch so much, Eudoxus, but the sequel of things doth in a manner prove and plainly speak so much, that the governors usually are envious one of another's greater glory; which if they would seek to excel by better governing, it should be a most laudable emulation; but they do quite otherwise. For this, as you may mark, is the common order of them, that who cometh next in place will not follow that course of government, however good, which his predecessors held, either for disdain of himself or doubt to have his doings drowned in another man's praise, but will straight take a way quite contrary to the former. As, if the former thought by keeping under the Irish to reform them, the next, by discountenancing the English, will curry favour with the Irish, and so make his government seem plausible, as having all the Irish at his command; but he that comes after will perhaps follow neither the one nor the other, but will dawdle the one and the other in such sort as he will suck sweet out of them both, and leave bitterness to the poor country; which if he that comes after shall seek to redress, he shall perhaps find such crosses as he shall hardly be able to bear, or do any good that might work the disgrace of his predecessors. Examples you may see hereof in the governors of late times sufficiently, and in others of former times more manifestly, when the government of that realm was committed sometimes to the Geraldines, as when the House of York had the crown of England; sometimes to the Butlers, as when the House of Lancaster got the same; and other whiles, when an English governor was appointed, he perhaps found enemies of both.

Eudox. I am sorry to hear so much as you report, and now I begin to conceive somewhat more of the cause of her continual wretchedness than heretofore I found, and wish that this inconvenience were well looked into; for sure, methinks, it is more weighty than all the former, and more hardly to be redressed in the governor than in the governed; as a malady in a vital part is more incurable than in an external.

Iren. You say very true; but now that we have thus ended all the abuses and inconveniences of that government, which was our First Part, it followeth now that we pass unto the Second Part, which was, of the means to cure and redress the same; which we must labour to reduce to the first beginning thereof.

Eudox. Right so, Ireneus; for by that which I have noted in all this your discourse you suppose that the whole ordinance and institution of that realm's government was both at first, when it was placed, evil plotted; and all sithence, through other oversights, came more out of square to that disorder which it is now come unto; like as two indirect lines, the farther they are drawn out, the farther they go asunder.

Iren. I do see, Eudoxus, and, as you say, so think, that the longer that government thus continueth, in the worse course will the realm be; for it is all in vain that they now strive and endeavour by fair means and peaceable plots to redress the same, without first removing all those inconveniences, and new-framing, as it were, in the forge all that is worn out of fashion; for all other means will be but as lost labour, by patching up one hole to make many. For the Irish do strongly hate and abhor all reformation and subjection to the English; by reason that, having been once subdued by them, they were thrust out of all their possessions. So as now they fear that if they were again brought under, they should likewise be expelled out of all; which is the cause that they hate the English government, according to the saying, *Quem metuunt oderunt.* Therefore the reformation must now be the strength of a greater power.

Eudox. But methinks that might be by making of good laws and establishing of new statutes, with sharp penalties and punishments, for amending of all that is presently amiss, and not, as you suppose, to begin all, as it were, anew, and to alter the whole form of the government; which how dangerous a thing it is to attempt you yourself must needs confess. And they which have the managing of the realm's whole policy cannot, without great cause, fear and refrain; for all innovation is perilous, insomuch as, though it be meant for the better, yet so many accidents and fearful events may come between, as that it may hazard the loss of the whole.

Iren. Very true, Eudoxus; all change is to be shunned where the affairs stand in such sort as that they may continue in quietness, or be assured at all to abide as they are. But that in the realm of Ireland we see much otherwise. For every day we perceive the troubles growing more upon us, and one evil growing upon another; insomuch as there is no part now found or ascertained but all have their ears upright, waiting when the watchword shall come, that they should all arise generally into rebellion and cast away the English subjection. To which there now little wanteth; for I think the word be already given, and there wanteth nothing but opportunity; which truly is the death of one noble person, who, being himself most steadfast to his sovereign Queen and his country, coasting upon the South Sea, stoppeth the ingate of all that evil which is looked for, and holdeth in all those which are at his beck, with the terror of his greatness and the assurance of his most immovable loyalty.[1] And, therefore, where you think that good and sound laws might amend and reform things there amiss, you think surely amiss. For it is vain to prescribe laws where no man careth for keeping of them, nor feareth the danger for breaking of them. But all the realm is first to be reformed, and laws are afterwards to be made for keeping and continuing it in that reformed estate.

Eudox. How then, do you think, is the reformation thereof to be begun, if not by laws and ordinances?

Iren. Even by the sword; for all these evils must first be cut

---

[1] Sir Walter Raleigh, who checked the Spaniards at sea, and in February 1595 attacked them in Trinidad on his way to the adventure of that year described in his "Discoverie of the Empyre of Guiana, with a Relation of the Citie of Manoa, which the Spaniards call El Dorado." Raleigh returned to London about July 1596.

away by a strong hand before any good can be planted; like as the corrupt branches and unwholesome boughs are first to be pruned and the foul moss cleansed and scraped away before the tree can bring forth any good fruit.

Eudox. Did you blame me even now for wishing of kern horseboys and carrows to be clean cut off as too violent a means, and do you yourself now prescribe the same medicine? Is not the sword the most violent redress that may be used for any evil?

Iren. It is so; but where no other remedy may be devised nor hope of recovery had, there must needs this violent means be used. As for the loose kind of people which you would have cut off, I blamed it; for that they might otherwise perhaps be brought to good, as, namely, by this way which I set before you.

Eudox. Is not your way all one with the former, in effect, which you found fault with, save only in this odds, that I said by the halter and you say by the sword? What difference is there?

Iren. There is surely great, when you shall understand it; for by the sword which I named I did not mean the cutting off all that nation with the sword; which far be it from me that I should ever think so desperately or wish so uncharitably. But by the sword I mean the royal power of the Prince, which ought to stretch itself forth in the chiefest strength, to the redressing and cutting off those evils which I before blamed, and not of the people which are evil. For evil people, by good ordinances and government, may be made good; but the evil that is of itself evil will never become good.

Eudox. I pray you, then, declare your mind at large how you would with that sword which you mean to be used to the reformation of all those evils.

Iren. The first thing must be to send over into that realm such a strong power of men as should perforce bring in all that rebellious rout and loose people, which either do now stand out in open arms, or, wandering in companies, do keep the woods, spoiling the good subjects.

Eudox. You speak now, Ireneus, of an infinite charge to Her Majesty to send over such an army as should tread down all that standeth before them on foot, and lay on the ground all the stiff-necked people of that land. For there is now but one outlaw of any great reckoning, to wit, the Earl of Tyrone, abroad in arms; against whom you see what huge charges she hath been at, this last year, in sending of men, providing of victuals, and making head against him. Yet there is little or nothing at all done, but the Queen's treasure spent, her people wasted, the poor country troubled, and the enemy nevertheless brought into no more subjection than he was, or list outwardly to show, which in effect is none, but rather a scorn of her power and embolding of a proud rebel, and an encouragement to all like lewdly disposed traitors that shall dare to lift up their heel against their Sovereign Lady. Therefore it were hard counsel to draw such an exceeding great charge upon her, whose event should be so uncertain.

Iren. True, indeed, if the event should be uncertain; but the certainty of the effect hereof shall be so infallible as that no reason can gainsay it; neither shall the charge of all this army, the which I demand, be much greater than so much as in these last two years' wars hath vainly been expended. For I dare undertake that it hath cost the Queen above £200,000 already; and for the present charge which she is at there amounteth to very near £12,000 a month, whereof cast you the account; yet nothing is done. The which sum, had it been employed as it should be, would have effected all this which now I go about.

Eudox. How mean you to have it employed, but to be spent in the pay of soldiers and provision of victuals?

Iren. Right so; but it is now not disbursed at once, as it might be, but drawn out into a long length by sending over now £20,000, and next half-year £10,000; so as the soldier in the meantime, for want of due provision of victual and good payment of his due, is starved and consumed; that of 1000 which came over lusty able men, in half a year there are not left 500. And yet is the Queen's charge never a whit the less, but what is not paid in present money is accounted in debt, which will not be long unpaid. For the captain, half of whose soldiers are dead and the other quarter never mustered nor seen, comes shortly to demand payment of his whole account, where by good means of some great ones, and privy sharings with the officers and servants of other some, he receiveth his debt, much less perhaps than was due, yet much more, indeed, than he justly deserved.

Eudox. I take this, sure, to be no good husbandry; for what must needs be spent, as good spend it at once where is enough, as to have it drawn out into long delays, seeing that thereby both the service is much hindered and yet nothing saved. But it may be, Ireneus, that the Queen's treasure, in so great occasions of disbursements as it is well known she hath been at lately, is not always so ready nor so plentiful as it can spare so great a sum together; but being paid as it is, now some and then some, it is no great burden unto her nor any great impoverishment to her coffers, seeing by such delay of time it daily cometh in as fast as she parteth it out.

Iren. It may be as you say; but for the going through of so honourable a course, I doubt not but if the Queen's coffers be not so well stored,—which we are not to look into,—but that the whole realm, which now, as things are used, do feel a continual burden of that wretched realm hanging upon their backs, would, for a small riddance of all that trouble, be once troubled for all, and put to all their shoulders and helping hands, and hearts also, to the defraying of that charge most gladfully and willingly. And surely the charge, in effect, is nothing to the infinite great good which should come thereby both to the Queen and all this realm, generally, as, when time serveth, shall be showed.

Eudox. How many men would you require to the furnishing of this which ye take in hand? And how long space would you have them entertained?

Iren. Verily, not above 10,000 footmen and 1000 horse, and all these not above the space of a year and a half; for I would still, as the heat of the service abateth, abate the number in pay, and make other provision for them, as I will show.

Eudox. Surely it seemeth not much which you require, nor no long time; but how would you have them used? Would you lead forth your army against the enemy and seek him where he is to fight?

Iren. No, Eudoxus, that would not be. For it is well known that he is a flying enemy, hiding himself in woods and bogs, from whence he will not draw forth but into some strait passage or perilous ford where he knows the army must needs pass; there will he lie in wait, and if he find advantage fit, will dangerously hazard the troubled soldier. Therefore, to seek him out that still flitteth, and follow him that can hardly be found, were vain and bootless. But I would divide my men in garrison upon his country, in such places as I should think might most annoy him.

Eudox. But how can that be, Ireneus, with so few men? For the enemy, as you may see, is not all in one country, but some in Ulster, some in Connaught, and others in Leinster. So as to plant strong garrisons in all those places should need many more men than you speak of; or to plant all in one and to leave the rest naked should be but to leave them to the spoil.

Iren. I would wish the chief power of the army to be garrisoned in one country that is strongest, and the other upon the rest that is weakest. As, for example, the Earl of Tyrone is now accounted the strongest; upon him would I lay 8000 men in garrison, 1000 upon Feagh MacHugh and the Cavanaghs, and 1000 upon some parts of Connaught, to be at the direction of the governor.

Eudox. I see now all your men bestowed; but in what places would you set their garrisons, that they might rise out most conveniently to service? And though perhaps I am ignorant of the places, yet I will take the map of Ireland and lay it before me, and make mine eyes, in the meantime, my schoolmasters, to guide my understanding to judge of your plot.

Iren. Those 8000 in Ulster I would divide likewise into four parts, so as there should be 2000 footmen in every garrison; the which I would thus place: upon the Blackwater, in some convenient place, as high upon the river as might be, I would lay one garrison; another would I put at Castle Liffer, or thereabouts, so as they should have all the passages upon the river to Lough Foyle; the third I would place about Fermanagh or Bundroise, so as they might lie between Connaught and Ulster, to serve upon both sides as occasion shall be offered; and this, therefore, would I have stronger than any of the rest, because it should be most enforced and most employed; and that they might put wards at Bally-Shannon and Belleek, and all those passages. The last would I set about Monaghan or Balturbut, so as it should front both upon the enemy that way and also keep the countries of Cavan and Meath in awe from passage of stragglers from those parts whence they used to come forth and oftentimes used to work much mischief. And to every of these garrisons of 2000 footmen I would have 200 horsemen added; for the one without the other can do but little service. The four garrisons thus being placed, I would have to be victualled beforehand for half a year, which you will say to be hard, considering the corruption and usual waste of victuals. But why should not they be as well victualled for so long time, as the ships are usually for a year, and sometimes two, seeing it is easier to keep victuals on land than water? Their bread I would have in flour, so as it might be baked still to serve their necessary want; their beer there also brewed within them from time to time, and their beef beforehand barrelled, the which may be used but as it is needed; for I make no doubt but fresh victuals they will sometimes purvey for themselves amongst their enemies. Hereunto, likewise, would I have them have a store of hose and shoes, with such other necessaries as may be needful for soldiers, so as they should have no occasion to look for relief from abroad, or occasion of such trouble for their continual supply, as I see and have often proved in Ireland to be more cumbrous to the Deputy, and dangerous to them that relieve them, than half the leading of an army. For the enemy, knowing the ordinary ways through which their relief must be brought them, useth commonly to draw himself into the strait passages thitherward, and oftentimes doth dangerously distress them. Besides the pay of such force as should be sent for their convoy, the charge of the carriages, the exactions of the country shall be spared. But only every half year the supply brought by the Deputy himself and his power, who shall then visit and overlook all those garrisons, to see what is needful to change, what is expedient, and to direct what he shall best advise. And those four garrisons, issuing forth at such convenient times as they shall have intelligence or espial upon the enemy, will so drive him from one side to another and tennis him amongst them, that he shall find nowhere safe to keep his creet [1] in nor hide himself, but flying from the fire shall fall into the water, and out of one danger into another; that in short space his creet, which is his chief sustenance, shall be wasted with preying or killed with driving, or starved for want of pasture in the woods, and he himself brought so low that he shall have no heart nor ability to endure his wretchedness, the which will surely come to pass in very short time; for one winter well followed upon him will so pluck him on his knees that he will never be able to stand up again.

Eudox. Do you then think the winter-time fittest for the services of Ireland? How falls it, then, that our most employments be in summer, and the armies then led commonly forth?

[1] *Creet*, stock of cattle.

Iren. It is surely misconceived, for it is not with Ireland as it is with other countries, where the wars flame most in summer and the helmets glister brightest in the fairest sunshine; but in Ireland the winter yieldeth best services, for then the trees are bare and naked, which use both to clothe and house the kern; the ground is cold and wet, which useth to be his bedding; the air is sharp and bitter to blow through his naked sides and legs; the kine are barren and without milk, which useth to be his only food; neither if he kill them will they yield him flesh, nor if he keep them will they give him food; besides, being all with calf, for the most part, they will, through much chasing and driving, cast all their calves and lose their milk which should relieve him the next summer.

Eudox. I do well understand your reason; but, by your leave, I have heard it otherwise said of some that were outlaws, that in summer they kept themselves quiet, but in winter they would play their parts, and when the nights were longest, then burn and spoil most, so that they might safely return before day.

Iren. I have likewise heard, and also seen proof thereof true; but that was of such outlaws as were either abiding in well-inhabited countries, as in Munster, or bordering on the English Pale, as Feagh MacHugh, the Cavanaghs, the Moores, the Dempseys, or such-like; for, for them the winter indeed is the fittest time for spoiling and robbing, because the nights are then, as you said, longest and darkest, and also the countries round about are then most full of corn, and good provision to be gotten everywhere by them. But it is far otherwise with a strong-peopled enemy that possess a whole country; for the other being but a few, and indeed privily lodged and kept in out-villages and corners nigh to the woods and mountains by some of their privy friends, to whom they bring their spoils and stealths and of whom they continually receive secret relief; but the open enemy having all his country wasted, what by himself and what by the soldiers, findeth them succour in no place. Towns there are none, of which he may get spoil; they are all burnt; bread he hath none—he plougheth not in summer; flesh he hath, but if he kill it in winter he shall want milk in summer, and shortly want life. Therefore, if they be well followed but one winter, you shall have little work with them the next summer.

Eudox. I do now well perceive the difference, and do verily think that the winter-time is their fittest for service; withal I conceive the manner of your handling of the service by drawing sudden draughts upon the enemy when he looketh not for you, and to watch advantages upon him, as he doth upon you. By which straight keeping of them in, and not suffering them at any time long to rest, I must needs think that they will soon be brought low and driven to great extremities. All which when you have performed, and brought them to the very last cast, suppose that they will offer either to come to you and submit themselves, or that some of them will seek to withdraw themselves; what is your advice to do? Will you have them received?

Iren. No. But at the beginning of those wars, and when the garrisons are well planted and fortified, I would wish a proclamation were made generally, to come to their knowledge, that what persons soever would within twenty days absolutely submit themselves, excepting only the very principals and ringleaders, should find grace. I doubt not but, upon the settling of the garrisons, such a terror and near consideration of their perilous state would be stricken into most of them, that they will covet to draw away from their leaders. And again, I well know that the rebels themselves, as I saw by proof in Desmond's wars, will turn away all their rascal people whom they think unserviceable; as old men, women, children, and hinds, which they call churls, which would only waste their victuals and yield them no aid; but their cattle they will surely keep away. These, therefore, though policy would turn them back again, that they might the rather consume and afflict the other rebels, yet in a pitiful commiseration I would wish them to be received; the rather, for that this sort of base people doth not for the most part rebel of themselves, having no heart thereunto, but are by force drawn by the grand rebels into their action, and carried away by the violence of the stream, else they should be sure to lose all that they have, and perhaps their lives too; the which they now carry unto them in hope to enjoy them there, but they are there by the strong rebels themselves soon turned out of all, so that the constraint hereof may in them deserve pardon. Likewise, if any of their able men or gentlemen shall then offer to come away, and to bring their cattle with them, as some no doubt may steal them away privily, I wish them also to be received, for the disabling of the enemy, but withal, that good assurance may be taken for their true behaviour and absolute submission; and that then they be not suffered to remain any longer in those parts, no, nor about the garrisons, but sent away into the inner parts of the realm, and dispersed in such sort as they may not come together, nor easily return if they would. For if they might be suffered to remain about the garrisons, and there inhabit, as they will offer to till the ground and yield a great part of the profit thereof and of their cattle to the colonel, wherewith they have heretofore tempted many, they would, as I have by experience known, be ever after such a gall and inconvenience to them as that their profit shall not recompense their hurt. For they will privily relieve their friends that are forth; they will send the enemy secret advertisements of all their purposes and journeys which they mean to make upon them; they will not also stick to draw the enemy privily upon them; yea, and to betray the fort itself, by discovery of all her defects and disadvantages, if any be, to the cutting of all their throats. For avoiding whereof and many other inconveniences, I wish that they should be carried far from thence into some other parts, so that, as I say, they come in and submit themselves upon the first summons. But afterwards I would have none received, but left to their fortune and miserable end; my reason is, for that those which will afterwards remain without are stout and obstinate rebels, such as will never be made dutiful and obedient, nor brought to labour or civil conversation; having once tasted that licentious life, and being acquainted with spoil and outrages, will ever after be ready for the like occasions, so as there is no hope of their amendment or recovery, and therefore needful to be cut off.

Eudox. Surely of such desperate persons as will follow the course of their own folly there is no compassion to be had, and for others you have proposed a merciful means, much more than they have deserved; but what then shall be the conclusion of this war, for you have prefixed a short time of its continuance?

Iren. The end will, I assure me, be very short, and much sooner than can be in so great a trouble, as it seemeth, hoped for; although there should none of them fall by the sword nor be slain by the soldier, yet thus being kept from manurance,[1] and their cattle from running abroad, by this hard restraint they would quickly consume themselves and devour one another. The proof whereof I saw sufficiently exampled in these late wars of Munster; for, notwithstanding that the same was a most rich and plentiful country, full of corn and cattle, that you would have thought they should have been able to stand long, yet ere one year and a half they were brought to such wretchedness as that any stony heart would have rued the same. Out of every corner of the woods and glens they came creeping forth upon their hands, for their legs could not bear them; they looked like anatomies of death; they spake like ghosts crying out of their graves; they did eat the dead carrions, happy where they could find them; yea, and one another soon after, insomuch as the very carcasses they spared not to scrape out of their graves; and if they found a plot of water-

[1] *Manurance*, cultivation.

cresses or shamrocks, there they flocked as to a feast for the time, yet not able long to continue there withal; that in short space there were none almost left, and a most populous and plentiful country suddenly left void of man and beast; yet, sure, in all that war there perished not many by the sword, but all by the extremity of famine which they themselves had wrought.

Eudox. It is a wonder that you tell, and more to be wondered how it should so shortly come to pass.

Iren. It is most true, and the reason also very ready, for you must conceive that the strength of all that nation is the kern, galloglasse, stocah,[1] horseman, and horse-boy; the which, having been never used to have anything of their own, and now being upon spoil of others, make no spare of anything, but havoc and confusion of all they meet with, whether it be their own friends' goods or their foes'. And if they happen to get never so great spoil at any time, the same they waste and consume in a trice, as naturally delighting in spoil, though it do themselves no good. On the other side, whatsoever they leave unspent, the soldier, when he cometh there, spoileth and havocketh likewise; so that, between both, nothing is very shortly left. And yet this is very necessary to be done for the soon finishing of the war; and not only this in this wise, but also those subjects which do border upon those parts are either to be removed and drawn away, or likewise to be spoiled, that the enemy may find no succour thereby; for what the soldier spares the rebel will surely spoil.

Eudox. I do now well understand you. But now, when all things are brought to this pass, and all filled with these rueful spectacles of so many wretched carcasses starving, goodly countries wasted, so huge desolation and confusion that even I that do but hear it from you, and do picture it in my mind, do greatly pity and commiserate it; if it shall happen that the state of this misery and lamentable image of things shall be told and feelingly

[1] *Stocah*, Irish, *stocach*, an idle fellow, a lounger; foot servant.

VIEW OF THE STATE OF IRELAND. 145

presented to her sacred Majesty, being by nature full of mercy and clemency, who is most inclinable to such pitiful complaints, and will not endure to hear such tragedies made of her poor people and subjects, as some about her may insinuate, then she perhaps, for very compassion of such calamities, will not only stop the stream of such violences, and return to her wonted mildness, but also con them little thanks which have been the authors and counsellors of such bloody platforms. So I remember that in the late government of that good Lord Grey,[1] when, after long travail and many perilous assays, he had brought things almost to this pass that you speak of, that it was even made ready for reformation, and might have been brought to what Her Majesty would, like complaint was made against him, that he was a bloody man, and regarded not the life of her subjects no more than dogs, but had wasted and consumed all, so as now she had nothing almost left but to reign in their ashes. Ear was soon lent thereunto, and all suddenly turned topside-turvy; the noble Lord eftsoons was blamed, the wretched people pitied, and new counsels plotted, in which it was concluded that a general pardon should be sent over to all that would accept of it. Upon which all former purposes were blanked, the governor at a bay, and not only all that great and long charge which she had before been at quite lost and cancelled, but also all that hope of good, which was even at the door, put back and clean frustrated. All which whether it be true or no yourself can well tell.

Iren. Too true, Eudoxus, the more the pity, for I may not forget so memorable a thing; neither can I be ignorant of that perilous devise, and of the whole means by which it was compassed and very cunningly contrived by sowing first dissension between him and another noble personage; wherein they both at length found how notably they had been abused, and how thereby underhand this universal alteration of things was brought

[1] Arthur Lord Grey of Wilton, in whose service Spenser first went to Ireland.

K

about, but then too late to stay the same; for in the meantime all that was formerly done with long labour and great toil was, as you say, in a moment undone, and that good Lord blotted with the name of a bloody man, whom who that well knew, knew to be most gentle, affable, loving, and temperate, but that the necessity of that present state of things enforced him to that violence, and almost changed his natural disposition. But otherwise he was so far from delighting in blood, that oftentimes he suffered not just vengeance to fall where it was deserved; and even some of them which were afterwards his accusers had tasted too much of his mercy, and were from the gallows brought to be his accusers. But his course indeed was this, that he spared not the heads and principals of any mischievous practices or rebellion, but showed sharp judgment on them chiefly for ensample sake, that all the meaner sort, which also were generally then infected with that evil, might, by terror thereof, be reclaimed and saved, if it were possible. For in the last conspiracy of some of the English Pale, think you not that there were many more guilty than they that felt the punishment? Yet he touched only a few of special note; and in the trial of them also, even to prevent the blame of cruelty and partial proceeding, and seeking their blood, which he, as in his great wisdom, as it seemeth, did foresee would be objected against him, he, for the avoiding thereof, did use a singular discretion and regard; for the jury that went upon their trial he made to be chosen out of their nearest kinsmen, and their judges he made of some of their own fathers; of others, their uncles and dearest friends; who, when they could not but justly condemn them, yet he uttered their judgment in abundance of tears; and yet he even herein was called bloody and cruel.

Eudox. Indeed, so have I heard it here often spoken, but I perceive, as I always verily thought, that it was most unjustly; for he was always known to be a most just, sincere, godly, and right noble man, far from such sternness, far from unrighteousness. But in that sharp execution of the Spaniards at the fort of Smerwick, I heard it specially noted, and if it were true as some reported, surely it was a great touch to him in honour; for some say that he promised them life; others, at least he did put them in hope thereof.

Iren. Both the one and the other are most untrue; for this I can assure you, myself being as near them as any, that he was so far either from promising or putting them in hope, that when first their secretary, called, as I remember, Signor Jeffrey, an Italian, being sent to treat with the Lord-Deputy for grace, was flatly refused; and afterwards their colonel, named Don Sebastian, came forth to entreat that they might part with their arms like soldiers, at least with their lives according to the custom of war and law of nations, it was strongly denied him, and told him by the Lord-Deputy himself that they could not justly plead either custom of war or law of nations, for that they were not any lawful enemies; and if they were, he willed them to show by what commission they came thither into another prince's dominions to war, whether from the Pope or the King of Spain, or any other. The which when they said they had not, but were only adventurers, that came to seek fortune abroad and to serve in wars amongst the Irish, who desired to entertain them, it was then told them that the Irish themselves, as the Earl and John of Desmond, with the rest, were no lawful enemies, but rebels and traitors, and therefore they that came to succour them no better than rogues and runagates, specially coming with no license nor commission from their own King; so as it should be dishonourable for him in the name of his Queen to condition or make any terms with such rascals, but left them to their choice, to yield and submit themselves or no. Whereupon the said colonel did absolutely yield himself and the fort, with all therein, and craved only mercy; which it being not thought good to show them for danger of them, if, being saved, they should afterward join with the Irish; and also for terror to the Irish, who are much emboldened by those foreign succours, and also put in hope of more ere long, there was no other way but to make that short end of them as was made. Therefore most untruly and maliciously do these evil tongues backbite and slander the sacred ashes of that most just and honourable personage, whose least virtue, of many most excellent that abounded in his heroic spirit, they were never able to aspire unto.

Eudox. Truly, Ireneus, I am right glad to be thus satisfied by you, in that I have often heard it questioned, and yet was never able till now to choke the mouth of such detractors with the certain knowledge of their slanderous untruths. Neither is the knowledge hereof impertinent to that which we formerly had in hand—I mean for the thorough prosecuting of that sharp course which you have set down for the bringing under of those rebels of Ulster and Connaught, and preparing a way for their perpetual reformation, lest, haply, by any such sinister suggestions of cruelty and too much bloodshed, all the plot might be overthrown, and all the cost and labour therein employed be utterly lost and cast away.

Iren. You say most true; for after that Lord's calling away from thence, the two Lords-Justices continued but a while; of which, the one was of mind, as it seemed, to have continued in the footing of his predecessors, but that he was curbed and restrained. But the other was more mildly disposed, as was meet for his profession, and willing to have all the wounds of that commonwealth healed and recured, but not with that heed as they should be. After, when Sir John Perrot succeeding, as it were, into another man's harvest, found an open way to what course he list, the which he bent not to that point which the former governors intended, but rather quite contrary, as it were in scorn of the former, and in vain vaunt of his own counsels, with the which he was too wilfully carried; for he did tread down and disgrace all the English, and set up and countenance the Irish all that he could; whether thinking thereby to make them more tractable and buxom[1] to his government, wherein he thought much amiss, or privily plotting some other purposes of his own, as it partly afterwards appeared. But surely his manner of government could not be sound nor wholesome for that realm, it being so contrary to the former; for it was even as two physicians should take one sick body in hand at two sundry times, of which the former would minister all things meet to purge and keep under the body, the other to pamper and strengthen it suddenly again; whereof what is to be looked for but a most dangerous relapse? That which we now see through his rule, and the next after him, happened thereunto, being now more dangerously sick than ever before. Therefore by all means it must be foreseen and assured, that after once entering into this course of reformation, there be afterwards no remorse nor drawing back for the sight of any such rueful objects as must thereupon follow, nor for compassion of their calamities, seeing that by no other means it is possible to cure them, and that these are not of will, but of very urgent necessity.

Eudox. Thus far, then, you have now proceeded to plant your garrisons and to direct their services; of the which, nevertheless, I must needs conceive that there cannot be any certain direction set down, so that they must follow the occasions which shall be daily offered, and diligently awaited. But, by your leave, Ireneus, notwithstanding all this your careful foresight and provision, methinks I see an evil lurk unespied, and that may chance to hazard all the hope of this great service if it be not very well looked into, and that is, the corruption of their captains; for though they be placed never so carefully, and their companies filled never so sufficiently, yet may they, if they list, discard whom they please, and send away such as will perhaps willingly be rid of that dangerous and hard service; the which, well I wot, is

[1] *Buxom,* bow-some, pliant, yielding.

their common custom to do when they are laid in garrison, for then they may better hide their defaults than when they are in camp, where they are continually eyed and noted of all men. Besides, when their pay cometh they will, as they say, detain the greatest portions thereof at their pleasure by a hundred shifts that need not here be named, through which they oftentimes deceive the soldier and abuse the Queen, and greatly hinder the service. So that, let the Queen pay never so fully, let the muster-master view them never so diligently, let the deputy or general look to them never so exactly, yet they can cozen them all. Therefore, methinks it were good if it be possible to make provision for this inconvenience.

Iren. It will surely be very hard, but the chiefest help for prevention hereof must be the care of the colonel that hath the government of all his garrison, to have an eye to their alterations, to know the numbers and names of the sick soldiers and the slain, to mark and observe their ranks in their daily rising forth to service, by which he cannot easily be abused, so that he himself be a man of special assurance and integrity. And therefore great regard is to be had in the choosing and appointing of them. Besides, I would not by any means that the captains should have the paying of their soldiers, but that there should be a paymaster appointed, of special truth, which should pay every man according to his captain's ticket and the accompt of the clerk of his band; for by this means the captain will never seek to falsify his alterations, nor to diminish his company, nor to deceive his soldiers, when nothing thereof shall be sure to come unto himself but what is his own bare pay. And this is the manner of the Spaniards' captain, who never hath to meddle with his soldiers' pay, and indeed scorneth the name as base to be counted his soldiers' *pagadore.* Whereas the contrary amongst us hath brought things to so bad a pass that there is no captain but thinks his band very sufficient if he can muster sixty, and sticks not to say openly that he is unworthy to have a captainship that cannot make it worth £500 by the year, the which they right well verify by the proof.

Eudox. Truly, I think this is a very good means to avoid that inconvenience of captains' abuses. But what say you to the colonel? What authority think you meet to be given him? Whether will you allow him to protect or safe-conduct, and to have martial laws, as they are accustomed?

Iren. Yea, verily; but all these to be limited with very strait instructions. As first, for protections; that they shall have authority, after the first proclamation, for the space of twenty days, to protect all that shall come in, and then to send to the Lord-Deputy with their safe-conduct or pass, to be at his disposition; but so as none of them return back again, being once come in, but be presently sent away out of the country to the next sheriff, and so conveyed in safety. And likewise for martial law, that to the soldier it be not extended, but by trial formally of his crime by a jury of his fellow-soldiers, as it ought to be, and not rashly at the will or displeasure of the colonel, as I have sometimes seen too lightly. And as for other of the rebels that shall light into their hands, that they be well aware of what condition they be and what holding they have. For in the last general wars there I knew many good freeholders executed by martial law, whose lands were thereby saved to their heirs which should have otherwise escheated to Her Majesty. In all which the great discretion and uprightness of the colonel himself is to be the chief stay, both for all those doubts and for many other difficulties that may in the service happen.

Eudox. Your caution is very good. But now, touching the arch-rebel himself, I mean the Earl of Tyrone, if he in all the time of these wars should offer to come in and submit himself to Her Majesty, would you not have him received, giving good hostages and sufficient assurance of himself?

Iren. No, marry; for there is no doubt but he will offer to come in, as he hath done divers times already; but it is without any intent of true submission, as the effect hath well showed; neither indeed can he now, if he would, come in at all, nor give that assurance of himself that should be meet. For being, as he is, very subtle-headed, seeing himself now so far engaged in this bad action, can you think that by his submission he can purchase to himself any safety, but that hereafter, when things shall be quieted, these his villanies will be ever remembered? And whensoever he shall tread awry, as needs the most righteous must sometimes, advantage will be taken thereof, as a breach of his pardon, and he brought to a reckoning for all former matters. Besides, how hard it is now for him to frame himself to subjection, that, having once set before his eyes the hope of a kingdom, hath thereunto not only found encouragement from the greatest King in Christendom, but also found great faintness in Her Majesty's withstanding him, whereby he is animated to think that his power is able to defend him, and offend further than he hath done whensoever he please, let every reasonable man judge. But if he himself should come, and leave all other his accomplices without, as O'Donnel, Macmahon, Maguire, and the rest, he must needs think that then even they will ere long cut his throat, which having drawn them all into this occasion, now in the midst of their trouble giveth them the slip; whereby he must needs perceive how impossible it is for him to submit himself. But yet, if he would do so, can he give any good assurance of his obedience? For how weak hold is there by hostages hath too often been proved; and that which is spoken of taking Shan O'Neill's sons from him, and setting them up against him, is a very perilous counsel, and not by any means to be put in proof; for were they let forth, and could overthrow him, who should afterwards overthrow them, or what assurance can be had of them? It will be like the tale in Æsop of the wild horse, who, having enmity with the stag, came to a man to desire his aid against his foe, who, yielding thereunto, mounted upon his back, and so following the stag, ere long slew him; but then when the horse would have him alight he refused, but ever after kept him in his subjection and service. Such, I doubt, would be the proof of Shan O'Neill's sons Therefore it is most dangerous to attempt any such plot; for even that very manner of plot was the means by which this traitorous Earl is now made great. For when the last O'Neill, called Terlagh Leinagh, began to stand upon some tickle terms, this fellow then, called Baron of Dungannon, was, set up as it were, to beard him, and countenanced and strengthened by the Queen so far as that he is now able to keep herself play; much like unto a gamester that, having lost all, borroweth of his next fellow-gamester somewhat to maintain play; which he setting unto him again, shortly thereby winneth all from the winner.

Eudox. Was this rebel then at first set up by the Queen, as you say, and now become so undutiful?

Iren. He was, I assure you, the most outcast of all the O'Neills then, and lifted up by Her Majesty out of the dust to that he hath now wrought himself unto; and now he playeth like the frozen snake, who, being for compassion relieved by the husbandman, soon after he was warm began to hiss and threaten danger even to him and his.

Eudox. He surely, then, deserveth the punishment of that snake, and should worthily be hewed to pieces. But if you like not the letting forth of Shan O'Neill's sons against him, what say you, then, of that advice which I heard was given by some, to draw in Scots to serve against him? How like you that advice?

Iren. Much worse than the former; for who that is experienced in those parts knoweth not that the O'Neills are nearly allied unto the MacNeils of Scotland and to the Earls of Argyle, from whence they used to have all succours of those Scots and Redshanks? Besides, all these Scots are, through long continuance, intermingled and allied to all the inhabitants of the north; so as there is no hope that they will ever be wrought to serve faithfully against their old friends and kinsmen. And though they would, how, when they have overthrown him and the wars are finished, shall they themselves be put out? Do we not all know that the Scots were the first inhabitants of all the north, and that those which now are called the North-Irish are indeed very Scots, which challenge the ancient inheritance and dominion of that country to be their own anciently? This, then, were but to leap out of the pan into the fire. For the chiefest caveat and provision in reformation of the north must be to keep out those Scots.

Eudox. Indeed, I remember that in your discourse of the first peopling of Ireland you showed that the Scythians or Scots were the first that sat down in the north, whereby it seems that they may challenge some right therein. How comes it, then, that O'Neills claim the dominion thereof, and this Earl of Tyrone saith that the right is in him? I pray you resolve me herein; for it is very needful to be known, and maketh unto the right of the war against him, whose success useth commonly to be according to the justness of the cause for which it is made. For if Tyrone have any right in that seigniory, methinks it should be wrong to thrust him out; or if, as I remember you said in the beginning, that O'Neill, when he acknowledged the King of England for his liege lord and sovereign, did, as he allegeth, reserve in the same submission his seigniories and rights unto himself, what should it be accounted to thrust him out of the same?

Iren. For the right of O'Neill in the seigniory of the north it is surely none at all; for, besides that the kings of England conquered all the realm, and thereby assumed and invested all the right of that land to themselves and their heirs and successors for ever,—so as nothing was left in O'Neill but what he received back from them,—O'Neill himself never had any ancient seigniory over that country, but what, by usurpation and encroachment after the death of the Duke of Clarence, he got upon the English, whose lands and possessions being formerly wasted by the Scots, under the leading of Edward le Bruce, as I formerly declared unto you, he eftsoons entered into, and sithence hath wrongfully detained, through the other occupations and great affairs which the kings of England soon after fell into here at home ; so as they could not intend to the recovery of that country of the north, nor restrain the insolency of O'Neill. Who, finding none now to withstand him, reigned in that desolation, and made himself lord of those few people that remained there, upon whom ever sithence he hath continued his first usurped power, and now exacteth and extorteth upon all men what he list; so that now to subdue or expel an usurper should be no unjust enterprise or wrongful war, but a restitution of ancient right unto the Crown of England, from whence they were most unjustly expelled and long kept out.

Eudox. I am very glad herein to be thus satisfied by you, that I may the better satisfy them whom I have often heard to object these doubts, and slanderously to bark at the courses which are held against that traitorous Earl and his adherents. But now that you have thus settled your service for Ulster and Connaught, I would be glad to hear your opinion for the prosecuting of Feagh MacHugh, who being but a base villain, and of himself of no power, yet so continually troubleth the State, notwithstanding that he lieth under their nose, that I disdain his bold arrogancy, and think it to be the greatest indignity to the Queen that may be to suffer such a caitiff to play such rex; and by his ensample, not only to give heart and encouragement to all such bad rebels, but also to yield them succour and refuge against Her Majesty, whensoever they fly unto his comerick.[1] Whereof I would first wish, before you enter into your plot of service against him, that you should lay open by what means he, being so base, first lifted him-

[1] *Comeric*, fellowship of warriors ; Old Irish, *comrac*, is a coming together, also battle.

self up to this dangerous greatness, and how he maintaineth his part against the Queen and her power, notwithstanding all that hath been done and attempted against him; and whether, also, ye have any pretence of right in the lands which he holdeth, or in the wars that he maketh for the same.

Iren. I will so, at your pleasure; and will further declare, not only the first beginning of his private house, but also the original of the sept of the Byrnes and Tooles, so far as I have learned the same from some of themselves and gathered the rest by reading. The people of the Byrnes and Tooles, as before I showed unto you my conjecture, descended from the ancient Britons, which first inhabited all those eastern parts of Ireland, as their names do betoken. For Brin in the British language signifieth woody, and Toole hilly; which names it seemeth they took of the countries which they inhabited, which is all very mountainous and woody. In the which it seemeth that ever since the coming in of the English with Dermot ni-Gall they have continued. Whether that their country, being so rude and mountainous, was of them despised and thought unworthy the inhabiting, or that they were received to grace by them, and suffered to enjoy their lands as unfit for any other; yet it seemeth that in some places of the same they have put foot and fortified with sundry castles, of which the ruins only do there now remain. Since which time they are grown to that strength that they are able to lift up hand against all that state; and now lately, through the boldness and late good success of this Feagh MacHugh, they are so far emboldened that they threaten peril even to Dublin, over whose neck they continually hang. But touching your demand of this Feagh's right unto that country which he claims, or the seigniory therein, it is most vain and arrogant. For of this you cannot be ignorant, that it was part of that which was given in inheritance by Dermot MacMorrough, King of Leinster, unto Strongbow, with his daughter, and which Strongbow gave over unto the King and his heirs; so as the right

VIEW OF THE STATE OF IRELAND.

is absolutely now in Her Majesty. And if it were not, yet could it not be in this Feagh, but in O'Brin, which is the ancient lord of all that country; for he and his ancestors were but followers unto O'Brin, and his grandfather, Shane MacTerlagh, was a man of meanest regard among them, neither having wealth nor power. But his son, Hugh MacShane, the father of this Feagh, first began to lift up his head, and through the strength and great fastness of Glan-Malor, which adjoineth unto his house of Ballinecor, drew unto him many thieves and outlaws, which fled unto the succour of that glen, as to a sanctuary, and brought unto him part of the spoil of all the country; through which he grew strong, and in short space got unto himself a great name thereby amongst the Irish. In whose footing this his son continuing, hath through many unhappy occasions increased his said name and the opinion of his greatness, insomuch that now he is become a dangerous enemy to deal withal.

Eudox. Surely I can commend him, that, being of himself of so mean condition, hath through his own hardiness lifted himself up to that height that he dare now front princes and make terms with great potentates. The which as it is to him honourable, so it is to them most disgraceful, to be bearded of such a base varlet, that, being but of late grown out of the dunghill, beginneth now to overcrow so high mountains and make himself the great protector of all outlaws and rebels that will repair unto him. But do you think he is now so dangerous an enemy as he is counted, or that it is so hard to take him down as some suppose?

Iren. No, verily; there is no great reckoning to be made of him; for had he ever been taken in hand, when the rest of the realm, or at least the parts adjoining, had been quiet; as the honourable gentleman that now governeth there—I mean Sir William Russell— gave a notable attempt thereunto, and had worthily performed it if his course had not been crossed unhappily; he could not have stood three months, nor ever have looked up against a very mean power. But now all the parts about him being up in a madding mood, as the Moores in Leix, the Cavanaghs in the county of Wexford, and some of the Butlers in the county of Kilkenny, they all flock unto him, and draw into his country as to a stronghold where they think to be safe from all that persecute them. And from thence they do at their pleasures break out into all the borders adjoining, which are well-peopled countries, as the counties of Dublin, of Kildare, of Catherlagh, of Kilkenny, of Wexford, with the spoils whereof they victual and strengthen themselves, which otherwise should in short time be starved and sore pined; so that what he is of himself you may hereby perceive.

Eudox. Then, by so much as I gather out of your speech, the next way to end the wars with him and to rout him quite should be to keep him from invading of those countries adjoining; which, as I suppose is to be done either by drawing all the inhabitants of those next borders away and leaving them utterly waste, or by planting garrisons upon all those frontiers about him, that when he shall break forth may set upon him and shorten his return.

Iren. You conceive very rightly, Eudoxus; but for that the dispeopling and driving away all the inhabitants from the country about him, which you speak of, should be a great confusion and trouble,—as well for the unwillingness of them to leave their possessions, as also for placing and providing for them in other countries,—methinks the better course should be by planting of garrisons about him, which, whensoever he shall look forth, or be drawn out with the desire of the spoil of those borders, or for necessity of victual, shall be always ready to intercept his going or coming.

Eudox. Where, then, do you wish those garrisons to be planted, that they may serve best against him, and how many in every garrison?

Iren. I myself, by reason that, as I told you, I am no martial man, will not take upon me to direct so dangerous affairs, but only as I understood by the purposes and plots which the Lord Grey, who was well experienced in that service, against him did lay down. To the performance whereof he only required 1000 men to be laid in six garrisons; that is, at Ballinecor 200 footmen and 50 horsemen, which should shut him out of his great glen, whereto he so much trusteth; at Knocklough 200 footmen and 50 horsemen, to answer the county of Catherlagh; at Arklow to Wicklow 200 footmen and 50 horsemen, to defend all that side towards the sea; in Shillelagh 100 footmen, which should cut him from the Cavanaghs and the county of Wexford; and about the three castles 50 horsemen, which should defend all the county of Dublin; and 100 footmen at Talbot's Town, which should keep him from breaking out into the county of Kildare, and be always on his neck on that side. The which garrisons, so laid, will so busy him that he shall never rest at home nor stir forth abroad but he shall be had. As for his creet, they cannot be above ground but they must needs fall into their hands or starve, for he hath no fastness nor refuge for them. And as for his partakers of the Moores, Butlers, and Cavanaghs, they will soon leave him, when they see his fastness and strong places thus taken from him.

Eudox. Surely this seemeth a plot of great reason and small difficulty, which promiseth hope of a short end. But what special directions will you set down for the services and risings out of these garrisons?

Iren. None other than the present occasions shall minister unto them; and as by good espials, whereof there they cannot want store, they shall be drawn continually upon him, so as one of them shall be still upon him, and sometimes all at one instant baiting him. And this, I assure myself, will demand no long time, but will be all finished in the space of one year, which how small a thing it is unto the eternal quietness which shall thereby be purchased to that realm, and the great good which should grow to Her Majesty, should, methinks readily draw on Her Highness to the undertaking of the enterprise.

Eudox. You have very well, methinks, Ireneus, plotted a course for the achieving [1] of those wars now in Ireland, which seems to ask no long time nor great charge, so as the effecting thereof be committed to men of sure trust and sound experience, as well in that country as in the manner of those services. For if it be left in the hands of such raw captains as are usually sent out of England, being thereunto only preferred by friendship and not chosen by sufficiency, it will soon fall to the ground.

Iren. Therefore it were meet, methinks, that such captains only were thereunto employed as have formerly served in that country and been at least lieutenants unto other captains there. For otherwise being brought and transferred from other services abroad, as in France, in Spain, and in the Low Countries, though they be of good experience in those, and have never so well deserved, yet in these they will be new to seek. And before they have gathered experience they shall buy it with great loss to Her Majesty, either by hazarding of their companies, through ignorance of the places and manner of the Irish services, or by losing a great part of the time which is required hereunto, being but short, in which it might be finished, almost before they have taken out a new lesson or can tell what is to be done.

Eudox. You are no good friend to new captains. It seems, Ireneus, that you bar them from the credit of this service. But, to say truth, methinks it were meet that any one before he came to be a captain should have been a soldier; for, *Parere qui nescit, nescit imperare.*[2] And besides, there is a great wrong done to the old soldier, from whom all means of advancement which is due unto him is cut off, by shuffling in these new-cutting captains into the place for which he hath long served, and perhaps better deserved.

[1] *Achieving*, finishing.   [2] He who cannot obey, cannot command.

VIEW OF THE STATE OF IRELAND. 161

But now that you have thus, as I suppose, finished all the war, and brought all things to that low ebb which you speak of, what course will you take for the bringing in of that Reformation which you intend, and recovering all things from this desolate estate in which methinks I behold them now left, unto that perfect establishment and new commonwealth which you have conceived of, by which so great good may redound unto Her Majesty and an assured peace be confirmed? For that is it whereunto we are now to look and do greatly long for, being long sithence made weary with the huge charge which you have laid upon us, and with the strong endurance of so many complaints, so many delays, so many doubts and dangers, as will hereof, I know well, arise. Unto the which, before we come, it were meet, methinks, that you should take some order for the soldier, which is now first to be discharged and disposed of some way. The which, if you do not well foresee, may grow to as great inconvenience as all this that I suppose you have quit us from, by the loose leaving off so many thousand soldiers, which from thenceforth will be unfit for any labour or other trade, but must either seek service and employment abroad, which may be dangerous, or else employ themselves here at home, as may be discommodious.

Iren. You say very true, and it is a thing much misliked in this our commonwealth, that no better course is taken for such as have been employed in service, but that returning, whether maimed and so unable to labour, or otherwise whole and sound, yet afterwards unwilling to work, or rather willing to set the hangman on work. But that needeth another consideration; but to this which we have now in hand, it is far from my meaning to leave the soldier so at random, or to leave that waste realm so weak and destitute of strength which may both defend it against others that might seek then to set upon it, and also keep it from that relapse which I before did forecast. For it is one special good of this plot which I would devise, that 6000 soldiers of these

L

whom I have now employed in this service and made thoroughly acquainted both with the state of the country and manners of the people, should henceforth be still continued and for ever maintained of the country without any charge to Her Majesty; and the rest, that are either old and unable to serve any longer, or willing to fall to thrift, as I have seen many soldiers after the service to prove very good husbands,[1] should be placed in part of the lands by them won, at such rate, or rather better than others, to whom the same shall be set out.

Eudox. Is it possible, Ireneus? Can there be any such means devised that so many men should be kept still in Her Majesty's service without any charge to her at all? Surely this were an exceeding great good, both to Her Highness to have so many old soldiers always ready at call to what purpose soever she list to employ them, and also to have that land thereby so strengthened that it shall neither fear any foreign invasion nor practice which the Irish shall ever attempt, but shall keep them under in continual awe and firm obedience.

Iren. It is so indeed; and yet this, truly, I do not take to be any matter of great difficulty, as I think it will also soon appear unto you. And first we will speak of the north part, for that the same is of more weight and importance. So soon as it shall appear that the enemy is brought down, and the stout rebel either cut off or driven to that wretchedness that he is no longer able to hold up his head, but will come into any conditions,—which I assure myself will be before the end of the second winter,—I wish that there be a general proclamation made that whatsoever outlaws will freely come in and submit themselves to Her Majesty's mercy shall have liberty so to do, where they shall either find that grace they desire or have leave to return again in safety. Upon which it is likely that so many as survive will come in to sue for grace; of which whoso are thought meet for subjection and fit to

[1] *Husbands,* husbandmen.

be brought to good may be received, or else all of them—for I think that all will be but a very few—upon condition and assurance that they will submit themselves absolutely to Her Majesty's ordinance for them, by which they shall be assured of life and liberty, and be only tied to such conditions as shall be thought by her meet for containing them ever after in due obedience. To the which conditions I nothing doubt but they will all most readily and upon their knees submit themselves, by the proof of that which I have seen in Munster; for upon the like proclamation there they all came in, both tag and rag;[1] and whenas afterwards many of them were denied to be received, they bade them do with them what they would, for they would not by any means return again nor go forth. For in that case who will not accept almost of any conditions rather than die of hunger and misery?

Eudox. It is very likely so. But what, then, is the ordinance, and what be the conditions which you will propose unto them, which shall reserve unto them an assurance of life and liberty?

Iren. So soon, then, as they have given the best assurance of themselves which may be required, which must be, I suppose, some of their principal men, to remain in hostage one for another, and some other for the rest; for other surety I reckon of none that may bind them, neither of wife nor of children, since then perhaps they would gladly be rid of both, from the famine; I would have them first unarmed utterly and stripped quite of all their warlike weapons, and then these conditions set down and made known unto them, that they shall be placed in Leinster and have land given them to occupy and to live upon, in such sort as shall become good subjects, to labour thenceforth for their living,

---

[1] *Tag and rag.* Stanyhurst translated Virgil's
"stridens Aquilone procella
Velum adversa ferit, fluctusque ad sidera tollit"
with
" the northern bluster approaching.
The sails tears tag rag, to the sky the wavés uphoising."
"Tag rag" is end and shred, the least and poorest; when "bobtail" is added, that is the dog with a cropped tail made part of the company.

and to apply themselves to honest trades of civility, as they shall every one be found meet and able for.

Eudox. Where, then, a God's name, will you place them in Leinster? Or will you find out any new land there for them that is yet unknown?

Iren. No; I will place them all in the country of the Byrnes and Tooles, which Feagh MacHugh hath, and in all the lands of the Cavanaghs, which are now in rebellion; and all the lands which will fall to Her Majesty thereabouts, which I know to be very spacious, and large enough to contain them, being very near twenty or thirty miles wide.

Eudox. But then what will you do with all the Byrnes, the Tooles, and the Cavanaghs, and all those that now are joined with them?

Iren. At the same very time and in the same very manner that I make that proclamation to them of Ulster will I also have it made to these; and upon their submission thereunto I will take like assurance of them as of the other; after which I will translate all that remain of them unto the places of the other in Ulster, with all their creet and what else they have left them; the which I will cause to be divided amongst them in some meet sort as each may thereby have somewhat to sustain himself a while withal, until by his further travail and labour of the earth he shall be able to provide himself better.

Eudox. But will you give the land then freely unto them, and make them heirs of the former rebels? So may you perhaps make them also heirs of all their former villanies and disorders, or how else will you dispose of them?

Iren. Not so; but all the lands will I give unto Englishmen, whom I will have drawn thither, who shall have the same, with such estates as shall be thought meet, and for such rent as shall eftsoons be rated. Under every of those Englishmen will I place some of those Irish to be tenants, for a certain rent, according to the quantity of such land as every man shall have allotted unto him and shall be found able to wield; wherein this special regard shall be had, that in no place under any landlord there shall be many of them placed together, but dispersed wide from their acquaintance, and scattered far abroad through all the country. For that is the evil which now I find in all Ireland, that the Irish dwell altogether by their septs and several nations, so as they may practise or conspire what they will; whereas if there were English well placed among them, they should not be able once to stir or to murmur but that it should be known, and they shortened according to their demerits.

Eudox. You have good reason. But what rating of rents mean you? To what end do you purpose the same?

Iren. My purpose is to rate the rent of all those lands of Her Majesty in such sort unto those Englishmen which shall take them, as they shall be well able to live thereupon, to yield Her Majesty reasonable chiefry,[1] and also give a competent maintenance unto the garrisons which shall be there left amongst them. For those soldiers, as I told you, remaining of the former garrisons I cast to maintain upon the rent of those lands which shall be escheated, and to have them divided through all Ireland in such places as shall be thought most convenient and occasion may require. And this was the course which the Romans observed in the conquest of England; for they planted some of their legions in all places convenient, the which they caused the country to maintain, cutting upon every portion of land a reasonable rent, which they called Romescot,[2] the which might not surcharge the tenant or freeholder, and might defray the pay of the garrison; and this hath been always observed by all princes in all countries to them newly subdued, to set garrisons amongst

---

[1] *Chiefry*, a small rent paid to the lord paramount. The word is used by Swift.
[2] *Romescot*, or Romeshot. The name was commonly applied to the Peter pence, or tax of a penny on every house formerly paid on Lammas Day to the Pope.

them, to contain them in duty, whose burden they made them to bear. And the want of this ordinance in the first conquest of Ireland by Henry the Second was the cause of the so short decay of that government and the quick recovery again of the Irish. Therefore, by all means, it is to be provided for. And this is that I would blame, if it should not misbecome me, in the late planting of Munster, that no care was had of this ordinance, nor any strength of garrison provided for by a certain allowance out of the said lands, but only the present profit looked into, and the safe continuance thereof for ever hereafter neglected.

Eudox. But there is a band of soldiers laid in Munster, to the maintenance of which what odds is there whether the Queen, receiving the rent of the country, do give pay at her pleasure, or that there be a settled allowance appointed unto them out of her lands there?

Iren. There are great odds; for now that said rent of the country is not appointed to the pay of the soldiers, but it is, by every other occasion coming between, converted to other uses, and the soldiers in time of peace discharged and neglected as unnecessary. Whereas if the said rent were appointed and ordained by an establishment to this end only, it should not be turned to any other; nor in troublous times, upon every occasion, Her Majesty be so troubled with sending over new soldiers as she is now; nor the country ever should dare to mutiny, having still the soldier in their neck; nor any foreign enemy dare to invade, knowing there is so strong and great a garrison always ready to receive them.

Eudox. Sith, then, you think that this Romescot of the pay of the soldiers to be both the readiest way to the soldiers, and least troublesome to Her Majesty, tell us, I pray you, how would you have the said lands rated, that both a rent may rise thereout unto the Queen, and also the soldiers receive pay? which, methinks will be hard.

VIEW OF THE STATE OF IRELAND. 167

Iren. First, we are to consider how much land there is in all Ulster, that according to the quantity thereof we may cess the said rent and allowance issuing thereout. Ulster, as the ancient records of that realm do testify, doth contain 9000 plough-lands, every of which plough-lands containeth 120 acres, after the rate of 21 feet to every perch of the acre; every of which plough-lands I will rate at 40s. by the year, the which yearly rent amounteth in the whole to £18,000, besides 6s. 8d. chiefly out of every plough-land. But because the county of Louth, being a part of Ulster, and containing in it 712 plough-lands, is not wholly to escheat to Her Majesty as the rest, they having in all their wars continued, for the most part, dutiful, though otherwise a great part thereof is now under the rebels; there is an abatement to be made thereout of 400 or 500 plough-lands, as I estimate the same, the which are not to pay the whole yearly rent of 40s. out of every plough-land, like as the escheated lands do, but yet shall pay for their composition of cess towards the keeping of soldiers 20s. out of every plough-land, so as there is to be deducted out of the former sum £200 or £300 yearly; the which may nevertheless be supplied by the rent of the fishings, which are exceeding great in Ulster, and also by an increase of rent in the best lands, and those that lie in the best places near the sea-coast. The which £18,000 will defray the entertainment of 1500 soldiers, with some overplus towards the pay of the victuallers which are to be employed in the victualling of these garrisons.

Eudox. So then, belike, you mean to leave 1500 soldiers in garrisons for Ulster to be paid principally out of the rent of those lands which shall be there escheated unto Her Majesty; the which, where, I pray you, will you have them garrisoned?

Iren. I will have them divided into three parts; that is, 500 in every garrison, the which I will have to remain in three of the same places where they were before appointed; to wit, 500 at Strabane and about Lough Foyle, so as they may hold all the passages of that part of the country; and some of them be put in wards upon all the straits thereabouts, which I know to be such as may stop all passages into the country on that side; and some of them also upon the Bann, up towards Lough Neagh, as I formerly directed. Also other 500 at the fort upon Lough Erne, and wards taken out of them, which shall be laid at Fermanagh, at Bellick, at Ballyshannon, and all the straits towards Connaught; the which, I know, do so strongly command all the passages that way as that none can pass from Ulster into Connaught without their leave. The last 500 shall also remain in their fort at Monaghan, and some of them be drawn into wards to keep the quays of all that country, both downwards and also towards O'Reilly's country and the Pale; and some at Enniskillen, some at Belturbet, some at the Black Fort, and so along that river, as I formerly showed in the first planting of them. And, moreover, at every of these forts I would have the seat of a town laid forth and encompassed, in the which I would wish that there should be inhabitants placed of all sorts, as merchants, artificers, and husbandmen, to whom there should charters and franchises be granted to incorporate them. The which, as it will be no matter of difficulty to draw out of England persons which would very gladly be so placed, so would it in short space turn those parts to great commodity, and bring ere long to Her Majesty much profit; for those places are so fit for trade and traffic, having most convenient out-gates by divers ways to the sea, and in-gates to the richest parts of the land, that they would soon be enriched and mightily enlarged; for the very seating of the garrisons by them, besides the safety and assurance which they shall work unto them, will also draw thither store of people and trade, as I have ensample at Maryborough and Philipstown in Leinster, where by reason of these two forts, though there be but small wards left in them, there are two good towns now grown, which are the greatest stay of both those two countries.

Eudox. Indeed, methinks, three such towns as you say would do very well in those places with the garrisons, and in short space would be so augmented as they would be able with little to inwall themselves strongly. But for planting of all the rest of the country what order would you take?

Iren. What other than, as I said, to bring people out of England, which should inhabit the same ; whereunto, though I doubt not but great troops would be ready to run, yet for that in such cases the worst and most decayed men are most ready to remove, I would wish them rather to be chosen out of all places of this realm, either by discretion of wise men thereunto appointed, or by lot, or by the drum, as was the old use in sending forth of colonies, or such other good means as shall in their wisdom be thought meetest. Amongst the chief of which I would have the land set into seigniories, in such sort as it is now in Munster, and divided into hundreds and parishes or wards, as it is in England, and laid out into shires, as it was anciently, viz., the county of Down, the county of Antrim, the county of Louth, the county of Armagh, the county of Cavan, the county of Coleraine, the county of Monaghan, the county of Tyrone, the county of Fermanagh, the county of Donegal, being in all ten. Over all which I wish a Lord President and a council to be placed, which may keep them afterwards in awe and obedience and minister unto them justice and equity.

Eudox. Thus I see the whole purpose of your plot for Ulster, and now I desire to hear your like opinion for Connaught.

Iren. By that which I have already said of Ulster you may gather my opinion for Connaught, being very answerable to the former. But for that the lands which shall therein escheat unto Her Majesty are not so entirely together as that they can be accompted in one sum, it needeth that they be considered severally. The province of Connaught in the whole containeth, as appeareth by the records of Dublin, 7200 plough-lands of the former measure, and is of late divided into six shires or counties—the county of Clare, the county of Leitrim, the county of Roscommon, the county of Galway, the county of Mayo, and the county of Sligo; of the which, all the county of Sligo, all the county of Mayo, the most part of the county of Roscommon, the most part of the county of Leitrim, a great part of the county of Galway, and some of the county of Clare are like to escheat to Her Majesty for the rebellion of their present possessors. The which two counties of Sligo and Mayo are supposed to contain almost 3000 plough-lands, the rent whereof rateably to the former I value almost at £6000 per annum. The county of Roscommon, saving that which pertaineth to the house of Roscommon and some few other English there lately seated, is all one, and therefore it is wholly likewise to escheat to Her Majesty, saving those portions of English inhabitants; and even those English do, as I understand by them, pay as much rent to Her Majesty as is set upon those in Ulster, counting their composition-money therewithal, so as it may all run into one reckoning with the former two counties. So that this county of Roscommon, containing 1200 plough-lands, as it is accompted, amounteth to £2400 by the year, which, with the former two counties' rent, maketh about £8300, for the former wanted somewhat. But what the escheated lands of the county of Galway and Leitrim will rise unto is yet uncertain to define till survey thereof be made, for that those lands are intermingled with the Earl of Clanricard's and other lands; but it is thought they be the one-half of both those counties, so as they may be counted to the value of one whole county, which containeth above 1000 plough-lands, for so many the least county of them all comprehendeth, which maketh £2000 more; that is, in all, ten or eleven thousand pounds. The other two counties must remain till their escheats appear; the which letting pass yet as unknown, yet this much is known to be accompted for certain, that the composition of these two counties being rated at 20s. every plough-land, will amount to above £2000 more; all which being laid together to the former may be reasonably estimated to rise unto £13,000; the which sum, together with the rent of the escheated lands in the two last counties, which cannot yet be valued, being, as I doubt not, no less than a thousand pounds more, will yield pay largely unto 1000 men and their victuallers, and a thousand pounds over towards the governor.

Eudox. You have, methinks, made but an estimate of those lands of Connaught even at a very venture, so as it should be hard to build any certainty of charge to be raised upon the same.

Iren. Not altogether upon uncertainties; for this much may easily appear unto you to be certain as the composition-money of every plough-land amounteth unto; for this I would have you principally to understand, that my purpose is to rate all the lands in Ireland at 20s. every plough-land for their composition towards the garrison; the which, I know, in regard of being freed from all other charges whatsoever, will be readily and most gladly yielded unto. So that there being in all Ireland, as appeareth by their old records, 43,920 plough-lands, the same shall amount to the sum likewise of £43,920; and the rest to be reared of the escheated lands which fall to Her Majesty in the said provinces of Ulster, Connaught, and that part of Leinster under the rebels, for Munster we deal not yet withal.

Eudox. But tell me this, by the way, do you then lay composition upon the escheated lands as you do upon the rest? For so methinks you reckon altogether; and that, sure, were too much to pay seven nobles out of every plough-land, and composition-money besides; that is, 20s. out of every plough-land.

Iren. No; you mistake me; I do put only seven nobles' rent and composition both upon every plough-land escheated; that is, 40s. for composition and 6s. 8d. for chiefry to Her Majesty.

Eudox. I do now conceive you; proceed then, I pray you, to the appointing of your garrisons in Connaught, and show us both how many and where you would have them placed.

Iren. I would have 1000 laid in Connaught in two garrisons; namely, 500 in the county of Mayo, about clan MacCostilagh, which shall keep all Mayo and the Bourkes of MacWilliam Eighter; the other 500 in the county of Galway, about Garandough, that they may contain the Connors and the Bourkes there, the Kellys and Murrays, with all them thereabouts; for that garrison which I formerly placed at Lough Erne will serve for all occasions in the county of Sligo, being near adjoining thereunto; so as in one night's march they may be almost in any place thereof when need shall require them. And like as in the former places of garrisons in Ulster I wished three corporate towns to be planted, which, under the safeguard of that strength, should dwell and trade safely with all the country about them; so would I also wish to be in this of Connaught; and that, besides, there were another established at Athlone, with a convenient ward in the castle there for their defence.

Eudox. What should that need, seeing the governor of Connaught useth to lie there always, whose presence will be a defence to all that township?

Iren. I know he doth so, but that is much to be disliked, that the governor should lie so far off in the remotest place of all the province, whereas it were meeter that he should be continually abiding in the midst of the charge; that he might both look out alike unto all places of his government and also be soon at hand in any place where occasion shall demand him; for the presence of the governor is, as you said, a great stay and bridle unto those that are ill-disposed; like as I see it is well observed in Munster, where the daily good thereof is continually apparent. And for this cause also do I greatly mislike the Lord-Deputy's seating at Dublin, being the outest corner of the realm and least needing the awe of his presence; whereas, methinks, it were fitter, since his proper care is of Leinster, though he have care of all besides generally, that he should seat himself at Athy, or thereabouts, upon the skirt of that unquiet country, so that he might sit, as it were, at the very mainmast of his ship; whence he might easily overlook and sometimes overreach the Moores, the Dempseys, the Connors, O'Carroll, O'Molloy, and all that heap of Irish nations which there lie huddled together without any to overawe them or contain them in duty. For the Irishman, I assure you, fears the government no longer than he is within sight or reach.

Eudox. Surely, methinks, herein you observe a matter of much importance, more than I have heard ever noted; but, sure, that seems so expedient as that I wonder that heretofore it hath been overseen or omitted; but I suppose the instance of the citizens of Dublin is the greatest let thereof.

Iren. Truly, then, it ought not so to be, for no cause have they to fear that it will be any hindrance to them, for Dublin will be still, as it is, the key of all passages and transportations out of England thither, to no less profit of those citizens than it now is; and besides other places will hereby receive some benefit. But let us now, I pray you, come to Leinster, in the which I would wish the same course to be observed that was in Ulster.

Eudox. You mean for the leaving of the garrisons in their forts and for planting of English in all those countries between the county of Dublin and the county of Wexford; but those waste wild places, I think, when they are won unto Her Majesty, that there is none which will be hasty to seek to inhabit.

Iren. Yes, enough, I warrant you; for though the whole tract of the country be mountainous and woody, yet there are many goodly valleys amongst them fit for fair habitations, to which those mountains adjoined will be a great increase of pasturage, for that country is a great soil of cattle and very fit for breed. As for corn, it is nothing natural, save only for barley and oats, and some places for rye, and therefore the larger pennyworths may be allowed to them; though otherwise the wideness of the mountain pasturage do recompense the badness of the soil, so as I doubt not but it will find inhabitants and undertakers enough.

Eudox. How much do you think that all those lands which Feagh MacHugh holdeth under him may amount unto, and what rent may be reared thereout, to the maintenance of the garrisons that shall be laid there?

Iren. Truly it is impossible by aim to tell it, and for experience and knowledge thereof, I do not think that there was ever any of the particulars thereof; but yet I will, if it please you, guess thereat, upon ground only of their judgment which have formerly divided all that country into two shires or counties; namely, the county of Wicklow and the county of Ferns; the which two I see no cause but that they should wholly escheat to Her Majesty, all save the baronry Arklow, which is the Earl of Ormond's ancient inheritance, and hath ever been in his possession. For all the whole land is the Queen's, unless there be some grant of any part thereof, to be showed from Her Majesty; as I think there is only of Newcastle to Sir Henry Harrington, and of the castle of Ferns to Sir Thomas Maisterson. The rest, being almost thirty miles over, I do suppose can contain no less than 2000 ploughlands, which I will estimate at £4000 rent by the year. The rest of Leinster, being seven counties; to wit, the county of Dublin, Kildare, Catherlagh, Wexford, Kilkenny, the King's and the Queen's County, do contain in them 7400 plough-lands, which amounteth to so many pounds for composition to the garrison; that makes in the whole £11,400, which sum will yield pay unto 1000 soldiers, little wanting, which may be supplied out of other lands of the Cavanaghs which are to be escheated to Her Majesty for the rebellion of their possessors, though otherwise indeed they be of her own ancient demesne.

Eudox. It is great reason. But tell us now where you will

wish those garrisons to be laid, whether all together, or to be dispersed in sundry places of the country?

Iren. Marry, in sundry places, viz., in this sort, or much the like as may be better advised; for 200 in a place I do think to be enough for the safeguard of that country, and keeping under all sudden upstarts that shall seek to trouble the peace thereof. Therefore I wish 200 to be laid at Ballincor, for the keeping of all bad persons from Glenmalor and all the fastnesses thereabouts, and also to contain all that shall be planted in those lands thenceforth. Another 200 at Knockloe, in their former place of garrison, to keep the Bracknagh and all those mountains of the Cavanaghs; 200 more to lie at Ferns, and upwards, inward upon the Slane; 200 to be placed at the fort of Leix, to restrain the Moores, Upper Ossory, and O'Carrol; other 200 at the fort of Ofaly, to curb the O'Connors, O'Molloys, MacCoghlan, MacGeoghegan, and all those Irish nations bordering thereabouts.

Eudox. Thus I see all your men bestowed in Leinster; wha` think you then of Meath?

Iren. Meath, which containeth both East Meath and West Meath, and of late the Annaly, now called the county of Longford, is counted thereunto; but Meath itself, according to the old records, containeth 4320 plough-lands, and the county of Longford 947, which in the whole makes 5267 plough-lands; of which the composition-money will amount likewise to £5267 to the maintenance of the garrison. But because all Meath, lying in the bosom of that kingdom, is always quiet enough, it is needless to put any garrison there, so as all that charge may be spared. But in the county of Longford I wish 200 footmen and 50 horsemen to be placed in some convenient seat, between the Annaly and the Breny, as about Lough Sillan or some like place of that river, so as they might keep both the O'Reillys and also the O'Farrels, and all that outskirt of Meath in awe; the which use upon every light occasion to be stirring, and having continual enmity amongst themselves, do thereby oftentimes trouble all those parts, the charge whereof, being 3400 and odd pounds, is to be cut out of that composition-money for Meath and Longford. The overplus, being almost £2000 by the year, will come in clearly to Her Majesty.

Eudox. It is worth the hearkening unto. But now that you have done with Meath, proceed, I pray you, to Munster, that we may see how it will rise there for the maintenance of the garrison.

Iren. Munster containeth, by record at Dublin, 16,000 ploughlands, the composition whereof, as the rest, will make £16,000 by the year; out of the which I would have 1000 soldiers to be maintained for the defence of that province, the charge whereof, with the victuallers' wages, will amount to £12,000 by the year; the other £4000 will defray the charge of the presidency and the council of that province.

Eudox. The reckoning is easy; but in this account, by your leave, methinks you are deceived, for in this sum of the composition-money you account the lands of the undertakers of that province, who are, by their grant from the Queen, to be freed from all such impositions whatsoever, excepting their only rent, which is surely enough.

Iren. You say true, I did so; but the same 20s. for every plough-land I mean to have deducted out of that rent due upon them to Her Majesty; which is no hindrance nor charge at all more to Her Majesty than it now is; for all that rent which she receives of them she putteth forth again to the maintenance of the presidency there, the charge whereof it doth scarcely defray; whereas in this account both that charge of the presidency and also of 1000 soldiers more shall be maintained.

Eudox. It should be well if it could be brought to that. But now where will you have your 1000 men garrisoned?

Iren. I would have 100 of them placed at the Bantry, where is a most fit place, not only to defend all that side of the west part from foreign invasion, but also to answer all occasions of troubles to which that country, being so remote, is very subject. And surely there also would be planted a good town, having both a good haven and a plentiful fishing, and the land being already escheated to Her Majesty, but being forcibly kept from her by one that proclaims himself the bastard son of the Earl of Clancar, being called Donell MacCarty, whom it is meet to foresee to. For whensoever the Earl shall die, all those lands, after him, are to come unto Her Majesty. He is like to make a foul stir there, though of himself no power, yet through supportance of some others who lie in the wind and look after the fall of that inheritance. Another 100 I would have placed at Castlemaine, which should keep all Desmond and Kerry, for it answereth them both most conveniently. Also about Kilmore, in the county of Cork, would I have 200 placed, the which should break that nest of thieves there, and answer equally both to the county of Limerick and also the county of Cork. Another 100 would I have lie at Cork, as well to command the town as also to be ready for any foreign occasion. Likewise at Waterford would I place 200 for the same reasons, and also for other privy causes that are no less important. Moreover, on this side of Arlo, near to Muskery Quirk, which is the country of the Burkes, about Kilpatrick, I would have 200 more to be garrisoned, which should scour both the White Knights' country and Arlo and Muskery Quirk; by which places all the passages of thieves do lie, which convey their stealth from all Munster downwards towards Tipperary and the English Pale; and from the English Pale also up unto Munster, whereof they used to make a common trade. Besides that, ere long I doubt that the county of Tipperary itself will need such a strength in it, which were good to be there ready before the evil fall, that is daily of some expected. And thus you see all your garrisons placed.

Eudox. I see it right well. But let me, I pray you, by the way, ask you the reason why in those cities of Munster, namely, Waterford and Cork, you rather placed garrisons than in all others in Ireland? for they may think themselves to have a great wrong to be so charged above all the rest.

Iren. I will tell you. Those two cities, above all the rest, do offer an in-gate to the Spaniard most fitly; but yet, because they shall not take exceptions to this, that they are charged above all the rest, I will also lay a charge upon the other likewise; for indeed it is no reason that the corporate towns, enjoying great franchises and privileges from Her Majesty, and living thereby not only safe, but drawing to them the wealth of all the land, should live so free as not to be partakers of the burthen of this garrison for their own safety, especially in this time of trouble, and seeing all the rest burthened; and therefore I will charge them all thus ratably according to their abilities, towards their maintenance; the which Her Majesty may, if she please, spare out of the charge of the rest, and reserve towards her own costs, or else add to the charge of the presidency in the north:—

Waterford	.	.	.	100	Kilkenny	.	.	.	25
Cork	.	.	.	50	Wexford	.	.	.	25
Limerick	.	.	.	50	Tredagh [Drogheda]	.	25
Galway	.	.	.	50	Ross	.	.	.	25
Dinglecush	.	.	.	10	Dundalk	.	.	.	10
Kinsale	.	.		10	Mullingar	.	.	.	10
Youghal	.	.	.	10	Newry	.	.	.	10
Kilmallock	.	.	.	10	Trim	.	.	.	10
Clonmel	.	.	.	10	Ardee	.	.	.	10
Cashel	.	.	.	10	Kells	.	.	.	10
Fedard	.	.	.	10	Dublin	.	.	.	100

In all 580

Eudox. It is easy, Ireneus, to lay a charge upon any town; but to foresee how the same may be answered and defrayed is the chief part of good advisement.

Iren. Surely this charge which I put upon them I know to be so reasonable as that it will not much be felt; for the port towns that have the benefit of shipping may cut it easily off their trading, and inland towns of their corn and cattle. Neither do I see but, since to them especially the benefit of peace doth redound, that they especially should bear the burthen of their safeguard and defence; as we see all the towns of the Low Countries do cut upon themselves an excise of all things towards the maintenance of the war that is made in their behalf; to which, though these are not to be compared in riches, yet are they to be charged according to their poverty.

Eudox. But now that you have thus set up these forces of soldiers, and provided well, as you suppose, for their pay, yet there remaineth to forecast how they may be victualled and where purveyance may thereof be made; for in Ireland itself I cannot see almost how anything is to be had for them, being already so pitifully wasted as it is with this short time of war.

Iren. For the first two years it is needful, indeed, that they be victualled out of England thoroughly, from half-year to half-year, aforehand. All which time the English Pale shall not be burthened at all, but shall have time to recover themselves. And Munster also, being reasonably well stored, will by that time, if God send seasonable weather, be thoroughly well furnished to supply a great part of that charge; for I know there is great plenty of corn sent over sea from thence, the which if they might have sale for at home, they would be glad to have money so near hand, specially if they were straightly restrained from transporting of it. Thereunto, also, there will be a great help and furtherance given in the putting forward of husbandry in all meet places, as hereafter shall in due place appear. But hereafter, when things shall grow unto a better strength and the country be replenished with corn, as in short space it will, if it be well followed, for the country people themselves are great ploughers and small spenders of corn; then would I wish that there should be good store of houses and magazines erected in all those great places of garrison and in all great towns, as well for the victualling of soldiers and ships as for all occasions of sudden services; as also for preventing of all times of dearth and scarcity. And this want is much to be complained of in England above all other countries, who, trusting too much to the usual blessing of the earth, do never forecast any such hard seasons nor any such sudden occasions as these troublous times may every day bring forth, when it will be too late to gather provision from abroad and to bring it perhaps from far, for the furnishing of ships or soldiers, which peradventure may need to be presently employed, and whose want may (which God forbid) hap to hazard a kingdom.

Eudox. Indeed, the want of those magazines of victuals I have oftentimes complained of in England, and wondered at in other countries; but that is nothing now to our purpose. But as for those garrisons which you have now so strongly planted throughout all Ireland, and every place swarming with soldiers, shall there be no end of them? For now thus being, methinks I do see rather a country of war than of peace and quiet, which you erst pretended to work in Ireland; for if you bring all things to that quietness that you said, what then needeth to maintain so great forces as you have charged upon it?

Iren. I will unto you, Eudoxus, in privity discover the drift of my purpose; I mean, as I told you, and do well hope thereby both to settle an eternal peace in that country, and also to make it very profitable to Her Majesty; the which I see must be brought in with a strong hand, and so continued till it run in a steadfast course of government, which in this sort will neither be difficult nor dangerous; for the soldier being once brought in for the service into Ulster, and having subdued it and Connaught, I will not have him to lay down his arms any more till he have effected that which I purpose; that is, first to have this general composition for maintenance of these throughout all the realm in regard of the troublous times and daily danger which is threatened to this realm by the King of Spain. And thereupon to bestow all my soldiers in such sort as I have done that no part of all that realm shall be able to dare so much as quinch.[1] Then will I eftsoons bring in my reformation, and thereupon establish such a form of government as I may think meetest for the good of that realm; which being once settled and all things put into a right way, I doubt not but they will run on fairly. And though they would ever seek to swerve aside, yet shall they not be able without foreign violence once to remove, as you yourself shall soon, I hope, in your own reason readily conceive; which if it shall ever appear, then may Her Majesty at pleasure withdraw some of the garrisons and turn their pay into her purse; or if she will never please so to do, which I would rather wish, then shall she have a number of brave old soldiers always ready for any occasion that she will employ them unto, supplying their garrisons with fresh ones in their stead; the maintenance of whom shall be no more charge to Her Majesty than now that realm is; for all the revenue thereof, and much more she spendeth, even in the most peaceable times that are there, as things now stand. And in time of war, which is now surely every seventh year, she spendeth infinite treasure besides to small purpose.

Eudox. I perceive your purpose. But now that you have thus strongly made way unto your Reformation, and that I see the people so humbled and prepared that they will and must yield to any ordinance that shall be given them, I do much desire to understand the same; for in the beginning you promised to show a means how to redress all those inconveniences and abuses

[1] *Quinch*, quiver, quake.

which you showed to be in that state of government which now stands there, as in the Laws, Customs, and Religion. Wherein I would gladly know first whether instead of those laws you would have new laws made ; for now, for aught that I see, you may do what you please.

Iren. I see, Eudoxus, that you well remember our first purpose, and do rightly continue the course thereof. First, therefore, to speak of Laws, since we first began with them. I do not think it now convenient, though it be in the power of the Prince, to change all the laws and make new; for that should breed a great trouble and confusion, as well in the English there dwelling and to be planted as also in the Irish. For the English, having been always trained up in the English government, will hardly be inured to any other, and the Irish will better be drawn to the English than the English to the Irish government. Therefore, sithence we cannot now apply laws fit to the people as in the first institutions of commonwealths it ought to be, we will apply the people and fit them unto the laws as it most conveniently may be. The laws, therefore, we resolve, shall abide in the same sort that they do, both Common Law and Statutes ; only such defects in the common law and inconveniences in the statutes as in the beginning we noted, and as men of deeper insight shall advise, may be changed by some other new acts and ordinances, to be by a Parliament there confirmed,—as those for trials of pleas of the crown, and private rights between parties, colourable conveyances, and accessaries.

Eudox. But how will those be redressed by Parliament, whenas the Irish, which sway most in Parliament, as you said, shall oppose themselves against them ?

Iren. That may well now be avoided. For now that so many freeholders of English shall be established, they, together with burgesses of towns and such other loyal Irishmen as may be preferred to be knights of the shire and such-like, will be able to beard and to counterpoise the rest, who also being now more brought in awe will the more easily submit to any such ordinances as shall be for the good of themselves and that realm generally.

Eudox. You say well, for by the increase of freeholders their numbers hereby will be greatly augmented; but how shall it pass through the higher House, which still must consist all of Irish?

Iren. Marry, that also may be redressed by ensample of that which I have heard was done in the like case by King Edward the Third, as I remember, who being greatly bearded and crossed by the lords of the clergy, they being there, by reason of the lords abbots and others, too many and too strong for him, so as he could not for their frowardness order and reform things as he desired, was advised to direct out his writs to certain gentlemen of the best ability and trust, entitling them therein barons, to serve and sit as barons in the next Parliament. By which means he had so many barons in his Parliament as were able to weigh down the clergy and their friends; the which barons, they say, were not afterwards lords, but only baronets,[1] as sundry of them do yet retain the name. And by the like device Her Majesty may now likewise curb and cut short those Irish and unruly lords that hinder all good proceedings.

Eudox. It seems no less than for reforming of all those inconvenient statutes that you noted in the beginning, and redressing of all those evil customs, and lastly, for settling of sound religion amongst them, methinks you shall not need any more to overgo those particulars again which you mentioned, nor any other which might besides be remembered, but to leave all to the reformation of such a Parliament, in which by the good care of the Lord-Deputy and council, they may all be amended. There-

---

[1] *Baronets*, lesser barons who did not rank as peers bore that name, as we here see, before 1611, when the name was applied to a new order of hereditary knights established by James I., professedly for the defence of the new plantation of Ulster. The first baronet was Sir Nicholas Bacon, of Redgrave, Suffolk, whose patent was dated May 22, 1611.

fore now you may come unto that general reformation which you spake of, and bringing in of that establishment by which you said all men should be contained in duty ever after without the terror of warlike forces or violent wresting of things by sharp punishments.

Iren. I will so at your pleasure; the which, methinks, can by no means be better plotted than by ensample of such other realms as have been annoyed with the like evils that Ireland now is and useth still to be. And first in this our realm of England it is manifest by report of the chronicles and ancient writers that it was greatly infested with robbers and outlaws, which, lurking in woods and fast places, used often to break forth into the highways, and sometimes into small villages to rob and spoil. For redress whereof it is written that King Alured or Alfred did divide the realm into shires, and the shires into hundreds, and the hundreds into lathes or wapentakes, and the wapentakes into tithings; so that ten tithings make an hundred, and five make a lathe or wapentake; of which ten each one was bound for another, and the eldest or best of them, whom they called the tithing-man or borsolder,[1] that is, the eldest pledge, became surety for all the rest. So that if any one of them did start into any undutiful action, the borsolder was bound to bring him forth, who joining eftsoons with all his tithing would follow that loose person through all places till they brought him in. And if all that tithing failed, then all that lathe was charged for that tithing; and if that lathe failed, then all that hundred was demanded for them; and if the hundred, then the shire, who joining eftsoons together would not rest till they had found out and delivered in that undutiful fellow which was not amenable to law. And herein it seems that that good Saxon King followed the counsel of Jethro to Moses, who advised him to divide the people into hundreds and to set captains and wise

[1] *Borsolder*, from First English *burhes-ealder*, chief of the borough, through the Anglo-Norman *borisalder*.

men of trust over them, who should take the charge of them and ease him of that burthen. And so did Romulus, as you may read, divide the Romans into tribes, and the tribes into centuries or hundreds. By this ordinance this King brought this realm of England, which before was most troublesome, unto that quiet state that no one bad person could stir but he was straight taken hold of by those of his own tithing and their borsolder, who, being his neighbour or next kinsman, were privy to all his ways and looked narrowly into his life. The which institution, if it were observed in Ireland, would work that effect which it did in England, and keep all men within the compass of duty and obedience.

Eudox. This is contrary to that you said before; for, as I remember, you said that there was a great disproportion between England and Ireland, so as the laws which were fitting for one would not fit the other. How comes it now, then, that you would transfer a principal institution from England to Ireland?

Iren. This law was not made by the Norman Conqueror, but by a Saxon king, at what time England was very like to Ireland as now it stands; for it was, as I told you, annoyed greatly with robbers and outlaws which troubled the whole state of the realm, every corner having a Robin Hood in it that kept the woods, that spoiled all passengers and inhabitants, as Ireland now hath; so as, methinks, this ordinance would fit very well and bring them all into awe.

Eudox. Then when you have thus tithed the commonalty, as you say, and set borsolders over them all, what would you do when you came to the gentlemen? Would you hold the same course.

Iren. Yea, marry, most especially; for this you must know, that all the Irish almost boast themselves to be gentlemen, no less than the Welsh; for if he can derive himself from the head of any sept, as most of them can,—they are so expert by their bards,—then he holdeth himself a gentleman, and thereupon scorneth to work or use any hard labour which he saith is the life of a peasant or churl; but thenceforth becometh either an horse-boy or a stocah to some kern, inuring himself to his weapon and to the gentlemanly trade of stealing, as they count it. So that if a gentleman or any wealthy yeoman of them have any children, the eldest of them, perhaps, shall be kept in some order, but all the rest shall shift for themselves and fall to this occupation. And, moreover, it is a common use amongst some of their gentlemen's sons that so soon as they are able to use their weapons they straight gather to themselves three or four stragglers or kern, with whom wandering a while up and down idly the country, taking only meat, he at last falleth unto some bad occasion that shall be offered; which being once made known, he is thenceforth counted a man of worth, in whom there is courage; whereupon there draw to him many other like loose young men, which stirring him up with encouragement, provoke him shortly to flat rebellion. And this happens not only sometimes in the sons of their gentlemen, but also of their noblemen, especially of them who have base sons. For they are not only not ashamed to acknowledge them, but also boast of them and use them to such secret services as they themselves will not be seen in; as to plague their enemies, to spoil their neighbours, to oppress and crush some of their own too stubborn freeholders which are not tractable to their wills.

Eudox. Then it seemeth that this ordinance of tithing them by the poll is not only fit for the gentlemen, but also for the noblemen, whom I would have thought to be of so honourable a mind as that they should not need such a kind of being bound to their allegiance, who should rather have held in and stayed all the others from undutifulness than need to be forced thereunto themselves.

Iren. Yea, so it is, Eudoxus; but because that noblemen cannot be tithed, there being not many tithings of them, and also because a borsolder over them should be not only a great indignity, but also a danger to add more power to them than they have, or to make one the commander of ten, I hold it meeter that there were only sureties taken of them, and one bound for another; whereby if any shall swerve, his sureties shall, for safeguard of their bonds, either bring him in or seek to serve upon him. And besides this, I would wish them all to be sworn to Her Majesty, which they never yet were but at the first creation; and that oath would sure contain them greatly, or the breach of it bring them to shorter vengeance, for God useth to punish perjury sharply. So I read that there was a corporal oath taken in the reigns of Edward the Second and of Henry the Seventh, when the times were very broken, of all the lords and best gentlemen, of fealty to the King; which now is no less needful, because many of them are suspected to have taken another oath privily to some bad purposes, and thereupon to have received the sacrament and been sworn to a priest, which they think bindeth them more than their allegiance to their Prince or love of their country.

Eudox. This tithing to the common people and taking sureties of lords and gentlemen I like very well, but that it will be very troublesome. Should it not be as well for to have them all booked, and the lords and gentlemen to take all the meaner sort upon themselves, for they are best able to bring them in, whensoever any of them starteth out?

Iren. This indeed, Eudoxus, hath been hitherto, and yet is a common order amongst them to have all the people booked by the lords and gentlemen, but yet the worst order that ever was advised; for by this booking of men all the inferior sort are brought under the command of their lords and forced to follow them into any action whatsoever. Now this you are to understand, that all the rebellions which you see from time to time happen in Ireland are not begun by the common people, but by the lords and captains of countries, upon pride or wilful obstinacy against the Government; which whensoever they will enter into, they draw with them all their people and followers, which think themselves bound to go with them, because they have booked them and undertaken for them. And this is the reason that in England you have such few bad occasions, by reason that the noblemen, however they should happen to be evil-disposed, have no command at all over the commonalty, though dwelling under them because that every man standeth upon himself, and buildeth his fortunes upon his own faith and firm assurance. The which this manner of tithing the polls will work also in Ireland; for by this the people are broken into many small parts, like little streams, that they cannot easily come together into one head, which is the principal regard that is to be had in Ireland, to keep them from growing unto such a head and adhering unto great men.

Eudox. But yet I cannot see how this can be brought about without doing great wrong unto the noblemen there. For at the first conquest of that realm those great seigniories and lordships were given them by the King, that they should be the stronger against the Irish by the multitudes of followers and tenants under them; all which hold their tenements of them by fealty and such services, whereby they are, by the first grant of the King, made bounden unto them, and tied to rise out with them into all occasions of service. And this I have often heard, that when the Lord-Deputy hath raised any general hostings,[1] the noblemen have claimed the leading of them by grant from the Kings of England under the Great Seal exhibited; so as the deputies could not refuse them to have the leading of them, or if they did, they would so work as none of their followers should rise forth to the hosting.

Iren. You say very true; but will you see the fruit of those grants? I have known when those lords have had the leading of their own followers under them to the general hostings, that

[1] *Hosting*, muster or review.

they have for the same cut upon every plough-land within their country forty shillings or more; whereby some of them have gathered together about seven or eight hundred pounds, and others much more into their purse; in lieu whereof they have gathered unto themselves a number of loose kern out of all parts, which they have carried forth with them, to whom they never gave any penny of entertainment, allowed by the country or forced by them, but let them feed upon the countries and extort upon all men where they come; for that people will never ask better entertainment than to have a colour of service or employment given them by which they will poll and spoil so outrageously as the very enemy cannot do much worse, and they also sometimes turn to the enemy.

Eudox. It seems the first intent of those grants was against the Irish, which now some of them use against the Queen herself. But now what remedy is there for this? Or how can those grants of the Kings be avoided without wronging of those lords which had those lands and lordships given them?

Iren. Surely they may be well enough, for most of those lords, since their first grants from the Kings, by which those lands were given them, have sithence bestowed the most part of them amongst their kinsfolk; as every lord perhaps hath given in his time one or another of his principal castles to his younger son, and other to others, as largely and as amply as they were given to him; and others they have sold, and others they have bought, which were not in their first grant, which now, nevertheless, they bring within the compass thereof; and take and exact upon them, as upon their first demesnes, all those kind of services, yea, and the very wild Irish exactions, as coigny and livery for him, and such-like; by which they poll and utterly undo the poor tenants and freeholders under them, which either through ignorance know not their tenures, or through greatness of their new lords dare not challenge them; yea, and some lords of countries also, as great ones as themselves, are now by strong hand brought under them and made their vassals. As, for example, Arundel of the Strande, in the county of Cork, who was anciently a great lord, and was able to spend £3500 by the year, as appeareth by good records, is now become the Lord Barry's man, and doth to him all those services which are due unto Her Majesty. For reformation of all which I wish that there were a commission granted forth under the Great Seal, as I have seen one recorded in the old council-book of Munster, that was sent forth in the time of Sir William Drury unto persons of special trust and judgment, to inquire throughout all Ireland, beginning with one county first, and so resting awhile till the same were settled by the verdict of a sound and substantial jury, how every man holdeth his land, of whom, and by what tenure; so that every one should be admitted to show and exhibit what right he hath and by what services he holdeth his land, whether in chief, or in socage, or by knight's service, or how else soever. Thereupon would appear, first, how all those great English lords do claim those great services, what seigniories they usurp, what wardships they take from the Queen, what lands of hers they conceal. And then, how those Irish captains of countries have encroached upon the Queen's freeholders and tenants, how they translated the tenures of them from English holding unto Irish tanistry, and defeated Her Majesty of all her rights and duties which are to accrue to her thereout; as wardships, liveries, marriages, fines of alienations, and many other commodities which now are kept and concealed from Her Majesty to the value of £40,000 per annum, I dare undertake, in all Ireland, by that which I know in one county.

Eudox. This, Ireneus, would seem a dangerous commission, and ready to stir up all the Irish in rebellion, who, knowing that they have nothing to show for all those lands which they hold but their swords, would rather draw them than suffer the lands to be thus drawn away from them.

Iren. Neither should their lands be taken away from them, nor the utmost advantages enforced against them. But this, by discretion of the commissioners, should be made known unto them, that it is not Her Majesty's meaning to use any such extremity, but only to reduce things into order of English law, and make them hold their lands of her, and to restore to her her due services which they detain out of those lands, which were anciently held of her. And that they should not only not be thrust out, but also have estates and grants of their lands new made to them from Her Majesty, so as they should thenceforth hold them rightfully, which they now usurp wrongfully. And yet, withal, I would wish that in all those Irish countries there were some land reserved to Her Majesty's free disposition for the better containing of the rest, and intermingling them with English inhabitants and customs, that knowledge might still be had of them and of all their doings, so as no manner of practice or conspiracy should be had in hand amongst them but notice should be given thereof by one means or another and their practices prevented.

Eudox. Truly, neither can the Irish nor yet the English lords think themselves wronged nor hardly dealt withal herein to have that which is indeed none of their own at all, but Her Majesty's, absolutely given to them, with such equal conditions as that both they may be assured thereof better than they are, and also Her Majesty not defrauded of her right utterly. For it is a great grace in a Prince to take that with conditions which is absolutely her own. Thus shall the Irish be well satisfied. And as for the great men which had such grants made to them at first by the Kings of England, it was in regard that they should keep forth the Irish and defend the King's right and his subjects; but now, seeing that, instead of defending them, they rob and spoil them, and instead of keeping out the Irish, they do not only make the Irish their tenants in those lands, and thrust out the English, but also some of themselves become mere Irish, with marrying with them, with fostering with them, and combining with them against the Queen, what reason is there but that those grants and privileges should be either revoked, or at least reduced to the first intention for which they were granted? For, sure, in mine opinion, they are more sharply to be chastised and reformed than the rude Irish, which, being very wild at the first, are now become more civil; whenas these, from civility, are grown to be wild and mere Irish.

Iren. Indeed, as you say, Eudoxus, these do need a sharper reformation than the Irish; for they are more stubborn and disobedient to law and government than the Irish be.

Eudox. In truth, Ireneus, this is more than ever I heard that any English there should be worse than the Irish.[1] Lord, how quickly doth that country alter men's natures! It is not for nothing, I perceive, which I have heard, that the Council of England think it no good policy to have that realm reformed or planted with English, lest they should grow so undutiful as the Irish and become more dangerous; as appeareth by the examples of the Lacys in the time of Edward the Second, which you spake of, that shook off their allegiance to their natural Prince, and turned to Edward le Bruce to make him King of Ireland.

Iren. No times have been without bad men. But as for that purpose of the Council of England which you spake of, that they should keep that realm from reformation, I think they are most lewdly abused; for their great carefulness and earnest endeavours do witness the contrary. Neither is it the nature of the country to alter men's manners, but the bad minds of the men, who, having been brought up at home under a strait rule of duty and obedience, being always restrained by sharp penalties from lewd behaviour, so soon as they come thither, where they see laws more slackly tended, and the hard restraint which they were used unto,

---

[1] "Ipsis Hibernicis hiberniores," first said of them, became a proverb.

now slacked, they grow more loose and careless of their duty; and as it is the nature of all men to love liberty, so they become flat libertines and fall to all licentiousness, more boldly daring to disobey the law, through the presumption of favour and friendship, than any Irish dareth.

Eudox. Then if that be so methinks your late advisement was very evil whereby you wished the Irish to be sowed and sprinkled with English, and in all the Irish countries to have English planted amongst them, for to bring them to English fashions, since the English sooner draw to the Irish than the Irish to the English. For, as you said before, if they must run with the stream, the greater number will carry away the less. Therefore, methinks, by this reason it should be better to part the Irish and English than to mingle them together.

Iren. Not so, Eudoxus; but where there is no good stay of government and strong ordinances to hold them, there indeed the fewer follow the more; but where there is due order of discipline and good rule, there the better shall go foremost and the worst shall follow. And therefore now, since Ireland is full of her own nation, that ought not to be rooted out, and somewhat stored with English already, and more to be, I think it best, by an union of manners and conformity of minds, to bring them to be one people and to put away the dislikeful conceit both of the one and the other, which will be by no means better than by this intermingling of them. For neither all the Irish may dwell together, nor all the English, but by translating of them and scattering them amongst the English, not only to bring them, by daily conversation, to better liking of each other, but also to make both of them less able to hurt. And, therefore, when I come to the tithing of them, I will tithe them one with another, and, for the most part, will make an Irishman the tithing-man, whereby he shall take the less exception to partiality, and yet be the more tied thereby. But when I come to the headborough, which is the head of the lathe, him will. I make an Englishman, or an Irishman of special assurance. As also when I come to appoint the alderman that is the head of the hundred, him will I surely choose to be an Englishman of special regard, that may be a stay and pillar of all the borough under him.

Eudox. What do you mean by your hundred, and what by your borough?' By that that I have read in ancient records of England, an hundred did contain an hundred villages, or, as some say, an hundred plough-lands, being the same which the Saxons called cantred;[1] the which cantred, as I find it recorded in the Black-book of the Exchequer of Ireland, did contain thirty *villatas terræ*, which some call quarters of land; and every *villata* can maintain 400 cows in pasture, and the 400 cows to be divided into four herds, so as none of them shall come near each other; every *villata* containing eighteen plough-lands, as is there set down. And by that which I have read of a borough, it signifieth a free town, which had a principal officer called a head-borough, to become ruler and undertake for all the dwellers under him, having for the same franchises and privileges granted them by the King, whereof it was called a free borough, and of the lawyers *franciplegium*.[2]

Iren. Both that which you said, Eudoxus, is true, and yet that which I say not untrue. For that which you spake of dividing the country into hundreds was a division of the lands of the realm; but this which I tell was of the people, which were thus divided by the poll; so that hundred in this sense signifieth a hundred pledges which were under the command and assurance of their alderman; the which, as I suppose, was also called a wapentake, so named of touching the weapon or spear of their alderman, and swearing to follow him faithfully and serve their

---

[1] *Cantred* was a word from the Welsh, *cant* (cent), a hundred, and *tref*, a dwelling.
[2] *Frankpledge*, having pledge or surety for the good behaviour of freemen.

*Prince truly.[1] But others think that a wapentake was ten hundreds or boroughs. Likewise a borough, as I here use it, and as the old laws still use, is not a borough town, as they now call it, that is, a franchised town, but a main pledge of a hundred free persons, therefore called a free borough, or, as you say, *franci plegium*. For borh in old Saxon signifieth a pledge or surety; and yet it is so used with us in some speeches, as Chaucer saith, St. John to boroh, that is, for assurance and warranty.

Eudox. I conceive the difference. But now that you have thus divided the people into these tithings and hundreds, how will you have them so preserved and continued? For people do often change their dwelling-places, and some must die, whilst other some do grow up into strength of years and become men.

Iren. These hundreds I would wish to assemble themselves once every year with their pledges, and to present themselves before the justices of the peace which shall be thereunto appointed, to be surveyed and numbered, to see what change hath happened since the year before; and the defects to supply, of young plants late grown up, the which are diligently to be overlooked and viewed, of what condition and demeanour they be, so as pledges may be taken for them, and they put into order of some tithing. Of all which alterations notes are to be taken and books made thereof accordingly.

Eudox. Now, methinks, Ireneus, you are to be warned to take heed, lest unawares you fall into that inconvenience which you formerly found fault with in others; namely, that by this booking of them you do not gather them into a new head, and having broken their former strength, do not unite them more strongly again. For every alderman, having all these free pledges of his hundred under his command, may, methinks, if he be evil-disposed, draw all his company into an evil action. And likewise

---

[1] This etymology is given in the Laws of Edward the Confessor.

by this assembling of them once a year unto their alderman by their wapentakes, take heed lest you also give them occasion and means to practise together in any conspiracies.

Iren. Neither of both is to be doubted; for their aldermen and head-boroughs will not be such men of power and countenance of themselves, being to be chosen thereunto, as need to be feared; neither, if he were, is his hundred at his command, further than his prince's service; and also every tithing-man may control him in such a case. And as for the assembling of the hundred, much less is any danger thereof to be doubted, seeing it is before some justice of peace or some high constable, to be thereunto appointed, so as of these tithings there can no peril ensue, but a certain assurance of peace and great good; for they are thereby withdrawn from their lords and subjected to the Prince. Moreover, for the better breaking of these heads and septs, which I told you was one of the greatest strengths of the Irish, methinks it should be very well to renew that old statute which was made in the reign of Edward the Fourth in England, by which it was commanded, that whereas all men then used to be called by the name of their septs, according to the several nations, and had no surnames at all, that from thenceforth each one should take upon himself a several surname, either of his trade and faculty, or of some quality of his body or mind, or of the place where he dwelt; so as every one should be distinguished from the other, or from the most part, whereby they shall not only not depend upon the head of their sept, as now they do, but also in time learn quite to forget his Irish nation. And herewithal would I also wish all the O's and the Macs, which the heads of septs have taken to their names, to be utterly forbidden and extinguished; for that the same being an ordinance, as some say, first made by O'Brien for the strengthening of the Irish, the abrogating thereof will as much enfeeble them.

Eudox. I like this ordinance very well. But now that you

have thus divided and distinguished them, what other order will you take for their manner of life?

Iren. The next thing that I will do shall be to appoint to every one that is not able to live of his freehold a certain trade of life, to which he shall find himself fittest and shall be thought ablest; the which trade he shall be bound to follow and live only thereupon. All trades, therefore, are to be understood to be of three kinds—manual, intellectual, and mixed. The first containeth all such as needeth exercise of bodily labour to the performance of their profession; the second consisting only of the exercise of wit and reason; the third sort, part of bodily labour and part of wit, but depending most of industry and carefulness. Of the first sort be all handicrafts and husbandry labour; of the second be all sciences and those which be called liberal arts; of the third is merchandise and chaffery[1]—that is, buying and selling. And without all these three there is no commonwealth can almost consist, or at the least be perfect. But the realm of Ireland wanteth the most principal of them, that is, the intellectual; therefore in seeking to reform her state it is specially to be looked unto. But because by husbandry, which supplieth unto us all things necessary for food, we chiefly live, therefore it is first to be provided for. The first thing, therefore, that we are to draw these new-tithed men into ought to be husbandry; first, because it is the most easy to be learned, needing only the labour of the body; next, because it is most general and most needful; then, because it is most natural; and lastly, because it is most enemy to war and most hateth unquietness. As the poet saith—

"*Bella execrata colonis.*"

For husbandry, being the nurse of thrift and the daughter of industry and labour, detesteth all that may work her scath and

[1] *Chaffery*, from First English "ceapan" (cheapen), to buy, and "faran," to fare or go.

destroy the travail of her hands, whose hope is all her life's comfort unto the plough. Therefore are those kern, stocaghs, and horse-boys to be driven and made to employ that ableness of body which they were wont to use to theft and villainy, henceforth to labour and industry. In the which, by that time they have spent but a little pain, they will find such sweetness and happy contentment, that they will afterwards hardly be haled away from it or drawn to their wonted lewd life in thievery and roguery. And being once thus inured thereunto, they are not only to be countenanced and encouraged by all good means, but also provided that their children after them may be brought up likewise in the same, and succeed in the rooms of their fathers. To which end there is a statute in Ireland already well provided, which commandeth that all the sons of husbandmen shall be trained up in their fathers' trades; but it is, God wot, very slenderly executed.

Eudox. But do you not count in this trade of husbandry pasturing of cattle and keeping of their cows? for that is reckoned as a part of husbandry.

Iren. I know it is, and needfully to be used; but I do not mean to allow any of those able bodies which are able to use bodily labour to follow a few cows grazing, but such impotent persons as, being unable for strong travail, are yet able to drive cattle to and fro to their pasture; for this keeping of cows is of itself a very idle life and a fit nursery for a thief. For which cause, you remember, I disliked the Irish manner of keeping boolies in the summer upon the mountains and living after that savage sort. But if they will algates feed many cattle or keep them on the mountains, let them make some towns near to the mountain's side, where they may dwell together with neighbours and be conversant in the view of the world. And, to say truth, though Ireland be by nature counted a great soil of pasture, yet had I rather have fewer cows kept and men better-mannered than to have such huge increase of cattle and no increase of good conditions. I would, therefore, wish that there were some ordinances made amongst them that whosoever keepeth twenty kine should keep a plough going; for otherwise all men would fall to pasturage and none to husbandry, which is a great cause of this dearth now in England and a cause of the usual stealths in Ireland; for look into all countries that live in such sort by keeping of cattle and you shall find that they are both very barbarous and uncivil, and also greatly given to war. The Tartarians, the Muscovites, the Norwegians, the Goths, the Armenians, and many others do witness the same. And, therefore, since now we purpose to draw the Irish from desire of war and tumults to the love of peace and civility, it is expedient to abridge their great custom of herding [1] and augment their trade of tillage and husbandry. As for other occupations and trades, they heed not be enforced to, but every man to be bound only to follow one that he thinks himself aptest for. For other trades of artificers will be occupied for very necessity and constrained use of them ; and so, likewise, will merchandise for the gain thereof; but learning and bringing up in liberal sciences will not come of itself, but must be drawn on with strait laws and ordinances. And, therefore, it were meet that such an Act were ordained, that all the sons of lords, gentlemen, and such others as are able to bring them up in learning should be trained up therein from their childhoods, and for that end, every parish should be forced to keep a petty schoolmaster adjoining unto the parish church, to be the more in view, which should bring up their children in the first elements of letters; and that in every country or barony they should keep another able schoolmaster, which should instruct them in grammar and in the principles of sciences, to whom they should be compelled to send their youth to be disciplined; whereby they will in short space grow up to that civil conversa-

[1] *Herding*, keeping herds.

tion, that both the children will loathe their former rudeness in which they were bred, and also their parents will, even by the ensample of their young children, perceive the foulness of their own behaviour compared to theirs. For learning hath that wonderful power in itself, that it can soften and temper the most stern and savage nature.

Eudox. Surely I am of your mind, that nothing will bring them from their uncivil life sooner than learning and discipline, next after the knowledge and fear of God. And, therefore, I do still expect that you should come thereunto and set some order for reformation of Religion, which is first to be respected; according to the saying of Christ, "Seek first the kingdom of heaven, and the righteousness thereof."

Iren. I have in mind so to do; but let me, I pray you, first finish that which I had in hand, whereby all the ordinances which shall afterwards be set for Religion may abide the more firmly and be observed more diligently. Now that this people is thus tithed and ordered, and every one bound unto some honest trade of life, which shall be particularly entered and set down in the tithing-book, yet perhaps there will be some stragglers and runagates which will not of themselves come in and yield themselves to this order; and yet, after the well-finishing of the present war and establishing of the garrisons in all strong places of the country where their wonted refuge was most, I suppose there will few stand out; or if they do, they will shortly be brought in by the ears. But yet, afterwards, lest any one of them should swerve, or any that are tied to a trade should afterwards not follow the same according to this institution, but should straggle up and down the country or mich[1] in corners amongst their friends idly, as carrows, bards, jesters, and such-like, I would wish that a provost-marshal should be appointed in every shire, which should continually walk about the country with half-a-dozen or half-a-score horsemen, to

[1] *Mich*, to lie hid, skulk. "Carrows," as we have seen, are strolling gamesters.

take up such loose persons as they should find thus wandering, whom he should punish by his own authority with such pains as the person shall seem to deserve; for if he be but once so taken idly roguing, he may punish him more lightly, as with stocks or such-like; but if he be found again so loitering, he may scourge him with whips or rods; after which, if he be again taken, let him have the bitterness of martial law. Likewise, if any relics of the old rebellion be found by any that either have not come in and submitted themselves to the law, or that, having once come in, do break forth again and walk disorderly, let them taste of the same cup, in God's name, for it was due to them for their first guilt; and now, being revived by their latter looseness, let them have their first desert, as now being found unfit to live in the commonwealth.

Eudox. This were a good ordinance; but methinks it is an unnecessary charge, and also unfit to continue the name or form of any martial law, whenas there is a proper officer already appointed for these turns, to wit, the sheriff of the shire, whose peculiar office it is to walk up and down his bailiwick, as you would have a marshal to snatch up all those runagates and unprofitable members, and to bring them to his gaol to be punished for the same. Therefore this may well be spared.

Iren. Not so, methinks; for though the sheriff have this authority of himself to take up all such stragglers and imprison them, yet shall he not do so much good nor work that terror in the hearts of them that a marshal will, whom they shall know to have power of life and death in such cases, and especially to be appointed for them. Neither doth it hinder but that, though it pertain to the sheriff, the sheriff may do therein what he can and yet the marshal may walk his course besides; for both of them may do the more good and more terrify the idle rogue, knowing that, though he have a watch upon the one, yet he may light upon the other. But this proviso is needful to be had in this case, that the sheriff may not have the like power of life as the marshal hath, and as heretofore they have been accustomed; for it is dangerous to give power of life into the hands of him which may have benefit by the party's death; as if any loose liver have any goods of his own, the sheriff is to seize thereupon, whereby it have come to pass that some who have not deserved judgment of death, though otherwise perhaps offending, have been, for their goods' sake, caught up and carried straight to the bough—a thing, indeed, very pitiful and horrible. Therefore by no means I would have the sheriff have such authority, nor yet to imprison that losel till the sessions, for so all gaols might soon be filled; but to send him to the marshal, who eftsoons finding him faulty, shall give him meet correction and send him away forthwith.

Eudox. I do now perceive your reason well. But come we now to that whereof we erst spake—I mean, to Religion and religious men. What order will you set amongst them?

Iren. For Religion little have I to say, myself being, as I said, not professed therein, and itself being but one, so as there is but one way therein; for that which is true only is, and the rest is not at all. Yet in planting of Religion thus much is needful to be observed, that it be not sought forcibly to be impressed into them with terror and sharp penalties, as now is the manner, but rather delivered and intimated with mildness and gentleness, so as it may not be hated before it be understood and their professors despised and rejected. And, therefore, it is expedient that some discreet ministers of their own countrymen be first sent over amongst them, which, by their meek persuasions and instructions, as also by their sober lives and conversations, may draw them first to understand, and afterwards to embrace, the doctrine of their salvation. For if that the ancient godly fathers which first converted them when they were infidels to the faith were able to pull them from idolatry and paganism to the true belief in Christ, as St. Patrick and St. Columba, how much more easily shall godly teachers bring them to the true understanding of that which they already professed! Wherein it is great wonder to see the odds which are between the zeal of Popish priests and the ministers of the Gospel. For they spare not to come out of Spain, from Rome and from Rheims, by long toil and dangerous travelling hither, where they know peril of death awaiteth them and no reward or riches are to be found, only to draw the people unto the Church of Rome: whereas some of our idle ministers, having a way for credit and estimation thereby opened unto them, and having the livings of the country offered unto them without pains and without peril, will neither for the same, nor any love of God, nor zeal of religion, nor for all the good they may do by winning souls to God, be drawn forth from their warm nests to look out into God's harvest, which is even ready for the sickle and all the fields yellow long ago. Doubtless those good old godly fathers will, I fear me, rise up in the Day of Judgment to condemn them.

Eudox. Surely it is great pity, Ireneus, that there are none chosen out of the ministers of England, good, sober, and discreet men, which might be sent over thither to teach and instruct them, and that there is not as much care had of their souls as of their bodies; for the care of both lieth upon the Prince.

Iren. Were there never so many sent over, they should do small good till one enormity be taken from them; that is, that both they be restrained from sending their young men abroad to other universities beyond the sea, as Rheims, Douay, Louvain, and the like; and others from abroad be restrained from coming into them; for they, lurking secretly in their houses and in corners of the country, do more hurt and hindrance to religion with their private persuasions than all the others can do good with their public instructions; and though for these latter there be a good statute there ordained, yet the same is not executed; and as for the former, there is no law nor order for their restraint at all.

Eudox. I marvel it is no better looked unto; and not only this, but that also which I remember you mentioned in your abuses concerning the profits and revenues of the lands of fugitives in Ireland, which, by pretence of certain colourable conveyances, are sent continually over unto them, to the comforting of them and others against Her Majesty, for which here in England there is good order taken; and why not, then, as well in Ireland? For though there be no statute there yet enacted therefor, yet might Her Majesty by her only prerogative seize the fruits and profits of those fugitive lands into her hands till they come over to testify their true allegiance.

Iren. Indeed she might so do, but the cumbrous times do perhaps hinder the regard thereof, and of many other good intentions.

Eudox. But why, then, did they not mend it in peaceable times?

Iren. Leave we that to their grave considerations, but proceed we forward. Next care in Religion is to build up and repair all the ruined churches, whereof the most part lie even with the ground; and some that have been lately repaired are so unhandsomely patched and thatched that men do even shun the places for the uncomeliness thereof. Therefore I would wish that there were order taken to have them built in some better form, according to the churches of England; for the outward show, assure yourself, doth greatly draw the rude people to the reverencing and frequenting thereof, whatever some of our late too nice fools say there is nothing in the seemly form and comely order of the Church. And for the keeping and continuing them there should likewise church-wardens of the gravest men in the parish be appointed, as they be here in England, which should take the yearly charge both hereof and also of the schoolhouses which I wish to be built near the said churches; for maintenance of both which it were meet that some small portion of lands were allotted, sith no more mortmains are to be looked for.

Eudox. Indeed, methinks it would be so convenient; but when all is done, how will you have your churches served and your ministers maintained, since the livings, as you say, are not sufficient scarce to make them gowns, much less to yield meet maintenance according to the dignity of their degree?

Iren. There is no way to help that but to lay two or three of them together until such time as the country grow more rich and better inhabited, at which time the tithes and other obventions will also be more augmented and better valued.

But now that we have thus gone through all the three sorts of trades, and set a course for their good establishment, let us, if it please you, go next to some other needful points of public matters, no less concerning the good of the commonwealth, though but accidentally depending on the former.

And first, I wish that order were taken for the cutting and opening of all places through woods, so that a wide way of the space of a hundred yards might be laid open in every of them for the safety of travellers, which use often in such perilous places to be robbed and sometimes murdered. Next, that bridges were built upon the rivers and all the fords marred and spilt,[1] so as none might pass any other way but by those bridges, and every bridge to have a gate and a gatehouse set thereon; whereof this good will come, that no night-stealths, which are commonly driven in byways and by blind fords unused of any but such-like, shall be conveyed out of one country into another, as they use, but

[1] *Spilt*, destroyed; First English "spillan" meant, to kill.

they must pass by those bridges, where they may either be haply encountered or easily tracked, or not suffered to pass at all, by means of those gatehouses thereon. Also, that in all straits [1] and narrow passages, as between two bogs or through any deep ford, or under any mountain-side, there should be some little fortilage or wooden castle set, which should keep and command that strait, whereby any rebels that should come into the country might be stopped that way or pass with great peril. Moreover, that all highways should be fenced and shut up on both sides, leaving only forty feet breadth for passage, so as none should be able to pass but through the highways; whereby thieves and night-robbers might be the more easily pursued and encountered, when there shall be no other way to drive their stolen cattle but therein, as I formerly declared. Further, that there should be in sundry convenient places by the highways towns appointed to be built, the which should be free boroughs and incorporate under bailiffs; to be by their inhabitants well and strongly intrenched or otherwise fenced with gates on each side thereof, to be shut nightly, like as there is in many places in the English Pale, and all the ways about it to be strongly shut up, so as none should pass but through those towns; to some of which it were good that the privilege of a market were given, the rather to strengthen and enable them to their defence. For there is nothing doth sooner cause civility in any country than many market towns, by reason that people repairing often thither for their needs will daily see and learn civil manners of the better sort. Besides, there is nothing doth more stay and strengthen the country than such corporate towns, as by proof in many rebellions hath appeared, in which when all the countries have swerved the towns have stood fast and yielded good relief to the soldiers on all occasions of services. And lastly, there is indeed nothing doth more enrich any country or realm than many towns; for to them

---

[1] *Straits* were narrow passages, whether of land or water.

will all the people draw and bring the fruits of their trades, as well to make money of them as to supply their needful uses; and the countrymen will also be more industrious in tillage and rearing of all husbandry commodities, knowing that they shall have ready sale for them at those towns. And in all those towns should there be convenient inns erected for the lodging and harbouring of travellers, which are now oftentimes spoiled by lodging abroad in weak thatched houses for want of such safe places to shroud them in.

Eudox. But what profit shall your market towns reap of their market when as each one may sell their corn and cattle abroad in the country and make their secret bargains amongst themselves, as now I understand they use?

Iren. Indeed, Eudoxus, they do so, and thereby no small inconvenience doth rise to the commonwealth; for now when any one hath stolen a cow or a garron [1] he may secretly sell it in the country without privity of any, whereas if he brought it to a market town it would perhaps be known and the thief discovered. Therefore it were good that a straight ordinance were made that none should buy or sell any cattle but in some open market,—there being now market towns everywhere at hand,—upon a great penalty. Neither should they, likewise, buy any corn to sell the same again unless it were to make malt thereof, for by such engrossing and regrating [2] we see the dearth that now commonly reigneth here in England to have been caused. Hereunto also is to be added that good ordinance which I remember was once proclaimed throughout all Ireland: that all men should mark their cattle with an open several mark upon their flanks or buttocks, so as if they happened to be stolen they might appear whose they were, and they which should buy them might thereby suspect the

---

[1] *Garron*, the Irish word for a horse put to common work.
[2] *Engrossing* was buying up in large quantities; *regrating* was selling again in small quantities, at an enhanced price, in or near the same market or fair.

owner, and be warned to abstain from buying them of a suspected person with such an unknown mark.

Eudox. Surely these ordinances seem very expedient, but specially that of free towns, of which I wonder there is so small store in Ireland, and that in the first peopling and planting thereof they were neglected and omitted.

Iren. They were not omitted, for there were through all places of the country convenient many good towns seated, which through that inundation of the Irish which I first told you of were utterly wasted and defaced, of which the ruins are yet in many places to be seen, and of some no sign at all remaining, save only their bare names, but their seats are not to be found.

Eudox. But how, then, cometh it to pass that they have never since been recovered, nor their habitations re-edified, as of the rest, which have been no less spoiled and wasted?

Iren. The cause thereof was, for that after their desolation they were begged by gentlemen of the Kings, under colour to repair them and gather the poor relics of the people again together. Of whom having obtained them, they were so far from re edifying them as that by all means they have endeavoured to keep them waste, lest that, being repaired, their charters might be renewed and their burgesses restored to their lands, which they had now in their possession, much like as in those old monuments of abbeys and religious houses we see them likewise use to do. For which cause it is judged that King Henry the Eighth bestowed them upon them, conceiving that thereby they should never be able to rise again. And even so do these lords, in these poor old corporate towns, of which I could name divers but for kindling of displeasure. Therefore, as I wished many corporate towns to be erected, so would I again wish them to be free, not depending upon the service nor under the command of any but the governor. And being so, they will both strengthen all the country round about them, which by their means will be the better replenished and enriched, and also be as continual holds for Her Majesty if the people should revolt or break out again; for without such it is easy to forage and overrun the whole land. Let be for ensample all those free boroughs in the Low Countries, which are now all the strength thereof. These and other like ordinances might be delivered for the good establishment of the realm after it is once subdued and reformed, in which it might afterwards be very easily kept and maintained, with small care of the governors and Council there appointed, so as it should in short space yield a plentiful revenue to the Crown of England, which now doth but suck and consume the treasure thereof, through those unsound plots and changeful orders which are daily devised for her good, yet never effectually prosecuted or performed.

Eudox. But in all this your discourse I have not marked anything by you spoken touching the appointment of the principal officer to whom you wish the charge and performance of all this to be committed. Only I observed some foul abuses by you noted in some of the late governors, the reformation whereof you left off for this present place.

Iren. I delight not to lay open the blames of great magistrates to the rebuke of the world, and therefore their reformation I will not meddle with, but leave unto the wisdom of greater heads to be considered. Only thus much I will speak generally thereof, to satisfy your desire, that the government and chief magistracy I wish to continue as it doth; to wit, that it be ruled by a Lord-Deputy or Justice, for that it is a very safe kind of rule; but therewithal I wish that over him there were placed also a Lord-Lieutenant of some of the greatest personages in England; such a one I could name, upon whom the eye of all England is fixed and our last hopes now rest, who being intituled with that dignity,

o

and being here always resident, may back and defend the good course of that government against all maligners which else will, through their cunning working underhand, deprave and pull back whatever thing shall be begun or intended there, as we commonly see by experience at this day, to the utter ruin and desolation of that poor realm. And this Lieutenancy should be no discountenancing of the Lord-Deputy, but rather a strengthening of all his doings. For now the chief evil in that government is that no governor is suffered to go on with any one course, but upon the least information here of this or that he is either stopped and crossed, or other courses appointed him from hence which he shall run, which how inconvenient it is, is at this hour too well felt. And therefore this should be one principle in the appointing of the Lord-Deputy's authority, that it should be more ample and absolute than it is, and that he should have uncontrolled power to do anything that he, with the advisement of the Council, should think meet to be done. For it is not possible for the Council here to direct a government there, who shall be forced oftentimes to follow the necessity of present actions and to take the sudden advantage of time, which being once lost will not be recovered; whilst through expecting direction from hence, the delays whereof are oftentimes through other greater affairs most irksome, the opportunities there in the meantime pass away and great danger often groweth, which by such timely prevention might easily be stopped. And this, I remember, is worthily observed by Machiavelli in his discourses upon Livy, where he commendeth the manner of the Romans' government in giving absolute power to all their counsellors and governors, which if they abused they should afterwards dearly answer. And the contrary thereof he reprehendeth in the states of Venice, of Florence, and many other principalities of Italy, who used to limit their chief officers so strictly as that thereby they have oftentimes lost such happy occasions as they could never come unto again; the

VIEW OF THE STATE OF IRELAND.

like whereof whoso hath been conversant in the government of Ireland hath too often seen, to their great hindrance and hurt. Therefore this I could wish to be redressed; and yet not so, but that in particular things he should be restrained, though not in the general government; as, namely, in this, that no offices should be sold by the Lord-Deputy for money, nor no pardons nor no protections bought for reward, nor no beeves taken for captainries of counties, nor no shares of bishoprics for nominating of bishops; nor no forfeitures nor dispensations with penal statutes given to their servants or friends, nor no selling of licenses for transportation of prohibited wares, and specially of corn and flesh, with many the like, which need some manner of restraint, or else very great trust in the honourable disposition of the Lord-Deputy.

Thus I have, Eudoxus, as briefly as I could and as my memory would serve me, run through the state of that whole country, both to let you see what it now is and also what it may be by good care and amendment. Not that I take upon me to change the policy of so great a kingdom or prescribe rules to such wise men as have the handling thereof, but only to show you the evils which in my small experience I have observed to be the chief hindrance of the reformation, and, by way of conference, to declare my simple opinion for the redress thereof and establishing a good course for government. Which I do not deliver as a perfect plot of mine own invention to be only followed; but as I have learned and understood the same by the consultations and actions of very wise governors and counsellors whom I have sometimes heard treat hereof, so have I thought good to set down a remembrance of them for my own good and your satisfaction, that whoso list to overlook them, although perhaps much wiser than they which have thus advised of that state, yet at least by comparison hereof may perhaps better his own judgment, and by the light of others foregoing him may follow after with more ease, and haply find a fairer way thereunto than they which have gone before.

Eudox. I thank you, Ireneus, for this your gentle pains, withal not forgetting now, in the shutting up, to put you in mind of that which you have formerly half promised; that hereafter, when we shall meet again upon the like good occasion, you will declare unto us those your observations which you have gathered of the antiquities of Ireland.

A

DISCOVERY OF THE TRUE CAUSES

WHY

IRELAND

WAS NEVER ENTIRELY SUBDUED NOR BROUGHT
UNDER OBEDIENCE

OF THE

CROWN OF ENGLAND

UNTIL THE BEGINNING OF

HIS MAJESTY'S HAPPY REIGN:

BY

SIR JOHN DAVIES

ATTORNEY-GENERAL FOR IRELAND UNDER JAMES THE FIRST.

MDCXII.

DEDICATED TO THE

KING,

BY HIS

MAJESTY'S ATTORNEY-GENERAL OF IRELAND,

SIR JOHN DAVIES.

Principis est virtus maxima, nôsse suos.

MDCXII.

A
DISCOVERY

OF THE

TRUE CAUSES WHY IRELAND WAS NEVER ENTIRELY SUBDUED AND
BROUGHT UNDER OBEDIENCE OF THE CROWN OF ENGLAND,
UNTIL THE BEGINNING OF HIS MAJESTY'S HAPPY REIGN.

DURING the time of my service in Ireland, which began in the first year of His Majesty's reign, I have visited all the provinces of that kingdom in sundry journeys and circuits; wherein I have observed the good temperature of the air; the fruitfulness of the soil; the pleasant and commodious seats for habitation; the safe and large ports and havens lying open for traffic into all the west parts of the world; the long inlets of many navigable rivers and so many great lakes and fresh ponds within the land, as the like are not to be seen in any part of Europe; the rich fishings and wild-fowl of all kinds; and lastly, the bodies and minds of the people endued with extraordinary abilities of nature. The observation whereof hath bred in me some curiosity to consider what were the true causes why this kingdom, whereof our kings of England have borne the title of sovereign lords for the space of four hundred and odd years, a period of time wherein divers great monarchies have risen from barbarism to civility, and fallen again to ruin, was not in all that space of time thoroughly subdued and reduced to obedience of the

Crown of England, although there hath been almost a continual war between the English and the Irish; and why the manners of the mere[1] Irish are so little altered since the days of King Henry the Second, as appeareth by the description made by Giraldus Cambrensis, who lived and wrote in that time, albeit there have been since that time so many English colonies planted in Ireland as that, if the people were numbered at this day by the poll, such as are descended of English race would be found more in number than the ancient natives.

And, truly, upon consideration of the conduct and passage of affairs in former times, I find that the state of England ought to be cleared of an imputation which a vulgar error hath cast upon it in one point; namely, that Ireland long since might have been subdued and reduced to civility if some statesmen in policy had not thought it more fit to continue that realm in barbarism. Doubtless this vulgar opinion or report hath no true ground, but did first arise either out of ignorance or out of malice. For it will appear by that which shall hereafter be laid down in this discourse, that ever since our nation had any footing in this land the state of England did earnestly desire, and did accordingly endeavour from time to time, to perfect the conquest of this kingdom, but that in every age there were found such impediments and defects in both realms as caused almost an impossibility that things should have been otherwise than they were.

The defects which hindered the perfection of the conquest of Ireland were of two kinds, and consisted, first, in the faint prosecution of the war, and next in the looseness of the civil government. For the husbandman must first break the land before it be made capable of good seed; and when it is thoroughly broken and manured, if he do not forthwith cast good seed into it, it will grow wild again and bear nothing but weeds. So a barbarous country must be first broken by a war before it will be

[1] *Mere*, unmixed; from the Latin. Mere wine was wine unmixed with water.

capable of good government; and when it is fully subdued and conquered, if it be not well planted and governed after the conquest, it will eftsoons return to the former barbarism.

Touching the carriage of the martial affairs from the seventeenth year of King Henry the Second, when the first overture was made for the conquest of Ireland—I mean, the first after the Norman conquest of England—until the nine-and-thirtieth year of Queen Elizabeth, when that royal army was sent over to suppress Tyrone's rebellion, which made in the end an universal and absolute conquest of all the Irishry, it is most certain that the English forces sent hither or raised here from time to time were ever too weak to subdue or master so many warlike nations or septs of the Irish as did possess this island; and, besides their weakness, they were ill paid and worse governed. And if at any time there came over an army of competent strength and power, it did rather terrify than break and subdue this people, being ever broken and dissolved by some one accident or other before the perfection of the conquest.

For that I call a perfect conquest of a country which doth reduce all people thereof to the condition of subjects; and those I call subjects which are governed by the ordinary laws and magistrates of the sovereign. For though the Prince doth bear the title of sovereign lord of an entire country, as our kings did of all Ireland, yet if there be two-third parts of that country wherein he cannot punish treasons, murders, or thefts unless he send an army to do it; if the jurisdiction of his ordinary courts of justice doth not extend into those parts to protect the people from wrong and oppression; if he have no certain revenue, no escheats or forfeitures, out of the same, I cannot justly say that such a country is wholly conquered.

First, then, that we may indulge and discern whether the English forces in Ireland were at any time of sufficient strength to make a full and final conquest of that land, let us see what extraordinary armies have been transmitted out of England thither, and what ordinary forces have been maintained there, and what service they have performed from time to time since the seventeenth year of King Henry the Second.

In that year MacMurrough, Lord of Leinster, being oppressed by the Lords of Meath and Connaught and expelled out of his territory, moved King Henry the Second to invade Ireland, and made an overture unto him for the obtaining of the sovereign lordship thereof. The King refused to undertake the war himself, to avoid the charge, as King Henry the Seventh refused to undertake the discovery of the Indies for the same cause, but he gave license by his Letters Patents that such of his subjects might pass over into Ireland as would at their own charge become adventurers in that enterprise.

So as the first attempt to conquer this kingdom was but an adventure of a few private gentlemen. Fitzstephen and Fitzgerald first brake the ice with a party of three hundred and ninety men. The Earl Strongbow followed them with twelve hundred more, whose good success upon the sea-coasts of Leinster and Munster drew over the King in person the next year after, *cum quingentis militibus*, as Giraldus Cambrensis reporteth, who was present in Ireland at that time; which, if they were but five hundred soldiers, seemeth too small a train for so great a Prince. But admit they were five hundred knights, yet because in those days every knight was not a commander of a regiment or company, but most of them served as private men, sometimes a hundred knights under a spear, as appeareth by the lists of the ancient armies, we cannot conjecture his army to have been so great as might suffice to conquer all Ireland, being divided into so many principalities, and having so many hydras' heads as it had at that time.

For, albeit Tacitus in the Life of Agricola doth report that Agricola, having subdued the greatest part of Great Britain, did signify to the Senate of Rome that he thought Ireland might also be conquered with one legion and a few aids, I make no doubt but that if he had attempted the conquest thereof with a far greater army he would have found himself deceived in his conjecture. For a barbarous country is not so easily conquered as a civil, whereof Cæsar had experience in his wars against the Gauls, Germans, and Britons, who were subdued to the Roman Empire with far greater difficulty than the rich kingdoms of Asia. And, again, a country possessed with many petty lords and states is not so soon brought under entirely as an entire kingdom governed by one prince or monarch. And, therefore, the late King of Spain could sooner win the kingdom of Portugal than reduce the states of the Low Countries.

But let us see the success of King Henry the Second. Doubtless his expedition was such as he might have said with Cæsar, " *Veni, vidi, vici.*" For upon his first arrival his very presence, without drawing his sword, prevailed so much as all the petty kings or great lords within Leinster, Connaught and Munster submitted themselves unto him, promised to pay him tribute, and acknowledged him their chief and sovereign lord. Besides the better to assure this inconstant sea-nymph, who was so easily won, the Pope would needs give her unto him with a ring, *conjugio jungam stabili, propriamque dicabo.* But as the conquest was but slight and superficial, so the Pope's donation and the Irish submissions were but weak and fickle assurances. For, as the Pope had no more interest in this kingdom than he which offered to Christ all the kingdoms of the earth, so the Irish pretend that by their law a tanist might do no act that might bind his successor. But this was the best assurance he could get from so many strong nations of people with so weak a power; and yet he was so well pleased with this title of the lordship of Ireland as he placed it in his royal style before the Duchies of Normandy and Aquitaine. And so, being advertised of some stirs raised by his unnatural sons in England, within five months after his first arrival he departed out of Ireland without striking one blow or building one castle or planting one garrison among the Irish; neither left he behind him one true subject more than those he found there at his coming over, which were only the English adventurers spoken of before, who had gained the port towns in Leinster and Munster and possessed some scopes of land thereunto adjoining, partly by Strongbow's alliance with the Lord of Leinster and partly by plain invasion and conquest.

And this is that conquest of King Henry the Second so much spoken of by so many writers, which though it were in no other manner than is before expressed, yet is the entire conquest of all Ireland attributed unto him.

But the truth is, the conquest of Ireland was made piece and piece by slow steps and degrees, and by several attempts in several ages. There were sundry revolutions as well of the English fortunes as of the Irish, somewhiles one prevailing, somewhiles the other, and it was never brought to a full period till His Majesty that now is came to the crown.

As for King Henry the Second, he was far from obtaining that monarchy royal and true sovereignty which His Majesty who now reigneth hath over the Irish; for the Irish lords did only promise to become tributaries to King Henry the Second. And such as pay only tribute, though they be placed by Bodin in the first degree of subjection, are not properly subjects but sovereigns. For, though they be less and inferior unto the Prince to whom they pay tribute, yet they hold all other points of sovereignty; and having paid their tribute which they promised, to have their peace, they are quit of all other duties, as the same Bodin writeth. And therefore, though King Henry the Second had the title of sovereign lord over the Irish, yet did he not put those things in execution which are the true marks and differences of sovereignty.

ON IRELAND BEFORE 1603. 223

For, to give laws unto a people, to institute magistrates and officers over them, to punish and pardon malefactors, to have the sole authority of making war and peace, and the like, are the true marks of sovereignty, which King Henry the Second had not in the Irish countries, but the Irish lords did still retain all these prerogatives to themselves.

For they governed their people by the Brehon law; they made their own magistrates and officers; they pardoned and punished all malefactors within their several countries; they made war and peace one with another without controlment; and this they did not only during the reign of King Henry the Second, but afterwards in all times, even until the reign of Queen Elizabeth. And it appeareth what manner of subjects these Irish lords were by the concord made between King Henry the Second and Roderick O'Connor, the Irish King of Connaught in the year 1175, which is recorded by Hoveden in this form: "*Hic est finis et Concordia, inter Dominum regem Angliæ Henricum, filium Imperatricis, et Rodoricum Regem Conactæ, scilicet, quod Rex, etc. Angliæ concessit prædict' Roderico Ligeo homini suo, ut sit Rex sub eo paratus ad servitium suum, ut homo suus, etc.*" And the commission whereby King Henry the Second made William Fitz-Adelme his Lieutenant of Ireland hath this direction: "*Archi-episcopis, Episcopis, Regibus, Comitibus, Baronibus, et omnibus fidelibus suis in Hibernia, Salutem.*" Whereby it is manifest that he gave those Irish lords the title and style of kings.

King John likewise did grant divers charters to the King of Connaught, which remain in the Tower of London. And afterwards, in the time of King Henry the Third, we find in the Tower a grant made to the King of Thomond in these words: "*Rex Regi Tosmond salutem. Concessimus vobis terram Tosmond quam prius tenuistis, per firmam centum et triginta marcarum; Tenendum de nobis usque ad ætatem nostram.*" And in the Pipe-Rolls remaining in Bremigham's Tower,[1] in the Castle of Dublin, upon sundry accounts of the seneschal of Ulster, when that earldom was in the King's hands, by reason of the minority of the Earl, the entry of all such charges as were made upon O'Neill for rent-beeves, or for aids towards the maintenance of the King's wars, are in this form: "*Oneal Regulus* 400 *vaccas pro arreragio reddit; Oneal Regulus,* 100 *li. de Auxilio Domini Regis ad guerram suam in Wasconia sustinendam.* And in one roll, the 36th of Henry the Third, *Oneale Rex,* 100 *li. de auxilio domini Regis ad guerram suam in Wallia sustinendam."* Which seemed strange to me, that the King's civil officer should give him that style upon record, unless he meant it in that sense as Maximilian the emperor did when speaking of his disobedient subjects. "The title," said he, "of *Rex Regum* doth more properly belong to me than to any mortal prince, for all my subjects do live as kings; they obey me in nothing, but do what they list." And truly in that sense these Irish lords might not unfitly be termed kings. But to speak in proper terms, we must say with the Latin poet, "*Qui Rex est, Regem, Maxime non habeat.*" But touching these Irish kings, I will add this note out of an ancient manuscript, the Black-book of Christ Church in Dublin: "*Isti Reges non fuerunt ordinati solemnitate alicuius ordinis, nec unctionis Sacramento, nec jure hæreditario, vel aliqua proprietatis successione, sed vi et armis quilibet Regnum suum obtinuit;*" and therefore they had no just cause to complain when a stronger king than themselves became a king and lord over them. But let us return to our purpose, and see the proceeding of the martial affairs.

King Henry the Second, being returned into England, gave the lordship of Ireland unto the Lord John, his youngest son, surnamed before that time *Sans Terre;* and the Pope, confirming

---

[1] *Bremigham's Tower.* The Birmingham Tower. The Irish Bremighams or Birminghams were of English descent, barons of Lowth, including Down and Antrim. One of them was executed after imprisonment in Dublin Castle.

that gift, sent him a crown of peacock's feathers, as Pope Clement the Eighth sent the feather of a phœnix, as he called it, to the traitor Tyrone. This young Prince, the King's son, being but twelve years of age, with a train of young noblemen and gentlemen, to the number of three hundred, but not with any main army, came over to take possession of his new patrimony; and being arrived at Waterford, divers Irish lords, who had submitted themselves to his father, came to perform the like duty to him. But that youthful company using them with scorn because their demeanours were but rude and barbarous, they went away much discontented, and raised a general rebellion against him; whereby it was made manifest that the submission of the Irish lords and the donation of the Pope were but slender and weak assurances for a kingdom.

Hereupon this young Lord was revoked and Sir John de Courcy sent over, not with the King's army, but with a company of voluntaries, in number four hundred or thereabout. With these he attempted the conquest of Ulster, and in four or five encounters did so beat the Irishry of that province as that he gained the maritime coasts thereof from the Boyne to the Bann, and thereupon was made Earl of Ulster. So as now the English had gotten good footing in all the provinces of Ireland; in the first three provinces of Leinster, Munster, and Connaught, part by the sword and part by submission and alliance; and, lastly, in Ulster by the invasion and victories of Sir John de Courcy.

From this time forward until the seventeenth year of King John, which was a space of more than thirty years, there was no army transmitted out of England to finish the conquest. Howbeit, in the meantime, the English adventurers and colonies already planted in Ireland did win much ground upon the Irish; namely, the Earl Strongbow, having married the daughter of MacMurrough, in Leinster; the Lacys in Meath; the Geraldines and other adventurers in Munster; the Audleys, Gernons, Clintons,

P

Russells, and other voluntaries of Sir John de Courcy's retinue in Ulster; and the Bourkes, planted by William FitzAdelme, in Connaught. Yet were the English reputed but part owners of Ireland at this time, as appeareth by the commission of the Pope's Legate in the time of King Richard the First, whereby he had power to exercise his jurisdiction in *Anglia, Wallia, ac illis Hiberniæ partibus, in quibus Johannes Moretonii Comes potestatem habet et dominium*, as it is recorded by Matthew Paris.

King John, in the twelfth year of his reign, came over again into Ireland, the stories of that time say with a great army, but the certain numbers are not recorded. Yet it is credible, in regard of the troubles wherewith this King was distressed in England, that this army was not of sufficient strength to make an entire conquest of Ireland; and if it had been of sufficient strength, yet did not the King stay a sufficient time to perform so great an action, for he came over in June and returned in September the same year. Howbeit, in that time the Irish lords for the most part submitted themselves to him, as they had done before to his father, which was but a mere mockery and imposture. For his back was no sooner turned but they returned to their former rebellion, and yet this was reputed a second conquest. And so this King, giving order for the building of some castles upon the borders of the English colonies, left behind him the Bishop of Norwich for the civil government of the land, but he left no standing army to prosecute the conquest; only the English colonies which were already planted were left to themselves to maintain what they had got, and to gain more if they could.

The personal presence of these two great Princes, King Henry the Second and King John, though they performed no great thing with their armies, gave such countenance to the English colonies, which increased daily by the coming over of new voluntaries and adventurers out of England, as that they enlarged their territories very much. Howbeit, after this time the Kings of England, either because they presumed that the English colonies were strong enough to root out the Irish by degrees, or else because they were diverted or disabled otherwise (as shall be declared hereafter), never sent over any royal army or any numbers of men worthy to be called an army into Ireland until the thirty-sixth year of King Edward the Third, when Lionel, Duke of Clarence, the King's second son, having married the daughter and heir of Ulster, was sent over with an extraordinary power in respect of the time (for the wars betwixt England and France were then in their heat), as well to recover his earldom of Ulster, which was then overrun and possessed by the Irish, as to reform the English colonies, which were become strangely degenerate throughout the whole kingdom.

For though King Henry the Third gave the whole land of Ireland to Edward the Prince, his eldest son and his heirs, *Ita quod non separetur a corona Angliæ;* whereupon it was styled the land of the Lord Edward, the King's eldest son, and all the officers of the land were called the officers of Edward, Lord of Ireland; and though this Edward was one of the most active Princes that ever lived in England, yet did he not, either in the lifetime of his father or during his own reign, come over in person or transmit any army into Ireland; but, on the other side, he drew sundry aids and supplies of men out of Ireland to serve him in his wars in Scotland, Wales, and Gascogne. And again, though King Edward the Second sent over Piers Gaveston with a great retinue, it was never intended he should perfect the conquest of Ireland, for the King could not want his company so long a time as must have been spent in the finishing of so tedious a work.

So then, in all that space of time, between the twelfth year of King John and the thirty-sixth year of King Edward the Third, containing a hundred and fifty years or thereabouts, although there were a continual bordering war between the English and the Irish, there came no royal army out of England to make an end of the war. But the chief governors of the realm, who were at first called *Custodes Hiberniæ*, and afterwards Lords-Justices, and the English lords who had gotten so great possessions and royalties, as that they presumed to make war and peace without direction from the State, did leave all their forces within the land. But those forces were weakly supplied and ill-governed, as I said before—weakly supplied with men and money, and governed with the worst discipline that ever was seen among men of war. And no marvel, for it is an infallible rule that an army ill-paid is ever unruly and ill-governed. The standing forces here were seldom or never reinforced out of England, and such as were either sent from thence or raised here did commonly do more hurt and damage to the English subjects than to the Irish enemies by their continual cess and extortion; which mischief did arise by reason that little or no treasure was sent out of England to pay the soldiers' wages. Only the King's revenue in Ireland was spent, and wholly spent, in the public service; and therefore in all the ancient Pipe-Rolls in the times of Henry the Third, Edward the First, Edward the Second, and Edward the Third, between the receipts and allowances there is this entry, "*In Thesauro nihil.*" For the officers of the State and the army spent all, so as there was no surplusage of treasure, and yet that all was not sufficient. For in default of the King's pay, as well the ordinary forces which stood continually as the extraordinary, which were levied by the chief governor, upon journeys and general hostings, were for the most part laid upon the poor subject descended of English race; howbeit this burden was in some measure tolerable in the time of King Henry the Third and King Edward the First; but in the time of King Edward the Second, Maurice Fitz-Thomas of Desmond, being chief commander of the army against the Scots, began that wicked extortion of coigny and livery and pay; that is, he and his army took horse-meat and man's-meat and money at their pleasure, without any ticket or any other satisfaction. And this was after that time the general fault of all the governors and commanders of the army in this land. Only the golden saying of Sir Thomas Rookesby, who was Justice in the thirtieth year of King Edward the Third, is recorded in all the annals of this kingdom, that he would eat in wooden dishes, but would pay for his meat gold and silver. Besides, the English colonies, being dispersed in every province of this kingdom, were enforced to keep continual guards upon the borders and marches round about them; which guards consisting of idle soldiers were likewise imposed as a continual burthen upon the poor English freeholders, whom they oppressed and impoverished in the same manner. And because the great English lords and captains had power to impose this charge when and where they pleased, many of the poor freeholders were glad to give unto those lords a great part of their lands, to hold the rest free from that extortion; and many others, not being able to endure that intolerable oppression, did utterly quit their freeholds and returned into England. By this means the English colonies grew poor and weak, though the English lords grew rich and mighty; for they placed Irish tenants upon the lands relinquished by the English; upon them they levied all Irish exactions; with them they married, and fostered, and made gossips; so as within one age the English, both lords and freeholders, became degenerate and mere Irish in their language, in their apparel, in their arms and manner of fight, and all other customs of life whatsoever.

By this it appeareth why the extortion of coigny and livery is called in the old statutes of Ireland a damnable custom, and the imposing and taking thereof made high treason. And it is said in an ancient discourse "Of the Decay of Ireland," that though it were first invented in hell, yet if it had been used and practised there as it hath been in Ireland, it had long since destroyed the very kingdom of Beelzebub. In this manner was the war of Ireland carried before the coming over of Lionel Duke of Clarence.

This young Prince, being Earl of Ulster and Lord of Connaught in right of his wife, who was daughter and heir of the Lord William Bourke, the last Earl of Ulster of that family, slain by treachery at Knockfergus, was made the King's Lieutenant of Ireland, and sent over with an army in the thirty-sixth year of King Edward the Third; the roll and list of which army doth remain of record in the King's Remembrancer's Office in England, in the press, *De Rebus tangentibus Hiberniam*, and doth not contain above fifteen hundred men by the poll; which, because it differs somewhat from the manner of this age, both in respect of the command and the entertainment, I think it not impertinent to take a brief view thereof.

The Lord Lionel was General, and under him, Ralph Earl of Stafford, James Earl of Ormond, Sir John Carew, Bart., Sir William Winsore, and other knights were commanders.

The entertainment of the General upon his first arrival was but 6s. 8d. per diem for himself; for five knights, 2s. a-piece per diem; for sixty-four esquires, 1s. a-piece per diem; for seventy archers, 6d. a-piece per diem. But being shortly after created Duke of Clarence, which honour was conferred upon him being here in Ireland, his entertainment was raised to 13s. 4d. per diem for himself, and for eight knights 2s. a-piece per diem, with an increase of the numbers of his archers, viz., 360 archers on horseback out of Lancashire at 6d. a-piece per diem, and twenty-three archers out of Wales at 2d. a-piece per diem.

The Earl of Stafford's entertainment was, for himself, 6s. 8d. per diem; for a baronet, 4s. per diem; for seventeen knights, 2s. a-piece per diem; for seventy-eight esquires, 1s. a-piece per diem; for one hundred archers on horseback, 6d. a-piece per diem. Besides, he had the command of twenty-four archers out of

Staffordshire, forty archers out of Worcestershire, and six archers out of Shropshire, at 4d. a-piece per diem.

The entertainment of James Earl of Ormond was, for himself, 4s. per diem; for two knights, 2s. a-piece per diem; for twenty-seven esquires, 1s. a-piece per diem; for twenty hobblers armed (the Irish horsemen were so called because they served on hobbies[1]), 6d. a-piece per diem; and for twenty hobblers not armed, 4d a-piece per diem.

The entertainment of Sir John Carew, Bart., was, for himself, 4s. per diem; for one knight, 2s. per diem; for eight esquires, 1s. a-piece per diem; for ten archers on horseback, 6d. a-piece per diem.

The entertainment of Sir William Winsore, was, for himself, 2s. per diem; for two knights, 2s. a-piece per diem; for forty-nine squires, 1s. a-piece per diem; for six archers on horseback, 6d. a-piece per diem.

The like entertainments, ratably, were allowed to divers knights and gentlemen upon that list, for themselves and their several retinues, whereof some were greater and some less, as they themselves could raise them among their tenants and followers.

For in ancient times the King himself did not levy his armies by his own immediate authority or commission, but the lords and captains did by indenture covenant with the King to serve him in his wars with certain numbers of men for certain wages and entertainments, which they raised in greater or less numbers as they had favour or power with the people. This course hath been changed in later times upon good reason of State; for the barons and chief gentlemen of the realm, having power to use the King's prerogative in that point, became too popular, whereby they were enabled to raise forces even against the Crown itself, which since the statutes made for levying and mustering of

---

[1] The Chronicle of Mathieu d'Escouchy speaks of "un hauby d'Ireland." Like words are found in Teutonic and classical languages. They may be allied to the Greek ἵππος.

soldiers by the King's special commission they cannot so easily perform, if they should forget their duties.

This Lord-Lieutenant, with this small army, performed no great service, and yet, upon his coming over, all men who had land in Ireland were by proclamation remanded back out of England thither, and both the clergy and laity of this land gave two years' profits of all their lands and tithes towards the maintenance of the war here; only he suppressed some rebels in Low Leinster and recovered the maritime parts of his earldom of Ulster. But his best service did consist in the well-governing of his army, and in holding that famous Parliament at Kilkenny wherein the extortion of the soldier and the degenerate manners of the English, briefly spoken of before, were discovered, and laws made to reform the same, which shall be declared more at large hereafter.

The next Lieutenant transmitted with any forces out of England was Sir William Winsore, who in the forty-seventh year of King Edward the Third undertook the custody, not the conquest, of this land, for now the English made rather a defensive than an invasive war, and withal to defray the whole charge of the kingdom for £11,213, 6s. 8d., as appeareth by the indenture between him and the King remaining of record in the Tower of London. But it appeareth by that which Froissart reporteth, that Sir William Winsore was so far from subduing the Irish as that himself reported that he could never have access to understand and know their countries, albeit he had spent more time in the service of Ireland than any Englishman then living.

And here I may well take occasion to show the vanity of that which is reported in the story of Walsingham touching the revenue of the Crown in Ireland in the time of King Edward the Third; for he, setting forth the state of things there in the time of King Richard the Second, writeth thus: "*Cum Rex Angliæ illustris, Edwardus tertius illic posuisset Bancum suum atque Judices, cum*

Scaccario, percepit inde ad Regalem Fiscum annuatim triginta millia librarum ; modò propter absentiam ligeorum, et hostium potentiam, nihil inde venit ; sed Rex per annos singulos, de suo marsupio, terræ defensoribus soluit triginta millia marcarum, ad regni sui dedecus et fisci gravissimum detrimentum."

If this writer had known that the King's Courts had been established in Ireland more than a hundred years before King Edward the Third was born, or had seen either the Parliament Rolls in England or the records of the receipts and issues in Ireland, he had not left this vain report to posterity. For both the Benches and the Exchequer were erected in the twelfth year of King John. And it is recorded in the Parliament Rolls of the twenty-first year of Edward the Third remaining in the Tower, that the Commons of England made petition that it might be inquired why the King received no benefit of his land of Ireland, considering he possessed more there than any of his ancestors had before him. Now, if the King at that time, when there were no standing forces maintained there, had received £30,000 yearly at his Exchequer in Ireland, he must needs have made profit by that land, considering that the whole charge of the kingdom in the forty-seventh year of Edward the Third, when the King did pay an army there, did amount to no more than £11,200 per annum, as appeareth by the contract of Sir William Winsore.

Besides, it is manifest by the Pipe-Rolls of that time, whereof many are yet preserved in Bremingham's Tower, and are of better credit than any monk's story, that during the reign of King Edward the Third the revenue of the Crown of Ireland, both certain and casual, did not rise unto 10,000 li. per annum, though the medium be taken of the best seven years that are to be found in that King's time. The like fable hath Holinshed touching the revenue of the earldom of Ulster, which, saith he, in the time of King Richard the Second was 30,000 marks by the year; whereas in truth, though the lordships of Connaught and Meath, which were then parcel of the inheritance of the Earl of Ulster, be added to the account, the revenue of that earldom came not to the third part of that he writeth. For the account of the profits of Ulster yet remaining in Bremingham's Tower, made by William Fitzwarren, seneschal and farmer of the lands in Ulster, seized into the King's hands after the death of Walter de Burgo, Earl of Ulster, from the fifth year of Edward the Third until the eighth year, do amount but to nine hundred and odd pounds, at what time the Irishry had not made so great an invasion upon the earldom of Ulster as they had done in the time of King Richard the Second.

As vain a thing it is that I have seen written in an ancient manuscript touching the customs of this realm in the time of King Edward the Third, that those duties in those days should yearly amount to 10,000 marks, which, by mine own search and view of the records here, I can justly control. For upon the late reducing of this ancient inheritance of the Crown, which had been detained in most of the port towns of this realm for the space of a hundred years and upwards, I took some pains, according to the duty of my place, to visit all the Pipe-Rolls wherein the accounts of customs are contained, and found those duties answered in every port for two hundred and fifty years together, but did not find that at any time they did exceed a thousand pounds per annum; and no marvel, for the subsidy of poundage was not then known and the greatest profit did arise by the cocquet of hides, for wool and wool-fells were ever of little value in this kingdom.[1]

But now, again, let us see how the martial affairs proceeded in Ireland. Sir William Winsore continued his government till the latter end of the reign of King Edward the Third, keeping, but not enlarging, the English borders.

[1] *Poundage*, a subsidy of twelvepence in the pound to the crown on all goods exported or imported. Aliens paid more. *Cocquet* or cocket was a certificate of custom-house duty paid, said to be named from the words '*quo quietus*' that made part of the form.

ON IRELAND BEFORE 1603.

In the beginning of the reign of King Richard the Second the State of England began to think of the recovery of Ireland; for then was the first statute made against absentees, commanding all such as had land in Ireland to return and reside thereupon upon pain to forfeit two-third parts of the profit thereof. Again, this King, before himself intended to pass over, committed the government of this realm to such great lords successively as he did most love and favour; first to the Earl of Oxford, his chief minion, whom he created Marquis of Dublin and Duke of Ireland; next to the Duke of Surrey, his half-brother; and, lastly, to the Lord Mortimer, Earl of March and Ulster, his cousin and heir-apparent.

Among the Patent-Rolls in the Tower the ninth year of Richard the Second we find five hundred men-at-arms at 1s. a-piece per diem, and a thousand archers at 6d. a-piece per diem, appointed for the Duke of Ireland, *Super conquestu illius terræ per duos annos*, for those are the words of that record; but for the other two Lieutenants, I do not find the certain numbers whereof their armies did consist. But certain it is that they were scarce able to defend the English borders, much less to reduce the whole island. For one of them, namely, the Earl of March, was himself slain upon the borders of Meath, for revenge of whose death the King himself made his second voyage into Ireland in the last year of his reign. For his first voyage in the eighteenth year of his reign, which was indeed a voyage royal, was made upon another motive and occasion, which was this. Upon the vacancy of the empire this King, having married the King of Bohemia's daughter, whereby he had great alliance in Germany, did, by his ambassadors, solicit the Princes-Electors to choose him Emperor; but another being elected and his ambassadors returned, he would needs know of them the cause of his repulse in that competition. They told him plainly that the Princes of Germany did not think him fit to command the empire, who was neither able to hold that which his ancestors had gained in France, nor to rule his insolent subjects in England, nor to master his rebellious people of Ireland. This was enough to kindle in the heart of a young Prince a desire to perform some great enterprise. And, therefore, finding it no fit time to attempt France, he resolved to finish the conquest of Ireland; and to that end he levied a mighty army, consisting of four thousand men-at-arms and thirty thousand archers, which was a sufficient power to have reduced the whole island if he had first broken the Irish with a war, and after established the English laws among them, and not have been satisfied with their light submissions only, wherewith in all ages they have mocked and abused the State of England. But the Irish lords, knowing this to be a sure policy to dissolve the forces which they were not able to resist—for their ancestors had put the same trick and imposture upon King John and King Henry the Second—as soon as the King was arrived with his army, which he brought over under St. Edward's banner, whose name was had in great veneration amongst the Irish, they all made offer to submit themselves. Whereupon the Lord Thomas Mowbray, Earl of Nottingham and Marshal of England, was authorised by special commission to receive the homages and oaths of fidelity of all the Irishry of Leinster. And the King himself having received humble letters from O'Neill, wherein he styleth himself Prince of the Irishry in Ulster, and yet acknowledgeth the King to be his sovereign lord, *perpetuus Dominus Hiberniæ*, removed to Drogheda, to accept the like submissions from the Irish of Ulster. The men of Leinster, namely, M'Murrough, O'Byrne, O'Moore, O'Murrough, O'Nolan, and the chief of the Kinshelaghs, in an humble and solemn manner did their homages and made their oaths of fidelity to the Earl Marshal, laying aside their girdles, their skeins, and their caps, and falling down at his feet upon their knees, which when they had performed, the Earl gave unto each of them *osculum pacis*.

Besides, they were bound by several indentures, upon great pains to be paid to the Apostolic Chamber, not only to continue loyal subjects, but that by a certain day prefixed they and all their swordmen should clearly relinquish and give up unto the King and his successors all their lands and possessions which they held in Leinster, and taking with them only their movable goods, should serve him in his wars against his other rebels; in consideration whereof the King should give them pay and pensions during their lives, and bestow the inheritance of all such lands upon them as they should recover from the rebels in any other part of the realm. And thereupon a pension of eighty marks per annum was granted to Art' MacMurrough, chief of the Cavanaghs, the enrolment whereof I found in the White-book of the Exchequer here. And this was the effect of the service performed by the Earl-Marshal by virtue of his commission. The King in like manner received the submissions of the Lords of Ulster, namely, O'Neill, O'Hanlon, M'Donnel, M'Mahon, and others, who with the like humility and ceremony did homage and fealty to the King's own person. The words of O'Neill's homage as they are recorded are not unfit to be remembered: "*Ego Nelanus Oneal Senior tam pro mcipso, quam pro filiis meis, et tota Natione mea et Parentelis meis, et pro omnibus subditis meis devenio Ligeus homo vester, etc.*" And in the indenture between him and the King, he is not only bound to remain faithful to the Crown of England, but to restore the bonaght[1] of Ulster to the Earl of Ulster, as of right belonged to that earldom, and usurped among other things by the O'Neills.

These indentures and submissions, with many other of the same kind—for there was not a chieftain or head of an Irish sept but submitted himself in one form or other—the King himself caused to be enrolled and testified by a notary public, and de-

[1] *Bonaght*, old Irish *bunad* (in the northern half of the island), family possession, place of origin.

livered the enrolments with his own hands to the Bishop of Salisbury, then Lord Treasurer of England, so as they have been preserved, and are now to be found in the office of the King's Remembrancer there.

With these humilities they satisfied the young King, and by their bowing and bending avoided the present storm, and so brake that army which was prepared to break them. For the King, having accepted their submissions, received them in *osculo pacis*, feasted them, and having given the honour of knighthood to divers of them, did break up and dissolve his army, and returned into England with much honour and small profit, saith Froissart. For though he had spent a huge mass of treasure in transporting his army, by the countenance whereof he drew on their submissions, yet did he not increase his revenue thereby one sterling pound, nor enlarged the English borders the breadth of one acre of land; neither did he extend the jurisdiction of his courts of justice one foot farther than the English colonies, wherein it was used and exercised before. Besides, he was no sooner returned into England but those Irish lords laid aside their masks of humility, and scorning the weak forces which the King had left behind him, began to infest the borders; in defence whereof the Lord Roger Mortimer, being then the King's Lieutenant and heir-apparent of the crown of England, was slain, as I said before. Whereupon the King, being moved with a just appetite of revenge, came over again in person, in the twenty-second year of his reign, with as potent an army as he had done before, with a full purpose to make a full conquest of Ireland. He landed at Waterford, and passed from thence to Dublin, through the waste countries of the Murroughs, Kinshelaghs, Cavanaghs, Byrnes, and Tooles. His great army was much distressed for want of victuals and carriages, so as he performed no memorable thing in that journey; only in the Cavanaghs' country he cut and cleared the paces, and bestowed the honour of knighthood upon the Lord Henry, the Duke of Lancaster's son, who was afterwards King Henry the Fifth, and so came to Dublin, where entering into counsel how to proceed in the war, he received news out of England of the arrival of the banished Duke of Lancaster at Ravenspurg, usurping the regal authority and arresting and putting to death his principal officers.

This advertisement suddenly brake off the King's purpose touching the prosecution of the war in Ireland, and transported him into England, where shortly after he ended both his reign and his life. Since whose time until the thirty-ninth year of Queen Elizabeth there was never any army sent over of a competent strength or power to subdue the Irish, but the war was made by the English colonies only to defend their borders; or if any forces were transmitted over, they were sent only to suppress the rebellions of such as were descended of English race, and not to enlarge our dominion over the Irish.

During the reign of King Henry the Fourth the Lord Thomas of Lancaster, the King's second son, was Lieutenant of Ireland, who for the first eight years of that King's reign made the Lord Scroope and others his deputies, who only defended the marches with forces levied within the land. In the eighth year that Prince came over in person with a small retinue; so as, wanting a sufficient power to attempt or perform any great service, he returned within seven months after into England. Yet during his personal abode there he was hurt in his own person within one mile of Dublin upon an encounter with the Irish enemy. He took the submissions of O'Byrne of the mountains, M'Mahon, and O'Reilly by several indentures, wherein O'Byrne doth covenant that the King shall quietly enjoy the manor of Newcastle; M'Mahon accepteth a state in the Ferny for life, rendering ten pounds a year; and O'Reilly doth promise to perform such duties to the Earl of March and Ulster as were contained in an indenture dated the eighteenth of Richard the Second.

In the time of King Henry the Fifth there came no forces out of England; howbeit the Lord Furnival, being the King's Lieutenant, made a martial circuit or journey round about the marches and borders of the Pale, and brought all the Irish to the King's peace, beginning with the Byrnes, Tooles, and Cavanaghs on the south, and so passing to the Moores, O'Connors, and O'Farrels in the west, and ending with the O'Reillys, MacMahons, O'Neills, and O'Hanlons in the north. He had power to make them seek the King's peace, but not power to reduce them to the obedience of subjects; yet this was then held so great and worthy a service as that the lords and chief gentlemen of the Pale made certificate thereof in French unto the King, being then in France, which I have seen recorded in the White-book of the Exchequer at Dublin. Howbeit his army was so ill-paid and governed as the English suffered more damage by the cess of his soldiers (for now that monster, coigny and livery, which the statute of Kilkenny had for a time abolished, was risen again from hell) than they gained profit or security by abating the pride of their enemies for a time.

During the minority of King Henry the Sixth, and for the space of seven or eight years after, the Lieutenants and Deputies made only a bordering war upon the Irish with small and scattered forces; howbeit, because there came no treasure out of England to pay the soldier, the poor English subject did bear the burthen of the men of war in every place, and were thereby so weakened and impoverished as the state of things in Ireland stood very desperate.

Whereupon the Cardinal of Winchester, who after the death of Humphrey Duke of Gloucester did wholly sway the State of England, being desirous to place the Duke of Somerset in the Regency of France, took occasion to remove Richard Duke of York from that government and to send him into Ireland, pretending that he was a most able and willing person to perform service there, because he had a great inheritance of his own in Ireland, namely, the earldom of Ulster and the lordships of Connaught and Meath, by descent from Lionel Duke of Clarence.

We do not find that this great Lord came over with any numbers of waged soldiers, but it appeareth upon what good terms he took that government by the covenants between the King and him which are recorded and confirmed by Act of Parliament in Ireland, and were to this effect:—

1. That he should be the King's Lieutenant of Ireland for ten years.

2. That to support the charge of that country he should receive all the King's revenues there, both certain and casual, without account.

3. That he should be supplied also with treasure out of England in this manner; he should have 4000 marks for the first year, whereof he should be impressed 2000 li. beforehand; and for the other nine years he should receive 2000 li. per annum.

4. That he might let to farm the King's lands, and place and displace all officers at his pleasure.

5. That he might levy and wage what numbers of men he thought fit.

6. That he might make a Deputy and return at his pleasure.

We cannot presume that this Prince kept any great army on foot, as well because his means out of England were so mean, and those ill-paid, as appeareth by his passionate letter written to the Earl of Salisbury, his brother-in-law, the copy whereof is registered in the story of this time; as also because the whole land except the English Pale and some part of the earldom of Ulster upon the sea-coasts were possessed by the Irish; so as the revenue of the kingdom which he was to receive did amount to little. He kept the borders and marches of the Pale with much ado; he held many parliaments, wherein sundry laws were made for erecting of castles in Louth, Meath, and Kildare to stop the incursions of the Irishry. And because the soldiers for want of pay were cessed and laid upon the subjects against their wills, upon the prayer and importunity of the Commons this extortion was declared to be high treason. But to the end that some means might be raised to nourish some forces for defence of the Pale, by another Act of Parliament every twenty pound land was charged with the furnishing and maintenance of one archer on horseback.

Besides, the native subjects of Ireland, seeing the kingdom utterly ruined, did pass in such numbers into England as one law was made in England to transmit them back again, and another law made here to stop their passage in every port and creek. Yet afterwards the greatest parts of the nobility and gentry of Meath passed over into England, and were slain with him at Wakefield in Yorkshire.

Lastly, the State of England was so far from sending an army to subdue the Irish at this time as among the articles of grievances exhibited by the Duke of York against King Henry the Sixth this was one, that divers lords about the King had caused His Highness to write letters unto some of his Irish enemies whereby they were encouraged to attempt the conquest of the said land, which letters the same Irish enemies had sent unto the Duke, marvelling greatly that such letters should be sent unto them, and speaking therein great shame of the realm of England.

After this, when this great Lord was returned into England, and making claim to the crown, began the war betwixt the two houses, it cannot be conceived but that the kingdom fell into a worse and weaker estate.

When Edward the Fourth was settled in the kingdom of England, he made his brother, George Duke of Clarence, Lieutenant of Ireland. This Prince was born in the Castle of Dublin during the government of his father, the Duke of York; yet did he never pass over into this kingdom to govern it in person, though he held the Lieutenancy many years. But it is manifest that King Edward the Fourth did not pay any army in Ireland during his reign, but the men of war did pay themselves by taking coigny and livery upon the country; which extortion grew so excessive and intolerable as the Lord Tiptoft, being Deputy to the Duke of Clarence, was enforced to execute the law upon the greatest Earl in the kingdom, namely, Desmond, who lost his head at Drogheda for this offence. Howbeit, that the State might not seem utterly to neglect the defence of the Pale, there was a fraternity of men-at-arms called the Brotherhood of St. George, erected by Parliament the fourteenth of Edward the Fourth, consisting of thirteen of the most noble and worthy persons within the four shires. Of the first foundation were Thomas, Earl of Kildare, Sir Rowland Eustace, Lord of Port Lester, and Sir Robert Eustace for the county of Kildare; Robert, Lord of Howth, the Mayor of Dublin, and Sir Robert Dowdall for the county of Dublin; the Viscount of Gormanstown, Edward Plunket, Seneschal of Meath, Alexander Plunket, and Barnaby Barnewale for the county of Meath; the Mayor of Drogheda, Sir Lawrence Taaffe, and Richard Bellewe for the county of Louth. These and their successors were to meet yearly upon St. George's Day, and to choose one of themselves to be captain of that brotherhood for the next year to come, which captain should have at his command 120 archers on horseback, forty horsemen, and forty pages to suppress outlaws and rebels. The wages of every archer should be sixpence per diem, and every horseman fivepence per diem, and four marks per annum. And to pay these entertainments and to maintain this new fraternity there was granted unto them by the same Act of Parliament a subsidy of poindage out of all merchandises exported or imported throughout the realm, hides and the goods of freemen of Dublin and Drogheda only excepted. These 200 men were all the standing forces that were then maintained in Ireland; and as they were natives of the kingdom, so the kingdom itself did pay their wages without expecting any treasure out of England.

But now the wars of Lancaster and York being ended, and Henry the Seventh being in the actual and peaceable possession of the kingdom of England, let us see if this King did send over a competent army to make a perfect conquest of Ireland. Assuredly, if those two idols or counterfeits which were set up against him in the beginning of his reign had not found footing and followers in this land, King Henry the Seventh had sent neither horse nor foot hither, but left the Pale to the guard and defence of the fraternity of St. George, which stood till the tenth year of his reign. And thereupon, upon the erection of the first idol, which was Lambert the priest's boy, he transmitted no forces, but sent over Sir Richard Edgecombe with commission to take an oath of allegiance of all the nobility, gentry, and citizens of this kingdom; which service he performed fully, and made an exact return of his commission to the King. And immediately after that the King sent for all the lords of Parliament in this realm, who, repairing to his presence, were first in a kingly manner reproved by him; for among other things he told them that if their King were still absent from them, they would at length crown apes; but at last entertained them, and dismissed them graciously. This course of clemency he held at first. But after, when Perkin Warbeck, who was set up and followed chiefly by the Geraldines in Leinster and the citizens of Cork in Munster, to suppress this counterfeit the King sent over Sir Edward Poynings with an army, as the histories call it, which did not consist of a thousand men by the poll; and yet it brought such terror with it as all the adherents of Perkin Warbeck were scattered, and retired for succour into the Irish countries. To the marches whereof he marched with his weak forces, but eftsoons returned and held a Parliament, wherein, among many good laws, one Act was made, that no subject should make any war or peace within the land without the special license of the King's Lieutenant or Deputy—a manifest argument that at that time the bordering wars in this kingdom were made altogether by voluntaries, upon their own head, without any pay or entertainment, and without any order or commission from the State. And though the lords and gentlemen of the Pale, in the nineteenth year of this King's reign, joined the famous battle of Knockroe in Connaught, wherein MacWilliam, with 4000 of the Irish and degenerate English were slain, yet was not this journey made by warrant from the King or upon his charge, as it is expressed in the Book of Howth, but only upon a private quarrel of the Earl of Kildare; so loosely were the martial affairs of Ireland carried during the reign of King Henry the Seventh.

In the time of King Henry the Eighth the Earl of Surrey, Lord Admiral, was made Lieutenant; and though he were the greatest captain of the English nation then living, yet brought he with him rather an honourable guard for his person than a competent army to recover Ireland. For he had in his retinue two hundred tall Yeomen of the King's Guard, but because he wanted means to perform any great action, he made means to return the sooner; yet in the meantime he was not idle, but passed the short time he spent here in holding a Parliament and divers journeys against the rebels of Leinster, insomuch as he was hurt in his own person upon the borders of Leix. After the revocation of this honourable personage, King Henry the Eighth sent no forces into Ireland till the rebellion of the Geraldines, which happened in the twenty-seventh year of his reign. Then sent he over Sir William Skeffington with five hundred men only to quench that fire, and not to enlarge the border or to rectify the government. This Deputy died in the midst of the service, so as the Lord Leonard Grey was sent to finish it; who, arriving with a supply of two hundred men or thereabouts, did so prosecute the rebels as the Lord Garret, their chieftain, and his five uncles submitted themselves unto him, and were by him transmitted into England.

But this service being ended, that active nobleman, with his little army and some aids of the Pale, did oftentimes repel O'Neill and O'Donnel attempting the invasion of the civil shires, and at last made that prosperous fight at Belahoo, on the confines of Meath, the memory whereof is yet famous, as that he defeated well-nigh all the power of the north, and so quieted the border for many years.

Hitherto, then, it is manifest that since the last transferation of King Richard the Second the Crown of England never sent over either numbers of men or quantities of treasure sufficient to defend the small territory of the Pale, much less to reduce that which was lost or to finish the conquest of the whole island.

After this Sir Anthony St. Leger was made chief governor, who performed great service in a civil course, as shall be expressed hereafter. But Sir Edward Bellingham, who succeeded him, proceeded in a martial course against the Irishry, and was the first Deputy, from the time of King Edward the Third till the reign of King Edward the Sixth, that extended the border beyond the limits of the English Pale, by beating and breaking the Moores and Connors and building the forts of Leix and Offaly. This service he performed with six hundred horse, the monthly charge whereof did arise to 770 li., and four hundred foot, whose pay did not amount to 446 li. per mensem, as appeareth upon the Treasurer's account remaining in the office of the King's Remembrancer in England. Yet were not these countries so fully recovered by this Deputy but that Thomas Earl of Sussex did put the last hand to this work, and rooting out these two rebellious septs, planted English colonies in their rooms, which in all the tumultuous times since have kept their habitations, their loyalty, and religion.

And now we are come to the time of Queen Elizabeth, who

sent over more men and spent more treasure to save and reduce the land of Ireland than all her progenitors since the conquest.

During her reign there arose three notorious and main rebellions which drew several armies out of England; the first of Shane O'Neill, the second of Desmond, the last of Tyrone; for the particular insurrections of the Viscount Baltinglass and Sir Edmund Butler, the Moores, the Cavanaghs, the Byrnes, and the Bourkes of Connaught were all suppressed by the standing forces here.

To subdue Shane O'Neill in the height of his rebellion, in the year 1566, Captain Randall transported a regiment of 1000 men into Ulster and planted a garrison at Lough Foyle; before the coming of which supply, viz., in the year 1565, the list of the standing army of horse and foot, English and Irish, did not exceed the number of 1200 men, as appeareth by the Treasurer's account of Ireland now remaining in the Exchequer of England. With these forces did Sir Henry Sidney, then Lord Deputy, march into the farthest parts of Tyrone, and joining with Captain Randall did much distress, but not fully defeat, O'Neill, who was afterwards slain upon a mere accident by the Scots, and not by the Queen's army.

To prosecute the wars in Munster against Desmond and his adherents there were transmitted out of England at several times three or four thousand men, which, together with the standing garrisons and some other supplies raised here, made at one time an army of six thousand and upwards, which, with the virtue and valour of Arthur Lord Grey and others the commanders, did prove a sufficient power to extinguish that rebellion. But that being done, it was never intended that these forces should stand till the rest of the kingdom were settled and reduced; only that army which was brought over by the Earl of Essex, Lord Lieutenant and Governor-General of this kingdom in the thirty-ninth year of Queen Elizabeth, to suppress the rebellion of Tyrone, which was spread universally over the whole realm—that army, I say (the command whereof, with the government of the realm, was shortly after transferred to the command of the Lord Mountjoy, afterwards Earl of Devonshire, who, with singular wisdom, valour, and industry, did prosecute and finish the war), did consist of such good men of war and of such numbers, being well-nigh 20,000 by the poll, and was so royally supplied and paid and continued in full strength so long a time as that it brake and absolutely subdued all the lords and chieftains of the Irishry and degenerate or rebellious English. Whereupon the multitude, who ever loved to be followers of such as could master and defend them, admiring the power of the Crown of England, being brayed, as it were, in a mortar with the sword, famine, and pestilence altogether, submitted themselves to the English Government, received the laws and magistrates, and most gladly embraced the King's pardon and peace in all parts of the realm with demonstration of joy and comfort, which made, indeed, an entire, perfect, and final conquest of Ireland. And though upon the finishing of the war this great army was reduced to less numbers, yet hath His Majesty, in his wisdom, thought it fit still to maintain such competent forces here as the Law may make her progress and circuit about the realm, under the protection of the sword, as Virgo, the figure of Justice, is by Leo in the zodiac, until the people have perfectly learned the lesson of obedience and the conquest be established in the hearts of all men.

Thus far have I endeavoured to make it manifest that from the first adventure and attempt of the English to subdue and conquer Ireland until the last war with Tyrone, which, as it was royally undertaken, so it was really prosecuted to the end, there hath been four main defects in the carriage of the martial affairs here. First, the armies for the most part were too weak for a conquest; secondly, when they were of a competent strength, as in both the journeys of Richard the Second, they were too soon broken up and dissolved; thirdly, they were ill-paid; and fourthly, they were ill-governed, which is always a consequent of ill-payment.

But why was not this great work performed before the latter end of Queen Elizabeth's reign, considering that many of the Kings her progenitors were as great captains as any in the world and had elsewhere larger dominions and territories? First, who can tell whether the Divine Wisdom, to abate the glory of those Kings, did not reserve this work to be done by a Queen, that it might rather appear to be His own immediate work, and yet for her greater honour made it the last of her great actions, as it were to crown all the rest? And to the end that a secure peace might settle the conquest and make it firm and perpetual to posterity, caused it to be made in that fulness of time when England and Scotland became to be united under one imperial crown, and when the monarchy of Great Britain was in league and amity with all the world. Besides, the conquest at this time doth perhaps fulfil that prophecy wherein the four great prophets of Ireland do concur, as it is recorded by Giraldus Cambrensis, to this effect, that after the first invasion of the English they should spend many ages in *crebris conflictibus, longoque certamine et multis cædibus;*[1] and that, *Omnes fere Anglici ab Hibernia turbabuntur: nihilominus orientalia maritima semper obtinebunt; sed vix paulo antè diem Judicii plenam Anglorum populo victoriam compromittunt; Insula Hibernica de mari usque ad mare de toto subacta et incastellata.*[2] If St. Patrick and the rest did not utter this prophecy, certainly Giraldus is a prophet who hath reported it. To this we may add the prophecy of Merlin, spoken of also by Giraldus, "*Sextus mœnia Hiberniæ subvertet, et regiones in Regnum*

[1] In frequent conflicts, with long strife and many slaughters.
[2] Nearly all Englishmen shall be disturbed from Ireland; nevertheless they will always hold the eastern shores, but there will scarcely be concession of full victory to the English people a little before Doomsday, Ireland from sea to sea wholly subdued and without castles.

redigentur,"[1] which is performed in the time of King James the Sixth, in that all the paces are cleared and places of fastness laid open, which are the proper walls and castles of the Irish, as they were of the British in the time of Agricola, and withal, the Irish countries being reduced into counties, make but one entire and undivided kingdom.

But to leave these high and obscure causes, the plain and manifest truth is, that the Kings of England in all ages had been powerful enough to make an absolute conquest of Ireland if their whole power had been employed in that enterprise, but still there arose sundry occasions which divided and diverted their power some other way.

Let us, therefore, take a brief view of the several impediments which arose in every King's time since the first overture of the conquest, whereby they were so employed and busied as they could not intend the final conquest of Ireland.

King Henry the Second was no sooner returned out of Ireland but all his four sons conspired with his enemies, rose in arms, and moved war against him, both in France and in England.

This unnatural treason of his sons did the King express in an emblem painted in his chamber at Winchester, wherein was an eagle with three eaglets tiring[2] on her breast, and the fourth pecking at one of her eyes. And the truth is, these ungracious practices of his sons did impeach[3] his journey to the Holy Land, which he had once vowed vexed him all the days of his life, and brought his grey hairs with sorrow to the grave. Besides, this King having given the lordship of Ireland to John, his youngest son, his ingratitude afterwards made the King careless to settle him in the quiet and absolute possession of that kingdom.

---

[1] Sextus shall overthrow the walls of Ireland, and the provinces shall be brought back into the kingdom.

[2] *Tiring*, of birds of prey, plucking and tearing flesh. First English "tyrigan" from "teran" to tear; or from French "tirer," to pull.

[3] *Impeach*, hinder.

Richard the First, which succeeded Henry the Second in the kingdom of England, had less reason to bend his power towards the conquest of this land, which was given in perpetuity to the Lord John, his brother; and therefore went he in person to the holy war, by which journey, and his captivity in Austria, and the heavy ransom that he paid for his liberty, he was hindered and utterly disabled to pursue any so great an action as the conquest of Ireland; and after his delivery and return hardly was he able to maintain a frontier war in Normandy, where by hard fortune he lost his life.

King John, his brother, had greatest reason to prosecute the war of Ireland, because the lordship thereof was the portion of his inheritance given unto him when he was called John *Sans-Terre*. Therefore he made two journeys thither; one when he was Earl of Morton, and very young, about twelve years of age; the other when he was King, in the twelfth year of his reign. In the first, his own youth, and his youthful company, Roboam's counsellors, made him hazard the loss of all that his father had won; but in the later he showed a resolution to recover the entire kingdom, in taking the submissions of all the Irishry and settling the estates of the English, and giving order for the building of many castles and forts, whereof some remain until this day. But he came to the crown of England by a defeasible title, so as he was never well settled in the hearts of the people, which drew him the sooner back out of Ireland into England, where shortly after he fell into such trouble and distress; the clergy cursing him on the one side, and the barons rebelling against him on the other; as he became so far unable to return to the conquest of Ireland, as besides the forfeituture of the territories in France he did in a manner lose both the kingdoms. For he surrendered both to the Pope, and took them back again to hold in fee-farm, which brought him into such hatred at home and such contempt abroad as all his lifetime after he was possessed rather with fear of losing his head than with hope of reducing the kingdom of Ireland.

During the infancy of Henry the Third the barons were troubled in expelling the French, whom they had drawn in against King John. But this Prince was no sooner come to his majority but the barons raised a long and cruel war against him.

Into these troubled waters the bishops of Rome did cast their nets, and drew away all the wealth of the realm by their provisions and infinite exactions, whereby the kingdom was so impoverished as the King was scarce able to feed his own household and train, much less to nourish armies for the conquest of foreign kingdoms. And albeit he had given this land to the Lord Edward, his eldest son, yet could not that worthy Prince ever find means or opportunity to visit this kingdom in person; for from the time he was able to bear arms he served continually against the barons, by whom he was taken prisoner at the battle of Lewes. And when that rebellion was appeased he made a journey to the Holy Land (an employment which in those days diverted all Christian Princes from performing any great actions in Europe), from whence he was returned when the crown of England descended upon him.

This King Edward the First, who was a Prince adorned with all virtues, did in the managing of his affairs show himself a right good husband, who, being owner of a lordship ill-husbanded, doth first enclose and manure his demesnes near his principal house before he doth improve his wastes afar off. Therefore, he began first to establish the commonwealth of England by making many excellent laws and instituting the form of public justice which remaineth to this day; next he fully subdued and reduced the dominion of Wales; then by his power and authority he settled the kingdom of Scotland; and lastly, he sent a royal army into Gascogne to recover the Duchy of Aquitaine. These four great actions did take up all the reign of this Prince. And therefore we find not in any record that this King transmitted any forces into Ireland; but, on the other side, we find it recorded both in the annals and in the Pipe-Rolls of this kingdom, that three several armies were raised of the King's subjects in Ireland, and transported one into Scotland, another into Wales, and the third into Gascogne, and that several aids were levied here for the setting forth of those armies.

The son and successor of this excellent Prince was Edward the Second, who much against his will sent one small army into Ireland, not with a purpose to finish the conquest, but to guard the person of his minion, Piers Gaveston, who, being banished out of England, was made Lieutenant of Ireland, that so his exile might seem more honourable.

He was no sooner arrived here but he made a journey into the mountains of Dublin, brake and subdued the rebels there, built Newcastle in the Byrnes' country, and repaired Castlekevin, and after passed up into Munster and Thomond, performing everywhere great service with much virtue and valour. But the King, who could not live without him, revoked him within less than a year. After which time the invasion of the Scots and rebellion of the barons did not only disable this King to be a conqueror, but deprived him both of his kingdom and life. And when the Scottish nation had overrun all this land under the conduct of Edward le Bruce, who styled himself King of Ireland, England was not then able to send either men or money to save this kingdom. Only Roger de Mortimer, then Justice of Ireland, arrived at Youghal, *cum* 38 *milit.*, saith Friar Cliun in his Annals.

But Bremingham, Verdon, Stapleton, and some other private gentlemen rose out with the commons of Meath and Vriell, and at Fagher, near Dundalk, a fatal place to the enemies of the Crown of England, overthrew a potent army of them. "*Et sic*," saith the Red-book of the Exchequer, wherein the victory was briefly recorded, "*per manus communis populi, et dextram dei, deliberatur populus dei a servitute machinata et præcogitata.*"

In the time of King Edward the Third the impediments of the conquest of Ireland are so notorious as I shall not need to express them; to wit, the wars which the King had with the realms of Scotland and of France, but especially the wars of France, which were almost continual for the space of forty years. And, indeed, France was a fairer mark to shoot at than Ireland, and could better reward the conqueror; besides, it was an inheritance newly descended upon the King, and therefore he had great reason to bend all his power and spend all his time and treasure in the recovery thereof. And this is the true cause why Edward the Third sent no army into Ireland till the thirty-sixth year of his reign, when the Lord Lionel brought over a regiment of 1500 men, as is before expressed, which that wise and warlike Prince did not transmit as a competent power to make a full conquest, but as an honourable retinue for his son, and withal to enable him to recover some part of his earldom of Ulster, which was then overrun with the Irish. But, on the other part, though the English colonies were much degenerate in this King's time and had lost a great part of their possessions, yet lying at the siege of Calais he sent for a supply of men out of Ireland, which were transported under the conduct of the Earl of Kildare and Fulco de la Freyn in the year 1347.

And now are we come again to the time of King Richard the Second, who for the first ten years of his reign was a minor, and much disquieted with popular commotions, and after that was more troubled with the factions that arose between his minions and the Princes of the blood. But at last he took a resolution to finish the conquest of this realm, and to that end he made two royal voyages hither. Upon the first he was deluded by the feigned submissions of the Irish; but upon the later, when he was fully bent to prosecute the war with effect, he was diverted and drawn from hence by the return of the Duke of Lancaster into England and the general defection of the whole realm.

As for Henry the Fourth, he being an intruder upon the Crown of England, was hindered from all foreign actions by sundry conspiracies and rebellions at home, moved by the House of Northumberland in the north, by the Dukes of Surrey and Exeter in the south, and by Owen Glendower in Wales; so as he spent his short reign in establishing and settling himself in the quiet possession of England, and had neither leisure nor opportunity to undertake the final conquest of Ireland. Much less could King Henry the Fifth perform that work, for in the second year of his reign he transported an army into France for the recovery of that kingdom, and drew over to the siege of Harfleur the Prior of Kilmainham with 1500 Irish, in which great action this victorious Prince spent the rest of his life.

And after his death the two noble Princes, his brothers, the Dukes of Bedford and Gloucester, who during the minority of King Henry the Sixth had the government of the kingdoms of England and France, did employ all their counsels and endeavours to perfect the conquest of France; the greater part whereof being gained by Henry the Fifth, and retained by the Duke of Bedford, was again lost by King Henry the Sixth—a manifest argument of his disability to finish the conquest of this land. But when the civil war between the two houses was kindled, the Kings of England were so far from reducing all the Irish under their obedience as they drew out of Ireland, to strengthen their parties, all the nobility and gentry descended of English race; which gave opportunity to the Irishry to invade the lands of the English colonies, and did hazard the loss of the whole kingdom. For, though the Duke of York did, while he lived in Ireland, carry himself respectively towards all the nobility, to win the general love of all, bearing equal favour to the Geraldines and the Butlers, as appeared at the christening of George Duke of Clarence, who was born in the Castle of Dublin, where he made both the Earl of Kildare and the Earl of Ormond his gossips; and having occasion divers times to pass into England, he left the sword with Kildare at one time, and with Ormond at another, and when he lost his life at Wakefield there were slain with him divers of both those families; yet afterwards those two noble houses of Ireland did severally follow the two royal houses of England, the Geraldines adhering to the House of York, and the Butlers to the House of Lancaster; whereby it came to pass that not only the principal gentlemen of both those surnames, but all their friends and dependents, did pass into England, leaving their lands and possessions to be overrun by the Irish. These impediments, or rather impossibilities of finishing the conquest of Ireland, did continue till the wars of Lancaster and York were ended, which was about the twelfth year of King Edward the Fourth.

Thus hitherto the Kings of England were hindered from finishing this conquest by great and apparent impediments, Henry the Second by the rebellion of his sons; King John, Henry the Third, and Edward the Second by the barons' wars; Edward the First by his wars in Wales and Scotland; Edward the Third and Henry the Fifth by the wars of France; Richard the Second, Henry the Fourth, Henry the Sixth, and Edward the Fourth by domestic contention for the crown of England itself.

But the fire of the civil war being utterly quenched, and King Edward the Fourth settled in the peaceable possession of the crown of England, what did then hinder that warlike Prince from reducing of Ireland also? First, the whole realm of England was miserably wasted, depopulated, and impoverished by the late civil dissensions; yet as soon as it had recovered itself with a little peace and rest this King raised an army and revived the title of France again; howbeit this army was no sooner transmitted and brought into the field but the two Kings also were brought to an interview. Whereupon, partly by the fair and white promises of Lewis the Second, and partly by the corruption of some of King Edward's minions, the English forces were broken and dismissed, and King Edward returned into England, where shortly after, finding himself deluded and abused by the French, he died with melancholy and vexation of spirit.

I omit to speak of Richard the Usurper, who never got the quiet possession of England, but was cast out by Henry the Seventh within two years and a half after his usurpation.

And for King Henry the Seventh himself, though he made that happy union of the two houses, yet for more than half the space of his reign there were walking spirits of the House of York as well in Ireland as in England, which he could not conjure down without expense of some blood and treasure. But in his later times he did wholly study to improve the revenues of the Crown in both kingdoms, with an intent to provide means for some great action which he intended, which doubtless, if he had lived, would rather have improved a journey into France than into Ireland, because in the eyes of all men it was a fairer enterprise.

Therefore King Henry the Eighth in the beginning of his reign made a voyage-royal into France, wherein he spent the greatest part of that treasure which his father had frugally reserved, perhaps for the like purpose. In the latter end of his reign he made the like journey, being enriched with the revenues of the Abbey lands. But in the middle time between these two attempts, the great alteration which he made in the state ecclesiastical caused him to stand upon his guard at home, the Pope having solicited all the Princes of Christendom to revenge his quarrel in that behalf. And thus was King Henry the Eighth detained and diverted from the absolute reducing of the kingdom of Ireland.

Lastly, the infancy of King Edward the Sixth and the coverture of Queen Mary, which are both non-abilities in the law, did in fact disable them to accomplish the conquest of Ireland.

So as now this great work did remain to be performed by Queen Elizabeth, who, though she were diverted by suppressing the open rebellion in the north, by preventing divers secret conspiracies against her person, by giving aids to the French and States of the Low Countries, by maintaining a naval war with Spain for many years together; yet the sundry rebellions, joined with foreign invasions upon this island, whereby it was in danger to be utterly lost and to be possessed by the enemies of the Crown of England, did quicken Her Majesty's care for the preservation thereof; and to that end, from time to time during her reign she sent over such supplies of men and treasure as did suppress the rebels and repel the invaders. Howbeit, before the transmitting of the last great army, the forces sent over by Queen Elizabeth were not of sufficient power to break and subdue all the Irishry and to reduce and reform the whole kingdom. But when the general defection came, which came not without a special providence for the final good of that kingdom—though the second causes thereof were the faint prosecution of the war against Tyrone, the practices of priests and Jesuits, and the expectation of the aids from Spain—then the extreme peril of losing the kingdom, the dishonour and danger that might thereby grow to the Crown of England, together with a just disdain conceived by that great-minded Queen that so wicked and ungrateful a rebel should prevail against her who had ever been victorious against all her enemies, did move and almost enforce her to send over that mighty army, and did withal inflame the hearts of the subjects of England cheerfully to contribute towards the maintaining thereof a million of sterling pounds at least, which was done with a purpose only to save and not to gain a kingdom; to keep and retain that sovereignty which the Crown of England had in Ireland, such as it was, and not to recover a more absolute dominion. But, as it falleth out many times that when a house is on fire the owner, to save it from burning, pulleth it down to the ground, but that pulling down doth give occasion of building it up again in a better form, so these last wars, which to save the kingdom did utterly break and destroy this people, produced a better effect than was at first expected. For every rebellion, when it is suppressed, doth make the subject weaker and the Prince stronger; so this general revolt, when it was overcome, did produce a general obedience and reformation of all the Irishry, which ever before had been disobedient and unreformed; and thereupon ensued the final and full conquest of Ireland.

And thus much may suffice to be spoken touching the defects in the martial affairs and the weak and faint prosecution of the war, and of the several impediments or employments which did hinder or divert every King of England successively from reducing Ireland to their absolute subjection.

It now remaineth that we show the defects of the civil policy and government which gave no less impediment to the perfection of this conquest.

The first of that kind doth consist in this, that the Crown of England did not from the beginning give Laws to the Irishry, whereas to give laws to a conquered people is the principal mark and effect of a perfect conquest. For albeit King Henry the Second, before his return out of Ireland, held a Council or Parliament at Lismore, "*Ubi leges Angliæ ab omnibus sunt gratanter receptæ, et juratoria cautione præstita confirmatæ,*"[1] as Matthew Paris writeth.

[1] Where the laws of England were thankfully accepted by all, sworn to, and established.

And though King John, in the twelfth year of his reign, did establish the English laws and customs here, and placed sheriffs and other ministers to rule and govern the people according to the law of England, and to that end, "*Ipse duxit secum viros discretos et legis peritos, quorum communi consilio statuit et præcepit leges Anglicanas teneri in Hibernia*," &c.,[1] as we find it recorded among the Patent-Rolls in the Tower, 11 Henry 3, m. 3; though, likewise, King Henry the Third did grant and transmit the like charter of liberties to his subjects of Ireland as himself and his father had granted to the subjects of England, as appeareth by another record in the Tower, 1 Hen. 3, Pat. m. 13; and afterwards, by a special Writ, did command the Lord-Justice of Ireland, "*Quod convocatis Archiepiscopis, Comitibus, Baronibus, etc. Coram eis legi faceret Chartam Regis Johannis; quam ipse legi fecit et jurari à Magnatibus Hiberniæ, de legibus et Constitutionibus Angliæ observandis, et quod leges illas teneant et observent*,[2] 12 Hen. 3, claus. m. 8. And after that again the same King, by Letters Patent under the Great Seal of England, did confirm the establishment of the English laws made by King John, in this form: "*Quia pro communi utilitate terræ Hiberniæ, ac unitate terrarum, de Communi Consilio provisum sit, quod omnes leges et consuetudines quæ in regno Angliæ tenentur, in Hiberniâ teneantur, eadem terra ejusdem legibus subjaceat, ac per easdem regatur, sicut Johannes Rex, cum illuc esset, statuit et firmiter mandavit; ideo volumus quod omnia brevia de Communi Jure, quæ currunt in Anglia, similiter currant in Hibernia, sub novo sigillo nostro, etc. Teste meipso apud Woodstock*," &c. ;[3] which confirmation is found

[1] He himself took with him discreet men learned in the law, by whose common counsel he appointed and ordained the English laws to be maintained in Ireland.

[2] That, having called together the archbishops, earls, barons, &c., he should cause the charter of King John to be read before them which he himself caused to be read before and sworn to by the Irish lords touching observance of the laws and constitutions of England, and that they should keep and obey these laws.

[3] Because for the common good of Ireland, and union of the lands, the Common Council has provided that all laws and customs which are observed in England

among the Patent-Rolls in the Tower, Anno 30, Hen. 3. Notwithstanding, it is evident by all the records of this kingdom that only the English colonies and some few septs of the Irishry which were enfranchised by special charters were admitted to the benefit and protection of the laws of England, and that the Irish generally were held and reputed aliens, or rather enemies to the Crown of England, insomuch as they were not only disabled to bring any actions, but they were so far out of the protection of the law as it was often adjudged no felony to kill a mere Irishman in the time of peace.

That the mere Irish were reputed aliens appeareth by sundry records wherein judgment is demanded, if they shall be answered in actions brought by them, and likewise by the Charters of Denization which in all ages were purchased by them.

In the Common Plea Rolls of the twenty-eighth of Edward the Third, which are yet preserved in Bremingham's Tower, this case is adjudged. Simon Neill brought an action of trespass against William Newlagh for breaking his close in Claudalkin, in the county of Dublin ; the defendant doth plead that the plaintiff is "*Hibernicus et non de quinque sanguinibus,*"[1] and demandeth judgment, if he shall be answered. The plaintiff replieth : "*Quod ipse est de quinque sanguinibus, viz., De les O'Neils de Ultonia, qui per concessionem progenitorum Domini Regis, Libertatibus Anglicis gaudere debent et utuntur, et pro liberis hominibus reputantur.*"[2] The defendant rejoineth that the plaintiff is not of the O'Neills of Ulster, "*Nec de quinque sanguinibus ;*" and therefore they are at

---

should be observed in Ireland, the said land be subject to the same laws and be ruled by them, as King John, when he was there, firmly ordained and commanded ; therefore it is our will that all briefs at common law current in England should likewise be current in Ireland, under the new seal. Witness my hand at Woodstock, &c.

[1] An Irishman, and not of the five kindreds.
[2] That he is of the five kindreds, namely, of the O'Neills of Ulton, who by concession of the ancestors of our lord the King, have enjoyment and use of English liberties, and are reputed to be free men.

issue. Which being found for the plaintiff, he had judgment to recover his damages against the defendant. By this record it appeareth that five principal bloods or septs of the Irishry were by special grace enfranchised and enabled to take benefit of the laws of England, and that the nation of O'Neills in Ulster was one of the five. And in the like case the third of Edward the Second, amongst the Plea Rolls in Bremingham's Tower, all the five septs or bloods, "*Qui gaudeant lege Anglicana quoad brevia portanda,*" are expressed, namely, *O'Neil de Ultonia, O'Molaghlin de Midia, O'Connoghor de Connacia, O'Brien de Thotmonia, et MacMurrogh de Lagenia.* And yet I find that O'Neill himself long after, viz., in the twentieth of Edward the Fourth, upon his marriage with a daughter of the House of Kildare, to satisfy the friends of the lady, was made denizen by a special Act of Parliament, 20 Ed. 4, c. 8.

Again, in the twenty-ninth of Edward the First, before the Justices in Eyre, at Drogheda, Thomas de Botteler brought an action of Detinue against Robert de Almain for certain goods. The defendant pleadeth: "*Quod non tenetur ei inde respondere eo, quod est Hibernicus, et non de libero sanguine. Et prædictus Thomas dicit, quod Anglicus est, et hoc petit quod inquiratur per patriam, ideo fiat inde jurat, etc. Jurat' dicunt super sacrament' suum, quod prædict' Thomas Anglicus est, ideo consideratum est quod recuperet,*" &c.[1]

These two records, among many other, do sufficiently show that the Irish were disabled to bring any actions at the Common Law. Touching their denizations, they were common in every king's reign since Henry the Second, and were never out of use till His Majesty that now is came to the crown.

Among the pleas of the Crown, fourth of Edward the Second, we

---

[1] That he is not bound to answer him in the matter, because he is an Irishman and not of free kin. And the before-named Thomas says that he is an Englishman, &c.

find a confirmation made by Edward the First of a Charter of Denization granted by Henry the Second to certain Oostmen, or Easterlings, who were inhabitants of Waterford long before Henry the Second attempted the conquest of Ireland : *"Edwardus Dei gratia, etc., Justitiario suo Hiberniæ, Salutem: Quia per inspectionem Chartæ Dom. Hen. Reg. filii Imperatricis quondam Dom. Hiberniæ proavi nostri nobis constat, quod Ostmanni de Waterford legem Anglicorum in Hibernia habere, et secundum ipsam legem Judicari et deduci debent: vobis mandamus quod Gillicrist MacGilmurrii Willielmum et Johannem MacGilmurrii et alios Ostmannos de civitate et comitatu Waterford, qui de predictis Ostmannis prædict. Dom. Henr. proavi nostri originem duxerunt, legem Anglicorum in partibus illis juxta tenorem Chartæ prædict. habere, et eos secundum ipsam legem, quantum in nobis est, deduci faciatis, donec aliud de consilio nostro inde duxerimus ordinand. In cuius rei, etc. Teste meipso apud Acton Burnell, 5 Octobris anno regni nostri undecimo."*

Again, among the Patent-Rolls of the first of Edward the Fourth remaining in the Chancery here, we find a Patent of Denization granted the thirteenth of Edward the First, in these words : *"Edwardus Dei gratia, Rex Angliæ, Dom. Hiberniæ, Dux Aquitaniæ, etc. Omnibus Ballivis et fidelibus suis in Hibernia, Salutem : Volentes Christophero filio Donaldi Hibernico gratiam facere specialem, concedimus pro nobis et hæredibus nostris, quod idem Christopherus hanc habeat libertatem, viz., Quod ipse de cætero in Hibernia utatur legibus Anglicanis, et prohibemus ne quisquam contra hanc concessionem nostram dictum Christopherum vexet in aliquo vel perturbet. In cuius rei testimonium, etc. Teste meipso apud West., 27 die Junii anno regni nostri* 13."

In the same roll we find another Charter of Denization granted in the first of Edward the Fourth, in a more large and beneficial form : *"Edw. Dei gratia, etc. Omnibus Ballivis, etc., Salutem. Sciatis quod nos volentes Willielmum O Bolgir capellanum de Hibernica natione existentem, favore prosequi gratioso, de gratia nostra speciali, etc. Concessimus eidem Willielmo quod ipse liberi sit status, et liberæ conditionis, et ab omni servitute Hibernicâ liber et quietus, et quod ipse legibus Anglicanis in omnibus et per omnia uti possit et gaudere, eodem modo quo homines Anglici infra dictam terram eas habent et iis gaudent et utuntur, quodque ipse respondeat, et respondeatur, in quibuscumque curiis nostris; ac omnimod. terras, tenementa, redditus, et servitia perquirere possit sibi et hæredibus suis in perpetuum, etc."*

If I should collect out of the records all the charters of this kind, I should make a volume thereof; but these may suffice to show that the mere Irish were not reputed free subjects nor admitted to the benefit of the Laws of England until they had purchased Charters of Denization.

Lastly, the mere Irish were not only accounted aliens but enemies, and altogether out of the protection of the law, so as it was no capital offence to kill them; and this is manifest by many records. At a gaol delivery at Waterford, before John Wogan, Lord-Justice of Ireland, the fourth of Edward the Second, we find it recorded among the pleas of the Crown of that year: *" Quod Robertus le Wayleys rectatus de morte Johannis filii Ivor Mac-Gillemory felonice per ipsum interfecti, etc. Venit et bene cognovit quod prædictum Johannem interfecit: dicit tamen quod per eius interfectionem feloniam committere non potuit, quia dicit, quod prædictus Johannes fuit purus Hibernicus, et non de libero sanguine, etc. Et cum Dominus dicti Johannis (cuius Hibernicus idem Johannes fuit) die quo interfectus fuit, solutionem pro ipso Johanne Hibernico suo sic interfecto petere voluerit, ipse Robertus paratus erit ad respondend' de solutione prædict. prout justitia suadebit. Et super hoc venit quidam Johannes le Poer, et dicit pro Domino Rege, quod prædict. Johannes filius Ivor MacGillemory, et antecessores sui de cognonime prædict. à tempore quo Dominus Henricus filius Imperatricis, quondam Dominus Hiberniæ, Tritavus Domini Regis nunc, fuit in Hibernia, legem Anglicorum in Hibernia usque ad hunc diem habere, et secundum ipsam legem judicari et deduci debent."* And so pleaded the Charter of Denization granted to the Oostmen recited before; all which appeareth at large in the said record, wherein we may note that the killing of an Irishman was not punished by our law as manslaughter, which is felony and capital, for our law did neither protect his life nor revenge his death, but by a fine or pecuniary punishment which is called an ericke according to the Brehon or Irish law.

Again, at the gaol-delivery before the same Lord-Justice at Limerick, in the roll of the same year, we find that " *Willielmus filius Rogeri rectatus de morte Rogeri de Cantcton felonice per ipsum interfecti, venit et dicit, quod feloniam per interfectionem prædictam committere non potuit, quia dicit quod prædict. Rogerus Hibernic. est, et non de libero sanguine; dicit etiam quod prædict. Rogerus fuit de cognomine de Ohederiscal et non de cognomine de Cantetons, et de hoc ponit se super patriam, etc. Et jurati dicunt super sacram. suum quod prædictus Rogerus Hibernicus fuit et de cognomine de Ohederiscal et pro Hibernico habebatur tota vita sua. Ideo prædict. Willielmus quoad feloniam prædict. dict. quietus. Sed quia prædictus Rogerus Ohederiscal fuit Hibernicus Domini Regis, prædict. Willielmus recommittatur gaolæ quousque plegios invenerit de quinque marcis solvendis Domino Regi pro solutione prædicti Hibernici."*

But, on the other side, if the jury had found that the party slain had been of English race and nation, it had been adjudged felony, as appeareth by a record of the twenty-ninth of Edward the First, in the Crown Office here: " *Coram Waltero Lenfant et sociis suis justitiariis itincrantibus apud Drogheda in Comitatu Louth. Johannes Laurens indictat. de morte Galfridi Dovedal venit et non dedicit mortem prædictam: sed dicit quod prædict. Galfridus fuit Hibernicus, et non de libero sanguine, et de bono et malo ponit se super patriam, etc. Et jurat. dicunt super sacram. suum quod prædict. Galfridus Anglicus fuit, et ideo prædict.*

Johannes culpabilis est de morte Galfridi prædict. Ideo suspend. Catalla 138 *unde Hugo de Clinton, Vicecom. respondet.*

Hence it is that in all the Parliament Rolls which are extant from the fortieth year of Edward the Third, when the Statutes of Kilkenny were enacted, till the reign of King Henry the Eighth, we find the degenerate and disobedient English called rebels; but the Irish, which were not in the King's peace, are called enemies (Statute Kilkenny, c. i. 10 and 11; 11 Hen. 4, c. 24; 10 Hen. 6, c. 1, 18; 18 Hen. 6, c. 4, 5; Edw. 4, c. 6; 10 Hen. 7, c. 17). All these Statutes speak of English rebels and Irish enemies, as if the Irish had never been in condition of subjects, but always out of the protection of the law, and were, indeed, in worse case than aliens of any foreign realm that was in amity with the Crown of England. For by divers heavy penal laws the English were forbidden to marry, to foster, to make gossips with the Irish, or to have any trade or commerce in their markets or fairs; nay, there was a law made no longer since than the twenty-eighth year of Henry the Eighth, that the English should not marry with any person of Irish blood, though he had gotten a Charter of Denization, unless he had done both homage and fealty to the King in the Chancery, and were also bound by recognisance with sureties to continue a loyal subject. Whereby it is manifest that such as had the government of Ireland under the Crown of England did intend to make a perpetual separation and enmity between the English and the Irish, pretending no doubt that the English should in the end root out the Irish; which the English, not being able to do, did cause a perpetual war between the nations, which continued four hundred and odd years, and would have lasted to the world's end if in the end of Queen Elizabeth's reign the Irishry had not been broken and conquered by the sword, and since the beginning of His Majesty's reign had not been protected and governed by the law.

But perhaps the Irishry in former times did wilfully refuse to be subject to the laws of England, and would not be partakers of the benefit thereof though the Crown of England did desire it, and therefore they were reputed aliens, outlaws, and enemies. Assuredly the contrary doth appear, as well by the Charters of Denization purchased by the Irish in all ages, as by a petition preferred by them to the King, anno 2 Edward the Third, desiring that an Act might pass in Ireland whereby all the Irishry might be enabled to use and enjoy the laws of England without purchasing of particular denizations. Upon which petition the King directed a special Writ to the Lord-Justice, which is found amongst the Close-Rolls in the Tower of London in this form :[1] *" Rex dilecto et fideli suo Johannis Darci le Nepieu Justic. suo Hiberniæ, Salutem. Ex parte quorundam hominum de Hibernia nobis extitit supplicatum, ut per Statutum inde faciendum concedere velimus quod omnes Hibernici qui voluerint legibus utātur Anglicanis, ita quod necesse non habeant super hoc chartas alienas à nobis impetrare : nos igitur certiorari volentes si sine alieno præjudicio præmissis annuere valeamus, vobis mandamus quod voluntatem magnatum terr. illius in proximo Parliamento nostro ibidem tenendo super hoc cum diligentia perscrutari facias : et de eo quod inde inveneritis una cum consilio et advisamento nobis certificetis,"* &c. Whereby I collect that the great lords of Ireland had informed the King that the Irishry might not be naturalised without damage and prejudice either to themselves or to the Crown.

But I am well assured that the Irishry did desire to be admitted to the benefit of the law, not only in this petition exhibited to King Edward the Third, but by all their submissions made to King Richard the Second and to the Lord Thomas of Lancaster before the wars of the two houses, and afterwards to the Lord Leonard Grey and Sir Anthony Saint Leger, when King Henry the Eighth began to reform this kingdom. In particular, the Byrnes of the mountains, in the thirty-

[1] Desiring the opinion to be taken of the Lords in Parliament.

fourth of Henry the Eighth, desire that their country might be made shire-ground and called the county of Wicklow; and in the twenty-third of Henry the Eighth, O'Donnell doth covenant with Sir William Skeffington, " *Quod si Dominus Rex velit reformare Hiberniam,*" whereof it should seem he made some doubt that he and his people would gladly be governed by the laws of England. Only that ungrateful traitor Tyrone, though he had no colour or shadow of title to that great lordship but only by grant from the Crown and by the law of England, for by the Irish law he had been ranked with the meanest of his sept, yet in one of his capitulations with the State he required that no sheriff might have jurisdiction within Tyrone, and consequently that the laws of England might not be executed there; which request was never before made by O'Neill or any other lord of the Irishry when they submitted themselves, but, contrariwise, they were humble suitors to have the benefit and protection of the English laws.

This, then, I note as a great defect in the civil policy of this kingdom, in that, for the space of 350 years at least after the conquest first attempted, the English laws were not communicated to the Irish, nor the benefit and protection thereof allowed unto them, though they earnestly desired and sought the same. For, as long as they were out of the protection of the law, so as every Englishman might oppress, spoil, and kill them without controlment, how was it possible they should be other than outlaws and enemies to the Crown of England? If the King would not admit them to the condition of subjects, how could they learn to acknowledge and obey him as their Sovereign? When they might not converse or commerce with any civil men, nor enter into any town or city without peril of their lives, whither should they fly but into the woods and mountains, and there live in a wild and barbarous manner? If the English magistrates would not rule them by the law which doth punish treason and murder and theft with death, but leave them to be ruled by their own lords and laws, why should they not embrace their own Brehon law, which punisheth no offence but with a fine or erick? If the Irish be not permitted to purchase estates of freeholds or inheritance, which might descend to their children, according to the course of our Common Law, must they not continue their custom of tanistry, which makes all their possessions uncertain, and brings confusion, barbarism, and incivility? In a word, if the English would neither in peace govern them by the law, nor could in war root them out by the sword, must they not needs be pricks in their eyes and thorns in their sides till the world's end, and so the conquest never be brought to perfection?

But, on the other side, if from the beginning the laws of England had been established, and the Brehon or Irish law utterly abolished, as well in the Irish countries as the English colonies; if there had been no difference made between the nations in point of justice and protection, but all had been governed by one equal, just, and honourable law, as Dido speaketh in Virgil, " *Tros, Tyriusve, mihi nullo discrimine habetur ;*" if upon the first submission made by the Irish lords to King Henry the Second, " *Quem in regem et dominum receperunt,*"[1] saith Matthew Paris; or upon the second commission made to King John, when, "*Plusquam viginti reguli maximo timore perterriti homagium ei et fidelitatem fecerunt,*"[2] as the same author writeth; or upon the third general submission made to King Richard the Second, when they did not only do homage and fealty, but bound themselves by indentures and oaths, as is before expressed, to become and continue loyal subjects to the Crown of England: if any of these three Kings, who came each of them twice in

---

[1] Whom they received for king and lord.
[2] More than twenty chiefs, overcome with the greatest fear, did homage and fealty to him.

person into this kingdom, had, upon these submissions of the Irishry, received them all, both lords and tenants, into their immediate protection, divided their several countries into counties; made sheriffs, coroners, and wardens of the peace therein; sent justices-itinerants half-yearly into every part of the kingdom, as well to punish malefactors as to hear and determine causes between party and party, according to the course of the laws of England; taken surrenders of their lands and territories, and granted estates unto them to hold by English tenures; granted them markets, fairs, and other franchises, and erected corporate towns among them—all which hath been performed since His Majesty came to the crown—assuredly the Irish countries had long since been reformed and reduced to peace, plenty, and civility, which are the effects of laws and good government. They had built houses, planted orchards and gardens, erected townships, and made provision for their posterities; there had been a perfect union betwixt the nations, and consequently a conquest of Ireland. For the conquest is never perfect till the war be at an end, and the war is not at an end till there be peace and unity; and there can never be unity and concord in any one kingdom but where there is but one King, one allegiance, and one law.

True it is that King John made twelve shires in Leinster and Munster, namely, Dublin, Kildare, Meath, Uriel, Catherlough, Kilkenny, Wexford, Waterford, Cork, Limerick, Kerry, and Tipperary; yet these counties did stretch no farther than the lands of the English colonies did extend. In them only were the English laws published and put in execution, and in them only did the itinerant judges make their circuits and visitations of justice, and not in the countries possessed by the Irishry, which contained two-third parts of the kingdom at least. And therefore King Edward the First, before the Court of Parliament was established in Ireland, did transmit the Statutes of England in this form:

"*Dominus Rex mandavit Breve suum in hæc verba: Edwardus Dei gratia, Rex Angliæ, Dominus Hiberniæ, etc. Cancellario suo Hiberniæ, Salutem. Quædam statuta per nos de assensu Prælatorum, Comitum, Baronum et Communitat. regni nostri nuper apud Lincolne et quædam alia statuta postmodum apud Eborum facta, quæ in dicta terra nostra Hiberniæ ad communem utilitatem populi nostri ejusdem terræ observari volumus, vobis mittimus sub sigillo nostro, mandantes quod statuta illa in dicta cancellaria nostra custodiri, ac in rotulis ejusdem cancellariæ irrotulari, et ad singulas placeas nostras in terra nostra Hiberniæ, et singulos comitatus ejusdem terræ mitti faciatis ministris nostris placearum illarum, et Vicecomitibus dictorum Comitatuum: mandantes, quod statuta illa coram ipsis publicari et ea in omnibus et singulis articulis suis observari firmiter faciatis. Teste meipso apud Nottingham*," &c. By which Writ, and by all the Pipe-Rolls of that time, it is manifest that the laws of England were published and put in execution only in the counties which were then made and limited, and not in the Irish countries, which were neglected and left wild, and have but of late years been divided in one-and-twenty counties more.

Again, true it is that by the Statute of Kilkenny, enacted in this kingdom in the fortieth year of King Edward the Third, the Brehon law was condemned and abolished, and the use and practice thereof made high treason. But this law extended to the English only, and not to the Irish; for the law is penned in this form: "Item, Forasmuch as the diversity of government by divers laws in one land doth make diversity of liegeance and debates between the people, it is accorded and established that hereafter no Englishman have debate with another Englishman but according to the course of the Common Law; and that no Englishman be ruled in the definition of their debates by the March Law or the Brehon Law, which by reason ought not to be named a law, but an evil custom, but that they be ruled as right is, by the

Common Law of the land, as the lieges of our Sovereign Lord the King; and if any do to the contrary, and thereof be attainted, that he be taken and imprisoned and lodged as a traitor, and that hereafter there be no diversity of liegeance between the English born in England, but that all be called and reputed English, and the lieges of our Sovereign Lord the King," &c. This law was made only to reform the degenerate English, but there was no care taken for the reformation of the mere Irish; no ordinance, no provision made for the abolishing of their barbarous customs and manners. Insomuch as the law then made for apparel and riding in saddles after the English fashion is penal only to Englishmen, and not to the Irish. But the Roman State, which conquered so many nations both barbarous and civil, and therefore knew by experience the best and readiest way of making a perfect and absolute conquest, refused not to communicate their laws to the rude and barbarous people whom they had conquered; neither did they put them out of their protection after they had once submitted themselves. But, contrariwise, it is said of Julius Cæsar, " *Qua vicit, victos protegit ille, manu*;"[1] and again, of another Emperor—

> "*Fecisti patriam diversis gentibus unam,*
> *Profuit invitis te dominante capi;*
> *Dumque offers victis proprii consortia juris,*
> *Urbem fecisti, quod prius orbis erat.*"[2]

And of Rome itself—

> "*Hæc est, in gremium victos quæ sola recepit,*
> *Humanumque genus communi nomine fovit,*

---

[1] His conquering hand protected the subdued.
[2] For differing tribes you made one fatherland,
Unwilling captives throve when ruled by you,
You gave the vanquished fellowship of laws,
And made one city where there was a world.

*Matris, non dominæ, ritu; civesque vocavit,
Quos domuit, neauque pio longinqua revinait.*[1]

Therefore, as Tacitus writeth, Julius Agricola, the Roman general in Brittany, used this policy to make a perfect conquest of our ancestors, the ancient Britons. They were, saith he, rude and dispersed, and therefore prone upon every occasion to make war, but to induce them by pleasure to quietness and rest, he exhorted them in private, and gave them helps in common, to build temples, houses, and places of public resort. The noblemen's sons he took and instructed in the liberal sciences, &c., preferring the wits of the Britons before the students of France, as being now curious to attain the eloquence of the Roman language, whereas they lately rejected that speech. After that the Roman attire grew to be in account and the gown to be in use among them; and so by little and little they proceeded to curiosity and delicacies in buildings and furniture of household, in baths and exquisite banquets; and so being come to the height of civility, they were thereby brought to an absolute subjection.

Likewise our Norman Conqueror, though he oppressed the English nobility very sore, and gave away to his servitors the lands and possessions of such as did oppose his first invasion, though he caused all his Acts of Counsel to be published in French, and some legal proceedings and pleadings to be framed and used in the same tongue, as a mark and badge of a conquest; yet he governed all, both English and Normans, by one and the same law, which was the ancient Common Law of England long before the Conquest. Neither did he deny any Englishman that submitted himself unto him the benefit of that law, though it

---

[1] She, only, took the vanquished to her breast,
Made her name common to the race of man;
As mother, not as queen, made citizens
Of men re-bound in love's enduring chain.

were against a Norman of the best rank and in greatest favour, as appeared in the notable controversy between Warren, the Norman, and Sherborne of Sherborne Castle in Norfolk. For the Conqueror had given that castle to Warren; yet when the inheritors thereof had alleged before the King that he never bore arms against him, that he was his subject as well as the other, and that he did inherit and hold his lands by the rules of that law which the King had established among all his subjects, the King gave judgment against Warren, and commanded that Sherborne should hold his lands in peace. By this means himself obtained a peaceable possession of the kingdom within few years; whereas, if he had cast all the English out of his protection and held them as aliens and enemies to the Crown, the Normans perhaps might have spent as much time in the conquest of ₊England as the English have spent in the conquest of Ireland.

The like prudent course hath been observed in reducing of Wales, which was performed partly by King Edward the First, and altogether finished by King Henry the Eighth. For we find by the Statute of Rutland made the twelfth of Edward the First, when the Welshmen had submitted themselves, *de alto et basso*, to that King, he did not reject and cast them off as outlaws and enemies, but caused their laws and customs to be examined, which were in many points agreeable to the Irish or Brehon law. " *Quibus diligenter auditis et plenius intellectis, quasdam illarum*," saith the King in that ordinance, "*consilio procerum delevimus, quasdam permissimus, quasdam correximus, ac etiam quasdam alias adjiciendas et faciend. decrevimus;*"[1] and so established a commonwealth among them, according to the form of the English government. After this, by reason of the sundry insurrections of the barons, the wars in France, and the dissension between the two

---

[1] These having been heard attentively, and fully understood, some of them by the counsel of our lords we abolished, some we allowed, some we revised, and some others also we ordered to be made and added.

Houses of York and Lancaster, the State of England neglected or omitted the execution of this Statute of Rutland, so as a great part of Wales grew wild and barbarous again. And therefore King Henry the Eighth, by the Statutes of the twenty-seventh and thirty-second of his reign, did revive and recontinue that noble work begun by King Edward the First, and brought it indeed to full perfection. For he united the dominion of Wales to the Crown of England and divided it into shires, and erected in every shire one borough, as in England, and enabled them to send knights and burgesses to the Parliament, established a Court of Presidency, and ordained that justices of assize and gaol-delivery should make their half-yearly circuits there as in England; made all the laws and statutes of England in force there, and, among other Welsh customs, abolished that of gavelkind, whereby the heirs-females were utterly excluded and the bastards did inherit as well as the legitimate, which is the very Irish gavelkind. By means whereof that entire country in a short time was securely settled in peace and obedience, and hath attained to that civility of manners and plenty of all things as now we find it not inferior to the best parts of England.

I will, therefore, knit up this point with these conclusions: First, that the Kings of England, which in former ages attempted the conquest of Ireland, being ill advised and counselled by the great men here, did not, upon the submissions of the Irish, communicate their laws unto them, nor admit them to the state and condition of free subjects. Secondly, that for the space of two hundred years at least after the arrival of Henry the Second in Ireland the Irish would gladly have embraced the laws of England, and did earnestly desire the benefit and protection thereof, which being denied them, did of necessity cause a continual bordering war between the English and the Irish. And lastly, if, according to the examples before recited, they had reduced as well the Irish countries as the English colonies under one form of civil government, as now they are, the meres and bounds of the marches and borders had been long since worn out and forgotten—for it is not fit, as Cambrensis writeth, that a King of an island should have any marches or borders but the four seas— both nations had been incorporated and united, Ireland had been entirely conquered, planted, and improved, and returned a rich revenue to the Crown of England.

The next error in the civil policy which hindered the perfection of the conquest of Ireland did consist in the distribution of the lands and possessions which were won and conquered from the Irish. For the scopes of land which were granted to the first adventurers were too large, and the liberties and royalties which they obtained therein were too great for subjects, though it stood with reason that they should be rewarded liberally out of the fruits of their own labours, since they did *militare propriis stipendiis*,[1] and received no pay from the Crown of England. Notwithstanding there ensued divers inconveniences, that gave great impediment to the conquest.

First, the Earl Strongbow was entitled to the whole kingdom of Leinster, partly by invasion and partly by marriage. Albeit he surrendered the same entirely to King Henry the Second, his Sovereign, for that with his license he came over, and with the aid of his subjects he had gained that great inheritance; yet did the King regrant back again to him and his heirs all that province, reserving only the city of Dublin and the cantreds next adjoining, with the maritime towns and principal forts and castles. Next, the same King granted to Robert Fitzstephen and Miles Cogan the whole kingdom of Cork, from Lismore to the sea. To Philip le Bruce he gave the whole kingdom of Limerick, with the donation and bishoprics and abbeys, except the city and one

[1] Serve in war at their own cost.

cantred of land adjoining; to Sir Hugh de Lacy all Meath; to Sir John de Courcy all Ulster; to William Burke Fitzadelm the greatest part of Connaught. In like manner, Sir Thomas de Clare obtained a grant of all Thomond; Otto de Grandison of all Tipperary; and Robert le Poer of the territory of Waterford, the city itself and the cantred of the Oostmen only excepted. And thus was all Ireland cantonised among ten persons of the English nation. And though they had not gained the possession of one-third part of the whole kingdom, yet in title they were owners and lords of all, so as nothing was left to be granted to the natives. And therefore we do not find in any record or story for the space of three hundred years after these adventurers first arrived in Ireland that any Irish lord obtained a grant of his country from the Crown, but only the King of Thomond, who had a grant but during King Henry the Third his minority; and Roderick O'Connor, King of Connaught, to whom King Henry the Second, before this distribution made, did grant, as is before declared, "*Ut sit Rex sub eo;*"[1] and, moreover, "*Ut teneat terram suam Conactiæ ita bene et in pace, sicut tenuit antequam Dominus Rex intravit Hiberniam.*"[2] And whose successor, in the twenty-fourth of Henry the Third, when the Bourkes had made a strong plantation there, and had well-nigh expelled him out of his territory, he came over into England, as Matthew Paris writeth, and made complaint to King Henry the Third of this invasion made by the Bourkes upon his land, insisting upon the grants of King Henry the Second and King John, and affirming that he had duly paid a yearly tribute of five thousand marks for his kingdom. Whereupon the King called unto him the Lord Maurice Fitzgerald, who was then Lord-Justice of Ireland and President in the Court, and commanded him that he should root out that unjust plantation

---

[1] That he should be king under him.
[2] That he should hold his land of Connaught as well and peacefully as he held it before the Lord King entered Ireland.

which Hubert Earl of Kent had in the time of his greatness planted in those parts, and wrote withal to the great men of Ireland to remove the Bourkes, and to establish the King of Connaught in the quiet possession of his kingdom. Howbeit, I do not read that the King of England's commandment or direction in this behalf was ever put in execution. For the truth is, Richard de Bargo had obtained a grant of all Connaught after the death of the King of Connaught then living, for which he gave a thousand pounds, as the record in the Tower reciteth, the third of Henry 3, claus. 2. And, besides, our great English lords could not endure that any Kings should reign in Ireland but themselves; nay, they could hardly endure that the Crown of England itself should have any jurisdiction or power over them. For many of these lords to whom our Kings had granted these petty kingdoms did, by virtue and colour of these grants, claim and exercise *jura regalia* within their territories, insomuch as there were no less than eight Counties Palatines in Ireland at one time.

For William Marshal, Earl of Pembroke, who married the daughter and heir of Strongbow, being Lord of all Leinster, had royal jurisdiction throughout all that province. This great Lord had five sons and five daughters. Every of his sons enjoyed that seigniory successively, and yet all died without issue. Then this great lordship was broken and divided, and partition made between the five daughters, who were married into the noblest houses of England. The county of Catherlough was allotted to the eldest, Wexford to the second, Kilkenny to the third, Kildare to the fourth, the greatest part of Leix, now called the Queen's County, to the fifth. In every of these portions the co-partners severally exercised the same jurisdiction royal which the Earl Marshal and his sons had used in the whole province. Whereby it came to pass that there were five Counties Palatines erected in Leinster. Then had the Lord of Meath the same royal liberty in all that territory, the Earls of Ulster in all that province, and the Lord of Desmond and Kerry within that county. All these appear upon record, and were all as ancient as the time of King John; only the Liberty of Tipperary, which is the only Liberty that remaineth at this day, was granted to James Butler, the first Earl of Ormond, in the third year of King Edward the Third.

These absolute Palatines made Barons and Knights, did exercise high justice in all points within their territories, erected courts for criminal and civil causes and for their own revenues, in the same form as the King's Courts were established at Dublin; made their own judges, seneschals, sheriffs, coroners, and escheators, so as the King's Writ did not run in those counties, which took up more than two parts of the English colonies, but only in the Church lands lying within the same, which were called the Cross, wherein the King made a sheriff. And so in each of these Counties Palatines there were two sheriffs, one of the Liberty and another of the Cross; as in Meath we find a sheriff of the Liberty and a sheriff of the Cross; and so in Ulster; and so in Wexford. And so at this day the Earl of Ormond maketh a sheriff of the Liberty, and the King a sheriff of the Cross, of Tipperary. Hereby it is manifest how much the King's jurisdiction was restrained and the power of these Lords enlarged by these high privileges. And it doth further appear by one Article among others preferred to King Edward the Third touching the reformation of the state of Ireland which we find in the Tower, in these words: "*Item les francheses grantes in Ireland, que sont Roialles, telles come Duresme et Cestre, vous oustont cybien de les profits, come de graunde partie de obeissance des persons enfrancheses; et en quescun franchese est Chancellerie, Chequer et Conusans de Pleas, cybien de la Coronne, come autres communes, et grantont auxi charters de pardon ; et sont souent per ley et reasonable cause seisses envostre main, a grand brofit de vous ; et leigerment restitues per maundement hors de Eng-*

leterre, a damage," &c. Unto which Article the King made answer:
"*Le Roy voet que les francheses que sont et serront per juste cause prises en sa main, ne soent my restitues, avant que le Roy soit certifie de la cause de la prise de icelles*" (26 Ed. 3, claus. m. 1). Again, these great undertakers were not tied to any form of plantation, but all was left to their discretion and pleasure; and although they builded castles and made freeholders, yet were there no tenures or services reserved to the Crown, but the Lords drew all the respect and dependency of the common people unto themselves. Now let us see what inconveniences did arise by these large and ample grants of lands and liberties to the first adventurers in the conquest.

Assuredly by these grants of whole provinces and petty kingdoms those few English Lords pretended to be proprietors of all the land, so as there was no possibility left of settling the natives in their possessions, and by consequence the conquest became impossible without the utter extirpation of all the Irish, which these English Lords were not able to do, nor perhaps willing if they had been able. Notwithstanding, because they did still hope to become lords of those lands which were possessed by the Irish, whereunto they pretended title by their large grants, and because they did fear that if the Irish were received into the King's protection and made liegemen and free subjects, the State of England would establish them in their possessions by grants from the Crown, reduce their countries into counties, ennoble some of them, and enfranchise all, and make them amenable to the law,—which would have abridged and cut off a great part of that greatness which they had promised unto themselves,—they persuaded the King of England that it was unfit to communicate the laws of England unto them; that it was the best policy to hold them as aliens and enemies, and to prosecute them with a continual war. Hereby they obtained another royal prerogative and power, which was to make war and peace at their pleasure in every part of the kingdom, which gave them an absolute command over the bodies, lands, and goods of the English subjects here; and, besides, the Irish inhabiting the lands fully conquered and reduced, being in condition of slaves and villains, did render a greater profit and revenue than if they had been made the King's free subjects.

And for these two causes last expressed they were not willing to root out all the Irishry. We may not, therefore, marvel that when King Edward the Third, upon the petition of the Irish, as is before remembered, was desirous to be certified, "*De voluntate magnatum suorum in proximo Parliamento in Hibernia tenend. si sine alieno præjudicio concedere possit, quod per statut. inde fact. Hibernici utantur legibus Anglicanis, sive chartis Regiis inde impetrandis,*"[1] that there was never any Statute made to that effect; for the truth is, that those great English Lords did to the uttermost of their power cross and withstand the enfranchisement of the Irish for the causes before expressed, wherein I must still clear and acquit the Crown and State of England of negligence or ill policy, and lay the fault upon the pride, covetousness, and ill counsel of the English planted here, which in all former ages have been the chief impediments of the final conquest of Ireland.

Again, those large scopes of land and great liberties, with the absolute power to make war and peace, did raise the English Lords to that height of pride and ambition as that they could not endure one another, but grew to a mortal war and dissension among themselves, as appeareth by all the records and stories of this kingdom. First, in the year 1204 the Lacys of Meath made war upon Sir John Courcy, who, having taken him by treachery, sent him prisoner into England. In the year 1210 King John, coming over in person, expelled the Lacys out of the kingdom

---

[1] Of the will of his lords in the next Parliament to be held in Ireland, whether it could be ordained, without prejudice to others, that the Irish should live under English laws and seek charters from England.

for their tyranny and oppression of the English; howbeit, upon payment of great fines, they were afterward restored. In the year 1228, that family being risen to a greater height—for Hugh de Lacy the younger was created Earl of Ulster after the death of Courcy without issue—there arose dissension and war between that House and William Marshal, Lord of Leinster, whereby all Meath was destroyed and laid waste. In the year 1264 Sir Walter Bourke, having married the daughter and heir of Lacy, whereby he was Earl of Ulster in right of his wife, had mortal debate with Maurice FitzMaurice the Geraldine for certain lands in Connaught; so as all Ireland was full of wars between the Bourkes and the Geraldines, say our annals. Wherein Maurice FitzMaurice grew so insolent, as that, upon a meeting at Thistledermot, he took the Lord-Justice himself, Sir Richard Capel, prisoner, with divers Lords of Munster being then in his company. In the year 1288 Richard Bourke, Earl of Ulster, commonly called the Red Earl, pretending title to the lordship of Meath, made war upon Sir Theobald de Verdun, and besieged him in the Castle of Athlone. Again, in the year 1292 John FitzThomas the Geraldine, having by contention with the Lord De Vesci gotten a goodly inheritance in Kildare, grew to that height of imagination, saith the story, as he fell into difference with divers great noblemen, and among many others with Richard the Red Earl, whom he took prisoner and detained him in Castle Lea; and by that dissension the English on the one side, and the Irish on the other, did waste and destroy all the country.

After, in the year 1311, the same Red Earl, coming to besiege Bonratty in Thomond, which was then held by Sir Richard de Clare as his inheritance, was again taken prisoner, and all his army, consisting for the most part of English, overthrown and cut in pieces by Sir Richard de Clare. And after this again, in the year 1327, most of the great Houses were banded one against another, viz., the Geraldines, Butlers, and Breminghams on the one side, and the Bourkes and Poers on the other, the ground of the quarrel being none other but that the Lord Arnold Poer had called the Earl of Kildare Rhymer; but this quarrel was prosecuted with such malice and violence as the counties of Waterford and Kilkenny were destroyed with fire and sword, till a Parliament was called of purpose to quiet this dissension.

Shortly after, the Lord John Bremingham, who was not long before made Earl of Louth for that notable service which he performed upon the Scots between Dundalk and the Faber, was so extremely envied by the Gernons, Verdons, and others of the ancient colony planted in the county of Louth, as that in the year 1329 they did most wickedly betray and murder that Earl, with divers principal gentlemen of his name and family, using the same speech that the rebellious Jews are said to use in the Gospel, "*Nolumus hunc regnare super nos.*"[1] After this the Geraldines and the Butlers, being become the most potent families in the kingdom (for the great lordship of Leinster was divided among co-partners, whose heirs for the most part lived in England; and the earldom of Ulster, with the lordship of Meath, by the match of Lionel Duke of Clarence, at last descended upon the Crown) had almost a continual war one with another. In the time of King Henry the Sixth, saith Baron Finglas in his "Discourse of the Decay of Ireland," in a fight between the Earls of Ormond and Desmond, almost all the townsmen of Kilkenny were slain. And as they followed contrary parties during the wars of York and Lancaster, so after that civil dissension ended in England these Houses in Ireland continued their opposition and feud still, even till the time of King Henry the Eighth, when by the marriage of Margaret Fitzgerald to the Earl of Ossory, the Houses of Kildare and Ormond were reconciled, and have continued in amity ever since.

Thus these great estates and royalties granted to the English

[1] We will not have this man to reign over us.

lords in Ireland begat pride, and pride begat contention among themselves, which brought forth divers mischiefs, that did not only disable the English to finish the conquest of all Ireland, but did endanger the loss of what was already gained, and of conquerors, made them slaves to that nation which they did intend to conquer. For whensoever one English lord had vanquished another, the Irish waited and took the opportunity, and fell upon that country which had received the blow, and so daily recovered some part of the lands which were possessed by the English colonies.

Besides, the English lords, to strengthen their parties, did ally themselves with the Irish, and drew them in to dwell among them, gave their children to be fostered by them, and having no other means to pay or reward them, suffered them to take coigny and livery upon the English freeholders; which oppression was so intolerable as that the better sort were enforced to quit their freeholds and fly into England, and never returned, though many laws were made in both realms to remand them back again; and the rest which remained became degenerate and mere Irish, as is before declared. And the English lords, finding the Irish exactions to be more profitable than the English rents and services, and loving the Irish tyranny, which was tied to no rules of law or honour better than a just and lawful seigniory, did reject and cast off the English law and government, received the Irish laws and customs, took Irish surnames, as MacWilliam, MacFeris, MacYoris, refused to come to the Parliaments which were summoned by the King of England's authority, and scorned to obey those English knights which were sent to command and govern this kingdom; namely, Sir Richard Capel, Sir John Morris, Sir John Darcy, and Sir Ralph Ufford. And when Sir Anthony Lucy, a man of great authority in the time of King Edward the Third, was sent over to reform the notorious abuses of this kingdom, the King, doubting that he should not be obeyed, directed a special writ or mandate to the Earl of Ulster and the rest of the nobility to assist him. And afterwards, the same King, upon good advice and counsel, resumed those excessive grants of lands and liberties in Ireland, by a special ordinance made in England, which remaineth of record in the Tower in this form :[1] "*Quia plures excessivæ donationes terrarum et libertatum in Hibernia ad subdolam machinationem petentium factæ sunt, etc. Rex delusorias huiusmodo machinationes volens elidere, de consilio peritorum sibi assistentium, omnes donationes terrarum et libertatum prædict. duxit revocandas, quousque de meritis donatariorum et causis ac qualitatibus donationum melius fuerit informat. et ideo mandatum est Justiciario Hiberni quod seisiri faciat,*" &c. Howbeit, there followed upon this resumption such a division and faction between the English of birth and the English of blood and race, as they summoned and held several Parliaments apart one from the other. Whereupon there had risen a general war betwixt them, to the utter extinguishing of the English name and nation in Ireland, if the Earl of Desmond, who was head of the faction against the English of birth, had not been sent into England, and detained there for a time. Yet afterwards, these liberties being restored by direction out of England the twenty-sixth of Edward the Third, complaint was made to the King of the easy restitution; whereunto the King made answer as is before expressed : so as we may conclude this point with that which we find in the annals published by Master Camden : "*Hibernici debellati et consumpti fuissent, nisi seditio Anglicorum impedivisset.*"[2] Whereunto I may add this note, that though some are of opinion that grants of extraordinary honours and liberties made by a King to his subjects do no more diminish his greatness than when one torch lighteth another, for it hath no less light than it had before—*Quis vetat apposito lumen de lumine sumi?*—yet many times inconveniences do arise there-

---

[1] Recalling excessive grants, which had often been made through underhand device of those who sought for them, until their origin had been inquired into.

[2] The Irish would have been wholly subdued if the sedition of the English had not hindered.

upon; and those Princes have held up their sovereignty best which have been sparing in those grants. And truly as these grants of little kingdoms and great royalties to a few private persons did produce the mischiefs spoken of before, so the true cause of the making of these grants did proceed from this, that the Kings of England, being otherwise employed and diverted, did not make the conquest of Ireland their own work, and undertake it not royally at their own charge; but as it was first begun by particular adventurers, so they left the prosecution thereof to them and other voluntaries who came to seek their fortunes in Ireland, wherein if they could prevail, they thought that in reason and honour they could do no less than make them proprietors of such scopes of land as they could conquer, people, and plant at their own charge, reserving only the sovereign lordship to the Crown of England. But if the lion had gone to hunt himself, the shares of the inferior beasts had not been so great. If the invasion had been made by an army transmitted, furnished, and supplied only at the King's charges and wholly paid with the King's treasure, as the armies of Queen Elizabeth and King James have been, as the conquest had been sooner achieved, so the servitors had been contented with lesser proportions.

For, when Scipio, Pompey, Cæsar, and other generals of the Roman armies, as subjects and servants of that State, and with the public charge, had conquered many kingdoms and commonwealths, we find them rewarded with honourable offices and triumphs at their return, and not made lords and proprietors of whole provinces and kingdoms which they had subdued to the Empire of Rome. Likewise, when the Duke of Normandy had conquered England, which he made his own work and performed it in his own person, he distributed sundry lordships and manors unto his followers but gave not away whole shires and countries in demesne to any of his servitors whom he most desired to advance. Only he made Hugh Lupus County Palatine of

Chester, and gave that earldom to him and his heirs, to hold the same, "*Ita liberè ad gladium, sicut Rex tenebat Angliam ad coronam;*" whereby that earldom indeed had a royal jurisdiction and seigniory, though the lands of that county in demesne were possessed for the most part by the ancient inheritors.

Again, from the time of the Norman Conquest till the reign of King Edward the First many of our English lords made war upon the Welshmen at their own charge. The lands which they gained they held to their own use, were called Lords Marchers, and had royal liberties within their lordships. Howbeit these particular adventurers could never make a perfect conquest of Wales.

But when King Edward the First came in person with his army thither, kept his residence and Court there, and made the reducing of Wales an enterprise of his own, he finished that work in a year or two, whereof the Lords Marchers had not performed a third part with their continual bordering war for two hundred years before. And withal, we may observe that though this King had now the dominion of Wales in *jure proprietatis*, as the Statute of Rutland affirmeth, which before was subject unto him, but in *jure feodali;* and though he had lost divers principal knights and noblemen in that war yet he did not reward his servitors with whole countries or counties but with particular manors and lordships; as to Henry Lacy, Earl of Lincoln, he gave the lordship of Denbigh, and to Reignold Gray the lordship of Ruthen, and so to others. And if the like course had been used in the winning and distributing of the lands of Ireland, that island had been fully conquered before the continent of Wales had been reduced. But the truth is, when private men attempt the conquest of countries at their own charge commonly their enterprises do perish without success; as when, in the time of Queen Elizabeth, Sir Thomas Smith undertook to recover the Ardes, and Chatterton to reconquer the Fues and Orier. The one lost his son, and the other himself, and both their adventures came to nothing. And as for the crown of England, it hath had the like fortune in the conquest of this land as some purchasers have who desire to buy land at too easy a rate; they find those cheap purchases so full of trouble as they spend twice as much as the land is worth before they get the quiet possession thereof.

And as the best policy was not observed in the distribution of the conquered lands, so I conceive that the first adventurers, intending to make a full conquest of the Irish, were deceived in the choice of the fittest places for their plantation. For they sat down and erected their castles and habitations in the plains and open countries, where they found most fruitful and profitable lands, and turned the Irish into the woods and mountains, which, as they were proper places for outlaws and thieves, so were they their natural castles and fortifications; thither they drave their preys and stealths; there they lurked and lay in wait to do mischief. These fast places they kept unknown by making the ways and entries thereunto impassable; there they kept their creaghts or herds of cattle, living by the milk of the cow, without husbandry or tillage; there they increased and multiplied unto infinite numbers by promiscuous generation among themselves; there they made their assemblies and conspiracies without discovery. But they discovered the weakness of the English dwelling in the open plains, and thereupon made their sallies and retreats with great advantage. Whereas, on the other side, if the English had built their castles and towns in those places of fastness, and had driven the Irish into the plains and open countries, where they might have had an eye and observation upon them, the Irish had been easily kept in order and in short time reclaimed from their wildness; there they would have used tillage, dwelt together in townships, learned mechanical arts and sciences. The woods had been wasted with the English habitations, as they are about the forts of Marlborough and

Phillipstown, which were built in the fastest places in Leinster, and the ways and passages throughout Ireland would have been as clear and open as they are in England at this day.

Again, if King Henry the Second, who is said to be the King that conquered this land, had made forests in Ireland, as he did enlarge the forests in England (for it appeareth by *Charta de Foresta* that he afforested many woods and wastes, to the grievance of the subject, which by that law were disafforested), or if those English lords amongst whom the whole kingdom was divided had been good hunters, and had reduced the mountains, bogs, and woods within the limits of forests, chases, and parks, assuredly the very Forest Law, and the law *de malefactoribus in parcis*, would in time have driven them into the plains and countries inhabited and manured,[1] and have made them yield up their fast places to those wild beasts which were indeed less hurtful and wild than they. But it seemeth strange to me that in all the records of this kingdom I seldom find any mention made of a forest, and never of any park or free-warren, considering the great plenty both of vert and venison within this land, and that the chief of the nobility and gentry are descended of English race; and yet at this day there is but one park stored with deer in all this kingdom, which is a park of the Earl of Ormond's near Kilkenny. It is, then, manifest, by that which is before expressed, that the not communicating of the English laws to the Irish; the over-large grants of lands and liberties to the English; the plantation made by the English in the plains and open countries, leaving the woods and mountains to the Irish, were great defects in the civil policy, and hindered the perfection of the conquest very much. Howbeit, notwithstanding these defects and errors, the English colonies stood and maintained themselves in a reasonable good estate as long as they retained their own ancient laws and customs, according to that of Ennius, "*Moribus antiquis res stat*

---

[1] *Manured*, cultivated.

Romana virisque." But when the civil government grew so weak and so loose as that the English lords would not suffer the English laws to be put in execution within their territorities and seigniories, but in place thereof both they and their people embraced the Irish customs, then the estate of things, like a game at Irish, was so turned about as the English, which hoped to make a perfect conquest of the Irish, were by them perfectly and absolutely conquered, because *Victi victoribus leges dedere*,[1] a just punishment to our nation, that would not give laws to the Irish when they might; and therefore now the Irish gave laws to them. Therefore, this defect and failing of the English justice in the English colonies, and the inducing of the Irish customs in lieu thereof, was the main impediment that did arrest and stop the course of the conquest, and was the only mean that enabled the Irishry to recover their strength again.

For, if we consider the nature of the Irish customs, we shall find that the people which doth use them must of necessity be rebels to all good government, destroy the commonwealth wherein they live, and bring barbarism and desolation upon the richest and most fruitful land of the world. For, whereas by the just and honourable law of England, and by the laws of all other well-governed kingdoms and commonweals, murder, manslaughter, rape, robbery, and theft are punished with death, by the Irish custom, or Brehon Law, the highest of these offences was punished only by fine, which they called an ericke. Therefore, when Sir William Fitzwilliams, being Lord-Deputy, told Maguire that he was to send a sheriff into Fermanagh, being lately before made a county, "Your sheriff," said Maguire, "shall be welcome to me; but let me know his ericke, or the price of his head, aforehand, that if my people cut it off I may cut the ericke upon the country." As for oppression, extortion, and other trespasses, the weaker had never any remedy against the stronger;

[1] The vanquished give laws to the victors.

whereby it came to pass that no man could enjoy his life, his wife, his lands or goods in safety if a mightier man than himself had an appetite to take the same from him. Wherein they were little better than cannibals, who do hunt one another, and he that hath most strength and swiftness doth eat and devour all his fellows.

Again, in England and all well-ordered commonweals men have certain estates in their lands and possessions, and their inheritances descend from father to son, which doth give them encouragement to build and to plant and to improve their lands, and to make them better for their posterities. But by the Irish custom of tanistry the chieftains of every country and the chief of every sept had no longer estate than for life in their chiefries, the inheritance whereof did rest in no man. And these chiefries, though they had some portions of land allotted unto them, did consist chiefly in cuttings and cosheries and other Irish exactions, whereby they did spoil and impoverish the people at their pleasure; and when their chieftains were dead their sons or next heirs did not succeed them, but their tanists, who were elective and purchased their elections by strong hand. And by the Irish custom of gavelkind the inferior tenantries were partible amongst all the males of the sept, both bastards and legitimate; and after partition made, if any one of the sept had died, his portion was not divided among his sons, but the chief of the sept made a new partition of all the lands belonging to that sept, and gave every one his part according to his antiquity.

These two Irish customs made all their possessions uncertain, being shuffled and changed and removed so often from one to another by new elections and partitions, which uncertainty of estates hath been the true cause of such desolation and barbarism in this land as the like was never seen in any country that professed the name of Christ; for though the Irishry be a nation of great antiquity and wanted neither wit nor valour, and though they had received the Christian faith above twelve hundred years since, and were lovers of music, poetry, and all kind of learning, and possessed a land abounding with all things necessary for the civil life of man, yet, which is strange to be related, they did never build any houses of brick or stone, some few poor religious houses excepted, before the reign of King Henry the Second, though they were lords of this island for many hundred years before and since the conquest attempted by the English. Albeit, when they saw us build castles upon their borders they have only, in imitation of us, erected some few piles for their captains of the country; yet I dare boldly say that never any particular person, either before or since, did build any stone or brick house for his private habitation but such as have lately obtained estates according to the course of the law of England. Neither did any of them in all this time plant any gardens or orchards, enclose or improve their lands, live together in settled villages or towns, nor make any provision for posterity, which, being against all common-sense and reason, must needs be imputed to those unreasonable customs which made their estates so uncertain and transitory in their possessions.

For who would plant or improve or build upon that land which a stranger whom he knew not should possess after his death? For that, as Solomon noteth, is one of the strangest vanities under the sun. And this is the true reason why Ulster and all the Irish countries are found so waste and desolate at this day, and so would they continue till the world's end if these customs were not abolished by the law of England.

Again, that Irish custom of gavelkind did breed another mischief, for thereby every man being born to land, as well bastard as legitimate, they all held themselves to be gentlemen; and though their portions were never so small and themselves never so poor—for gavelkind must needs in the end make a poor gentility—yet did they scorn to descend to husbandry or merchandise or to learn any mechanical art or science. And this is the true cause why there were never any corporate towns erected in the Irish countries. As for the maritime cities and towns, most certain it is that they were built and peopled by the Oostmen or Easterlings, for the natives of Ireland never performed so good a work as to build a city. Besides, these poor gentlemen were so affected unto their small portions of land as they rather chose to live at home by theft, extortion, and coshering than to seek any better fortunes abroad, which increased their septs or surnames into such numbers as there are not to be found in any kingdom of Europe so many gentlemen of one blood, family, and surname as there are of the O'Neills in Ulster, of the Bourkes in Connaught, of the Geraldines and Butlers in Munster and Leinster. And the like may be said of the inferior bloods and families. Whereby it came to pass in times of trouble and dissension that they made great parties and factions adhering one to another with much constancy because they were tied together *vinculo sanguinis;* whereas rebels and malefactors which are tied to their leaders by no band, either of duty or blood, do more easily break and fall off one from another; and, besides, their cohabitation in one country or territory gave them opportunity suddenly to assemble and conspire and rise in multitudes against the Crown. And even now, in the time of peace, we find this inconvenience, that there can hardly be an indifferent trial had between the King and the subject, or between party and party, by reason of this general kindred and consanguinity.

But the most wicked and mischievous custom of all others was that of coigny and livery, often before mentioned, which consisted in taking of man's-meat, horse-meat, and money of all the inhabitants of the country at the will and pleasure of the soldier, who, as the phrase of Scripture is, "did eat up the people as it were bread," for that he had no other entertainment. This extortion was originally Irish, for they used to lay bonaght upon their people and never gave their soldier any other pay. But when the English had learned it they used it with more insolency and made it more intolerable; for this oppression was not temporary or limited either to place or time, but because there was everywhere a continual war, either offensive or defensive, and every lord of a country and every marcher made war and peace at his pleasure, it became universal and perpetual, and was indeed the most heavy oppression that ever was used in any Christian or heathen kingdom. And therefore, *vox oppressorum*, this crying sin did draw down as great or greater plagues upon Ireland than the oppression of the Israelites did draw upon the land of Egypt; for the plagues of Egypt, though they were grievous, were but of a short continuance, but the plagues of Ireland lasted four hundred years together. This extortion of coigny and livery did produce two notorious effects. First, it made the land waste; next it made the people idle. For when the husbandman had laboured all the year, the soldier in one night did consume the fruits of all his labour, *longique perit labor irritus anni*. Had he reason then to manure the land for the next year? Or rather might he not complain as the shepherd in "Virgil:"—

> "*Impius hæc tam culta novalia miles habebit?*
> *Barbarus has segetes? En, quo discordia cives*
> *Perduxit miseros! his nos consevimus agros!*"[1]

And hereupon of necessity came depopulation, banishment, and extirpation of the better sort of subjects, and such as remained became idle and lookers-on, expecting the event of those miseries and evil times; so as this extreme extortion and oppression hath been the true cause of the idleness of this Irish nation, and that rather the vulgar sort have chosen to be beggars

---

[1] Did we for these barbarians plant and sow?
On these, on these, our happy fields bestow?
Good heaven, what dire effects from civil discord flow!
—*Dryden's Virgil*, Ecl. 1.

in foreign countries than to manure[1] their own fruitful land at home.

Lastly, this oppression did of force and necessity make the Irish a crafty people; for such as are oppressed and live in slavery are ever put to their shifts, *Ingenium mala sæpe movent;*[2] and therefore in the old comedies of Plautus and Terence the bond-slave doth always act the cunning and crafty part. Besides, all the common people have a whining tune or accent in their speech, as if they did still smart or suffer some oppression. And this idleness, together with fear of imminent mischiefs which did continually hang over their heads, have been the cause that the Irish were ever the most inquisitive people after news of any nation in the world; as St. Paul himself made observation upon the people of Athens, that they were an idle people, and did nothing but learn and tell news. And because these news-carriers did by their false intelligence many times raise troubles and rebellions in this realm, the Statute of Kilkenny doth punish news-tellers, by the name of skelaghes,[3] with fine and ransom.

This extortion of coigny and livery was taken for the maintenance of their men of war; but their Irish exactions, extorted by the chieftains and tanists by colour of their barbarous seigniory, were almost as grievous a burthen as the other, namely, cosherings, which were visitations and progresses made by the lord and his followers among his tenants, wherein he did eat them, as the English proverb is, out of house and home; cessings of the kern, of his family, called kernety, of his horses and horse-boys, of his dogs and dog-boys, and the like; and lastly, cuttings, tallages, or spendings, high or low, at his pleasure; all which made the lord an absolute tyrant and the tenant a very slave and villain, and in one respect more miserable than bond-slaves. For com-

---

[1] *Manure*, cultivate. Manure, contracted from manœuvre, meant originally working with the hands. [2] Ills often stir the wit.
[3] *Scelaighe* in Irish was a historian or story-teller; "sgeulach," historical narrative.

monly the bond-slave is fed by his lord, but here the lord was fed by his bond-slave.

Lastly, there were two other customs proper and peculiar to the Irishry, which being the cause of many strong combinations and factions, do tend to the utter ruin of a commonwealth; the one was fostering, the other gossipred, both which have ever been of greater estimation among this people than with any other nation in the Christian world. For fostering, I did never hear or read that it was in that use or reputation in any other country, barbarous or civil, as it hath been and yet is in Ireland, where they put away all their children to fosterers, the potent and rich men selling, the meaner sort buying, the alterage[1] of their children. And the reason is because in the opinion of this people fostering hath always been a stronger alliance than blood, and the foster-children do love and are beloved of their foster-fathers and their sept more than of their own natural parents and kindred, and do participate of their means more frankly, and do adhere unto them in all fortunes with more affection and constancy. And though Tully in his book of Friendship doth observe that children of Princes being sometimes, in cases of necessity, for saving of their lives, delivered to shepherds to be nourished and bred up, when they have been restored to their great fortunes have still retained their love and affection to their fosterers, whom for many years they took to be their parents; yet this was a rare case, and few examples are to be found thereof.

But such a general custom in a kingdom, in giving and taking children to foster, making such a firm alliance as it doth in Ireland, was never seen or heard of in any other country of the world besides.

The like may be said of gossipred or compaternity, which though by the Canon Law it may be a spiritual affinity, and a juror

---

[1] *Alterage*, fostering, from "alere," to nourish; or possibly from the changing as from one mother to another.

that was gossip to either of the parties might in former times have been challenged as not indifferent by our law, yet there was no nation under the sun that ever made so religious account thereof as the Irish.

Now, these two customs, which of themselves are indifferent in other kingdoms, became exceeding evil and full of mischief in this realm by reason of the inconveniences which followed thereupon. For they made, as I said before, strong parties and factions, whereby the great men were enabled to oppress their inferiors and to oppose their equals; and their followers were borne out and countenanced in all their lewd and wicked actions. For fosterers and gossips, by the common custom of Ireland, were to maintain one another in all causes lawful and unlawful, which, as it is a combination and confederacy punishable in all well-governed commonweals, so was it not one of the least causes of the common misery of this kingdom.

I omit their common repudiation of their wives; their promiscuous generation of children; their neglect of lawful matrimony; their uncleanness in apparel, diet, and lodging; and their contempt and scorn of all things necessary for the civil life of man.

These were the Irish customs which the English colonies did embrace and use after they had rejected the civil and honourable laws and customs of England, whereby they became degenerate and metamorphosed like Nebuchadnezzar, who, although he had the face of a man, had the heart of a beast; or like those who had drunk of Circe's cup, and were turned into very beasts, and yet took such pleasure in their beastly manner of life as they would not return to their shape of men again; insomuch as within less time than the age of a man they had no marks or differences left amongst them of that noble nation from which they were descended. For, as they did not only forget the English language and scorn the use thereof, but grew to be ashamed of their very English names, though they were noble and of great antiquity, and took Irish surnames and nicknames. Namely, the two most potent families of the Bourkes in Connaught, after the House of the Red Earl failed of heirs-males, called their chiefs MacWilliam Eighter and MacWilliam Oughter. In the same province, Bremingham, Baron of Athenrie, called himself MacYoris; Dexecester, or De'exon, was called MacJordan; Dangle, or De Angulo, took the name of MacCostelo. Of the inferior families of the Bourkes, one was called MacHubbard, another MacDavid. In Munster, of the great families of the Geraldines planted there, one was called MacMorice, chief of the House of Lixnaw; and another MacGibbon, who was also called the White Knight. The chief of the Baron of Dunboyne's house, who is a branch of the House of Ormond, took the surname of MacFeris. Condon, of the county of Waterford, was called MacMaioge; and the Archdeacon of the county of Kilkenny, MacOdo. And this they did in contempt and hatred of the English name and nation, whereof these degenerate families became more mortal enemies than the mere Irish. And whereas the State and Government, being grown weak by their defection, did, to reduce them to obedience, grant them many protections and pardons, the cheapness whereof in all ages hath brought great dishonour and damage to this commonweal, they grew so ungrateful and unnatural as in the end they scorned that grace and favour, because the acceptance thereof did argue them to be subjects, and they desired rather to be accounted enemies than rebels to the Crown of England.

Hereupon was that old verse made which I find written in the White-book of the Exchequer, in a hand as ancient as the time of King Edward the Third :—

> "By graunting charters of peas
> To false English, withouten leas,
>   This land shall be mich undoo.
> But gossipred, and alterage,
> And leesing of our language,
>   Have mickly holp theretoo."

And therefore, in a Close-Roll in the Tower, bearing this title, "*Articuli in Hibernia observand:*," we find these two articles among others—" 1. *Justiciarius Hiberniæ non concedat perdonationes de morte hominis, nec de Roberiis, seu incendiis, et quod de cætero certificet dominum regem de nominibus petentium.* 2. *Item, Quod nec Justiciarius nec aliquis Magnas Hiberniæ concedat protectiones alicui contra pacem Regis existent.*"[1] &c. But now it is fit to look back and consider when the old English colonies became so degenerate, and in what age they fell away into that Irish barbarism, rejecting the English laws and customs. Assuredly, by comparing the ancient annals of Ireland with the records remaining here and in the Tower of London, I do find that this general defection fell out in the latter end of the reign of King Edward the Second and in the beginning of the reign of King Edward the Third. And all this great innovation grew within the space of thirty years, within the compass of which time there fell out divers mischievous accidents, whereby the whole kingdom was in a manner lost. For, first, Edward de Bruce invaded Ireland with the Scottish army, and prevailed so far as that he possessed the maritime parts of Ulster, marched up to the walls of Dublin, spoiled the English Pale, passed through Leinster and Munster as far as Limerick, and was master of the field in every part of the kingdom.

This happened in the tenth year of King Edward the Second, at what time the Crown of England was weaker and suffered more dishonour in both kingdoms than it did at any time since the Norman Conquest. Then did the State of England send over John de Hotham to be Treasurer here, with commission to call the great lords of Ireland together, and to take of them an oath of association, that they should loyally join together in life and

[1] The Lord Justice of Ire'and shall grant no pardons for murder, robbery, or arson, and report to the king the names of those who ask for them. Also he shall grant no protections to any one against the king's peace.

death to preserve the right of the King of England and to expel the common enemy. But this Treasurer brought neither men nor money to perform this service.

At that time, though Richard Bourke, Earl of Ulster, commonly called the Red Earl, was of greater power than any other subject in Ireland, yet was he so far stricken in years as that he was unable to manage the martial affairs, as he had done during all the reign of King Edward the First, having been General of the Irish forces, not only in this kingdom, but in the wars of Scotland, Wales, and Gascogne. And therefore Maurice Fitz-Thomas of Desmond, being then the most active nobleman in this realm, took upon him the chief command in this war, for the support whereof the revenue of this land was far too short, and yet no supply of treasure was sent out of England.

Then was there no mean to maintain the army but by cessing the soldiers upon the subject, as the Irish were wont to impose their bonaght. Whereupon grew that wicked extortion of coigny and livery spoken of before, which in short time banished the greatest part of the freeholders out of the county of Kerry, Limerick, Cork, and Waterford; into whose possessions Desmond and his kinsmen, allies, and followers, which were then more Irish than English, did enter and appropriate these lands unto themselves, Desmond himself taking what scopes he best liked for his demesnes in every country, and reserving an Irish seigniory out of the rest. And here, that I may verify and maintain by matter of record that which is before delivered touching the nature of this wicked extortion called coigny and livery, and the manifold mischiefs it did produce, I think it fit and pertinent to insert the preamble of the Statute of the tenth of Henry the Seventh, c. 4, not printed, but recorded in Parliament Rolls of Dublin, in these words : "At the request and supplication of the Commons of this land of Ireland, that where of long time there hath been used and exacted by the lords and gentlemen of this land many and

divers damnable customs and usages, which being called coigny
and livery and pay; that is, horse-meat and man's-meat, for the
finding of their horsemen and footmen; and over that 4d. or 6d.
daily to every of them to be had and paid of the poor earth-
tillers and tenants, inhabitants of the said land, without anything
doing or paying thereof; besides many murders, robberies, rapes,
and other manifold extortions and oppressions by the said horsemen and footmen, daily and mightily committed and done; which
being the principal causes of the desolation and destruction of
the said land, and hath brought the same into ruin and decay, so
as the most part of the English freeholders and tenants of this
land being departed out thereof, some into the realm of England,
and other some to other strange lands; whereupon the foresaid
lords and gentlemen of this land have intruded into the said
freeholders' and tenants' inheritances, and the same keepeth and
occupieth as their own inheritances, and setting under them in
the same land the King's Irish enemies, to the diminishing of Holy
Church's rites, the disherison of the King and his obedient subjects, and the utter ruin and desolation of the land: For reformation whereof be it enacted, that the King shall receive a
subsidy of 26s. 8d. out of every hundred and twenty acres of
arable land manured," &c.

But to return to Maurice Fitz-Thomas of Desmond; by this
extortion of coigny and livery he suddenly grew from a mean to
a mighty estate; insomuch as the Baron Finglas, in his discourse
of the decay of Ireland, affirmeth that his ancient inheritance
being not one thousand marks yearly, he became able to dispend
every way ten thousand pounds per annum.

These possessions, being thus unlawfully gotten, could not be
maintained by the just and honourable law of England, which
would have restored the true owners to their land again. And
therefore this great man found no means to continue and uphold
his ill-purchased greatness but by rejecting the English law and

government, and assuming in lieu thereof the barbarous customs of the Irish. And hereupon followed the defection of those four shires containing the greatest part of Munster from the obedience of the law.

In like manner, saith Baron Finglas, the Lord Tipperary, perceiving how well the House of Desmond had thrived by coigny and livery and other Irish exactions, began to hold the like course in the counties of Tipperary and Kilkenny, whereby he got great scopes of land, especially in Ormond, and raised many Irish exactions upon the English freeholders there, which made him so potent and absolute among them as at that time they knew no other law than the will of their Lord. Besides, finding that the Earl of Desmond excluded the ordinary ministers of justice, under colour of a Royal Liberty which he claimed in the counties of Kerry, Cork, and Waterford, by a grant of King Edward the First, as appeareth in a *Quo warranto?* brought against him, anno 12, Edward the First, the record whereof remaineth in Bremingham's Tower, among the Common Plea Rolls there, this Lord also, in the third of Edward the Third, obtained a grant of the like Liberty in the county of Tipperary, whereby he got the law into his own hands and shut out the Common Law and justice of the realm.

And thus we see that all Munster fell away from the English law and government in the end of King Edward the Second his reign, and in the beginning of the reign of King Edward the Third. Again, about the same time, viz., in the twentieth year of King Edward the Second, when the state of England was well-nigh ruined by the rebellion of the Barons, and the government of Ireland utterly neglected, there arose in Leinster one of the Cavanaghs named Donald MacArt, who named himself Mac-Murrough, King of Leinster, and possessed himself of the county of Catherlough, and of the greatest part of the county of Wexford. And shortly after, Lisagh O'Moore called himself O'Moore, took eight castles in one evening, destroyed Dunamase, the principal house of the Lord Mortimer in Leix, recovered that whole country, "*de servo dominus, de subjecto princeps effectus*,"[1] saith Friar Clynne in his annals.

Besides, the Earl of Kildare, imitating his cousin of Desmond, did not omit to make the like use of coigny and livery in Kildare and the west part of Meath, which brought the like barbarism into those parts. And thus a great part of Leinster was lost and fell away from the obedience of the Crown near about the time before expressed.

Again, in the seventh year of King Edward the Third the Lord William Bourke, Earl of Ulster and Lord Connaught, was treacherously murdered by his own squires at Knockfergus, leaving behind him "*unicam et unius anni filiam*,"[2] saith Friar Clynne. Immediately upon the murder committed, the Countess with her young daughter fled into England, so as the government of that country was wholly neglected until that young lady being married to Lionel Duke of Clarence, that Prince came over with an army to recover his wife's inheritance and to reform this kingdom, anno 36 of Edward the Third. But in the meantime what became of that great inheritance both in Ulster and Connaught? Assuredly, in Ulster the sept of Hugh-Boy O'Neill, then possessing Glaucoukeyn and Killeightra in Tyrone, took the opportunity, and passing over the Bann did first expel the English out of the Barony of Tuscard, which is now called the Rout, and likewise out of the glynnes and other lands up as far as Knockfergus, which country or extent of land is at this day called the Lower Clan Hugh-Boy. And shortly after that they came up into the Great Ardes, which the Latin writers call *Altitudines Ultoniæ*, and was then the inheritance of the Savages, by whom they were valiantly resisted for divers years; but at last, for

---

[1] From servant lord, from subject grown a prince.
[2] An only daughter who was one year old.

want of castles and fortifications—for the saying of Henry Savage mentioned in every story is very memorable, that a castle of bones was better than a castle of stones—the English were overrun by the multitude of the Irishry. So as about the thirtieth of King Edward the Third, some few years before the arrival of the Duke of Clarence, the Savages were utterly driven out of the Great Ardes into a little nook of land near the river of Strangford, where they now possess a little territory called the Little Ardes; and their greater patrimony took the name of the Upper Clan Hugh-Boy from the sept of Hugh-Boy O'Neill, who became invaders thereof.

For Connaught, some younger branches of the family of the Bourkes being planted there by the Red Earl and his ancestors, seeing their chief to be cut off and dead without heir-male and no man left to govern or protect that province, intruded presently into all the Earl's lands, which ought to have been seized into the King's hands by reason of the minority of the heir. And within a short space two of the most potent among them divided that great seigniory betwixt them, the one taking the name of MacWilliam Oughter and the other of MacWilliam Eighter, as if the Lord William Bourke, the last Earl of Ulster, had left two sons of one name behind him to inherit that lordship in course of gavelkind. But they well knew that they were but intruders upon the King's possession during the minority of the heir; they knew those lands were the rightful inheritance of that young lady, and, consequently, that the law of England would speedily evict them out of their possession; and therefore they held it the best policy to cast off the yoke of English law and to become mere Irish, and according to their example drew all the rest of the English in that province to do the like, so as from thenceforth they suffered their possessions to run in course of tanistry and gavelkind. They changed their names, language, and apparel, and all their civil manners and customs of living. Lastly, about the twenty-fifth year of King Edward the Third, Sir Richard de Clare was slain in Thomond, and all the English colonies there utterly supplanted.

Thus in that space of time which was between the tenth year of King Edward the Second and the thirtieth year of King Edward the Third (I speak within compass), by the concurrence of the mischiefs before recited, all the old English colonies in Munster, Connaught, and Ulster, and more than a third part of Leinster became degenerate and fell away from the Crown of England; so as only the four shires of the English Pale remained under the obedience of the law; and yet the borders and marches thereof were grown unruly and out of order too, being subject to black-rents and tribute of the Irish, which was a greater defection than when ten of twelve tribes departed and fell away from the Kings of Judah.

But was not the State of England sensible of this loss and dishonour? Did they not endeavour to recover the land that was lost and to reduce the subjects to their obedience?

Truly, King Edward the Second, by the incursions of the Scottish nation and by the insurrection of his barons, who raised his wife and his son against him, and in the end deposed him, was diverted and utterly disabled to reform the disorders of Ireland. But as soon as the Crown of England was transferred to King Edward the Third, though he were yet in his minority, the State there began to look into the desperate estate of things here, and finding such a general defection, letters were sent from the King to the great men and prelates requiring them particularly to swear fealty to the Crown of England.

Shortly after, Sir Anthony Lucy, a person of great authority in England in those days, was sent over to work a reformation in this kingdom by a severe course, and to that end the King wrote expressly to the Earl of Ulster and others of the nobility to assist him, as is before remembered. Presently upon his arrival he arrested Maurice Fitz-Thomas, Earl of Desmond, and Sir William Bremingham, and committed them prisoners to the castle of Dublin, where Sir William Bremingham was executed for treason, though the Earl of Desmond was left to mainprise, upon condition he should appear before the King by a certain day and in the meantime to continue loyal.

After this, the King being advertised that the over-large grants of lands and liberties made to the lords of English blood in Ireland made them so insolent as they scorned to obey the law, the magistrate did absolutely resume all such grants, as is before declared. But the Earl of Desmond above all men found himself grieved with this resumption or repeal of liberties, and declared his dislike and discontent, insomuch as he did not only refuse to come to a Parliament at Dublin summoned by Sir William Morris, Deputy to the Lord John Darcy, the King's Lieutenant; but, as we have said before, he raised such dissension between the English of blood and the English of birth as the like was never seen from the time of the first planting of our nation in Ireland. And in this factious and seditious humour, he drew the Earl of Kildare and the rest of the nobility, with the citizens and burgesses of the principal towns, to hold a several Parliament by themselves at Kilkenny, where they framed certain articles against the Deputy, and transmitted the same into England to the King.

Hereupon Sir Ralph Ufford, who had lately before married the Countess of Ulster, a man of courage and severity, was made Lord-Justice, who forthwith calling a Parliament, sent a special commandment to the Earl of Desmond to appear in that great Council; but the Earl wilfully refused to come. Whereupon the Lord-Justice raised the King's standard, and marching with an army into Munster, seized into the King's hands all the possessions of the Earl, took and executed his principal followers, Sir Eustace le Poer, Sir William Grant, and Sir John Cotterell; enforced the Earl himself to fly and lurk, till twenty-six noblemen and knights became mainpernors[1] for his appearance at a certain day prefixed; but he making default the second time, the uttermost advantage was taken against his sureties. Besides, at the same time, this Lord-Justice caused the Earl of Kildare to be arrested and committed to the Castle of Dublin, indited and imprisoned many other disobedient subjects, called in and cancelled such Charters as were lately before resumed, and proceeded every way so roundly and severely as the nobility, which were wont to suffer no controlment, did much distaste him; and the commons, who in this land have ever been more devoted to their immediate lords here, whom they saw every day, than unto their Sovereign Lord and King, whom they never saw, spake ill of this governor as of a rigorous and cruel man, though in truth he were a singular good Justicer, and if he had not died in the second year of his government, was the likeliest person of that age to have reformed and reduced the degenerate English colonies to their natural obedience of the Crown of England.

Thus much, then, we may observe, by the way, that Maurice Fitz-Thomas, the first Earl of Desmond, was the first English Lord that imposed coigny and livery upon the King's subjects, and the first that raised his estate to immoderate greatness by that wicked extortion and oppression; that he was the first that rejected the English laws and government, and drew others by his example to do the like; that he was the first peer of Ireland that refused to come to the Parliament summoned by the King's authority; that he was the first that made a division and distinction between the English of blood and the English of birth.

And as this Earl was the only author and first actor of these mischiefs which give the greatest impediment to the full conquest

[1] *Mainpernors*, sureties by mainprise, takers in hand, from French *main* and *preneurs*. Mainprise differed from bail, in being an obligation to produce the accused by a given day, without the power bail had of imprisoning or surrendering before the given day.

of Ireland, so it is to be noted that, albeit others of his rank afterwards offended in the same kind, whereby their houses were many times in danger of ruin, yet was there not ever any noble house of English race in Ireland utterly destroyed and finally rooted out by the hand of justice but the House of Desmond only, nor any peer of this realm ever put to death—though divers have been attainted—but Thomas Fitz-James, the Earl of Desmond, only; and only for those wicked customs brought in by the first Earl and practised by his posterity, though by several laws they were made high treason. And therefore, though in the seventh of Edward the Fourth, during the government of the Lord Tiptoft, Earl of Worcester, both the Earls of Desmond and Kildare were attainted by Parliament at Drogheda for alliance and fostering with the Irish, and for taking coigny and livery of the King's subjects, yet was Desmond only put to death, for the Earl of Kildare received his pardon. And albeit the son of this Earl of Desmond who lost his head at Drogheda was restored to the earldom, yet could not the King's grace regenerate obedience in that degenerate house, but it grew rather more wild and barbarous than before. For from thenceforth they reclaimed a strange privilege, that the Earls of Desmond should never come to any Parliament or Grand Council or within any walled town but at their will and pleasure. Which pretended privilege James Earl of Desmond, the father of Gerald, the last Earl, renounced and surrendered by his deed in the Chancery of Ireland in the thirty-second of Henry the Eighth. At what time, among the mere Irishry, he submitted himself to Sir Anthony Saint-Leger, then Lord-Deputy, took an oath of allegiance, covenanted that he would suffer the law of England to be executed in his country and assist the King's judges in their circuits, and if any subsidies should be granted by Parliament, he would permit the same to be levied upon his tenants and followers. Which covenants are as strange as the privilege itself spoken of before. But that which

I conceive most worthy of observation upon the fortunes of the House of Desmond is this, that as Maurice Fitz-Thomas, the first Earl, did first raise the greatness of that house by Irish exactions and oppressions, so Gerald, the last Earl, did at last ruin and reduce it to nothing by using the like extortions. For certain it is that the first occasion of this rebellion grew from hence, that when he attempted to charge the Decies in the county of Waterford with coigny and livery, black-rents and cosheries, after the Irish manner, he was resisted by the Earl of Ormond, and upon an encounter overthrown and taken prisoner, which made his heart so unquiet as it easily conceived treason against the Crown and brought forth actual and open rebellion, wherein he perished himself and made a final extinguishment of his house and honour. Oppression and extortion did maintain the greatness, and oppression and extortion did extinguish the greatness, of that house. Which may well be expressed by the old emblem of a torch turned downwards with these words, *Quod me alit, extinguit.*[1]

Now let us return to the course of reformation held and pursued here after the death of Sir Ralph Ufford, which happened in the twentieth year of King Edward the Third; after which time, albeit all the power and counsel of England was converted towards the conquest of France, yet was not the work of reformation altogether discontinued. For, in the twenty-fifth year of King Edward the Third, Sir Thomas Rookeby, another worthy governor whom I have once before named, held a Parliament at Kilkenny, wherein many excellent laws were propounded and enacted for the reducing of the English colonies to their obedience, which laws we find enrolled in the Remembrancer's Office here, and differ not much in substance from those other Statutes of Kilkenny which not long after, during the government of Lionel Duke of Clarence, were not only enacted but put in execution. This noble Prince, having married the daughter and heir of Ulster, and being like-

[1] What I live by kills me.

wise a copartner [1] of the county of Kilkenny, in the thirty-sixth year of King Edward the Third came over the King's Lieutenant, attended with a good retinue of martial men, as is before remembered, and a grave and honourable counsel as well for peace as for war. But because this army was not of a competent strength to break and subdue all the Irishry, although he quieted the borders of the English Pale and held all Ireland in awe with his name and presence, the principal service that he intended was to reform the degenerate English colonies and to reduce them to obedience of the English law and magistrate. To that end, in the fortieth year of King Edward the Third, he held that famous Parliament at Kilkenny wherein many notable laws were enacted, which do show and lay open (for the law doth best discover enormities) how much the English colonies were corrupted at that time, and do infallibly prove that which is laid down before, that they were wholly degenerate and fallen away from their obedience. For first, it appeareth by the preamble of these laws that the English of this realm, before the coming over of Lionel Duke of Clarence, were at that time become mere Irish in their language, names, apparel, and all their manner of living, and had rejected the English laws and submitted themselves to the Irish, with whom they had many marriages and alliances, which tended to the utter ruin and destruction of the commonwealth. Therefore, alliance by marriage, nurture of infants, and gossipred with the Irish are by this Statute made high treason. Again, if any man of English race should use an Irish name, Irish language, or Irish apparel, or any other guise or fashion of the Irish, if he had lands or tenements, the same should be seized till he had given security to the Chancery to conform himself in all points to the

---

[1] Sir John Davies always uses the old spelling of this word, *coparcener*. Cotgrave gives in his Dictionary, for Old French *parsonnier*, "a partener or co-parcener." Prof. Skeat, in his Etymological Dictionary, suggests that parcener became partener by confusion between the old written *c* and *t*, as cityen became citizen by confusion of the old letter for *y* with *z*.

English manner of living; and if he had no lands, his body was to be taken and imprisoned till he found sureties as aforesaid.

Again, it was established and commanded that the English in all their controversies should be ruled and governed by the Common Law of England, and if any did submit himself to the Brehon Law or March Law he should be adjudged a traitor.

Again, because the English at that time made war and peace with the bordering enemy at their pleasure, they were expressly prohibited to levy war upon the Irish without special warrant and direction from the State.

Again, it was made penal to the English to permit the Irish to creaght or graze upon their lands; to present them to ecclesiastical benefices, to receive them into any monasteries or religious houses, or to entertain any of their minstrels, rhymers, or newstellers. To impose or cess any horse or foot upon the English subjects against their wills was made felony. And because the great liberties or franchises spoken of before were become sanctuaries for all malefactors, express powers were given to the King's sheriffs to enter into all franchises, and there to apprehend all felons and traitors. And lastly, because the great lords, when they levied forces for the public service, did lay unequal burdens upon the gentlemen and freeholders, it was ordained that four wardens of the peace in every county should set down and appoint what men and armour every man should bear according to his freehold or other ability of estate.

These and other laws tending to a general reformation were enacted in that Parliament. And the execution of these laws, together with the presence of the King's son, made a notable alteration in the state and manners of this people within the space of seven years, which was the term of this Prince's Lieutenancy.

For all the discourses that I have seen of the decay of Ireland do agree in this, that the presence of the Lord Lionel and these statutes of Kilkenny did restore the English government in the degenerate colonies for divers years. And the Statute of the tenth of Henry the Seventh, which reviveth and confirmeth the Statutes of Kilkenny, doth confirm as much. For it declareth, that as long as these laws were put in use and execution, this land continued in prosperity and honour; and since they were not executed, the subjects rebelled and digressed from their allegiance and the land fell to ruin and desolation. And, withal, we find the effect of these laws in the Pipe-Rolls and Plea-Rolls of this kingdom; for, from the thirty-sixth of Edward the Third, when this Prince entered into his government, till the beginning of Richard the Second his reign, we find the revenue of the Crown, both certain and casual, in Ulster, Munster, and Connaught accounted for; and that the King's Writ did run and the Common Law was executed in every of these provinces. I join with these laws the personal presence of the King's son as a concurrent cause of this reformation; because the people of this land, both English and Irish, out of a natural pride, did ever love and desire to be governed by great persons. And therefore I may here justly take occasion to note, that the absence first of the Kings of England, and next the absence of those great lords who were inheritors of those mighty seigniories of Leinster, Ulster, Connaught, and Meath, have been main causes why this kingdom was not reduced in so many ages.

Touching the absence of our Kings, three of them only since the Norman Conquest have made royal journeys into this land; namely, King Henry the Second, King John, and King Richard the Second. And yet they no sooner arrived here but that all the Irishry, as if they had been but one man, submitted themselves, took oaths of fidelity, and gave pledges and hostages to continue loyal. And if any of those kings had continued here in person a competent time, till they had settled both English and Irish in their several possessions, and had set the law in a due course throughout the kingdom, these times wherein we live had not gained the honour of the final conquest and reducing of Ireland. For the King, saith Solomon, *dissipat omne malum intuitu suo*.[1] But when Moses was absent in the mount the people committed idolatry, and when there was no King in Israel every man did what seemed best in his own eyes.

And therefore, when Alexander had conquered the East part of the world and demanded of one what was the fittest place for the seat of his empire, he brought and laid a dry hide before him, and desired him to set his foot on the one side thereof; which being done, all the other parts of the hide did rise up; but when he did set his foot in the middle of the hide, all the other parts lay flat and even. Which was a lively demonstration that if a Prince keep his residence in the border of his dominions, the remote parts will easily rise and rebel against him; but if he make the centre thereof his seat, he shall easily keep them in peace and obedience.

Touching the absence of the great lords, all writers do impute the decay and loss of Leinster to the absence of the English lords who married the five daughters of William Marshal, Earl of Pembroke, to whom that great seigniory descended, when his five sons, who inherited the same successively, and during their times held the same in peace and obedience to the law of England, were all dead without issue, which happened about the fortieth year of King Henry the Third. For, the eldest being married to Hugh Bigot, Earl of Norfolk, who in right of his wife had the Marshalship of England; the second to Warren de Mountchensey, whose sole daughter and heir was matched to William de Valentia, half-brother to King Henry the Third, who by that match was made Earl of Pembroke; the third to Gilbert de Clare, Earl of Gloucester; the fourth to William Ferrers, Earl of Derby; the fifth to William de Bruce, Lord of Brecknock,

[1] "A king that sitteth in the throne of judgment scattereth away all evil with his eyes."—Proverbs xx. 8.

these great lords, having greater inheritances in their own right in England than they had in Ireland in right of their wives—and yet each of the coparceners had an entire county allotted for her purparty,[1] as is before declared—could not be drawn to make their personal residence in this kingdom, but managed their estates here by their seneschals and servants. And to defend their territories against the bordering Irish they entertained some of the natives, who pretended a perpetual title to those great lordships; for the Irish, after a thousand conquests and attainders by our law, would in those days pretend title still, because by the Irish law no man could forfeit his land. These natives, taking the opportunity in weak and desperate times, usurped those seigniories; and so Donald MacArt Cavanagh, being entertained by the Earl of Norfolk, made himself lord of the county of Catherlough; and Lisagh O'Moore, being trusted by the Lord Mortimer, who married the daughter and heir of the Lord Bruce, made himself lord of the lands in Leix in the latter end of King Edward the Second's reign, as is before declared.

Again, the decay and loss of Ulster and Connaught is attributed to this, that the Lord William Bourke, the last Earl of that name, died without issue male, whose ancestors, namely, the Red Earl and Sir Hugh de Lacy, before him, being personally resident, held up their greatness there and kept the English in peace and the Irish in awe. But when those provinces descended upon an heir-female and an infant, the Irish overran Ulster and the younger branches of the Bourkes usurped Connaught. And, therefore, the ordinance made in England the third of Richard the Second against such as were absent from their lands in Ireland, and gave two-third parts of the profits thereof unto the King until they returned or placed a sufficient number of men to defend the same, was grounded upon good reason of State; which ordinance was put in execution for many years after, as appeareth

[1] *Purparty*, a share of an estate allotted by partition; *pour partie*, for a part.

by sundry seizures made thereupon in the time of King Richard the Second, Henry the Fourth, Henry the Fifth, and Henry the Sixth, whereof there remain records in the Remembrancer's Office here. Among the rest the Duke of Norfolk himself was not spared, but was impleaded upon this ordinance for two parts of the profits of Dorburies Land and other lands in the county of Wexford in the time of King Henry the Sixth; and afterwards, upon the same reason of State, all the lands of the House of Norfolk, of the Earl of Shrewsbury, the Lord Barkly, and others, who, having lands in Ireland, kept their continual residence in England, were entirely resumed by the Act of Absentees made in the twenty-eighth year of King Henry the Eighth.

But now again let us look back and see how long the effect of that reformation did continue which was begun by Lionel Duke of Clarence in the fortieth year of King Edward the Third, and what courses have been held to reduce and reform this people by other Lieutenants and governors since that time.

The English colonies, being in some good measure reformed by the Statutes of Kilkenny, did not utterly fall away into barbarism again till the wars of the two houses had almost destroyed both these kingdoms; for in that miserable time the Irish found opportunity, without opposition, to banish the English law and government out of all the provinces, and to confine it only to the English Pale. Howbeit, in the meantime, between the government of the Duke of Clarence and the beginning of those civil wars of York and Lancaster, we find that the State of England did sundry times resolve to proceed in this work of reformation.

For, first, King Richard the Second sent over Sir Nicholas Dagworth to survey the possessions of the Crown and to call to account the officers of the Revenue. Next, to draw his English subjects to manure and defend their lands in Ireland, he made that ordinance against absentees spoken of before. Again, he, showed an excellent example of justice upon Sir Philip Courtney, being his Lieutenant of that kingdom, when he caused him to be arrested by special Commissioners, upon complaint made of sundry grievous oppressions and wrongs which during his government he had done unto that people.

After this the Parliament of England did resolve that Thomas Duke of Gloucester, the King's uncle, should be employed in the reformation and reducing of that kingdom; the same whereof was no sooner bruited in Ireland but all the Irishry were ready to submit themselves before his coming; so much the very name of a great personage, specially of a Prince of the blood, did ever prevail with this people. But the King and his minions, who were ever jealous of this Duke of Gloucester, would not suffer him to have the honour of that service. But the King himself thought it a work worthy of his own presence and pains, and thereupon himself in person made those two royal journeys mentioned before. At what time he received the submissions of all the Irish lords and captains, who bound themselves both by indenture and oath to become and continue his loyal subjects; and withal laid a particular project for a civil plantation of the mountains and maritime counties between Dublin and Wexford, by removing all the Irish septs from thence, as appeareth by the covenants between the Earl Marshal of England and those Irish septs, which are before remembered, and are yet preserved and remain of record in the King's Remembrancer's Office at Westminster. Lastly, this King, being present in Ireland, took special care to supply and furnish the courts of justice with able and sufficient judges; and to that end he made that grave and learned judge, Sir William Hankford, Chief-Justice of the King's Bench here, who afterwards for his service in this realm was made Chief-Justice of the King's Bench in England by King Henry the Fourth, and did withal associate unto him William Sturmy, a well-learned man in the law, who likewise came out of England with the King, that the legal proceedings, which were out of order too, as all other things in that realm were, might be amended and made formal, according to the course and precedents of England. But all the good purposes and projects of this King were interrupted and utterly defeated by this sudden departure out of Ireland and unhappy deposition from the Crown of England.

Howbeit, King Henry the Fourth, intending likewise to prosecute this noble work in the third year of his reign, made the Lord Thomas of Lancaster, his second son, Lieutenant of Ireland, who came over in person, and accepted again the submissions of divers Irish lords and captains, as is before remembered; and held also a Parliament, wherein he gave new life to the Statutes of Kilkenny and made other good laws tending to the reformation of the kingdom. But the troubles raised against the King his father in England drew him home again so soon, as that seed of reformation took no root at all ; neither had his service in that kind any good effect or success.

After this the State of England had no leisure to think of a general reformation in this realm till the civil dissensions of England were appeased and the peace of that kingdom settled by King Henry the Seventh.

For, albeit in the time of King Henry the Sixth, Richard Duke of York, a Prince of the blood, of great wisdom and valour, and heir to a third part of the kingdom at least, being Earl of Ulster and Lord of Connaught and Meath, was sent the King's Lieutenant into Ireland to recover and reform that realm, where he was resident in person for the greatest part of ten years, yet the truth is he aimed at another mark, which was the Crown of England. And therefore he thought it no policy to distaste either the English or Irish by a course of reformation, but sought by all means to please them, and by popular courses to steal away their hearts, to the end he might strengthen his party when he should set on foot his title, as is before declared. Which policy of his took such effect as that he drew over with him into England the flower of all the English colonies, specially of Ulster and Meath, whereof many noblemen and gentlemen were slain with him at Wakefield, as is likewise before remembered. And after his death, when the wars between the houses were in their heat, almost all the good English blood which was left in Ireland was spent in those civil dissensions, so as the Irish became victorious over all without blood or sweat. Only that little canton of land called the English Pale, containing four small shires, did maintain a bordering war with the Irish and retain the form of English government.

But out of that little precinct there were no lords, knights, or burgesses summoned to the Parliament; neither did the King's Writ run in any other part of the kingdom; and yet upon the marches and borders, which at that time were grown so large as they took up half Dublin, half Meath, and a third part of Kildare and Louth, there was no law in use but the March Law, which in the Statutes of Kilkenny is said to be no law, but a lewd custom.

So as upon the end of these civil wars in England the English law and government was well banished out of Ireland, so as no footstep or print was left of any former reformation.

Then did King Henry the Seventh send over Sir Edward Poynings to be his Deputy, a right worthy servitor both in war and peace. The principal end of his employment was to expel Perkin Warbeck out of this kingdom; but that service being performed, that worthy Deputy, finding nothing but a common misery, took the best course he possibly could to establish a commonwealth in Ireland; and to that end he held a Parliament no less famous than that of Kilkenny, and more available for the reformation of the whole kingdom. For, whereas all wise men did ever concur in opinion that the readiest way to reform Ireland is to settle a form of civil government there conformable to that of

England, to bring this to pass Sir Edward Poynings did pass an Act whereby all the Statutes made in England before that time were enacted, established, and made of force in Ireland. Neither did he only respect the time past, but provided also for the time to come. For he caused another law to be made, that no Act should be propounded in any Parliament of Ireland but such as should be first transmitted into England and approved by the King and Council there as good and expedient for that land, and so returned back again, under the Great Seal of England. This Act, though it seemed *primâ facie* to restrain the liberty of the subjects of Ireland, yet was it made at the prayer of the Commons upon just and important cause.

For the governors of that realm, specially such as were of that country birth, had laid many oppressions upon the commons; and amongst the rest they had imposed laws upon them, not tending to the general good, but to serve private turns, and to strengthen their particular factions. This moved them to refer all laws that were to be passed in Ireland to be considered, corrected, and allowed, first by the State of England, which had always been tender and careful of the good of this people, and had long since made them a civil, rich, and happy nation if their own lords and governors there had not sent bad intelligence into England. Besides this, he took special order that the summons of Parliament should go into all the shires of Ireland, and not to the four shires only; and for that cause specially he caused all the Acts of a Parliament lately before holden by the Viscount of Gormanstown to be repealed and made void. Moreover, that the Parliaments of Ireland might want no decent or honourable form that was used in England, he caused a particular Act to pass that the lords of Ireland should appear in the like Parliament robes as the English lords are wont to wear in the Parliaments of England. Having thus established all the Statutes of England in Ireland and set in order the great Council of that realm, he did not omit to pass other laws as well for the increase of the King's revenue as the preservation of the public peace.

To abundance[1] the profits of the Crown, first he obtained a subsidy of 26s. 8d. out of every six score acres manured, payable yearly for five years; next he resumed all the Crown land which had been aliened, for the most part, by Richard Duke of York; and lastly, he procured a subsidy of poundage out of all merchandises imported and exported, to be granted to the Crown in perpetuity.

To preserve the public peace he revived the Statutes of Kilkenny. He made wilful murder high treason. He caused the Marchers to book their men for whom they should answer; and restrained the making war or peace without special commission from the State.

These laws, and others as important as these, for the making of a commonwealth in Ireland, were made in the government of Sir Edward Poynings. But these laws did not spread their virtue beyond the English Pale, though they were made generally for the whole kingdom. For the provinces without the Pale, which during the war of York and Lancaster had wholly cast off the English government, were not apt to receive this seed of reformation, because they were not first broken and mastered again with the sword. Besides, the Irish countries, which contained two-third parts of the kingdom, were not reduced to shireground, so as in them the laws of England could not possibly be put in execution. Therefore these good laws and provisions made by Sir Edward Poynings were like good lessons set for a lute that is broken and out of tune, of which lessons little use can be made till the lute be made fit to be played upon.

And that the execution of all these laws had no greater latitude than the Pale is manifest by the Statute of the thirteenth of Henry the Eighth, c. 3, which reciteth that at that time the

[1] *Abundance*, make to abound. Perhaps a misprint for *advance*.

King's laws were obeyed and executed in the four shires only; and yet then was the Earl of Surrey Lieutenant of Ireland, a governor much feared of the King's enemies and exceedingly honoured and beloved of the King's subjects. And the instructions given by the State of Ireland to John Allen, Master of the Rolls, employed into England near about the same time, do declare as much; wherein, among other things, he is required to advertise the King, that his land of Ireland was so much decayed that the King's laws were not obeyed twenty miles in compass. Whereupon grew that byword used by the Irish, viz., that they dwelt by-west the law which dwelt beyond the river of the Barrow, which is within thirty miles of Dublin. The same is testified by Baron Finglas in his discourse of the decay of Ireland, which he wrote about the twentieth year of King Henry the Eighth. And thus we see the effect of the reformation which was intended by Sir Edward Poynings.

The next attempt of reformation was made in the twenty-eigthth year of King Henry the Eighth by the Lord Leonard Gray, who was created Viscount of Garny in this kingdom, and held a Parliament wherein many excellent laws were made. But to prepare the minds of the people to obey these laws, he began first with a martial course; for, being sent over to suppress the rebellion of the Geraldines, which he performed in a few months, he afterwards made a victorious circuit round about the kingdom, beginning in Ofaly against O'Connor, who had aided the Geraldines in their rebellion; and from thence passing along through all the Irish countries in Leinster, and so into Munster, where he took pledges of the degenerate Earl of Desmond; and thence into Connaught, and thence into Ulster; and then concluded this warlike progress with the battle of Belahoo in the borders of Meath, as is before remembered.

The principal septs of the Irishry being all terrified, and most of them broken in this journey, many of their chief lords upon this Deputy's return came to Dublin and made their submissions to the Crown of England, namely, the O'Neills and O'Reillys of Ulster, MacMurrough, O'Byrne, and O'Carrol of Leinster, and the Bourkes of Connaught.

This preparation being made, he first propounded and passed in Parliament these laws which made the great alteration in the State Ecclesiastical, namely, the Act which declared King Henry the Eighth to be supreme head of the Church of Ireland; the Act prohibiting appeals to the Church of Rome; the Act for first-fruits and twentieth part to be paid to the King; the Act for faculties and dispensations; and lastly, the Act that did utterly abolish the usurped authority of the Pope. Next, for the increase of the King's revenue, by one Act he suppressed sundry abbeys and religious houses, and by another Act resumed the lands of the absentees, as is before remembered.

And for the civil government a special Statute was made to abolish the black-rents and tributes exacted by the Irish upon the English colonies; and another law enacted that the English apparel, language, and manner of living should be used by all such as would acknowledge themselves the King's subjects. This Parliament being ended, the Lord Leonard Gray was suddenly revoked and put to death in England, so as he lived not to finish the work of reformation which he had begun; which, notwithstanding, was well pursued by his successor, Sir Anthony Saint-Leger, unto whom all the lords and chieftains of the Irishry and of the degenerate English throughout the kingdom made their several submissions by indenture: which was the fourth General Submission of the Irish made since the first attempt of the conquest of Ireland, whereof the first was made to King Henry the Second, the second to King John, the third to King Richard the Second, and this last to Sir Anthony Saint-Leger in the thirty-third of Henry the Eighth.

In these indentures of submission all the Irish lords do acknowledge King Henry the Eighth to be their Sovereign Lord and King, and desire to be accepted of him as subjects. They confess the King's supremacy in all causes, and do utterly renounce the Pope's jurisdiction, which I conceive to be worth the noting, because when the Irish had once resolved to obey the King they made no scruple to renounce the Pope. And this was not only done by the mere Irish, but the chief of the degenerate English families did perform the same; as Desmond, Barry, and Roche in Munster, and the Bourkes, which bore the title of MacWilliam, in Connaught.

These submissions being thus taken, the Lord Deputy and Council for the present government of those Irish countries made certain ordinances of State not agreeable altogether with the rules of the law of England, the reason whereof is expressed in the preamble of those ordinances: "*Quia nondum sic sapiunt leges et jura, ut secundum ea iam immediatè vivere et regi possint;*"[1] the chief points or articles of which orders registered in the Council-book are these: That King Henry the Eighth should be accepted, reputed, and named KING OF IRELAND by all the inhabitants of the kingdom; that all archbishops and bishops should be permitted to exercise their jurisdiction in every diocese throughout the land; that tithes should be duly set out and paid; that children should not be admitted to benefices; that for every manslaughter and theft above 14d. committed in the Irish countries the offender should pay a fine of 40 li. to the King, and 20 li. to the captain of the country; and for every theft under 14d. a fine of 5 marks should be paid, 46s. 8d. to the captain and 20s. to the tanister; that horsemen and kern should not be imposed upon the common people to be fed and maintained by them; that the master should answer for his servants and the father for his children; that cuttings should not be made by the lord upon his

---

[1] That they do not yet know the laws well enough for immediate obedience to them.

tenants to maintain war with his neighbours, but only to bear his necessary expenses, &c.

These ordinances of State being made and published, there were nominated and appointed in every province certain orderers or arbitrators, who, instead of these Irish Brehons, should hear and determine all their controversies. In Connaught, the Archbishop of Tuam, the Bishop of Clonfert, Captain Wakeley, and Captain Ovington; in Munster, the Bishop of Waterford, the Bishop of Cork and Ross, the Mayor of Cork, and Mayor of Youghal; in Ulster, the Archbishop of Armagh and the Lord of Louth. And if any difference did arise which they could not end, either for the difficulty of the cause or for the obstinacy of the parties, they were to certify the Lord Deputy and Council, who would decide the matter by their authority.

Hereupon the Irish captains of lesser territories, which had ever been oppressed by the greater and mightier—some with risings out, others with bonaght, and others with cuttings and spendings at pleasure—did appeal for justice to the Lord Deputy, who, upon hearing their complaints, did always order that they should all immediately depend upon the King, and that the weaker should have no dependency upon the stronger.

Lastly, he prevailed so much with the greatest of them, namely, O'Neill, O'Brien, and MacWilliam, as that they willingly did pass into England and presented themselves to the King, who thereupon was pleased to advance them to the degree and honour of Earls, and to grant unto them their several countries by Letters Patents. Besides, that they might learn obedience and civility of manners by often repairing unto the State, the King, upon the motion of the same Deputy, gave each of them a house and lands near Dublin for the entertainment of their several trains.

This course did this governor take to reform the Irishry, but withal he did not omit to advance both the honour and profit of the King. For, in the Parliament which he held the thirty-third of Henry the Eighth, he caused an Act to pass which gave unto King Henry the Eighth, his heirs and successors, the name, style, and title of KING OF IRELAND; whereas before that time the Kings of England were styled but Lords of Ireland; albeit, indeed, they were absolute monarchs thereof, and had in right all royal and imperial jurisdiction and power there as they had in the realm of England. And yet, because in the vulgar conceit the name of King is higher than the name of Lord, assuredly the assuming of this title hath not a little raised the sovereignty of the King of England in the minds of this people. Lastly, this Deputy brought a great augmentation to the King's revenue by dissolving of all the monasteries and religious houses in Ireland, which was done in the same Parliament, and afterward by procuring Min and Cavendish, two skilful auditors, to be sent over out of England, who took an exact survey of all the possessions of the Crown, and brought many things into charge which had been concealed and subtracted for many years before. And thus far did Sir Anthony Saint-Leger proceed in the course of reformation, which, though it were a good beginning, yet was it far from reducing Ireland to the perfect obedience of the Crown of England. For all this while the provinces of Connaught and Ulster and a good part of Leinster were not reduced to shire-ground; and though Munster were anciently divided into counties, the people were so degenerate as no justice of assize durst execute his commission amongst them. None of the Irish lords or tenants were settled in their possessions by any grant or confirmation from the Crown, except the three great Earls before named, who, notwithstanding, did govern their tenants and followers by the Irish or Brehon Law, so as no treason, murder, rape, or theft committed in those countries was inquired of or punished by the law of England; and, consequently, no escheat, forfeiture, or fine, no revenue, certain or casual, did acrue to the Crown out of those provinces.

The next worthy governor that endeavoured to advance this reformation was Thomas Earl of Sussex, who, having thoroughly broken and subdued the two most rebellious and powerful Irish septs in Leinster, namely, the Moores and O'Connors, possessing the territories Leix and Ofaly, did by Act of Parliament third and fourth Philip and Mary, reduce those countries into two several counties, naming the one the King's and the other the Queen's County, which were the first two counties that had been made in this kingdom since the twelfth year of King John, at what time the territories then possessed by the English colonies were reduced into twelve shires, as is before expressed.

This noble Earl, having thus extended the jurisdiction of the English law into two counties more, was not satisfied with that addition, but took a resolution to divide all the rest of the Irish countries unreduced into several shires; and to that end he caused an Act to pass in the same Parliament authorising the Lord Chancellor, from time to time, to award commissions to such persons as the Lord Deputy should nominate and appoint to view and perambulate those Irish territories, and thereupon to divide and limit the same into such and so many several counties as they should think meet; which being certified to the Lord Deputy and approved by him, should be returned and enrolled in the Chancery, and from thenceforth be of like force and effect as if it were done by Act of Parliament.

Thus did the Earl of Sussex lay open a passage for the civil government into the unreformed parts of this kingdom, but himself proceeded no further than is before declared.

Howbeit, afterwards, during the reign of Queen Elizabeth, Sir Henry Sidney, who hath left behind him many monuments of a good governor in this land, did not only pursue that course which the Earl of Sussex began in reducing the Irish countries into shires and placing therein sheriffs and other ministers of the law : for first he made the Annaly, a territory in Leinster, possessed by the sept of O'Farrels, one entire shire by itself, and called it the county of Longford; and after that he divided the whole province of Connaught into six counties more; namely, Clare, which containeth all Thomond, Galway, Sligo, Mayo, Roscommon, and Leitrim. But he also had caused divers good laws to be made, and performed sundry other services tending greatly to the reformation of this kingdom. For, first, to diminish the greatness of the Irish lords, and to take from them the dependency of the common people, in the Parliament which he held eleventh of Elizabeth, he did abolish their pretended and usurped captainships and all exactions and extortions incident thereunto. Next, to settle their seigniories and possessions in a course of inheritance according to the course of the Common Law, he caused an Act to pass whereby the Lord Deputy was authorised to accept their surrenders and to regrant estates unto them, to hold of the Crown by English tenures and services. Again, because the inferior sort were loose and poor and not amenable to the law, he provided by another Act that five of the best and eldest persons of every sept should bring in all the idle persons of their surname to be justified by the law. Moreover, to give a civil education to the youth of this land in the time to come, provision was made by another law that there should be one free school, at least, erected in every diocese of the kingdom. And lastly, to inure and acquaint the people of Munster and Connaught with the English government again, which had not been in use among them for the space of two hundred years before, he instituted two Presidency Courts in those two provinces, placing Sir Edward Fitton in Connaught and Sir John Perrot in Munster.

To augment the King's revenue in the same Parliament, upon the attainder of Shane O'Neill he resumed and vested in the Crown more than half the province of Ulster; he raised the customs upon the principal commodities of the kingdom; he reformed the abuses of the Exchequer by many good orders and instructions sent out of England; and lastly, he established the composition of the Pale, in lieu of purveyance and cess of soldiers.

These were good proceedings in the work of reformation, but there were many defects and omissions withal; for though he reduced all Connaught into counties, he never sent any justices of assize to visit that province, but placed commissioners there, who governed it only in a course of discretion, part martial and part civil. Again, in the law that doth abolish the Irish captainships, he gave way for the reviving thereof again, by excepting such as should be granted by the Letters Patents from the Crown, which exception did indeed take away the force of that law. For no governor during Queen Elizabeth's reign did refuse to grant any of those captainships to any pretended Irish lord who would desire and with his thankfulness deserve the same. And again, though the greatest part of Ulster were vested by Act of Parliament in the actual and real possession of the Crown, yet was there never any seizure made thereof, nor any part thereof brought into charge, but the Irish were permitted to take all the profits without rendering any duty or acknowledgment for the same. And though the name of O'Neill were damned by that Act, and the assuming thereof made high treason, yet after that was Tirlagh Leynnagh suffered to bear that title and to intrude upon the possessions of the Crown, and yet was often entertained by the State with favour. Neither were these lands resumed by Act of eleventh of Elizabeth neglected only, for the abbeys and religious houses in Tyrone, Tyrconnel, and Fermanagh, though they were dissolved in the thirty-third of Henry the Eighth were never surveyed nor reduced into charge, but were continually possessed by the religious persons, until His Majesty, that now is, came to the Crown. And that which is more strange,—the donations of bishoprics being a flower of the Crown which the Kings of England did ever retain in all their dominions when the

Pope's usurped authority was at the highest,—there were three bishoprics in Ulster, namely, Derry, Rapho, and Clogher, which neither Queen Elizabeth, nor any of her progenitors did ever bestow, though they were the undoubted patrons thereof. So as King James was the first King of England that did ever supply those sees with bishops; which is an argument either of great negligence or of great weakness in the State and governors of those times. And thus far proceeded Sir Henry Sidney.

After him, Sir John Perrot, who held the last Parliament in this kingdom, did advance the reformation in three principal points. First, in establishing the great composition of Connaught, in which service the wisdom and industry of Sir Richard Bingham did concur with him; next, in reducing unreformed parts of Ulster into seven shires, namely, Armagh, Monaghan, Tyrone, Colerain, Donegal, Fermanagh, and Cavan; though in his time the law was never executed in these new counties by any sheriffs or justices of assize, but the people left to be ruled still by their own barbarous lords and laws. And lastly, by vesting in the Crown the lands of Desmond and his adherents in Munster, and planting the same with English, though that plantation were imperfect in many points.

After Sir John Perrot, Sir William Fitzwilliams did good service in two other points. First, in raising a composition in Munster, and then settling the possessions both of the lords and tenants in Monaghan, which was one of the last acts of State tending to the reformation of the civil government which was performed in the reign of Queen Elizabeth.

Thus we see by what degrees and what policy and success the governors of this land from time to time, since the beginning of the reign of King Edward the Third, have endeavoured to reform and reduce this people to the perfect obedience of the Crown of England. And we find that before the civil wars of York and Lancaster they did chiefly endeavour to bring back the degenerate English colonies to their duty and allegiance, not respecting the mere Irish, whom they reputed as aliens or enemies of the Crown. But after King Henry the Seventh had united the Roses, they laboured to reduce both English and Irish together, which work to what pass and perfection it was brought in the latter end of Queen Elizabeth's reign hath been before declared.

Whereof sometimes when I do consider, I do in mine own conceit compare these later governors who went about to reform the civil affairs in Ireland unto some of the Kings of Israel, of whom it is said that they were good Kings, but they did not cut down the groves and high places, but suffered the people still to burn incense and commit idolatry in them. So Sir Anthony Saint-Leger, the Earl of Sussex, Sir Henry Sidney, and Sir John Perrot were good governors, but they did not abolish the Irish customs nor execute the law in the Irish countries, but suffered the people to worship their barbarous lords and to remain utterly ignorant of their duties to God and the King.

And now I am come to the happy reign of my Most Gracious Lord and Master King James, in whose time, as there hath been a concurrence of many great felicities, so this, among others, may be numbered in the first rank, that all the defects in the government of Ireland spoken of before have been fully supplied in the first nine years of his reign, in which time there hath been more done in the work and reformation of this kingdom than in the 440 years which are past since the conquest was first attempted.

Howbeit, I have no purpose in this discourse to set forth at large all the proceedings of the State here in reforming of this kingdom since His Majesty came to the Crown, for the parts and passages thereof are so many as to express them fully would require a several treatise. Besides, I, for my part, since I have not flattered the former times, but have plainly laid open the negligence and errors of every age that is past, would not willingly seem to flatter the present by amplifying the diligence and true judgment of those servitors that have laboured in this vineyard since the beginning of His Majesty's happy reign.

I shall therefore summarily, without any amplification at all, show in what manner and by what degrees all the defects which I have noted before in the government of this kingdom have been supplied since His Majesty's happy reign began, and so conclude these observations concerning the state of Ireland.

First, then, touching the martial affairs I shall need to say little, in regard that the war which finished the conquest of Ireland was ended in almost the instant when the crown descended upon His Majesty; and so there remained no occasion to amend the former errors committed in the prosecution of the war. Howbeit, sithence His Majesty hath still maintained an army here, as well for a seminary of martial men as to give strength and countenance to the civil magistrate, I may justly observe that this army hath not been fed with coigny and livery or cess, with which extortions the soldier hath been nourished in the times of former Princes, but hath been as justly and royally paid as ever Prince in the world did pay his men of war. Besides, when there did arise an occasion of employment for this army against the rebel O'Dogherty, neither did His Majesty delay the reinforcing thereof, but instantly sent supplies out of England and Scotland; neither did the martial men dally or prosecute the service faintly, but did forthwith quench that fire whereby themselves would have been the warmer the longer it had continued, as well by the increase of their entertainment as by booties and spoil of the country. And thus much I thought fit to note touching the amendment of the errors in the martial affairs.

Secondly, for the supply of the defects in the civil government these courses have been pursued since His Majesty's prosperous reign began.

First, albeit upon the end of the war whereby Tyrone's universal rebellion was suppressed the minds of the people were broken and prepared to obedience of the law, yet the State, upon good reason, did conceive that the public peace could not be settled till the hearts of the people were also quieted by securing them from the danger of the law, which the most part of them had incurred one way or other in that great and general confusion.

Therefore, first by a general Act of State, called the Act of Oblivion, published by proclamation under the Great Seal, all offences against the Crown and all particular trespasses between subject and subject done at any time before His Majesty's reign were, to all such as would come in to the justices of assize by a certain day and claim the benefit of this Act, pardoned, remitted, and utterly extinguished, never to be revived or called in question. And by the same proclamation, all the Irishry, who for the most part in former times were left under the tyranny of their lords and chieftains, and had no defence or justice from the Crown, were received into His Majesty's immediate protection. This bred such comfort and security in the hearts of all men as thereupon ensued the calmest and most universal peace that ever was seen in Ireland.

The public peace being thus established, the State proceeded next to establish the public justice in every part of the realm; and to that end, Sir George Cary, who was a prudent governor and a just, and made a fair entry into the right way of reforming this kingdom, did in the first year of His Majesty's reign make the first sheriffs that ever were made in Tyrone and Tyrconnel, and shortly after sent Sir Edmund Pelham, Chief Baron, and myself thither, the first justices of assize that ever sat in those countries; and in that circuit we visited all the shires of that province. Besides, which visitation, though it were somewhat distasteful to the Irish lords, was sweet and most welcome to the common people, who, albeit they were rude and barbarous, yet did they quickly apprehend the difference between the tyranny and oppression under which they lived before and the just government and protection which we promised unto them for the time to come.

The law having made her progress into Ulster with so good success, Sir Arthur Chichester, who with singular industry, wisdom, and courage hath now for the space of seven years and more prosecuted the great work of reformation, and brought it well near to an absolute perfection, did in the first year of his government establish two other new circuits for justices of assize, the one in Connaught and the other in Munster. I call them new circuits, for that, although it be manifest by many records that justices itinerent have in former times been sent into all the shires of Munster and some part of Connaught, yet certain it is that in two hundred years before—I speak much within compass —no such commission had been executed in either of these two provinces. But now, the whole realm being divided into shires, and every bordering territory whereof any doubt was made in what county the same should lie being added or reduced to a county certain;—among the rest, the mountains and glynnes on the south side of Dublin were lately made a shire by itself, and called the county of Wicklow, whereby the inhabitants, which were wont to be thorns in the side of the Pale, are become civil and quiet neighbours thereof;—the streams of the public justice were derived into every part of the kingdom, and the benefit and protection of the law of England communicated to all, as well Irish as English, without distinction or respect of persons; by reason whereof the work of deriving the public justice grew so great as that there was *Magna messis, sed operarii pauci*.[1] And therefore the number of the judges in every Bench was increased, which do now every half-year, like good planets in their several spheres or circles, carry the light and influence of justice round about the kingdom ; whereas the circuits in former times went

---

[1] "The harvest truly is great, but the labourers are few."—*Luke* x. 2.

but round about the Pale, like the circuit of the Cynosura about the Pole—

"*Quæ cursu nitentiore, brevi convertitur orbe.*"

Upon these visitations of justice, whereby the just and honourable law of England was imparted and communicated to all the Irishry, there followed these excellent good effects :—

First, the common people were taught by the justices of assize that they were free subjects to the Kings of England, and not slaves and vassals to their pretended lords; that the cuttings, cosheries, cessings, and other extortions of their lords were unlawful, and that they should not any more submit themselves thereunto, since they were now under the protection of so just and mighty a Prince as both would and could protect them from all wrongs and oppressions. They gave a willing ear unto these lessons; and thereupon the greatness and power of those Irish lords over the people suddenly fell and vanished when their oppressions and extortions were taken away which did maintain their greatness. Insomuch as divers of them, who formerly made themselves owners of all by force, were now by the law reduced to this point, that, wanting means to defray their ordinary charges, they resorted ordinarily to the Lord Deputy, and made petition that by license and warrant of the State they might take some aid and contribution from their people, as well to discharge their former debts as for competent maintenance in time to come. But some of them, being impatient of this diminution, fled out of the realm to foreign countries. Whereupon we may well observe, that as extortion did banish the old English freeholder who could not live but under the law, so the law did banish the Irish lord who could not live but by extortion.

Again, these circuits of justice did, upon the end of the war, more terrify the loose and idle persons than the execution of the martial law, though it were more quick and sudden; and in a short time after did so clear the kingdom of thieves and other capital offenders as I dare affirm that for the space of five years last past there have not been found so many malefactors worthy of death in all the six circuits of this realm, which is now divided into thirty-two shires at large, as in one circuit of six shires, namely, the western circuit in England. For the truth is, that in time of peace the Irish are more fearful to offend the law than the English or any other nation whatsoever.

Again, whereas the greatest advantage that the Irish had of us in all their rebellions was our ignorance of their countries, their persons, and their actions; since the law and her ministers have had a passage among them, all their places of fastness have been discovered and laid open, all their paces cleared, and notice taken of every person that is able to do either good or hurt. It is known not only how they live and what they do, but it is foreseen what they purpose or intend to do; insomuch as Tyrone hath been heard to complain that he had so many eyes watching over him as he could not drink a full carouse of sack but the State was advertised thereof within few hours after. And, therefore, those allowances which I find in the ancient Pipe-Rolls, *Pro guidagio et spiagio*, may be well spared at this day. For the under-sheriffs and bailiffs-errant are better guides and spies in the time of peace than any were found in the time of war.

Moreover, these civil assemblies at assizes and sessions have reclaimed the Irish from their wildness, caused them to cut off their glibs and long hair, to convert their mantles into cloaks, to conform themselves to the manner of England in all their behaviour and outward forms. And because they find a great inconvenience in moving their suits by an interpreter, they do for the most part send their children to schools, especially to learn the English language; so as we may conceive an hope that the next generation will in tongue and heart and every way else become English, so as there will be no difference or distinction but the

Irish Sea betwixt us. And thus we see a good conversion and the Irish game turned again.

For heretofore the neglect of the law made the English degenerate and become Irish; and now, on the other side, the execution of the law doth make the Irish grow civil and become English.

Lastly, these general sessions now do teach the people more obedience and keep them more in awe than did the general hostings in former times. These progresses of the law renew and confirm the conquest of Ireland every half-year, and supply the defect of the King's absence in every part of the realm, in that every judge sitting in the seat of justice doth represent the person of the King himself.

These effects hath the establishment of the public peace and justice produced since His Majesty's happy reign began.

Howbeit, it was impossible to make a Commonweal in Ireland without performing another service; which was, the settling of all the estates and possessions, as well of Irish as English, throughout the kingdom. For, although that in the twelfth year of Queen Elizabeth a special law was made which did enable the Lord Deputy to take surrenders and regrant estates unto the Irishry, upon signification of Her Majesty's pleasure in that behalf, yet were there but few of the Irish lords that made offer to surrender during her reign; and they which made surrenders of entire countries obtained grants of the whole again to themselves only and to no other, and all in demesne. In passing of which grants there was no care taken of the inferior septs of people inhabiting and possessing these countries under them, but they held their several portions in the course of tanistry and gavelkind, and yielded the same Irish duties or exactions as they did before. So that upon every such surrender and grant there was but one freeholder made in a whole country, which was the lord himself; all the rest were but tenants at will, or rather tenants in villeinage, and were neither fit to be sworn in juries nor to perform any public service; and by reason of the uncertainty of their estates, did utterly neglect to build or to plant or to improve the land. And therefore, although the lord were become the King's tenant, his country was no whit reformed thereby, but remained in the former barbarism and desolation.

Again, in the same Queen's time there were many Irish lords which did not surrender, yet obtained Letters Patents of the captainships of their countries, and of all lands and duties belonging to those captainships; for the Statute which doth condemn and abolish these captainries usurped by the Irish doth give power to the Lord Deputy to grant the same by Letters Patents. Howbeit, these Irish captains, and likewise the English which which were made seneschals of the Irish countries, did by colour of these grants, and under pretence of government claim an Irish seigniory and exercise plain tyranny over the common people. And this was the fruit that did arise of the Letters Patents granted of the Irish countries in the time of Queen Elizabeth, where before they did extort and oppress the people only by colour of a lewd and barbarous custom, they did afterwards use the same extortions and oppressions by warrant under the Great Seal of the realm.

But now, since His Majesty came to the crown, two special Commissions have been sent out of England for the settling and quieting of all the possessions in Ireland, the one for accepting surrenders of the Irish and degenerate English, and for regranting estates unto them according to the course of the Common Law; the other for strengthening of defective titles. In the execution of which commissions there hath ever been had a special care to settle and secure the under-tenants, to the end there might be a repose and establishment of every subject's estate, lord and tenant, freeholder and farmer, throughout the kingdom.

Upon surrenders, this course hath been held from the beginning. When an Irish lord doth offer to surrender his country his surrrender is not immediately accepted, but a Commission is first awarded to inquire of three special points; first, of the quantity and limits of the land whereof he is reputed owner; next, how much himself doth hold in demesne and how much is possessed by his tenants and followers; and thirdly, what customs, duties, and services he doth yearly receive out of those lands. This inquisition being made and returned, the lands which are found to be the lord's proper possessions in demesne are drawn into a particular, and his Irish duties, as cosherings, cessings, rents of butter and oatmeal, and the like, are reasonably valued and reduced into certain sums of money, to be paid yearly in lieu thereof. This being done the surrender is accepted, and thereupon a grant passed, not of the whole country, as was used in former times, but of those lands only which are found in the lord's possession, and of those certain sums of money as rents issuing out of the rest. But the lands which are found to be possessed by the tenants are left unto them respectively, charged with these certain rents only in lieu of all uncertain Irish exactions.

In like manner, upon all grants which have passed by virtue of the Commission for defective titles, the Commissioners have taken special caution for preservation of the estates of all particular tenants.

And as for grants of captainships or seneschalships in the Irish countries, albeit this Deputy had as much power and authority to grant the same as any other governors had before him, and might have raised as much profit by bestowing the same if he had respected his private more than the public good, yet hath he been so far from passing any such in all his time as he hath endeavoured to resume all the grants of that kind that have been made by his predecessors, to the end the inferior subjects of the realm should make their only and immediate dependency upon the Crown. And thus we see how the greatest part of the possessions, as well of the Irish as of the English, in Leinster, Connaught, and Munster, are settled and secured since His Majesty came to the crown; whereby the hearts of the people are also settled, not only to live in peace, but raised and encouraged to build, to plant, to give better education to their children, and to improve the commodities of their lands, whereby the yearly value thereof is already increased double of that it was within these few years, and is like daily to rise higher, till it amount to the price of our land in England.

Lastly, the possessions of the Irishry in the province of Ulster, though it were the most rude and unreformed part of Ireland, and the seat and nest of the last great rebellion, are now better disposed and established than any the lands in the other provinces which have been passed and settled upon surrenders. For, as the occasion of the disposing of those lands did not happen without the special providence and finger of God, which did cast out those wicked and ungrateful traitors who were the only enemies of the reformation of Ireland; so the distribution and plantation thereof hath been projected and prosecuted by the special direction and care of the King himself; wherein His Majesty hath corrected the errors before spoken of committed by King Henry the Second and King John in distributing and planting the first conquered lands. For, although there were six whole shires to be disposed, His Majesty gave not an entire country or county to any particular person; much less did he grant *Jura Regalia* or any extraordinary liberties. For the best British undertaker had but a proportion of 3000 acres for himself, with power to create a manor and hold a Court Baron; albeit many of these undertakers were of as great birth and quality as the best adventurers in the first conquest. Again, His Majesty did not utterly exclude the natives out of this plantation with a purpose to root them out, as the Irish were excluded out of the first English colonies, but made a mixed plantation of British and Irish, that they might grow up together in one nation; only, the Irish were in some places transplanted from the woods and mountains into the plains and open countries, that, being removed, like wild fruit-trees, they might grow the milder and bear the better and sweeter fruit. And this, truly, is the masterpiece and most excellent part of the work of reformation, and is worthy indeed of His Majesty's royal pains. For when this plantation hath taken root and been fixed and settled but a few years, with the favour and blessing of God— for the Son of God Himself hath said in the Gospel, "*Omnis plantatio, quam non plantavit pater meus, eradicabitur*"[1]—it will secure the peace of Ireland, assure it to the Crown of England for ever, and, finally, make it a civil and a rich, a mighty and a flourishing, kingdom.

I omit to speak of the increase of the revenue of the Crown, both certain and casual, which is raised to a double proportion, at least, above that it was, by deriving the public justice into all parts of the realm, by settling all the possessions both of the Irish and English, by re-establishing the compositions, by restoring and resuming the customs, by reviving the tenures *in capite* and knights-service, and reducing many other things into charge which by the confusion and negligence of former times became concealed and subtracted from the Crown. I forbear likewise to speak of the due and ready bringing in of the revenue, which is brought to pass by the well-ordering of the Court of Exchequer and the authority and pains of the Commissioners for Accounts.

I might also add hereunto the encouragement that hath been given to the maritime towns and cities, as well to increase their trade of merchandise as to cherish mechanical arts and sciences, in that all their charters have been renewed and their liberties more enlarged by His Majesty than by any of his progenitors since the conquest. As likewise the care and course that hath been taken to make civil commerce and intercourse between the

[1] "Every plant which My heavenly Father hath not planted shall be rooted up."

subjects newly reformed and brought under obedience, by granting markets and fairs to be holden in their countries, and by erecting of corporate towns among them.

Briefly, the clock of the civil government is now well set, and all the wheels thereof do move in order. The strings of this Irish harp which the civil magistrate doth finger are all in tune;—for I omit to speak of the State Ecclesiastical;—and make a good harmony in this Commonweal. So as we may well conceive a hope that Ireland, which heretofore might properly be called the Land of Ire, because the irascible power was predominant there for the space of four hundred years together, will from henceforth prove a Land of Peace and Concord. And though heretofore it hath been like the lean cow of Egypt in Pharaoh's dream, devouring the fat of England, and yet remaining as lean as it was before, it will hereafter be as fruitful as the land of Canaan; the description whereof in the eighth of Deuteronomy doth in every part agree with Ireland, being,[1] "*Terra rivorum, aquarumque, et fontium; in cuius campis, et montibus, erumpunt fluviorum abyssi; terra frumenti, et hordei; terra lactis, et mellis; ubi absque ulla penuria comedes panem tuum, et rerum abundantia perfrueris.*"

And thus I have discovered and expressed the defects and errors as well in the managing of the martial affairs as of the civil, which in former ages gave impediment to the reducing of all Ireland to the obedience and subjection of the Crown of England. I have likewise observed what courses have been taken to reform the defects and errors in government and to reduce the people of this land to obedience since the beginning of the reign of King Edward the Third till the latter end of the reign of Queen Elizabeth.

[1] "A land of brooks of water, of fountains and depths that spring out of valleys and hills; a land of wheat and barley, a land of milk and honey; a land wherein thou shalt eat bread without scarceness, thou shalt not lack anything in it." Sir John Davies, omitting from the quotation vines, figs, pomegranates, and olives, fitly puts milk in their place.

And, lastly, I have declared and set forth how all the said errors have been corrected and the defects supplied under the prosperous government of His Majesty. So as I may positively conclude in the same words which I have used in the title of this discourse, that until the beginning of His Majesty's reign Ireland was never entirely subdued and brought under the obedience of the Crown of England. But since the crown of this kingdom, with the undoubted right and title thereof, descended upon His Majesty, the whole island from sea to sea hath been brought into His Highness's peaceable possession, and all the inhabitants in every corner thereof have been absolutely reduced under his immediate subjection. In which condition of subjects they will gladly continue without defection or adhering to any other Lord or King, as long as they may be protected and justly governed without oppression on the one side or impunity on the other. For there is no nation of people under the sun that doth love equal and indifferent justice better than the Irish, or will rest better satisfied with the execution thereof, although it be against themselves; so as they may have the protection and benefit of the law when upon just cause they do desire it.

A LETTER

FROM

SIR JOHN DAVIES, Knight,

ATTORNEY-GENERAL OF IRELAND,

TO

ROBERT EARL OF SALISBURY,

TOUCHING THE STATE OF MONAGHAN, FERMANAGH, AND CAVAN, WHEREIN IS A DISCOURSE CONCERNING THE CORBES AND IRENAHS OF IRELAND.

MDCVII.

A LETTER.

My most honourable good Lord,—

I AM not ignorant how little my advertisements do add unto your Lordship's knowledge of the affairs of this kingdom; forasmuch as I know your Lordship doth receive such frequent despatches from the Lord Deputy and Council here as nothing worthy of any consideration is left by them unadvertised. Besides, they knowing things *a priori*, in that they see the causes and grounds of all accidents, can give your Lordship more full and perfect intelligence than such an inferior Minister as I am, which come to understand things *a posteriori* only by the effect and by the success. Notwithstanding, because the diligence of others cannot excuse my negligence if I omit duty in this behalf, I presume still to write to your Lordship; and though I write the same things to your Lordship as are written by others in substance, yet perhaps I may sometimes add a circumstance which may give light to the matter of substance and make it clearer unto your Lordship.

After the end of the last term my Lord Deputy took a resolution to visit three counties in Ulster, namely, Monaghan, Fermanagh, and Cavan, which, being the most unsettled and unreformed parts of that province, did most of all need his Lordship's visitation at this time.

For Monaghan, otherwise called M'Mahon's country: Sir William Fitzwilliams, upon the attainder and execution of Hugh

Ro M'Mahon, chief of his name, did with good wisdom and policy divide the greatest part of that county among the natives thereof, except the Church lands, which he gave to English servitors. In which division he did allot unto five or six gentlemen sundry large demesnes, with certain rents and services; and to the inferior sort several freeholds; and withal reserved a yearly rent unto the Crown of four hundred and odd pounds; whereby the county seemed to be well settled for a year or two. Notwithstanding, the late rebellion, wherein the M'Mahons were the first actors, reversed all that was done, and brought things in this country to the old chaos and confusion. For they erected a M'Mahon among them, who became master of all; they revived the Irish cuttings and exactions, detained the Queen's rent, reduced the poor freeholders into their wonted slavery, and, in a word, they broke all the covenants and conditions contained in their Letters Patent, and thereby entitled the Crown to resume all again; they having now no other title to pretend but only the late Lord Lieutenant's promise and the King's mercy. I speak of the chief lords and gentlemen, whose estates were subject to conditions; albeit there was yet no office found[1] of the breach of those conditions. But as for the petty freeholders, whose estates were absolute, many of them, whose names were yet unknown, were slain in the late rebellion, and so attainted in law if any inquisitions thereof had been taken. Of such as did survive the wars and had their pardons, some were removed and transplanted by the tyranny of the lords, and some were driven out of the country, not daring to return to their freeholds without special countenance of the State. And thus stood the state of Monaghan.

Touching Fermanagh, otherwise called M'Guire's country: that country was never reduced to the Crown since the conquest of

---

[1] *Office found*, a law term for the finding of certain facts upon official inquest or inquisition.

Ireland, neither by attainder, surrender, or other resumption whatsoever, until Sir John Perrot's government, who caused Coconagh M'Guire, father of Hugh M'Guire, who was a principal actor in the late rebellion, and slain in Munster upon an encounter with Sir Warham St. Leger, to surrender all the country of Fermanagh, in general words, unto the late Queen, and to take Letters Patent back again, of all the country, in the like general words, to him and his heirs; whereupon was reserved a rent of one hundred and twenty beeves, arising out of certain horse and foot, and a tenure *in capite*. But this English tenure did not take away his Irish customs and exactions. He was suffered still to hold his title of M'Guire and to exercise his tyranny over the Queen's poor subjects, of whom the State took no care nor notice. Albeit there are many gentlemen who claim estate of freehold in that country by a more ancient title than M'Guire himself doth claim the chiefry. Coconagh M'Guire, having thus obtained Letters Patent, died seized of the country; and after his death, Hugh M'Guire, being his eldest son, took possession thereof, not as heir at Common Law, but as tanist and chief of his name was created M'Guire, and held it as an Irish lord until he was slain in actual rebellion, which we hold an attainder in law in this kingdom.

Hereupon, an office being found that Hugh M'Guire was killed in rebellion, one Connor Ro M'Guire, whose ancestors had been chief lords of the country, and who, being received to grace, had performed good service in those parts, had a Patent of the whole country granted unto him by the late Lord Lieutenant, and held it accordingly during the wars. Howbeit, when young Coconagh M'Guire, brother to Hugh M'Guire and second son to the old Coconagh, submitted himself to the late Lord Lieutenant, his Lordship promised him to divide the country betwixt him and Connor Ro. In performance of which promise the State here, by direction out of England, persuaded Connor Ro to surrender his Patent, which he did, and thereupon set down a division of the country allotting the greater portion to Coconagh; according to which division they have since held their several portions, but hitherto they have obtained no Letters Patent, my Lord Deputy having made stay thereof till he had seen and understood the state of the country, and established a competent number of freeholders there, which will be more conveniently and easily effected now while the land is in His Majesty's disposition than it would be if these Irish lords had estates executed or passed unto them. Upon these terms stood the estate of the chief lords of Fermanagh. But touching the inferior gentlemen and inhabitants, it was not certainly known to the State here whether they were only tenants-at-will to the chief lords, whereof the uncertain cutting which the lords used upon them might be an argument, or whether they were freeholders yielding of right to their chief lord certain rights and services, as many of them do allege, affirming that the Irish cutting was an usurpation and a wrong. This was a point wherein the Lord Deputy and Council did much desire to be resolved, the resolution whereof would give them much light how to make a just and equal distribution of the country, and to settle every particular inhabitant thereof. Thus much concerning the state of Fermanagh.

As for Cavan, otherwise called Breny Orelye or O'Reilly's country, the late troubles had so unsettled the possessions thereof, which indeed were never well distinguished and established, as it was doubtful in whom the chiefry of that country rested; or if the chief lord had been known, yet was it as uncertain what demesnes or duties he ought to have. And for the particular tenants, they were so many times removed and rejected, as their titles and possessions were as doubtful as the lord's. True it is that Sir John Perrot, being Deputy, purposed the reformation and settling of this country; and to that end indentures were drawn between himself, in behalf of the late Queen on the one part, and Sir John O'Reilly, then chief lord of the country, on the other; whereby Sir John O'Reilly did covenant to surrender the whole unto the Queen, and Sir John Perrott, on the other part, did covenant that Letters Patent should be made unto him of the whole. Howbeit, there followed no effect of this; for neither was there any surrender made by Sir John O'Reilly, neither was there any Patent granted unto him during Sir John Perrot's time. Marry, afterwards, when the late Lord Chancellor and Sir Henry Wallop were Lords Justices, certain Commissioners were sent down to divide the country into baronies and to settle the chief septs and families therein, which they did in this manner:—The whole country being divided into seven baronies, they assigned two unto Sir John O'Reilly, free from all public charges and contributions; a third barony they allotted to Philip O'Reilly, brother to Sir John O'Reilly; a fourth to Edmond O'Reilly, uncle to Sir John O'Reilly; a fifth to the sons of one Hugh O'Reilly, surnamed the Prior; and out of the three baronies whereof Sir John O'Reilly was not possessed, they reserved unto him a chief rent of 10s. out of every poll, being a portion of land containing threescore acres or thereabouts, in lieu of all Irish cuttings and taxes. As for the other two baronies possessed by the septs of M'Rernon and M'Gaurol, being remote and bordering upon O'Rorke's country, they were neglected and left subject still to the Irish exactions of the chief lord; but to the Crown they reserved upon the whole country 220 beeves, which the Deputy ever since hath taken for his provision. This division or establishment was made and reduced to writing, as one of the Commissioners who is yet living told me; who told me withal that they were well paid for their pains, for he that had least had an hundred fat beeves given him by the country; yet cannot we find any return of this Commission either in the Council-book or in the Chancery. So as hitherto there were only projects made for the settling of the country, but nothing was really and effectually done; none of the rules and ceremonies of the law observed, either by accepting surrenders or regranting the land back again, or by any other lawful conveyance or execution of estates. After this Sir John O'Reilly died in rebellion, whereupon his brother, Philip O'Reilly, took upon him the name of O'Reilly, and possessed himself of the country as tanist and chief lord, according to the Irish custom; and being so possessed, was slain in rebellion. After his death Edmond O'Reilly, his uncle, entered in like manner, and was killed in actual rebellion. Since the death of Edmond none of that sept was elected or created O'Reilly, but the chiefry of the country stood doubtful till the end of the wars. Then a niece of the Earl of Ormond, being the widow of Mulmora O'Reilly, eldest son of Sir John O'Reilly, which Mulmora had been always loyal, and was slain on the Queen's part, supposing that Sir John O'Reilly held the country by grant from the late Queen—which, indeed, he never did—caused an inquisition to be taken, whereby it was found that Sir John O'Reilly was seized of the country in fee, and died seized; after whose death the country descended to Mulmora, who likewise died seized, his heir being within age and His Majesty's ward. Thereupon she made suit to Sir George Cary, then Lord Deputy, as well for the grant of the wardship as for the assignment of her dower; whereas, indeed, the land never descended, according to the course of the Common Law, but now was ever held by tanis, according to the Irish custom, whereby there could grow neither wardships nor dower; for, the tanist coming in by election, neither did his heir ever inherit, neither was his wife ever endowed. Howbeit, Sir George Cary, by a warrant from the Council Table only, did assign unto her the third part of the profit of the country, and gave her withal the custody of the body of her son; but the custody of the land during the King's pleasure he committed unto one Mulmora O'Reilly, great-uncle to the supposed ward, whereof the poor gentleman hath made little benefit, because, not being created O'Reilly by them, they would not suffer him to cut and exact, like an Irish lord, neither would they suffer him to receive the establishment made by the Commissioners, because it had been broken and rejected by Philip and Edmond, who since held the country as tanist or Irish chieftains. In these uncertain terms stood the possessions of Brevye, which we now call the county of Cavan.

I thought it not impertinent to show unto your Lordship how unsettled the possessions of these countries were before my Lord Deputy began his journey, that it may appear how needful it was that the Lord Deputy should descend in person to visit those countries, whereby he might have opportunity to discover and understand the true and particular state, both of the possessions and possessors thereof, before he gave warrants for passing the same by Letters Patent unto any, and thereby prevent that error which hath formerly been committed in passing all Tyrone to one, and Tyrconnel to another, and other large territories to O'Dogherty and Randal M'Sorley, without any respect of the King's poor subjects who inhabit and hold the lands under them, whereby the patentees are made little kings, or rather tyrants, over them. Insomuch as they now being wooed and prayed by the State, cannot yet be drawn to make freeholders for the service of the Commonwealth, which, before the passing of their Patents, they would gladly and humbly have yielded unto.

The state, therefore, of the three counties before named standing in such terms as I have before expressed, my Lord Deputy, accompanied with the Lord Chancellor, the Lord Chief-Justice, Sir Oliver Lambert, and Sir Garret Moore, and being also waited upon by myself, who was for this service joined in commission of assize and gaol delivery with the Chief-Justice, began this journey the nineteenth day of July last, being Saturday, and lodged that night and the next at the Abbey of Mellifont, Sir

Garret Moore's house. On Monday night his Lordship camped in the field upon the borders of Ferney, which is the inheritance of the Earl of Essex; and albeit we were to pass through the wastest and wildest parts of all the north, yet had we only for our guard six or seven score foot and fifty or threescore horse, which is an argument of a good time and of a confident Deputy; for in former times, when the State enjoyed the best peace and security, no Lord Deputy did ever venture himself into those parts without an army of eight hundred or one thousand men. The third night after our departure from Mellifont we came to the town of Monaghan, which doth not deserve the name of a good village, consisting of divers scattered cabins or cottages, whereof the most part are possessed by the cast soldiers of that garrison. In the northmost part thereof there is a little fort, which is kept by the foot-company of Sir Edward Blaney, who is seneschal or governor of that county by patent. In the midst of this village there is a foundation of a new castle, which, being raised ten or twelve feet from the ground, and so left and neglected for the space of almost two years, is now ready to fall into ruin again, albeit His Majesty's charge in building hath already been twelve hundred pounds at least. My Lord Deputy was as much displeased at the sight thereof as the chief lords of the country are pleased and comforted therewith, because if it were erected and finished in that form as was intended, it would at all times be a bridle unto their insolency; for the M'Mahons undoubtedly are the proudest and most barbarous sept among the Irish, and do ever soonest repine and kick and spurn at the English government. My Lord Deputy, having pitched his tents about a quarter of a mile from the town, did presently distinguish the business that was to be done. The determining of matters of the Crown and the hearing of personal petitions touching debt and trespass he left wholly to the justices of the assize and gaol delivery, and referred only to himself and the Lord Chancellor the consideration of such petitions as should be made unto him touching the lands and possessions of that country; which business, because it was the principal, and taken in hand by my Lord Deputy himself, I will first trouble your Lordship with the relation thereof.

His Lordship first propounded to the inhabitants of the country two principal questions in writing, viz., first, what lands they were at that instant possessed of; and secondly, what lands they claimed, either by Patent from the Crown or by promise from the State. When they had given in their several answers to these questions, my Lord Deputy thought meet to inform himself of the particular state of the country by perusing the Book of Division made by Sir William Fitzwilliams, which remaining among the Rolls in the Chancery, the Lord Chancellor had brought with him of purpose for this service. By that book it did appear that the county of Monaghan was divided into five baronies, viz., Dartrey, Monaghan, Cremorne, Trough, and Donamayn; that these five baronies contain an hundred ballibetaghs, viz., Dartrey twenty-one, Monaghan twenty-one, Cremorne twenty-two, Trough fifteen, and Donamayn twenty-two; that every ballibetagh,[1] which signifieth in the Irish tongue a town able to maintain hospitality, containeth sixteen taths; every tath containeth threescore English acres or thereabouts; so as every ballibetagh containeth nine hundred and sixty acres. The extent of the whole country, containing one hundred ballibetaghs, is eighty-six thousand acres, beside the Church land. All this country, albeit it were resumed and rested actually in the Crown, by the act of attainder of Shane O'Neill, notwithstanding the M'Mahons being still permitted to hold the possession, no man sought to have any grant thereof until Walter Earl of Essex obtained the whole barony of Donamayn, otherwise called the Ferry and Clankawell, to himself and his

---

[1] *Ballibetagh. Balli* or *baile* as prefix indicates an inhabited place; *biatach* distinguished in Old Irish a farmer who held his land rent-free, in return for which he was bound to entertain travellers and the soldiers of his chief when on a march.

heirs; and afterwards, upon the execution of Hugh Ro M'Mahon, chief of his name, Sir William Fitzwilliams divided and disposed the other baronies in this manner: in the Dartrey, five ballibetaghs were granted in demesne unto Brian M'Hugh Oge M'Mahon, then reputed chief of his name, and the heirs-males of his body, rendering thirty pounds rent, viz., six pounds for every ballibetagh; the other sixteen ballibetaghs were divided among the ancient inhabitants of that barony, some having a great portion allotted, and some a less. Howbeit, every one did render a yearly rent of twenty shillings out of every tath, whereof twelve shillings and sixpence was granted to Brian M'Hugh Oge M'Mahon as a chief-rent in lieu of all other duties, and seven and sixpence was reserved to the Crown, which plot was observed in every of the other baronies; so as out of every ballibetagh containing sixteen taths the Lord had ten pounds and the King six.

In Monaghan, Rosse Bane M'Mahon had likewise five ballibetaghs granted unto him with the like estate, rendering to the Queen £30 rent, and the like chief-rents as aforesaid out of nine ballibetaghs more. And in the same baronies Patrick M'Art Moyle had three ballibetaghs allotted unto him with the like estate, rendering £18 rent to the Queen, and the like chief-rent out of all the other four.

In Cremorne, Euer M'Collo M'Mahon, who was the first of that name that entered into the late rebellion, and is now farmer to my Lord of Essex of all his land in that country, had five ballibetaghs in demesne granted unto him and the heirs-male of his body, rendering £30 rent to the Crown, and the like chief-rent out of twelve other ballibetaghs; and in the same barony one Patrick Duffe M'Collo M'Mahon had two ballibetaghs and a half assigned to him in demesne, rendering £15 rent, and the like chief-rent out of two other baronies and a half.

In the Trough, containing only fifteen ballibetaghs, Patrick M'Rena had three ballibetaghs and twelve taths in demesne given

IN MONAGHAN.

unto him with the like estate, rendering £22 rent as aforesaid, and the like chief-rent out of seven other ballibetaghs; and in the same barony one Brian Oge M'Mahon, brother to Hugh Ro, who was executed, had the like estate granted unto him in three ballibetaghs, rendering £18 rent in like manner, and the like chief-rent out of two other ballibetaghs; and under this condition, that if the patentee or the assigns did not within five years build a castle upon some part of the land contained in their Patents, their several grants to be void.

Thus it appeared that these four baronies were then bestowed among the chief lords or gentlemen of that country; and as they had their demesnes and rents allotted unto them, so the inferior inhabitants, which were so many in number as it is not fit to trouble your Lordship with the list of their particular names, were all named in the Book of Division, and had their several portions of land granted unto them and to their heirs. Howbeit, the estates made to these petty freeholders were not subject to any conditions to defeat the same, but only *nomine pœnæ* for nonpayment of their several rents; whereas in every grant made to the lords there was a threefold proviso, viz., that if any of them took upon him the name of M'Mahon, or did fail of payment of the Queen's rent, or entered into rebellion and were thereof attainted, their Letters Patent should be void.

Thus the temporal lands were disposed. For the Church land, the Abbey of Clones, which was the only abbey of any value in that country, was formerly demised to Sir Henry Drake for years; but the rest of the spiritual lands, which the Irish call termons, they were granted to sundry servitors, rendering ten shillings to the Crown for every tath, which out of all the Church land amounted to £70 per annum or thereabouts; but as well these patentees as the former did all fail in their performance of the conditions whereupon their several estates depended, so as there wanted nothing but an office to be found thereof for the making void of all their Patents. And therefore as soon as the state of the possessions of this country did appear unto my Lord Deputy to stand in such sort as is before expressed, his Lordship forthwith commanded me to draw a special commission, directed among others to the Chief-Justice and myself, to inquire as well of the breach of the conditions contained in the grants before mentioned, as also of all escheated and concealed lands in that county. Accordingly, the commission was drawn and sealed in the haniper, in the execution whereof we impannelled as many of the patentees themselves as appeared at that sessions to inquire of the articles contained in the commission; so as they themselves found their own Letters Patent void, some for non-payment of the King's rent, and others for not building of castles within the time prescribed. Besides, they found divers of the inferior freeholders to have been slain in the late rebellion, whereby eight or nine ballibetaghs were escheated to the Crown, every ballibetagh, as I said before, containing nine hundred and fifty acres or thereabouts; which office being found, there rested in the possession of the Crown the greatest part of that county. This being done, my Lord Deputy entered into council in what manner he might best dispose and resettle the same again, according to his instructions received out of England in that behalf. Wherein, albeit his Lordship did resolve to determine of nothing finally before his return to Dublin, where, with the rest of the Council, he proposed to digest all the business of this journey; yet, having an intent to make some alterations of the former division, his Lordship acquainted the principal gentlemen and lords therewith, moving them to give their free consents thereunto, to the end that those small alterations might not breed any difference or discord among them. And thereupon his Lordship did in a manner conclude that Brian M'Hugh Oge should be restored to all that he had by the former division, except one or two ballibetaghs, which he was well contented should be disposed to two young children, his near kinsmen, for which he was promised to receive recompense out of the lands escheated within his barony. That Patrick M'Art Moyle should likewise be restored *in integram*. Howbeit, he was not well contented therewith, alleging That my Lord Lieutenant, when he received him into grace, promised to make him equal in possessions with Brian M'Hugh Oge; but my Lord Deputy found no easy way to perform that promise, notwithstanding his Lordship designed unto him one ballibetagh more, being a parcel of the barony of Trough, which, lying upon the border of Tyrone, hath been possessed of late by the Earl, who pretended that it is a parcel of his country. That Rosse Bane M'Mahon should likewise be re-established in all his former possessions, one ballibetagh excepted, which he frankly gave to one of his kinsmen, who was forgotten in the last division. That Patrick M'Renna and Brian Oge M'Mahon should hold all their lands and rents without any alteration at all. But the greatest change was to be made in the barony of Cremorne, the greatest part whereof was by the former division assigned to Euer M'Collo, who, notwithstanding, never enjoyed any part thereof; because one Art M'Rory M'Mahon, an active and desperate fellow, who had a very small portion given him by Sir William Fitzwilliams, making claim to that whole barony, did ever since with strong hand withhold the possession thereof from Euer M'Collo; therefore, not without consent of Euer himself, his Lordship assigned to Art M'Rory five ballibetaghs in that barony. And because a place called Ballilargan, containing two ballibetaghs, lieth in the midway between Monaghan and the Newry, which two towns are distant the one from the other twenty-four miles; and forasmuch as Monaghan, being an inland town, cannot be supplied with victuals but from the Newry, and that it is a matter of great difficulty in time of war to convey victuals twenty-four miles, having no place of safety to rest in by the way, therefore his Lordship thought it very necessary for the service of the State to reserve those two ballibetaghs, and to pass some estate thereof to the governor of Monaghan, who doth undertake within short time to build a castle thereupon at his own charges.

These seven ballibetaghs being resumed from Euer M'Collo, he hath yet allotted to him and his sons in demesne and in chief ten ballibetaghs or thereabouts; albeit Patrick Duffy M'Collo, his kinsman, doth still hold his five ballibetaghs according to the first division. This resumption was made upon Euer M'Collo for two causes; first, in regard the State shall now put him in quiet possession of a good part of the barony, whereas before he did not enjoy any part thereof; secondly, because he holdeth a whole barony in farm from my Lord of Essex, wherein he hath so good a pennyworth as he is grown since the wars to be of greater wealth than all the rest of his name besides.

Thus much was intended for the principal gentlemen and lords of the country. As for the petty freeholders, such of them as have survived the wars, and not been since pardoned, do own good estates in law still, and need only to be established in their several possessions; all which his Lordship hath a purpose to do by a general order. But the lands of such as were slain in rebellion, his Lordship allotted two or three ballibetaghs thereof, lying in the barony of Monaghan, unto divers cast soldiers dwelling in that poor town, which will be a good strength to that garrison; the remnant, being scattered in the other baronies, his Lordship hath disposed to such of the inhabitants as were commended for their inclination to prove civil and loyal subjects. Lastly, the patentees of the spiritual or termon lands, making suit to his Lordship to be restored to their several portions granted unto them upon the former division, his Lordship thought fit to extend the like favour unto them as he had done to the Irish. And this is the effect of that business which his Lordship reserved unto himself, wherein his Lordship doth make this a year of jubilee to the poor inhabitants of this county of Monaghan, because every man shall return to his own house, be restored to his ancient possessions, and withal have the arrear of rent to the King remitted; which is indeed a great matter, for the arrear of this country doth amount to £6000 at least.

Touching the service performed in this country by the justices of assize : albeit they found few prisoners in the gaols, the most part being bailed by Sir Edward Blaney, to the end the fort where the gaol is kept might not be pestered with them, yet when such as were bailed came in upon their recognisances, the number was greater than we expected. One Grand Jury was so well chosen as they found with good expedition all the bills of indictment true ; but, on the other side, the juries that were impanneled for trial of the prisoners did acquit them as fast, and found them not guilty, which, whether it was done for favour or for fear it is hard to judge. For the whole county consisting of three or four names only, viz., M'Mahon, M'Rena, M'Cabe, and O'Connaly, the chief was ever of one of those names, and of these names the jury did consist; so that it was impossible to try him but by his kinsmen, and therefore it was probable that the malefactors were acquitted for favour. But, on the other part, we were induced to think that fear might be the cause, forasmuch as the poor people seemed very unwilling to be sworn of the juries, alleging that, if they condemned any man, his friends, in revenge, would rob or burn or kill them for it, and that the like mischief had happened to divers jurors since the last session holden there : such is the barbarous malice and impiety of this people. Notwithstanding, when we had punished one jury with good round fines and imprisonment for acquitting some prisoners contrary to direct and pregnant evidence, another jury being impanneled for the trial of others found two notorious malefactors guilty, whereof one was a notable thief and the other a receiver of thieves, both which were presently executed, and their execution struck some terrror in the best men of the country; for the beef which they eat in their houses is for the most part stolen out of the English Pale, and for that purpose every one of them keepeth a cunning thief, which he calleth his cater. Brian Oge M'Mahon and Art M'Rory, two of the principal gentlemen before named, were indicted for the receiving of such stealths; but they acknowledging their faults upon their knees before my Lord Deputy, had their pardon granted unto them. So that I believe stolen flesh will not be so sweet unto them hereafter.

When we had delivered the gaol we impanneled another jury, to inquire of the state of the Church in that county, giving them these special articles in charge, viz., how many parish churches there were in that county, who were patrons, who were incumbents, which of the churches were sufficiently repaired and what decayed, of what yearly value they were, what glebe, tithes, or other duties belonged unto every church, and who took the profits thereof.

This we did by virtue of that great Commission which was sent out of England about twelve months since, whereby the Commissioners have authority, among other things, to inquire of these points, and thereupon to take order for the re-edifying and the repairing of the churches, and for the placing of sufficient incumbents therein. This point of that Commission was not beforetime put in execution anywhere, albeit it was sundry times moved at the Council table that somewhat might be done therein; but my Lords the Bishops that sit at the board, being not very well pleased that laymen should intermeddle with ecclesiastical matters, did ever answer that motion in this manner: Let us alone with that business; take you no care for that; we will see it effected, we warrant you. Notwithstanding, there hath been so little care taken as that the greatest part of the churches within the Pale lie still in their ruins, so as the common people (whereof many without doubt would conform themselves) have no place to resort unto where they may hear Divine Service. This consideration moved us to inquire of the state of the Church in these

IN MONAGHAN.

unreformed counties. The inquisition presented unto us in this county was in Latin, because the principal jurors were vicars and clerks. It appeared that the churches for the most part are utterly waste, that the King is patron of all, and that the incumbents are Popish priests, instituted by bishops authorised from Rome, yet many of them, like other old priests of Queen Mary's time in England, ready to yield to conformity.

When we had received this particular information it was thought meet to reserve it, and to suspend and stay all proceedings thereupon until the Bishop of Derry, Raphoe, and Clogher (which three dioceses comprehend the greatest part of Ulster, albeit they be now united for one man's benefit) shall arrive out of England, whose absence, being two years since he was elected by His Majesty, hath been the chief cause that no course hath been hitherto taken to reduce this poor people to Christianity; and therefore *majus peccatum habet.*

Lastly, for the civil government of this county we made several orders; first, for the building of a gaol and sessions-house, we imposed a tax upon the country, by consent of the chief gentlemen and freeholders, of £40 sterling, and for the surplusage of the charge we moved my Lord Deputy and Council to promise an allowance out of the fines and casualties of that county; next, for the erecting of a free school and maintenance of a schoolmaster in Monaghan, we prevailed with the chief lords, so far as they yielded, to contribute £20 a year to that use; finally, we revived and enlarged sundry former orders made for the mending of highways, clearing of paths, and the bringing of lazy and idle men to justice, &c.

This is the effect of all our proceedings in the county of Monaghan.

From Monaghan we went the first night to the ruins of the Abbey of Clones, where we camped; and passing from thence through ways almost impassable for our carriages by reason of the woods and bogs, we came the second night after to the south side of Lough Erne, and pitched our tents over against the island of Devenish, a place being prepared for the holding of our sessions for Fermanagh in the ruins of an abbey there. Here my Lord Deputy distinguished the business, as he had formerly done in the county of Monaghan, reserving unto himself the disposition and settling of the lands of inheritance, and leaving unto us the ordinary matters, both criminal and civil.

For the lands of inheritance in Fermanagh, they stood not in the same terms as the lands of Monaghan; for the seigniory or chiefry and the demesne lands that were the inheritance of M'Guire himself were reduced and rested in the Crown, by two several inquisitions found after the death of Hugh M'Guire, the arch-rebel, of whom I have spoken before—the one found in Munster (where shortly after he was slain in actual rebellion) by special commission, and the other in Fermanagh, by the late Lord Chief Baron, by virtue of his office of Chief Baron, two years since, when he was justice of assize in that county; both which offices are returned and remain of record, the one in the Chancery and the other in the Exchequer. But forasmuch as the greatest part of the inhabitants of that country did claim to be freeholders of their several possessions, who, surviving the late rebellion, had never been attainted, but having received His Majesty's pardon, stood upright in law,—so as we could not clearly entitle the Crown to their lands, except it were in point of conquest, a title which the State here hath not at any time taken hold of for the King against the Irish which upon the conquest were not dispossessed of their lands, but were permitted to die seized thereof in the King's allegiance; albeit they hold the same, not according to the course of the Common Law, but by the custom of tanistry, whereby the eldest of every sept claimed a chiefry over the rest, and the inferior sort divided their possessions after the manner of gavelkind,—therefore it was thought meet to impannel a jury of the most sufficient inhabitants to inquire and present how many freeholds there were, and what lands they held in this county, and what certain rents and services they yielded to the M'Guires or other chieftains and tanists in ancient time. Though this was a business of some labour, because the custom of gavelkind had made such petty fractions and divisions of the possessions of this county as the number of freeholders was exceeding great, yet within two days they brought in their inquisition in Irish, which, being translated into English, appeared to be confused in general and without method; wherewith my Lord Deputy not being satisfied, his Lordship having taken a resolution to visit the fort and castle of Ballyshannon in Tyrconnel, being situate on the north-west end of Lough Erne, and not distant from our camp above twenty English miles, commanded me, in the meantime of his Lordship's absence, to call the Grand Jury who had made the former presentment, and with them the chief inhabitants of every barony, and, by conference with them, to digest the business against his return, which was done in this order.

First we thought meet to distinguish the possessions; next to inquire of the particular possessors thereof. Touching the possessions, we found Fermanagh to be divided into seven baronies, viz., Maghera Boy, Clanauley, Clankelley, Maghera Stephanagh, Tirecannada, Knockninney, and Turath. Every of these baronies containeth seven ballibetaghs and a half of land, chargeable with M'Guire's rent and other contributions of the country; every ballibetagh is divided into four quarters of lands, and every quarter into four taths, so as a ballibetagh containeth sixteen taths, as it doth in Monaghan. But the measure of this country is far larger. Besides, the freeland, whereof there is good quantity in every barony, is no parcel of the seven ballibetaghs and a half whereof the barony is said to consist. For these reasons Fermanagh, containing but fifty-one ballibetaghs and a half of chargeable lands, is well-nigh of as large an extent as Monaghan, which hath in it an hundred ballibetaghs.

Touching the free land, we found it to be of three kinds; Church land or termon land, as the Irish call it; secondly, the mensall land of M'Guire; thirdly, lands given to certain septs privileged among the Irish, viz., the lands of the chroniclers, rhymers, and galloglasses.

For the monastery land, we found no other than that which belonged to the Abbey of Lisgoole, which doth not exceed the quantity of two ballibetaghs, and lieth for the most part in the barony of Clanauley. The Church land was either monastery land, corbe land, or herinachs' land; for it did not appear unto us the Bishop had any land in demesne, but certain mensall duties of the corbes and herinachs; neither did we find the parsons and vicars had any glebe lands at all in this country.

But the lands belonging to the corbes and herinachs are of a far greater quantity, and are found in every barony. I had heard of the name of a corbe and of an herinach divers times since I came into this kingdom, and would gladly have learned of our clergymen at Dublin what kind of religious persons they were, but could never be satisfied by any; and therefore at this time I was the more curious and inquisitive to inform myself of these ecclesiastical persons, the like whereof are not to be found in any other part of Christendom, nor in Ireland neither, but only in the countries that are mere Irish. When, therefore, we came to inquire of the quantity of termon lands, I called unto me one of the best-learned vicars in all the country, and one that had been a brehon and had some skill in the Civil and Common Laws, and with much ado I got from him thus much light for the understanding of this matter. He told me that the word termon doth signify in the Irish tongue a liberty or freedom, and that all Church lands whatsoever are called termon lands by the Irish, because they were ever free from all impositions and cuttings of the temporal lords and had the privilege of sanctuary; so as no temporal serjeant or officer might enter to arrest any person upon these lands, but the bishops' officers only; howbeit, in common understanding among us that are English we call such only termon lands as were in the possession of corbes or herinachs. For the name of corbe, I could not learn that it had any signification in the Irish tongue; some call him in Latin *Converbius*, but such as are of best understandings call him *Plebanus*, and they yield the reason of that name, *Quia plebi ecclesiasticæ præest*. I collect by that which they tell me, that he was a prior or a resident of a collegiate church; for he did not only possess a good quantity of glebe lands, the tenants and occupiers whereof were called termon-men, and had privilege of clergy, but he had also some rectories appropriate, whereof he had that portion of tithes which belonged to the parson, and had withal the presentation of the vicarage. He had always his place or seat in a mother-church, where he had a certain number of priests serving with him; in the cathedral church he had a stall in the choir and a voice in the chapter. And this corbship is named a dignity in the register at Rome; for all dignities in cathedral churches and all benefices of value in this kingdom are contained in a register at Rome, and the Pope at this day doth collate unto them; and until this day the parsons presented have enjoyed the benefices in this mere Irish country by colour of the Pope's collation. Lastly, this corbeship was in a manner hereditary; for though the corbe were ever in orders, yet was he in this Irish country usually married, or if he were not married he had children; and after his death, if any of his sons were qualified with learning, he was chosen by the Dean and Chapter to be corbe; and, if none of his sons were capable, another of that sept or surname was chosen. Without doubt these corbeships, being in the nature of collegiate churches, are vested in the Crown by the Statute of dissolution of monasteries, and accordingly some of them have been reduced into charge; but there are many whereof no inquisition hath been found, but concealed as detained by the Irish unto this day. And that your Lordship may perceive I weave not this web out of my own brain, but that I have authority for that which I deliver, I will here insert a certificate in Latin made unto me by an Irish scholar whose opinion I required in this matter, which by chance I have now among my papers; for the most part of these things I have set down out of my own memory, being now at Waterford, and having left the notes of our former journey at Dublin.

The scholar's opinion was this : "*Corbanatus, sive plebanatus, dignitas est; et modo ad regem pertinet, sed antea ad papam; in matrici ecclesia debet necessario esse, initiatus sacris ordinibus, omnesque decimas pertinentes ad hunc debet habere et beneficia adjuncta huic ipsius sunt, eorumque conferentiam habet et presentationem. Dictum hoc nomen, quia populo et plebi ecclesiasticæ matricis ecclesiæ præfuit, certum numerum sacerdotum quasi collegialium debet habere secum, primum stallum in sua ecclesia habet. Habet etiam stallum vacuum in ecclesia cathedrali, et vocem in omni capitulo, tam publico, quam privato. Inscribitur Romano registro, ideoque dignitas est.*"[1]

Of these corbeships, the best in these parts is at Clones, in the county of Monaghan, which M'Mahon himself procured to be conferred upon his eldest son, being but a boy, in the time of the late rebellion. It was long before granted unto Sir Henry Duke for years, and is now in the possession of Sir Francis Rushe, who married one of Sir Henry Duke's daughters. There is another at Derough in Fermanagh, which is likewise brought

---

[1] The sense of this is embodied in the previous description. Usher described the herenach as in deacon's orders, with office partly ecclesiastical and partly lay. He lived on the Church land, and distributed its profits to the bishop and clergy, and to the repair of churches and maintenance of hospitality. He presided over the inferior clergy, and was almost a bishop. Herenach or Erenach (there was no *k*) may be air-inech, as the head or manager.

into charge. There are others in O'Rourke's country; others in Upper Ossory and in Ormond, and in many other places which are not yet discovered. Thus much touching the nature and name of a corbe and of a herinach.

For the herinach, there are few parishes of any compass in extent where there is not an herinach, which, being an officer of the Church, took beginning in this manner: When any lord or gentleman had a direction to build a church, he did first dedicate some good portion of land to some saint or other whom he chose to be his patron; then he founded the church, and called it by the name of that saint, and then gave the land to some clerk not being in orders, and to his heirs for ever with this intent, that he should keep the church clean and well repaired, keep hospitality, and give alms to the poor for the soul's health of the founder. This man and his heirs had the name of errenagh. The errenagh was also to make a weekly commemoration of the founder in the church.

He had always *primam tonsuram*, but took no other orders; he had a voice in the Chapter, when they consulted about their revenues, and paid a certain yearly rent to the Bishop. Besides a fine upon marriage of every one of his daughters, which they call a loughhimpy, he gave a subsidy to the Bishop at his first entrance into his bishopric.

The certainty of all which duties appear in the Bishop's register, and these duties grew unto the Bishop; first, because the herinach could not be created nor the church dedicated without the consent of the Bishop. We are yet doubtful whether these lands possessed by the herinachs be yet reduced to the Crown, because the Statute of Chauntries is not yet enacted in this kingdom; but certain it is that these men possessed all the glebe lands, which belongeth yearly to such as have care of souls, and therefore when they shall be resumed it were meet they should be added to the parsonages and vicarages, whereby they may be found competent livings for able ministers which may be placed hereafter in these parts; for now, albeit there be in every parish both a parson and a vicar, yet both their livings being put together are not sufficient to feed an honest man. For the tithes of every parish within the diocese of Clogher, which comprehendeth Monaghan and almost all Fermanagh, are divided into four parts, whereof the parson, being commonly no priest, hath two parts; the vicar, who is ever a priest and serveth the cure, hath one-fourth part; and the Bishop hath another fourth part, which God knoweth in these poor waste countries doth arise to very small portions. And thus we found the state of the Church land in this country.

Touching M'Guire's mensal lands, which were free from all common charges and contributions of the country, because they yielded a large proportion of butter and meal and other provisions for M'Guire's table; albeit the jury and other inhabitants did set forth these mensal lands in certainty, which, lying in several baronies, did not in quantity exceed four ballibetaghs, the greatest thereof being in the possession of one M'Manus and his sept, yet touching the certainty of the duties or provisions yielded unto M'Guire out of these mensal lands, they referred themselves unto an old parchment roll, which they called an indenture, remaining in the hands of one O'Bristan, a chronicler and principal brehon of that country. Whereupon O'Bristan was sent for, who lived not far from the camp, but was so aged and decrepit as he was scarce able to repair unto us. When he was come we demanded of him the sight of that ancient roll, wherein, as we were informed, not only the certainty of M'Guire's mensal duties did appear, but also the particular rents and other services which were answered to M'Guire out of every part of the country. The old man, seeming to be much troubled with this demand, made answer that he had such a roll in his keeping before the war, but that in the late rebellion it was burned among other of his papers and books by certain English soldiers. We were told by some that were present that this was not true; for they affirmed that they had seen the roll in his hands since the war. Thereupon my Lord Chancellor, being then present with us—for he did not accompany my Lord Deputy to Ballyshannon, but stayed behind in the camp—did minister an oath unto him, and gave him a very serious charge to inform us truly what was become of the roll. The poor old man, fetching a deep sigh, confessed that he knew where the roll was, but that it was dearer to him than his life, and therefore he would never deliver it out of his hands unless my Lord Chancellor would take the like oath that the roll should be restored unto him again. My Lord Chancellor, smiling, gave him his word and his hand that he should have the roll redelivered unto him if he would suffer us to take a view and a copy thereof. And thereupon the old brehon drew the roll out of his bosom, where he did continually bear it about him. It was not very large, but it was written on both sides in a fair Irish character; howbeit, some part of the writing was worn and defaced with time and ill-keeping. We caused it forthwith to be translated into English, and then we perceived how many vessels of butter and how many measures of meal and how many porks and other such gross duties did arise unto M'Guire out of his mensal lands, the particulars whereof I could have expressed if I had not lost the translated copy of the roll at Dublin; but these trifles are not worthy to be presented to your Lordship's knowledge. It is sufficient to show of what *qualis* those mensal duties are. And for the quantity thereof, though it were great in respect of the land out of which these provisions were taken, which being laid altogether doth not exceed four ballibetaghs, as I said before, yet such commodities in those parts are of little or no value, and therefore he never made any civil use of them, but spent them wastefully in a sordid and barbarous manner among his loose and idle followers. Beside these mensals M'Guire had 240 beeves or thereabouts yearly paid unto him out of all the seven baronies, and about his Castle of Enniskillen he had almost a ballibetagh of land, which he manured with his own churls; and this was M'Guire's whole estate in certainty; for in right he had no more, and in time of peace he did exact no more; marry in time of war he made himself owner of all, cutting what he listed, and imposing as many bonaghts or hired soldiers upon them as he had occasion to use. For albeit Hugh M'Guire that was slain in Munster were indeed a valiant rebel and the stoutest that ever was of his name, notwithstanding generally the natives of this county are reputed the worst swordsmen of the north, being rather inclined to be scholars or husbandmen than to be kern or men of action, as they term rebels in this kingdom. And for this cause M'Guire in the late wars did hire and wage the greatest part of his soldiers out of Connaught and out of the Breny O'Reilly, and made his own countrymen feed them and pay them; and therefore the jury inquiring of escheats found only two freeholders in this country, besides Hugh M'Guire himself, to have been slain in the late rebellion. Hereby your Lordship may perceive what manner of Lord M'Guire should have been, and what means and power he should have had to do hurt, if the State here had in former times but looked into the state of this country and had established the English laws and justice among them, whereby every man might have enjoyed his own. And your Lordship may likewise conjecture of what greatness the best of this surname will be, when the chiefry of this country shall be divided between two M'Guires, and the freeholders shall be established in their possessions without any dependency upon the lords, paying only their certain rents and duties. Assuredly these Irish lords appear to us like glowworms, which afar off seem to be all fire, but, being taken up in a man's hands, are but silly worms. And yet this young Coconagh M'Guire (whose brother Hugh was the alpha and himself the omega of the last rebellion; for Hugh was the first that went out, and himself the last that came in) will in no wise be satisfied with the greatest part of the chiefry of his country; such is the pride of his own heart and such is the encouragement he receives from some of place and power in this kingdom. And to the end he might be thought a person fit to be pleased with extraordinary good terms, he gave out a false alarm, some few days before our coming into Fermanagh, that himself with the Earl of Tyrconnel were going into Spain—a common and poor Irish policy practised in this realm ever since the conquest, to amuse the State with rumours that are utterly false, which notwithstanding, in former times, hath prevailed to do hurt in this kingdom, according to the observation and saying of the old Cardinal of Lorraine, *that a lie, believed but for an hour, doth many times produce effects of seven years' continuance.* I have digressed a little too much in this place, for which I humbly crave pardon, if your Lordship shall not think it pertinent to this discourse, wherein I meant to set forth the quality and quantity of M'Guire's mensal duties.

Concerning the free lands of the third kind, viz., such lands as are possessed by the Irish officers of this country, viz., chroniclers, galloglasses, and rhymers, the entire quantity of it, laid together as it is scattered in sundry baronies, doth well-nigh make two ballibetaghs, and no more; which land, in respect of the persons, that merit no respect but rather discountenance from the State—for they are enemies to the English government—may perhaps be thought meet to be added to the demesne lands of the chief lords.

In this manner we distinguished the possessions of Fermanagh, which being drawn into method, we presented to my Lord Deputy upon his return.

For the several possessions of all these lands we took this course to find them out and set them down for his Lordship's information. We called unto us the inhabitants of every barony severally, beginning with the barony of Maghera Boy, wherein we camped; and so calling one barony after another, we had present certain of the clerks or scholars of the country who know all the septs and families and all their branches, and the dignity of one sept above another, and what families or persons were chief of every sept, and who were next, and who were of a third rank, and so forth, till they descended to the most inferior man in all the baronies. Moreover, they took upon them to tell what quantity of land every man ought to have by the custom of their country, which is of the nature of gavelkind; whereby, as their septs or families did multiply, their possessions have been from time to time divided and subdivided, and broken into so many small parcels as almost every acre of land hath a several owner, which termeth himself a lord and his portion of land his country. Notwithstanding, as M'Guire himself had a chiefry over all the country, and some demesnes that did ever pass to him only who carried that title, so was there a chief of every sept, who had certain services, duties, or demesnes, that ever passed to the tanist of that sept and never were subject to division. When this was understood, we first inquired whether one or more septs did possess that barony which we had in hand; that being set down, we took the names of the chief parties of the sept or septs that did possess the baronies, and also the names of such as were second in them, and so of others that were inferior unto them again in rank and in possessions.

Then, whereas every barony containeth seven ballibetaghs and a half, we caused the name of every ballibetagh to be written down, and thereupon we made inquiry what portion of land or services every man held in every ballibetagh, beginning with such first as had land and services, and after naming such as had the greatest quantity of land, and so descending unto such as possess only two taths. There we stayed, for lower we could not go, because we knew the purpose of the State was only to establish such freeholders as were fit to serve on juries; at least we had found by experience in the county of Monaghan that such as had less than two taths allotted unto them had not 40s. freehold per annum, *ultra reprisalem*, and therefore were not of competent ability for that service; and yet the number of freeholders named in this county was above 200.

And in this order and method we digested the business touching the possessors and possessions of this county of Fermanagh, which we presented to my Lord Deputy upon his return from Ballyshannon. His Lordship, having received it and taken some consideration of it, called the principal inhabitants before him in the camp, told them that he came on purpose to understand the state of every particular man in that country, to the end he might establish and settle the same according to His Majesty's directions out of England, and that he had received some information thereof, which gave him some good satisfaction; howbeit, that he would not suddenly take any final order touching the same, but would resolve what was fit to be done, and finish his service the next term at Dublin. His Lordship's speech and good demonstration to the people gave them great contentment.

It remains I should inform your Lordship somewhat of the service performed by the justices of assize in this county, albeit they had little to do here, no matter being prepared for them to work upon; for the gaol delivery must needs be quickly despatched where there were no justices of peace that had either the will or the skill to commit malefactors, and where there was no gaol of any fastness to keep them, being committed. Howbeit, we had full appearance of all the country, and there came in, upon recognisances taken unskilfully enough by the sheriff and other Irish justices of peace, twenty persons in number or thereabouts, the greatest part whereof were loose and idle people bound over to find masters or sureties for their behaviour; others were committed for felonies, whereof some few were indited; but in the end all were acquitted for want of evidence, which happened by the negligence of the justices of the peace, who had not bound their accusers to prosecute against them. We rebuked the justices of peace for this omission and imposed fines upon them; and so ended our gaol delivery. Then made we the like inquisition here touching ecclesiastical livings, and published the like orders for the civil government of their country as we had done in Monaghan, and so dissolved our sessions. The erecting of a free school in this county was deferred till the coming of the Bishop of Clogher. The building of a gaol and sessions-house was likewise respited until my Lord Deputy had resolved of a fit place for a market and a corporate town, for the habitations of this people are so wild and transitory as there is not one fixed village in all this county. His Lordship took a view of two or three places for that purpose, of which he conceiveth the Abbey of Lisgoole to be the fittest; and I conjecture that the next term, when the principal gentlemen of this country shall repair to Dublin to settle their estates, his Lordship will make choice of that place for the shire-town of this county, and then take order for the erecting of a gaol and house of sessions there.

Having spent six or seven days in this waste country, we raised our camp, and returned the same way which we had passed before into the county of Monaghan; and lodging the second night not far from the Abbey of Clones, we came the third day to Cavan, and pitched our tents on the south side of this poor Irish town. The appearance of this place was very full, for not only the natives of the county of Cavan, but also many inhabitants of Westmeath and other parts of the Pale bordering upon this country,—whereof some pretended title to land, others came to demand debts, and others to give evidence against felons,—repaired to this sessions, the chief of which was the Baron of Delvin, who came attended with many followers.

My Lord Deputy, having a purpose to pursue the same course in the service here which had been holden in the other two counties, caused forthwith a commission to be drawn and passed the Seal, whereby the judges of assize and others were authorised to inquire of all lands escheated to the Crown in this county by attainder, outlawry, or actual killing in rebellion of any person, or by any other means whatsoever. For the despatch of this business a jury was impanneled of the best knights and gentlemen that were present, whereof some were foreign inhabitants of the Pale, and yet freeholders of this county, and the rest were the chief of every Irish sept natives of this county. We received two presentments from them, the first of sundry freeholders who were slain in the late rebellion, and of such lands as they were severally seized of at the same time of their killings. The second was that Philip O'Reilly, who was, according to the custom of the country, created O'Reilly, and was lord or chieftain of the whole country, being seized of all lands, tenements, and hereditaments in Breny O'Reilly, *in dominio suo ut de foedo et jure* (for these are the words of the inquisition), was slain in actual rebellion; and again, they found that after the death of Philip, one Edmund O'Reilly was, after the like custom of the country, created O'Reilly, and was in like manner seized of the country, and being so seized, was slain in rebellion. Also they found, lastly, that Sir John O'Reilly, who was chieftain and tanist of the country long before Philip and Edmund, did adhere to the Earl of Tyrone and other rebels, and died an actual rebel against the Crown. This inquisition was found with some difficulty, because the jurors themselves, all claiming and pretending be freeholders of land within that county, were jealous lest their particular freeholds might be found escheated by this office, because in time of rebellion these lords or chieftains, by their Irish cuttings and exactions, took the profits of the whole country at their pleasure, and so might be said to be seized of all the country in demesne when they were slain in rebellion. But some of the jury, being learned in the law, informed the rest that by the words *in dominio suo ut de foedo et jure* not only lands in demesne or possession, but a seigniory or chiefry may be understood, and thereupon they were content to put their seals to the inquisition, which, being drawn and engrossed in parchment by one of the Commissioners, was presented unto them. By these two offices the greatest part of this county, if not all, is vested in possession of the Crown. But because my Lord Deputy conceived His Majesty's pleasure to be that' the natives of the country, to whom His Highness had granted his general pardon, shall be re-established in their possessions which they peaceably held before the late war—albeit I do not understand that his Lordship hath any particular direction touching the disposition of this country of Breny O'Reilly; his Lordship therefore thought fit to look back to the time before the rebellion, and to inform himself how every man's possession stood at that time, and thereupon commanded of us to take the like pains as were taken in Fermanagh, and in the like order and method to distinguish the possessors and possessions of this country, which was the more easily performed because in the Irish countries where the custom of tanistry is not extinguished the tenures are everywhere alike. There is, first, a general chieftain of every country or territory, which hath some demesnes and many household provisions yielded unto him by all the inhabitants; under him every sept or surname hath a particular chieftain or tanist, which has likewise his peculiar demesnes and duties, and their possessions go by succession or election entirely, without any division; but all the other lands holden by the inferior inhabitants are partible in course of gavelkind, wherein there is no difference made between legitimate sons and bastards; and therefore both these customs, both of tanistry and gavelkind, in this kingdom are lately, by the opinion of all the judges here, adjudged to be utterly void in law; and as they are void, so shall they be shortly avoided and extinguished, either by surrender or resumption of all the lands which are so holden.

My Lord Deputy, having received the like survey of the lands and the like distinction or list of the freeholders in this country as was presented to his Lordship in M'Guire's country, deferred the disposition and settling thereof until his return to Dublin, having a purpose in Michaelmas term to make a perfect establishment of these three counties.

The state of the lay possessions being discovered, we did not omit to inquire of the number and value of parsonages and vicarages, of the reparation of the churches, and of the quality of their incumbents. By which inquisition we found that the greatest number of the parsonages are appropriate unto two great abbeys lying within the English Pale, viz., the Abbey of Fore in Westmeath, granted to the Baron of Delvin, and the Abbey of Kells, whereof one Gerard Flemynge is farmer. To the first of these fourteen parsonages within this country are appropriate, and to the other eight; besides, there are two or three more belonging in like manner to the Abbey of Cavan, in this county, being now in possession of Sir James Dillon. As for the vicarages, they are so poorly endowed as ten of them being united will scarce suffice to maintain an honest minister. For the churches, they are for the most part in ruins; such as were presented to be in reparation are covered only with thatch. But the incumbents, both parsons and vicars, did appear to be such poor, ragged, ignorant creatures—for we saw many of them in the camp—as we could not esteem any of them worthy of the meanest of those livings, albeit many of them are not worth above forty shillings per annum. This country doth lie within the diocese of Kilmore, whose bishop, Robert Draper, was and is parson of Trim in Meath, which is the best parsonage in all the kingdom, and is a man of this country birth worth well-nigh £400 a year. He doth live now in these parts, where he hath two bishoprics;

THE LORD DEPUTY'S SERVICE.

This is the effect of the service which was performed in that journey which my Lord Deputy made into Ulster this summer vacation, whereof I have made unto your Lordship a broken and disjointed relation, for which I humbly crave pardon; the rather because I was continually interrupted in the writing thereof, being employed, upon my return out of the North, together with my Lord Chief-Justice, in a new commission of assize and *nisi prius* for the counties of Waterford, Wexford, and Wicklow. So as I have been enforced to take fractions and starts, and almost instants of time, to finish the several periods of this rude discourse; which, notwithstanding, I hope your Lordship will, according to your wonted noble disposition to me, accept in good part. And so, with the presentation of my humble service, I leave your Lordship to the Divine preservation.

JO. DAVIES.

THE PLANTATION OF ULSTER.

A

LETTER

FROM

SIR JOHN DAVIES

TO

ROBERT EARL OF SALISBURY,

CONCERNING THE STATE OF IRELAND.

1610.

A LETTER.

My most honourable good Lord :—

THOUGH I perform this duty of advertising your Lordship how we proceed in the plantation of Ulster very late, yet cannot I accuse myself either of sloth or forgetfulness in that behalf; but my true excuse is the slow despatch of Sir Oliver Lambert from hence, into whose hands I thought to have given these letters more than a month since.

In the perambulation which we made this summer over the escheated counties in Ulster we performed four principal points of our commission.

1. First, the land assigned to the natives we distributed among the natives in different quantities and portions, according to their different qualities and deserts.

2. Next, we made the like distribution of the lands allotted to the servitors.

3. Thirdly, we published by proclamation in each county what lands were granted to British undertakers, and what to servitors, and what to natives; to the end that the natives should remove from the precincts allotted to the Britons, whereupon a clear plantation is to be made of English and Scottish without Irish, and to settle upon the lands assigned to natives and servitors, where there shall be a mixed plantation of English and Irish together.

4. Lastly, to the British undertakers, who are for the most part

come over, we gave seizin and possession of their several portions, and assigned them timber for their several buildings.

We began at the Cavan, where, as it falleth out in all matters of importance, we found the first access and entry into the business the most difficult. Of our proceeding here my report to your Lordship shall be the larger, because the best precinct in this county fell to your Lordship's lot to be disposed; and the undertakers thereof do still expect to be by your Lordship countenanced and protected. The inhabitants of this country do border upon the English Pale, where they have many acquaintances and alliances; by means whereof they have learned to talk of a freehold and of estates of inheritance, which the poor natives of Fermanagh and Tyrconnel could not speak of, although these men had no other nor better estate than they; that is, only a scambling and transitory possession at the pleasure of the chief of every sept.

When the proclamation was published touching their removal (which was done in the public session-house, the Lord Deputy and Commissioners being present), a lawyer of the Pale retained by them did endeavour to maintain that they had estates of inheritance in their possessions which their chief lords could not forfeit, and therefore, in their name, desired two things: first, that they might be admitted to traverse the offices which had been found of those lands; secondly, that they might have the benefit of a proclamation made about five years since, whereby the persons, lands, and goods of all His Majesty's subjects were taken into his royal protection.

To this the King's attorney, being commanded by the Lord Deputy, made answer, that he was glad that this occasion was offered of declaring and setting forth His Majesty's just title, as well for His Majesty's honour (who, being the most just Prince living, would not dispossess the meanest of his subjects wrongfully to gain many such kingdoms) as for the satisfaction of the

THE PLANTATION OF ULSTER. 385

natives themselves and of all the world; for His Majesty's right, it shall appear, said he, that His Majesty may and ought to dispose of these lands in such manner as he hath done, and is about to do, in law, in conscience, and in honour.

In law; whether the case be to be ruled by our law of England which is in force, or by their own Brehon Law, which is abolished and adjudged no law, but a lewd custom.

It is our rule in our law that the King is Lord Paramount of all the land in the kingdom, and that all his subjects hold their possessions of him, mediate or immediate.

It is another rule of our law that where the tenant's estate doth fail and determine, the lord of whom the land is holden may enter and dispose thereof at his pleasure.

Then those lands in the county of Cavan, which was O'Reilly's country, are all holden of the King; and because the captainship or chiefry of O'Reilly is abolished by Act of Parliament by Statute second of Elizabeth, and also because two of the chief lords elected by the country have been lately slain in rebellion, which is an attainder in law, these lands are holden immediately of His Majesty.

If, then, the King's Majesty be immediate chief lord of these lands, let us see what estates the tenants or possessors have by the rules of the Common Law of England.

Either they have an estate of inheritance or a lesser estate. A lesser estate they do not claim; or if they did, they ought to show the creation thereof, which they cannot do.

If they have an estate of inheritance their lands ought to descend to a certain heir; but neither their chiefries nor their tenancies did ever descend to a certain heir; therefore they have no estate of inheritance.

Their chiefries were ever carried in a course of tanistry to the eldest and strongest of the sept, who held the same during life if he were not ejected by a stronger.

2 B

This estate of the chieftain or tanist hath been lately adjudged no estate in law, but only a transitory and scambling possession.

Their inferior tenancies did run in another course, like the old gavelkind in Wales, where the bastards had their portions as well as the legitimate; which portion they held not in perpetuity, but the chief of the sept did once in two or three years shuffle and change their possessions by new partitions and divisions; which made their estates so uncertain as that, by opinion of all the judges in this kingdom, this pretended custom of gavelkind is adjudged and declared void in law.

And as these men had no certain estates of inheritance, so did they never till now claim any such estate, nor conceive that their lawful heirs should inherit the land which they possessed, which is manifest by two arguments:—(1) They never esteemed lawful matrimony, to the end they might have lawful heirs; (2) they never did build any houses, nor plant orchards or gardens, nor take any care of their posterities. If these men had no estates in law, either in their mean chiefries or in their inferior tenancies, it followeth that if His Majesty, who is the undoubted Lord Paramount, do seize and dispose these lands, they can make no title against His Majesty or his patentees, and consequently cannot be admitted to traverse any office of those lands; for without showing a title no man can be admitted to traverse an office.

Then have they no estates by the rules of the Common Law; for the Brehon Law, if it were a law in force and not an unreasonable custom, is abolished; yet even by that Irish custom, His Majesty, having the supreme chiefry, may dispose the profits of all the lands at his pleasure, and consequently the land itself; for the land and the profit of the land are all one. For he that was O'Reilly, or chieftain of the country, had power to cut upon all the inhabitants, high or low, as pleased him; which argues they held their lands of the chief lord in villeinage, and therefore they are properly called natives; for *nativus* in our old register or writs doth signify a villein; and the writ to recover a villein is entitled *De nativo habendo;* and in that action the plaintiff doth declare that he and his ancestors, time out of mind, were wont *tallier haut et bas* upon the villein and his ancestors; and thence comes the phrase of *cutting*, used among the Irish at this day.[1]

Thus, then, it appears that, as well by the Irish custom as the law of England, His Majesty may, at his pleasure, seize these lands and dispose thereof. The only scruple which remains consists in this point, whether the King may, in conscience or honour, remove the ancient tenants and bring in strangers among them.

Truly, His Majesty may not only take this course lawfully, but is bound in conscience so to do.

For, being the undoubted rightful King of this realm, so as the people and land are committed by the Divine Majesty to his charge and government, His Majesty is bound in conscience to use all lawful and just courses to reduce his people from barbarism to civility; the neglect whereof heretofore hath been laid as an imputation upon the Crown of England. Now civility cannot possibly be planted among them but by this mixed plantation of civil men, which likewise could not be without removal and transplantation of some of the natives and settling of their possessions in a course of Common Law; for if themselves were suffered to possess the whole country, as their septs have done for many hundred of years past, they would never, to the end of the world, build houses, make townships or villages, or manure or improve the land as it ought to be; therefore it stands neither with Christian policy nor conscience to suffer so good and fruitful a country to lie waste like a wilderness, when His Majesty may lawfully dispose it to such persons as will make a civil plantation thereupon.

Again, His Majesty may take this course in conscience, because

[1] *Cutting* is only an English form of the word *tallage,* a tax on tenants towards public expenses.

it tendeth to the good of the inhabitants many ways; for half their land doth now lie waste, by reason whereof that which is habited is not improved to half the value; but when the undertakers are planted among them, there being place and scope enough both for them and for the natives, and that all the land shall be fully stocked and manured, 500 acres will be of better value than 5000 are now. Besides, where before their estates were altogether uncertain and transitory, so as their heirs did never inherit, they shall now have certain estates of inheritance, the portions allotted unto them, which they, and their children after them, shall enjoy with security.

Again, His Majesty's conscience may be satisfied, in that his Majesty seeks not his own profit, but doth suffer loss by this plantation, as well in expense of his treasure as in the diminution of his revenue; for the entertainment of Commissioners here and in England, and the extraordinary charge of the army for the guard of the Lord Deputy and Council in several journeys made into Ulster about this business only, hath drawn no small sum of money out of His Majesty's coffers within these three years; and whereas Tyrone did the last year yield unto His Majesty £2000, for four years to come it will yield nothing; and afterwards the fee-farm of the undertakers will not amount to £600 per annum.

Again, when a project was made for the division of that country about twenty years since, Sir John O'Reilly being then chief lord and captain, they all agreed, before divers Commissioners sent from the State to settle that country, that Sir John O'Reilly should have two entire baronies in demesne, and ten shillings out of every poll in the other five baronies; which is much more than His Majesty, who hath title to all the land in demesne as well as to the chiefry, hath now given to undertakers or reserved to himself.

Lastly, this transplantation of the natives is made by His Majesty rather like a father than like a lord or monarch. The

THE PLANTATION OF ULSTER. 389

Romans transplanted whole nations out of Germany into France; the Spaniards lately removed all the Moors out of Grenada into Barbary, without providing them any new seats there. When the English Pale was first planted all the natives were clearly expelled, so as not one Irish family had so much as an acre of freehold in all the five counties of the Pale; and now, within those four years past, the Graemes were removed from the borders of Scotland to this kingdom, and had not one foot of land allotted unto them here; but these natives of Cavan have competent portions of land assigned unto them, many of them in the same barony where they dwelt before, and such as are removed are planted in the same county, so as His Majesty doth in this imitate the skilful husbandman, who doth remove his fruit-trees, not with a purpose to extirpate and destroy them, but that they may bring better and sweeter fruit after the transplantation.

Those and other arguments were used by the attorney to prove that His Majesty might justly dispose of those lands both in law, in conscience, and in honour; wherewith the natives seemed not unsatisfied in reason, though they remained in their passions discontented, being much grieved to leave their possessions to strangers, which they had so long after their manner enjoyed. Howbeit, my Lord Deputy did so mix threats with entreaty, *precibusque minas regaliter addit*, as they promised to give way to the undertakers, if the sheriff, by warrant of the Commissioners, did put them in possession, which they have performed like obedient and loyal subjects. Howbeit, we do yet doubt that some of them will appeal unto England, and therefore I have presumed to trouble your Lordship with this rude discourse at large, that your Lordship may understand upon what grounds we have proceeded, especially in that county where your Lordship's precinct doth lie.

The eyes of all the natives in Ulster were turned upon this county. Therefore, when they saw the difficulty of the business overcome here, their minds were the better prepared to submit themselves to the course prescribed by His Majesty for the plantation; and the service was afterwards performed in the rest of the counties with less contradictions. The British undertakers are preparing their materials for the erection of their buildings the next spring; the servitors and natives are taking out their Letters Patent with as much expedition as is possible. The agents for London have made better preparation for the erection of their new city at Coleraine than expected; for we found there such store of timber and other materials brought in places, and such a number of workmen so busy in several places about their several tasks, as methought I saw Dido's colony erecting of Carthage in Virgil—

> "*Instant ardentes Tyrii: pars ducere muros,*
> *Molirique arcem, et manibus subvolvere saxa:*
> *Pars optare locum tecto, et concludere sulco.*
> . . . .
> *Fervet opus,*" &c.

Thus, craving pardon, and presenting my humble service to your Lordship, I leave the same to the Divine preservation, and continue your Lordship's in all humble duties,

JO. DAVIES.

DUBLIN, 8th *November* 1610.

POSTSCRIPT.

This worthy servitor, Sir Oliver Lambert, is like to prove a good planter in the county of Cavan; whereof he hath made better proof than any man of our nation, having at his own charge voluntarily made a singularly good plantation in the wild and most dangerous places in Leinster, more for the Commonwealth than his own profit.

THE IRISH PARLIAMENT.

SIR JOHN DAVIES'S

SPEECH

TO THE

LORD DEPUTY OF IRELAND,

WHEN HE APPROVED OF HIM AS SPEAKER OF THE COMMONS,

THE 2ND MAY 1613.

SPEECH

TO

THE LORD DEPUTY OF IRELAND.

MOST HONOURABLE AND RIGHT NOBLE LORD,—

SINCE your high wisdom, unto which I humbly made my appeal, hath not thought it fit to repeal, but rather to ratify and confirm, the judgment of these worthy knights and burgesses in electing me, yet still unworthy in my own opinion, to be their Speaker, which your Lordship, I doubt not, hath been pleased to do, not in regard of any worthiness appearing in me, but for the honourable respect you worthily bear to that grave and wise assembly that made the election, I do humbly and absolutely submit myself to your Lordship's pleasure; and since these gentlemen have first conferred upon me, and now your Lordship hath confirmed unto me, the name and office of a Speaker, I will presume, with your Lordship's grace and favour, to speak somewhat in this great and entire assembly of all the states of this kingdom that shall be proper and agreeable to the circumstances of the time, of the place, and of the persons that are here assembled.

It is a saying and a rule of the wisest King that ever lived, "*Ubi multa consilia, ibi salus populi;*" and it is the direction of the wisest King now living that a Common Council shall be holden at this time and at this place for the common good of the kingdom of Ireland.

Such Common Councils, or Assemblies of States, are usual in all States and Commonwealths in one form or another, and in divers countries are called by divers names; but under the English monarchy and the French, which are the two best-tempered monarchies in the world, they are called Parliaments.

These Parliaments, though they consist of three different estates —the King, the Nobility, and the Commons—yet as in music distinct and several notes do make a perfect harmony, so these Councils, compounded of divers states and degrees, being well ordered and timed, do make a perfect concord in a Commonwealth. "*Nam quæ harmonia dicitur a musicis in cantu, ea est in civitate concordia*," saith Cicero; and this concord and harmony of hearts doth ever produce the safety and security of the people which is the *salus populi* that Solomon speaks of.

Whereof there cannot be a more certain demonstration than this, that these two kingdoms, which have been ruled by these Parliaments, are now the most ancient imperial monarchies of Christendom, and are withal two of the most flourishing Commonwealths that are to be seen upon the face of the earth.

But what doth this concern this kingdom of Ireland, or what application hath it to the place and persons present? Assuredly, when I speak of the monarchy of England I include the kingdom of Ireland within the circle of that imperial crown.

For the Kings of England no sooner were lords of Ireland but they made a real union of both these kingdoms, as is manifest by authentic records of the time of King John and King Henry the Third, so as Ireland became but as a member, *quasi membrum Angliæ*, as it is resolved by all the justices in third of Henry the Seventh. It became a member appendant and belonging, as the Act of Faculties twenty-eighth of Henry the Eighth calls it, or united and annexed to the imperial crown of the

THE IRISH PARLIAMENT. 395

realm of England, as the Statute of thirty-third of Henry the Eighth, which gave to that Prince the title of King of Ireland, doth term it.

And now at this day, God be blessed, the subjects of both realms have but one King, which is the renowned King of England, and are ruled and governed by one Common Law, which is the just and honourable Common Law of England; and as there is now but one Common Law, so for the space of one hundred and forty years after King Henry the Second had taken possession of the lordship of Ireland there was but one Parliament for both kingdoms, which was the . . . all that time. But the laws made in the Parliaments of England were from time to time transmitted hither under the Great Seal of that kingdom to be proclaimed, enrolled, and executed as laws of this realm.

In this manner was the great Charter of the ancient liberties of the English subjects, the Statutes of Merton and Marlebridge, sent over by King John and King Henry the Third, the Statutes of Westminster, the first, second, and third, and the Statute of Gloucester by King Edward the First, the Statutes of Lincoln and of York by King Edward the Second.

Among the rest, that of Westminster the second and that of York in their several preambles do make express mention of the people and land of Ireland as well as of England, where the laws were made.

All which Statutes, together with the warrants and writs whereby they were transmitted, we find enrolled and preserved to this day among the records of this kingdom.

But when, then, how long since, in what King's reign, was this great Common Council, this High Court of Parliament, erected first and established in Ireland?

Doubtless, though the rest of the ordinary courts of justice began with the first plantation of the English colonies here, yet the wisdom of the State of England thought it fit to reserve the power of making laws to the Parliaments of England for many years after.

So as this high extraordinary Court was not established in Ireland by authority out of England for many years after in the form that now it is till towards the declining of King Edward the Second's reign. For before that time the meetings and consultations of the great Lords with some of the Commons for appeasing of dissensions among themselves, though they be called Parliaments in the ancient annals, yet, being without orderly summons or formal proceedings, are rather to be called parleys than Parliaments.

But by what reason of State was the State of England moved to establish this Court of Parliament in Ireland at that time?

Assuredly this Common Council was then instituted when Ireland stood most in need of counsel, for under the conduct of Edward le Bruce the Scottish nation had overrun the whole realm, England had the same enemy at her back and the Barons' Rebellion in her bowels; and so, being distracted in herself, could give neither consilium nor auxilium to the distressed subjects here, so as they, being left to their own strength and council, did then obtain authority from the State of England to hold this Common Council of the realm among themselves for the quenching of that common fire that had almost consumed the whole kingdom.

And this, by the testimony of the best antiquaries, was the first time and first occasion of instituting this High Court of Parliament in Ireland.

But now why should I not, with your Lordship's favour, proceed further, and take a brief view of the principal Parliaments that have been holden in Ireland since that time, and therein note and observe what were the motives from time to time of calling these Common Councils, and what and how many the persons were that were wont to be called thereunto, that it may

THE IRISH PARLIAMENT.

appear by way of comparison how far this Parliament is like to excel all former Parliaments holden in this kingdom, not only in the felicity of the time, but in all their circumstances whatsoever.

Certain it is that the incursion of the Scots and the insurrection of the Irish concurring with it, and the intolerable oppression and extortion of the great lords of the realm, under colour of maintaining that army that should repel the one and repress the other, brought such misery and desolation upon this land about the latter end of Edward the Second's reign, as the English colonies of the provinces without the English Pale fell for the most part into such corruption of manners as it became a greater labour to reform them by the law than to conquer their enemies by the sword.

Therefore, in the beginning of the reign of King Edward the Third, Sir Anthony Lucy did summon and hold one Parliament, and Sir Ralph Ufford another, and the principal cause of holding both these Parliaments was to repress the insolencies and reform the abuses of the great lords descended of English race, of which the Earl of Desmond was the most exorbitant offender.

And after that, during the same King's reign, Sir Thomas Rookesby at one time, and Lionel Duke of Clarence at another, held several Parliaments at Kilkenny, which tended to no other end but to reduce the degenerate English in general from the barbarous customs of the Irish to their ancient civil manners and the obedience of their true mother, the State of England.

After this we find the same cause still to continue of calling the succeeding Parliaments in this realm, until the wars of Lancaster and York began, which made a great alteration in both kingdoms.

For if you look into the Parliament rolls of those times, which are mean between the fortieth year of King Edward the Third and the thirtieth year of King Henry the Sixth, we shall first find the Statutes of Kilkenny confirmed in every Parliament, and then the laws of principal consideration are against coigny and livery, cess of soldiers, night suppers, cumrick, and the like extortions and lewd customs which the English had learned among the Irish.

So as for the space of 140 years after the first erecting of this High Court in Ireland it is apparent that never any Parliament was called to reduce the Irish to obedience or to perfect the conquest of the whole island, but only to reform the English colonies that were become degenerate, and to retain the sovereignty of the Crown of England over them only, and to no other end or purpose.

But when the civil war in England between the two houses was thoroughly kindled, that fiery constellation made such an impression upon this realm also, as the nobility, following the several factions of England, fell into the like dissension here, which gave the Irish opportunity to reconquer the greatest part of the English colonies, who thereupon fell into such a relapse of barbarism as the fruit of the former Parliaments was utterly lost, and no part of the realm but these four shires of the Pale left under the obedience of the law of England.

But what did the governors of this kingdom then, when the jurisdiction of the law was drawn into so narrow a compass? Did they summon any more Parliaments, or did they omit to call the Common Council of the realm, for that the greatest part of the realm had rejected the English law and government?

Assuredly, they were so far from that neglect or omission as Parliaments were never called so often nor so thick one upon another as in the times of King Henry the Sixth and King Edward the Fourth, for scarce there passed a year without a Parliament, and sometimes two or three Parliaments were summoned and held within the compass of a year, which was such a trouble and charge to the subject as a special law was made that there should be but one Parliament held in a year.

But to what end did they call so many Parliaments? What

THE IRISH PARLIAMENT.

matters did they handle in these Common Councils? Did they consult about the recovery of the provinces that were lost or about final subduing of all the Irish? We find no such matter at all propounded; but we find in the Parliaments, in the rolls of that time, an extraordinary number of private Bills and petitions answered and ordered in Parliament, containing such mean and ordinary matters as, but for want of other business, were not fit to be handled in so high a court.

And such were the motives of calling the Parliaments in this kingdom, and the matters therein debated, during the wars of York and Lancaster, and after that likewise until the tenth year of King Henry the Seventh.

In that year, which was the tenth year after the uniting of the Roses, as now it is full ten years since the uniting of the kingdoms under one imperial crown—a happy period of time, we hope, for holding of a Parliament in this kingdom—in that year did Sir Edward Poynings summon and hold this famous Parliament, wherein doubtless he showed a large heart and a great desire of a general reformation, and to that end procured many general laws to pass which we find most profitable and necessary for the Commonweal at this day.

Among the rest, he caused two laws to be made which may rightly be called *leges legum*, being excellent laws concerning the laws themselves, whereof one did look backward to the time past and gave a great supply to the defects of former Parliaments by confirming and establishing at once in this realm all the Statutes formerly made in England.

The other looked forward to the time to come, by providing that from henceforth there should be no Parliament holden here until the Acts which should be propounded were first certified into England and approved by the King and his Council there, and there returned hither under the Great Seal of that realm.

This latter Act is that we call Poynings' Act, and is indeed that

Act of Parliament which is a rule for our Parliaments until this day.

But these Acts passed by Sir Edward Poynings, though they were made and meant for the general good, and gave indeed the first overture for the general reformation that has followed since that time, yet could they not produce so good and great an effect as was intended by those laws, because that more than three parts of four of this kingdom at least were then and long after possessed by the Irish and unreformed English, which were not answerable to the law.

As for the principal Parliaments which have been holden since that time, during the reigns of King Henry the Eighth, Queen Mary, and Queen Elizabeth—for King Edward the Sixth did call no Parliament in Ireland—they were all summoned upon special and particular occasions, and not for the general settlement of the whole kingdom.

For to what end was the Parliament holden by the Lord Leonard Gray in the twenty-eighth of Henry the Eighth but to attaint the Geraldines and to abolish the usurped authority of the Pope?

Wherefore did Sir Anthony St. Leger call the next Parliament after, in the thirty-eighth of Henry the Eighth, but to invest that Prince with the title of King of Ireland, and to suppress the abbeys and religious houses?

To what purpose did Thomas Earl of Sussex hold his first Parliament in the third and fourth of King Philip and Queen Mary but to settle Leix and Ofaly in the Crown?

And his second in the second year of Queen Elizabeth but to re-establish the reformed religion in this kingdom?

What was the principal cause that Sir Henry Sidney held a Parliament in the eleventh year of Queen Elizabeth but to extinguish the name of O'Neill and entitle the Crown to the greatest part of Ulster?

And lastly, what was the chief motive of the last Parliament holden by Sir John Perrot but the attainder of two great peers of this realm, the Viscount Baltinglas and the Earl of Desmond, and for vesting of their lands and the lands of their adherents in the actual possession of the Crown?

And now having made a summary collection of the principal causes of summoning the former Parliaments which from time to time have been holden since the first institution of this High Court in Ireland, I must not forget to note also unto your Lordship what and how many persons were called in former times to make up the body of this great Council.

For the persons before the thirty-third year of King Henry the Eighth, we do not find any to have had place in Parliament but the English of blood or English of birth only. For the mere Irish in those days were never admitted, as well because their countries, lying out of the limits of counties, could send no knights, and having neither cities nor boroughs in them, could send no burgesses to the Parliament. Besides, the State did not then hold them fit to be trusted with the counsel of the realm.

For the number since before the thirty-fourth year of King Henry the Eighth, when Meath was divided into shires, there were no more than twelve counties in Ireland besides the liberty of Tipperary. The number of knights must needs have been few; and since the ancient cities were but four and the boroughs which sent burgesses not above thirty, the entire body of the whole House of Commons could not then consist of one hundred persons; and though Queen Mary did add two shires, and Queen Elizabeth seventeen more, to increase the number of knights in that House, yet all did not send knights to the Parliament, for the remote shires of Ulster returned none at all.

For the lords temporal, though they are yet but few, yet was the number less before King Henry the Eighth was styled King of Ireland, for since that time divers of the Irish nobility and some descended of the English race have been created both earls and barons.

And lastly, for the bishops and archbishops, though their number was greater than now it is, in respect to the divers unions made of latter years, yet such as were resident in the mere Irish countries and did not acknowledge the King to be their patron were never summoned to any Parliament.

And now, by way of comparison, it may easily appear unto your Lordship how much this first Parliament now begun under the blessed government of our most gracious King James is like to excel all former Parliaments, as well in respect of the cause and time of calling it as of the persons that are called unto it.

For this Parliament (God be blessed!) is not called to repel an invasion, or to suppress a rebellion, or to reduce degenerate subjects to their obedience. It is not summoned to pass private Bills only or to serve private turns, or for any one special service for the Crown, though such have been the occasions and causes of calling the most part of the former Parliaments.

But now since God hath blessed the whole island with an universal peace and obedience, together with plenty, civility, and other felicities, more than ever it enjoyed in any former age, this general Council of the whole realm is called now principally to confirm and establish these blessings unto us and to make them perpetual to our posterities.

Again, this Parliament is not called in such a broken and miserable time that we need complain in our Bills and petitions of the miseries and calamities of this kingdom, whereas the rolls of former Parliaments are full of such complaint; but it is called, as it were, in the year of Jubilee, or upon the Sabbath of this land, being now at rest after all her travails, which lasted 400 years together.

It is called in the time of greatest security and in the most joyful and happy time that ever did shine upon the inhabitants of this kingdom.

Again, it is not called in such a time as when the four shires of the Pale only did send their barons, knights, and burgesses to the Parliament, when they alone took upon them to make laws to bind the whole kingdom, neglecting to call the subjects residing in other parts of the realm unto them, as appeareth by that Parliament holden by the Viscount of Gormanstown, which Sir Edward Poynings, in the tenth year of King Henry the Seventh, caused to be utterly repealed and the Acts thereof made void, chiefly for that the summons of Parliament went forth to the four shires of the Pale only, and not to all the rest of the counties.

But it is called in such a time when this great and mighty kingdom, being wholly reduced to shire ground, containeth thirty-three counties at large; when all Ulster and Connaught, as well as Leinster and Munster, have voices in Parliament by their knights and burgesses; when all the inhabitants of the kingdom, English of birth, English of blood, the new British colony, and the old Irish natives, do all meet together to make laws for the common good of themselves and their posterities.

To this end His Majesty hath most graciously and justly erected divers new boroughs in sundry parts of this kingdom. I say His Majesty hath done it most justly, even as His Highness himself hath been pleased to say that he was obliged in justice and honour to give all his free subjects of this kingdom indifferent and equal voices in making of their laws, so as one half of them should not make laws alone which should bind the other subjects half without their consents.

Neither is this a new or strange precedent, for His Majesty doth but follow the steps herein of his next predecessors which went before him.

Queen Mary made two counties of Leix and Ofaly, whereby they were enabled to send knights to the Parliament; but she

erected boroughs in these new counties also, that they might send burgesses as well as knights.

In Queen Elizabeth's time Sir Henry Sidney made sundry counties in Connaught, immediately before the Parliament which he held in the eleventh year of that Queen.

And after him Sir John Perrot did the like in Ulster near about the beginning of the last Parliament. Out of these new counties so many knights were added to the Lower House, yet no man took exception thereunto.

This did Queen Elizabeth in her time. What hath King James done now? Whereas the Queen had omitted to make boroughs in these new counties, the King hath now supplied that defect, by making these new corporations we speak of; for why should all your old shires have cities and boroughs in them and these new counties be without them; or shall Queen Elizabeth be able to make a county, and shall not King James be able to make a borough?

But what proportion is there now observed between the number of the counties that before this time had no boroughs in them and the number of boroughs newly erected?

Certainly the number of these new boroughs, compared with the counties that never had any burgesses before this time, doth carry a less proportion than the ancient boroughs, compared with the number of the ancient counties; for in those twelve or thirteen old shires there are thirty cities and boroughs at least, which send citizens and burgesses to the Parliament.

Whereas for seventeen counties at large, being more than half the shires of this kingdom, which had not one borough in them before this new erection, His Majesty hath now lately erected but forty new boroughs or thereabouts, which in the judgment of all indifferent men must needs seem reasonable, just, and honourable.

Lastly, this Parliament is called in such a time when all the lords spiritual and temporal do acknowledge the King of England to be their undoubted patron, and when all the lords temporal do appear in an honourable fashion like themselves, none of them (God be thanked!) claiming any such privilege as the undutiful Earl of Desmond was wont to claim, that he should never be summoned to come within any walled town nor to any Parliament or Grand Council but at his own will and pleasure.

Whereupon I may positively conclude that this present Parliament now begun by your Lordship doth pass and excel all former Parliaments that ever were holden in this kingdom, as well in the happiness of the time wherein it is called, and the importance of the cause for which it is called, as in the number and worthiness of the persons which are called thereunto.

And this, doubtless, is a great honour and happiness unto your Lordship, above all the former Viceroys of this kingdom, for that your Lordship doth now hold the first Parliament that may justly be called a Common Council, wherein all the commons throughout the kingdom are present, and have free voices by their knights and burgesses, a felicity and a glory that many of your predecessors, zealous of the reformation of this kingdom, did exceedingly desire, but could never attain unto it.

How glad would Sir Henry Sidney have been to have seen this day—he that so much desired to reduce Ulster, but could never perfectly perform it! What honour would he have thought it unto himself if he might have held a Parliament unto which that province should have sent so many worthy knights and burgesses as now it doth!

How joyful would Thomas Earl of Sussex have been to have seen the Statute he caused to be made for reducing the Irish countries into shire ground to have taken so good effect as now it hath, since all these countries are now brought into counties and do all send knights to serve in this Parliament!

In a word, Sir Edward Poynings in the time of King Henry

the Seventh, and Lionel Duke of Clarence in Edward the Third's time, if they could have seen but half such an assembly in their Parliaments, would have thought themselves happy and highly honoured; and yet those Parliaments holden by them are the most famous Parliaments that have been formerly holden in this kingdom.

And truly, as your Lordship hath more honour in this respect than any of your predecessors, so I may justly say without adulation that your Lordship hath merited this particular honour more than any of them that have gone before you.

For if it be an honour unto you to hold such a Parliament, you do but reap the fruit of your own labours, since yourself principally have prepared the way to this Parliament, as well by your martial virtue in time of war as by your justice and policy in the time of peace.

For hath not your Lordship—I humbly crave your Lordship's pardon, I will not presume to ask you the question, but I will ask these reverend prelates and noble lords, these grave and learned judges, these worthy knights and burgesses—I will ask them the question: Hath not this most noble Deputy been a principal author of the reformation of this kingdom, was not his fortitude one of the chief instruments for suppressing the late rebellion, and hath not his justice since that time established the public peace of the kingdom?

Hath he not acted his part so well upon this theatre of honour as no man is ambitious to come upon the stage after him, knowing it is more easy to succeed him in his place than to follow him in his painful and prudent course of government, and that he must be as strong as Hercules to undergo the burthen that such an Atlas hath borne before him?

Nay, hath not himself performed Hercules labours in suppressing more monstrous enormities in Ireland than Hercules himself did destroy monsters when he sought adventures over all Europe?

I ask not these questions as if any man here were doubtful or ignorant of his noble virtues and deserts; but as praise is nothing but a reflection of virtue, so should it be delivered rather collaterally than directly, to avoid suspicion of direct flattery, which I know your Lordship loveth not, as I know your Lordship needs it not.

Nevertheless, Right Honourable Lord—for now I must convert my speech to your Lordship—though you have no need of my praise, yet it is most needful, in respect of the place you hold, that your Lordship should be adorned with all praiseworthy virtues. You had need be a virtuous and most worthy Deputy, since you sit in the throne and represent the person of the most virtuous and excellent King in the world.

For he that doth fight with the sword of a King, write with the pen of a King—he that hath the justice, mercy, and bounty of a King in his hands—had need be furnished with those noble powers and virtues as are fit for the rule and government of a kingdom, especially if he hold the place of such a King as our most renowned and gracious Sovereign is, who is the greatest and best King that now reigneth upon the face of the earth.

I call him the greatest King, not so much for the largeness and extent of his territories, nor for the multitude of his subjects, though he be in possession of three great kingdoms, and doth command more martial and able men than any King in Europe at this day.

But I will call him indeed the greatest King for his exceeding great measure of goodness and virtue, and for the great grace and favour that His Majesty standeth in with the Divine Majesty, the King of Kings.

For if that man be accounted the greatest subject of a kingdom that is in highest favour with a King upon earth, why should not that King be the greatest King on earth that is in greatest favour with the King of Heaven?

And that our most gracious Sovereign standeth in highest favour with Almighty God doth not only appear by the innumerable blessings poured from heaven upon him and upon his kingdoms for his sake, by the special providence and care God hath always had of his sacred person by protecting and delivering him from his enemies.

Again, I will call His Majesty the best King for that he is a most just King, and justice is the best of all kingly virtues; and for that also he is a most bountiful King, resembling therein the Divine goodness, ever spreading and communicating his riches unto others, which we must needs remember in this kingdom; for we cannot forget it without ingratitude, since we all know that His Majesty doth not only expend the whole revenue of this land upon itself, but spares yearly out of England a great mass of treasure to support the extraordinary charge thereof, out of which the greater number of us here present, by entertainments, pensions, or rewards, do taste every day of His Majesty's bounty.

Lastly, His Majesty ought to be called the best King, as well for his sweet inclination to peace, whereby he doth make happy both his own dominions and also his neighbour kingdoms round about him, as for his singular piety and religion towards God, which is the best and highest praise that can be given to any Prince.

But I should launch forth into a main sea that hath neither bottom nor shore if I should proceed further in the praise of such a Prince, whose worthiness exceeds all degrees of comparison. It is a theme too high and too large for me to handle; it becometh me better to give thanks than praise.

And, therefore, I will conclude with most humble thanks, first unto Almighty God for giving us such an excellent King; then unto our most gracious King for appointing us so worthy a Deputy; and lastly, unto our noble Deputy for all his good services and endeavours, tending so much to the honour of God and the King and the general good of the whole kingdom.

THE IRISH PARLIAMENT.

And now I descend unto these humble petitions which I am to make, &c.

(Wherein he most humbly requesteth that the ancient rights and privileges of the House of Commons, in freely delivering their speech and minds and of being free from arrests, as well themselves as their servants, during the time of Parliament, might be kept whole and untouched; and if that in anything not well by them understood they should happen to offend, he requesteth eave, as well for himself as for the rest, to have access unto his Lordship.)

A DESCRIPTION

OF

IRELAND

BY

FYNES MORYSON,

SECRETARY TO THE LORD MOUNTJOY, THEN LORD DEPUTY.

1600–1603.

FYNES MORYSON'S
DESCRIPTION OF IRELAND.

THE longitude of Ireland extends four degrees, from the meridian of eleven degrees and a half to that of fifteen and a half; and the latitude extends also four degrees, from the parallel of fifty-four degrees to that of fifty-eight degrees. In the geographical description I will follow Camden, as formerly.

This famous island in the Virginian Sea is by old writers called Ierna, Inverna, and Iris; by the old inhabitants Erin, by the old Britons Yuerdhen, by the English at this day Ireland, and by the Irish bards at this day Banno, in which sense of the Irish word, Avicen calls it the Holy Island; besides, Plutarch of old called it Ogygia, and after him Isidore named it Scotia. This Ireland, according to the inhabitants, is divided into two parts,—the wild Irish and the English-Irish living in the English Pale; but of the old kingdoms, five in number, it is divided into five parts.

1. The first is by the Irish called Mowne, by the English MUNSTER, and is subdivided into six counties, of *Kerry*, of *Limerick*, of *Cork*, of *Tipperary*, of the *Holy Cross*, and of *Waterford*, to which the seventh County of *Desmond* is now added. The Gangavi, a Scythian people, coming into Spain, and from thence into Ireland, inhabited the County of Kerry, full of woody mountains, in which the Earls of Desmond had the dignity of Palatines, having their houses in Tralee, a little town now almost uninhabited. Not far thence lies St. Mary Wick, vulgarly

called Smerwick, where the Lord Arthur Grey, being Lord Deputy, happily overthrew the aiding troops sent to the Earl of Desmond from the Pope and the King of Spain. On the south side of Kerry lies the County of Desmond, of old inhabited by three kinds of people, the Luceni (being Spaniards), the Velebri (so called of their seat upon the sea-water or marshes), and the Iberni or upper Irish, inhabiting about Bear Haven and Ballimore, two havens well known by the plentiful fishing of herrings, and the late invasion of the Spaniards in the year 1601. Next to these is the country of M'Carty Moore, of Irish race, whom, as enemy to the Fitzgeralds, Queen Elizabeth made Earl of Glencar in the year 1566. For of the Fitzgeralds of the family of the Earls of Kildare the Earls of Desmond descended, who, being by birth English and created Earls by King Edward the Third, became hateful rebels in our time. The third county hath the name of the City Cork, consisting almost all of one long street, but well known and frequented, which is so compassed with rebellious neighbours as, they of old not daring to marry their daughters to them, the custom grew, and continues to this day, that by mutual marriages one with another all the citizens are of kin in' some degree of affinity. Not far thence is Youghal, having a safe haven, near which the Viscounts of Barry, of English race, are seated. In the fourth County, of Tipperary, nothing is memorable but that it is a Palatinate. The little town Holy Cross, in the County of the same name, hath many great privileges. The sixth County hath the name of the City Limerick, the seat of a Bishop, wherein is a strong castle built by King John. Not far thence is Awne, the seat of a Bishop, and the Lower Ossory, giving the title of an Earl to the Butlers, and the town Thurles, giving them also the title Viscount. And there is Cassiles, now a poor city, but the seat of an Archbishop. The seventh County hath the name of the City Waterford, which the Irish call Porthlargi, of the commodious haven, a rich and well-inhabited city, esteemed the second to Dublin. And because the inhabitants long faithfully helped the English in subduing Ireland, our Kings gave them excessive privileges; but they rashly failing in their obedience at King James's coming to the crown, could not in long time obtain the confirmation of their old charter.

2. Leinster, the second part of Ireland, is fertile and yields plenty of corn, and hath a most temperate mild air, being divided into ten Counties, of Catherlough, Kilkenny, Wexford, Dublin, Kildare, the King's County, the Queen's County, the Counties of Longford, of Ferns, and of Wicklow. The Carcondi of old inhabited Catherlough (or Carlow) County, and they also inhabited great part of Kilkenny, of Upper Ossory, and of Ormond, which have nothing memorable but the Earls of Ormond, of the great family of the Butlers, inferior to no Earl in Ireland (not to speak of Fitzpatrick, Baron of Upper Ossory). It is ridiculous which some Irish, who will be believed as men of credit, report of men in these parts yearly turned into wolves, except the abundance of melancholy humour transports them to imagine that they are so transformed. Kilkenny, giving name to the second County, is a pleasant town, the chief of the towns withinland, memorable for the civility of the inhabitants, for the husbandman's labour, and the pleasant orchards. I pass over the walled town Thomastown, and the ancient city Rheban, now a poor village with a castle, yet of old giving the title of Baronet. I pass over the village and strong Castle of Leighlin, with the country adjoining, usurped by the sept of the Cavanaghs, now surnamed O'Moores. Also I omit Ross, of old a large city, at this day of no moment. The third County, of Wexford (called by the Irish County Reogh), was of old inhabited by the Menapii, where, at the town called Banna, the English made their first descent into Ireland; and upon that coast are very dangerous flats in the sea, which they vulgarly call Grounds. The City Weshford, Weisford, or Wexford, is the chief

of the County, not great, but deserving praise for their faithfulness towards the English, and frequently inhabited by men of English race. The Cauci, a sea-bordering nation of Germany, and the Menapii aforesaid, of old inhabited the territories now possessed by the O'Moores and O'Byrnes. Also they inhabited the fourth County of Kildare, a fruitful soil, having the chief town of the same name, greatly honoured in the infancy of the Church by St. Bridget. King Edward the Second created the Geralds Earls of Kildare. The Eblani of old inhabited the Territory of Dublin, the fifth County, having a fertile soil and rich pastures, but wanting wood, so as they burn turf, or sea-coal brought out of England. The City Dublin, called Divelin by the English, and Balacleigh (as seated upon hurdles) by the Irish, is the Chief City of the Kingdom, and seat of justice; fairly built, frequently inhabited, and adorned with a strong Castle, fifteen churches, an Episcopal seat, and a fair College,—an happy foundation of an University laid in our age,—and endowed with many privileges; but the haven is barred and made less commodious by those hills of sands. The adjoining promontory, Howth-head, gives the title of a Baron to the family of St. Lawrence. And towards the north lies Fingal, a little territory, as it were the garner of the kingdom, which is environed by the sea and great rivers, and this situation hath defended it from the incursion of rebels in former Civil Wars. I omit the King's and Queen's Counties (namely, Ofaly and Leix), inhabited by the O'Connors and O'Moores, as likewise the Counties of Longford, Ferns, and Wicklow, as less affording memorable things.

3. The third part of Ireland is Midia or Media, called by the English Meath, in our fathers' memory divided in Eastmeath and Westmeath. In Eastmeath is Drogheda, vulgarly called Tredagh, a fair and well-inhabited town. Trim is a little town upon the confines of Ulster, having a stately castle but now much ruinated, and it is more notable for being the ancient (as

DESCRIPTION OF IRELAND.   417

it were) barony of the Lacies. Westmeath hath the town Deloin, giving the title Baron to the English family of the Nugents; and Westmeath is also inhabited by many great Irish septs, as the O'Maddens, the MacGeoghegans, O'Mallaghans, and MacCoghlans, which seem barbarous names. Shannon is a great river, in a long course making many and great lakes (as the large lake or Lough Regith), and yields plentiful fishing, as do the frequent rivers and all the seas of Ireland. Upon this river lies the town Athlone, having a very fair bridge of stone, the work of Sir Henry Sidney, Lord Deputy, and a strong fair castle.

4. Connaught is the fourth part of Ireland, a fruitful Province, but having many bogs and thick woods; and it is divided into six Counties, of Clare, of Leitrim, of Galway, of Roscommon, of Mayo, and of Sligo. The County of Clare, or Thomond, hath his Earls of Thomond, of the family of the O'Brenes, the old kings of Connaught, and Tuam is the seat of an Archbishop,—only part, but the greatest, of this county was called Clare, of Thomas Clare, Earl of Gloucester. The adjoining territory, Clan-Richard (the land of Richard's sons) hath his Earls called Clanricarde of the land, but being of the English family De Burgo, vulgarly Burke, and both these Earls were first created by Henry the Eighth. In the same territory is the barony Atterith, belonging to the barons of the English family Birmingham, of old very warlike, but their posterity have degenerated to the Irish barbarism. The City Galway, giving name to the County, lying upon the sea, is frequently[1] inhabited with civil people, and fairly built. The northern part of Connaught is inhabited by these Irish septs, O'Connor, O'Rourke, and M'Diermod. Upon the western coast lies the Island Arran, famous for the fabulous long life of the inhabitants.

5. Ulster, the fifth part of Ireland, is a large Province, woody, fenny, in some parts fertile, in other parts barren, but in all parts

[1] *Frequently*, here and in other places, numerously.

green and pleasant to behold, and exceedingly stored with cattle. The next part to the Pale and to England is divided into three counties, Lowth, Down, and Antrim; the rest contains seven counties, Monaghan, Tyrone, Armagh, Coleraine, Donegal, Fermanagh, and Cavan. Lowth is inhabited by English-Irish (Down and Antrim being contained under the same name), and the barons thereof be of the Birmingham's family, and remain loving to the English. Monaghan was inhabited by the English family Fitzurse, and these are become degenerate and barbarous, and in the sense of that name are in the Irish tongue called Mac-Mahon, that is, the Sons of Bears. I forbear to speak of Tyrone and of the Earl thereof, infamous for his rebellion which I have at large handled in this work. Armagh is the seat of an Archbishop, and the Metropolitan City of the whole island, but in time of the rebellion was altogether ruinated. The other Counties have not many memorable things, therefore it shall suffice to speak of them briefly. The neck of land called Lecaile is a pleasant little territory, fertile, and abounding with fish and all things for food, and therein is Down, at this time a ruined town, but the seat of a Bishop, and famous for the burial of St. Patrick, St. Bridget, and St. Columb. The town of Carrickfergus is well known by the safe haven. The river Bann, running through the Lake Evagh into the sea, is famous for the fishing of salmons, the water being most clear, wherein the salmons much delight. The great families or septs of Ulster are thus named, O'Neill, O'Donnell (whereof the chief was lately created Earl of Tyrconnel), O'Buil, MacGuire, O'Kane, O'Dogherty, MacMahon, MacGennis, MacSurley, &c. The Lake Erne, compassed with thick woods, hath such plenty of fish as the fishermen fear the breaking of their nets rather than want of fish. Towards the north, in the midst of vast woods, and, as I think, in the County Donegal, is a Lake, and therein an Island in which is a Cave famous for the apparition of spirits, which the inhabitants

DESCRIPTION OF IRELAND.

call Ellanvi frugadory, that is, the Island of Purgatory, and they call it Saint Patrick's Purgatory, fabling that he obtained of God by prayer that the Irish seeing the pains of the damned might more carefully avoid sin.

The Land of Ireland is uneven, mountainous, soft, watery, woody, and open to winds and floods of rain, and so fenny as it hath bogs upon the very tops of mountains, not bearing man or beast, but dangerous to pass, and such bogs are frequent all over Ireland. Our mariners observe the sailing into Ireland to be more dangerous, not only because many tides meeting make the sea apt to swell upon any storm, but especially because they ever find the coast of Ireland covered with mists, whereas the coast of England is commonly clear and to be seen far off. The air of Ireland is unapt to ripen seeds, yet, as Mela witnesseth, the earth is luxurious in yielding fair and sweet herbs. Ireland is little troubled with thunder, lightning, or earthquakes, yet— I know not upon what presage—in the year 1601, and in the month of November, almost ended at the siege of Kinsale, and a few days before the famous battle in which the rebels were happily overthrown, we did mightily hear and see great thunderings and lightnings, not without some astonishment what they should presage. The fields are not only most apt to feed cattle, but yield also great increase of corn. I will freely say that I observed the winter's cold to be far more mild than it is in England, so as the Irish pastures are more green, and so likewise the gardens all winter-time, but that in summer, by reason of the cloudy air and watery soil, the heat of the sun hath not such power to ripen corn and fruits, so as their harvest is much later than in England. Also I observed that the best sorts of flowers and fruits are much rarer in Ireland than in England, which notwithstanding is more to be attributed to the inhabitants than to the air; for Ireland being often troubled with rebellions, and

The Situation.

the rebels not only being idle themselves, but in natural malice destroying the labours of other men, and cutting up the very trees or fruit for the same cause or else to burn them, for these reasons the inhabitants take less pleasure to till their grounds or plant trees, content to live for the day, in continual fear of like mischiefs. Yet is not Ireland altogether destitute of these flowers and fruits, wherewith the County of Kilkenny seems to abound more than any other part. And the said humidity of the air and land making the fruits for food more raw and moist, hereupon the inhabitants and strangers are troubled with looseness of body, the country disease. Yet for the rawness they have an excellent remedy by their *Aqua Vitæ*, vulgarly called Usquebaugh,[1] which binds the belly and drieth up moisture more than our *Aqua Vitæ*, yet inflameth not so much. Also inhabitants as well as strangers are troubled there with an ague which they call the Irish ague, and they who are sick thereof, upon a received custom, do not use the help of the physician, but give themselves to the keeping of Irish women, who starve the ague, giving the sick man no meat, who takes nothing but milk and some vulgarly known remedies at their hand.

Ireland after much blood spilt in the Civil Wars became less populous, and as well great lords of countries as other inferior gentlemen laboured more to get new possessions for inheritance than by husbandry and peopling of their old lands to increase their revenues; so as I then observed much grass, wherewith the island so much abounds, to have perished without use, and either to have rotted or in the next springtime to be burnt, lest it should hinder the coming of new grass. This plenty of grass makes the Irish have infinite multitudes of cattle, and in the heat of the last rebellion the very vagabond rebels

The Fertility and Traffic.

---

[1] Usquebaugh is from *Uisge*, water, and *Beatha*, life. *Uisge* for water gives its names to rivers, Usk, Esk, Exe, &c., and in modern English spelling it is whisky, or whiskey.

DESCRIPTION OF IRELAND.

had great multitudes of cows, which they still, like the nomades, drove with them whithersoever themselves were driven, and fought for them as for their altars and families. By this abundance of cattle the Irish have a frequent though somewhat poor traffic for their hides, the cattle being in general very little, and only the men and the greyhounds of great stature. Neither can the cattle possibly be great, since they eat only by day, and then are brought at evening within the bawns of castles, where they stand or lie all night in a dirty yard without so much as a lock of hay; whereof they make little, for sluggishness, and that little they altogether keep for their horses. And they are thus brought in by nights for fear of thieves, the Irish using almost no other kind of theft, or else for fear of wolves, the destruction whereof being neglected by the inhabitants, oppressed with greater mischiefs, they are so much grown in number as sometimes in winter nights they will come to prey in villages and the suburbs of cities. The Earl of Ormond in Munster, and the Earl of Kildare in Leinster, had each of them a small park enclosed for fallow deer, and I have not seen any other part in Ireland, nor have heard that they had any other at that time; yet in many woods they have many red deer loosely scattered, which seem more plentiful because the inhabitants used not then to hunt them, but only the governors and commanders had them sometimes killed with the piece. They have also about Ofalia and Wexford and in some parts of Munster some fallow deer scattered in the woods; yet in the time of the war I did never see any venison served at the table, but only in the houses of the said Earls and of the English commanders. Ireland hath great plenty of birds and fowls, but by reason of their natural sloth they had little delight or skill in birding or fowling. But Ireland hath neither singing nightingale, nor chattering pie, nor undermining mole, nor black crow, but only crows of mingled colour such as we call Royston crows. They have such plenty of pheasants as I have known sixty served at one feast, and abound much more with rails, but partridges are somewhat rare. There be very many eagles, and great plenty of hares, conies, hawks called goshawks, much esteemed with us, and also of bees, as well in hives at home as in hollow trees abroad, and in caves of the earth. They abound in flocks of sheep, which they shear twice in the year, but their wool is coarse, and merchants may not export it, forbidden by a law made on behalf of the poor, that they may be nourished by working it into cloth, namely, rugs (whereof the best are made at Waterford) and mantles generally worn by men and women and exported in great quantity. And of old they had such plenty of linen cloth as the wild Irish used to wear thirty or forty ells in a shirt, all gathered and wrinkled, and washed in saffron, because they never put them off till they were worn out. Their horses called hobbies are much commended for their ambling pace and beauty; but Ireland yields few horses good for service in war, and the said hobbies are much inferior to our geldings in strength to endure long journies, and being bred in the fenny soft ground of Ireland are soon lamed when they are brought into England. The hawks of Ireland, called goshawks, are, as I said, much esteemed in England, and they are sought out by money and all means to be transported thither. Ireland yields excellent marble near Dublin, Kilkenny, and Cork; and I am of their opinion who dare venture all they are worth that the mountains would yield abundance of metals, if this public good were not hindered by the inhabitants' barbarousness, making them apt to seditions, and so unwilling to enrich their Prince and Country; and by their slothfulness, which is so singular as they hold it baseness to labour; and by their poverty not being able to bear the charge of such works; besides that the wiser sort think their poverty best for the public good, making them peaceable, as nothing sooner makes them kick against authority than riches. Ireland hath in all parts pleasant rivers, safe

DESCRIPTION OF IRELAND.

and long havens, and no less frequent lakes of great circuit, yielding great plenty of fish; and the sea on all sides yields like plenty of excellent fish, as salmons, oysters (which are preferred before the English), and shell fishes, with all other kinds of sea fish; so as in all parts the Irish might have abundance of excellent sea and fresh-water fish, if the fishermen were not so possessed with the natural fault of slothfulness, as no hope of gain, scarcely the fear of authority, can in many places make them come out of their houses and put to sea. Hence it is that in many places they use Scots for fishermen, and they, together with the English, make profit of the inhabitants' sluggishness; and no doubt if the Irish were industrious in fishing they might export salted and dried fish with great gain. In time of peace the Irish transport good quantity of corn; yet they may not transport it without licence, lest in any sudden rebellion the King's forces and his good subjects should want corn. Ulster and the western parts of Munster yield vast woods, in which the rebels cutting up trees and casting them on heaps used to stop the passages, and therein, as also in fenny and boggy places, to fight with the English. But I confess myself to have been deceived in the common fame that all Ireland is woody, having found in my long journey from Armagh to Kinsale few or no woods by the way, except the great woods of Ofaly, and some low shrubby places which they call Glins. Also I did observe many boggy and fenny places, whereof great part might be dried by good and painful husbandry. I may not omit the opinion commonly received that the earth of Ireland will not suffer a snake or venomous beast to live, and that the Irish wood transported for building is free of spiders and their webs. Myself have seen some, but very few, spiders, which the inhabitants deny to have any poison, but I have heard some English of good credit affirm by experience the contrary. The Irish having in most parts great woods or low shrubs and thickets, do use the same for fire, but in other parts they burn turf and sea coals brought out of England. They export great quantities of wood to make barrels, called pipe-staves, and make great gain thereby. They are not permitted to build great ships for war, but they have small ships, in some sort armed to resist pirates, for transporting of commodities into Spain and France, yet no great number of them. Therefore, since the Irish have small skill in navigation, as I cannot praise them for this art, so I am confident that the nation, being bold and warlike, would no doubt prove brave seamen if they shall practise navigation and could possibly prove industrious therein. I freely profess that Ireland in general would yield abundance of all things to civil and industrious inhabitants. And when it lay wasted by the late rebellion, I did see it after the coming of the Lord Mountjoy daily more and more to flourish, and in short time after the rebellion appeared, like the new spring, to put on the wonted beauty.

Touching the Irish diet, some lords and knights and gentlemen of the English-Irish, and all the English there abiding, having competent means, use the English diet, but some more some less cleanly, few or none curiously; and no doubt they have as great and for their part greater plenty than the English of flesh, fowl, fish, and all things for food, if they will use like art of cookery. Always I except the fruits, venison, and some dainties proper to England and rare in Ireland. And we must conceive that venison and fowl seem to be more plentiful in Ireland, because they neither so generally affect dainty food nor so diligently search it as the English do. Many of the English-Irish have by little and little been infected with the Irish filthiness, and that in the very cities, excepting Dublin, and some of the better sort in Waterford, where, the English continually lodging in their houses, they more retain the English diet. The English-Irish, after our manner, serve to the table joints of flesh cut after our fashion, with geese, pullets, pigs, and like roasted meats; but

The Diet.

their ordinary food for the common sort is of white-meats, and they eat cakes of oat for bread, and drink not English beer made of malt and hops, but ale. At Cork I have seen with these eyes young maids stark naked grinding of corn with certain stones to make cakes thereof, and striking off into the tub of meal such reliques thereof as stick upon their belly, thighs, and more unseemly parts. And for the cheese and butter commonly made by the English-Irish, an Englishman would not touch it with his lips though he were half-starved; yet many English inhabitants make very good of both kinds. In cities they have such bread as ours, but of a sharp savour, and some mingled with aniseeds and baked like cakes, and that only in the houses of the better sort.

At Dublin and in some other cities they have taverns wherein Spanish and French wines are sold, but more commonly the merchants sell them by pints and quarts in their own cellars. The Irish *aqua vitæ*, vulgarly called usquebaugh, is held the best in the world of that kind; which is made also in England, but nothing so good as that which is brought out of Ireland. And the usquebaugh is preferred before our *aqua vitæ* because the mingling of raisins, fennel-seed, and other things, mitigating the heat and making the taste pleasant, makes it less inflame, and yet refresh the weak stomach with moderate heat and a good relish. These drinks the English-Irish drink largely, and in many families —especially at feasts—both men and women use excess therein. And since I have in part seen, and often heard from others' experience, that some gentlewomen were so free in this excess as they would, kneeling upon the knee and otherwise, carouse health after health with men; not to speak of the wives of Irish lords or to refer it to the due place, who often drink till they be drunken, or at least till they void urine in full assemblies of men. I cannot, though unwilling, but note the Irish women more specially with this fault, which I have observed in no other part to be a woman's vice, but only in Bohemia. Yet, so accusing them, I mean not to excuse the men, and will also confess that I have seen virgins, as well gentlewomen as citizens, commanded by their mothers to retire after they had in courtesy pledged one or two healths.

In cities passengers may have feather beds, soft and good, but most commonly lousy, especially in the highways, whether that came by their being forced to lodge common soldiers or from the nasty filthiness of the nation in general. For even in the best city, as at Cork, I have observed that my own and other Englishmen's chambers, hired of the citizens, were scarce swept once in the week, and the dust then laid in a corner, was perhaps cast out once in a month or two. I did never see any public inns with signs hanged out, among the English or English-Irish; but the officers of cities and villages appoint lodgings to the passengers, and perhaps in each city they shall find one or two houses where they will dress meat, and these be commonly houses of Englishmen, seldom of the Irish, so as these houses having no signs hung out, a passenger cannot challenge right to be entertained in them, but must have it of courtesy and by entreaty.

The wild and (as I may say) mere Irish, inhabiting many and large provinces, are barbarous and most filthy in their diet. They scum the seething pot with an handful of straw, and strain their milk taken from the cow through a like handful of straw, none of the cleanest, and so cleanse, or rather more defile, the pot and milk. They devour great morsels of beef unsalted, and they eat commonly swine's flesh, seldom mutton, and all these pieces of flesh, as also the entrails of beasts unwashed, they seethe in a hollow tree, lapped in a raw cow's hide, and so set over the fire, and therewith swallow whole lumps of filthy butter. Yea (which is more contrary to nature) they will feed on horses dying of themselves, not only upon small want of flesh, but even for pleasure; for I remember an accident in the army, when the Lord Mountjoy, the Lord Deputy, riding to take the air out of the camp, found the buttocks of dead horses cut off, and suspecting that some soldiers had eaten that flesh out of necessity, being defrauded of the victuals allowed them, commanded the men to be searched out, among whom a common soldier, and that of the English-Irish, not of the mere Irish, being brought to the Lord Deputy, and asked why he had eaten the flesh of dead horses, thus freely answered, "Your Lordship may please to eat pheasant and partridge, and much good do it you that best likes your taste; and I hope it is lawful for me without offence to eat this flesh, that likes me better than beef." Whereupon the Lord Deputy, perceiving himself to be deceived, and further understanding that he had received his ordinary victuals (the detaining whereof he suspected, and purposed to punish for example), gave the soldier a piece of gold to drink in usquebaugh for better digestion, and so dismissed him.

The foresaid wild Irish do not thresh their oats, but burn them from the straw, and so make cakes thereof; yet they seldom eat this bread, much less any better kind, especially in the time of war. Whereof a Bohemian baron complained who, having seen the Courts of England and Scotland, would needs, out of his curiosity, return through Ireland in the heat of the rebellion; and having letters from the King of Scots to the Irish lords then in rebellion, first landed among them in the furthest north, where for eight days' space he had found no bread, not so much as a cake of oats, till he came to eat with the Earl of Tyrone; and after obtaining the Lord Deputy's pass to come into our army, related this their want of bread to us as a miracle, who nothing wondered thereat. Yea, the wild Irish in time of greatest peace impute covetousness and base birth to him that hath any corn after Christmas, as if it were a point of nobility to consume all within those festival days. They willingly eat the herb Shamrock, being of a sharp taste, which, as they run and are chased to and fro, they snatch like beasts out of the ditches.

Neither have they any beer made of malt or hops, nor yet any ale, no, nor the chief lords, except it be very rarely. But they drink milk like nectar, warmed with a stone first cast into the fire, or else beef broth mingled with milk. But when they come to any market town to sell a cow or horse, they never return home till they have drunk the price in Spanish wine (which they call the King of Spain's daughter) or in Irish usquebaugh, and till they have outslept two or three days' drunkenness. And not only the common sort, but even the lords and their wives, the more they want this drink at home the more they swallow it when they come to it, till they be as drunk as beggars.

Many of these wild Irish eat no flesh but that which dies of disease or otherwise of itself, neither can it scape them for stinking. They desire no broth, nor have any use of a spoon. They can neither seethe artichokes nor eat them when they are sodden. It is strange and ridiculous, but most true, that some of our carriage horses[1] falling into their hands, when they found soap and starch carried for the use of our laundresses, they, thinking them to be some dainty meats, did eat them greedily, and when they stuck in their teeth cursed bitterly the gluttony of us English churls, for so they term us. They feed most on white-meats, and esteem for a great dainty sour curds, vulgarly called by them Bonaclabbe. And for this cause they watchfully keep their cows, and fight for them as for religion and life; and when they are almost starved, yet they will not kill a cow except it be old and yield no milk. Yet will they upon hunger, in time of war, open a vein of the cow and drink the blood, but in no case kill or much weaken it. A man would think these men to be Scythians, who let their horses blood under their ears and for nourishment drink their blood; and indeed, as I have formerly said, some of the Irish are of the race of Scythians, coming into Spain and from thence into Ireland. The wild Irish, as I said, seldom kill a cow to eat, and if perhaps

[1] Sumpter horses.

they kill one for that purpose, they distribute it all to be devoured at one time; for they approve not the orderly eating at meals, but so they may eat enough when they are hungry, they care not to fast long. And I have known some of these Irish footmen serving in England (where they are nothing less than sparing in the food of their families) to lay meat aside for many meals, to devour it all at one time.

These wild Irish, as soon as their cows have calved, take the calves from them and thereof feed some with milk, to rear for breed, some of the rest they flay, and seethe them in a filthy poke, and so eat them, being nothing but froth, and send them for a present one to another. But the greatest part of these calves they cast out to be eaten by crows and wolves, that themselves may have more abundance of milk. And the calves being taken away, the cows are so mad among them as they will give no milk till the skin of the calf be stuffed and set before them, that they may smell the odour. Yea, when these cows thus madly deny their milk, the women wash their hands in cows' dung, and so gently stroke their dugs; yea, put their hands into the cow's tail and with their mouths blow into their tails, that with this manner, as it were, of enchantment, they may draw milk from them. Yea, these cows seem as rebellious to their owners as the people are to their Kings, for many times they will not be milked but of some one old woman only, and of no other. These wild Irish never set any candles upon tables—what do I speak of tables? since indeed they have no tables, but set their meat upon a bundle of grass, and use the same grass as napkins to wipe their hands. But I mean that they do not set candles upon any high place to give light to the house, but place a great candle made of reeds and butter upon the floor in the midst of a great room. And in like sort the chief men in their houses make fires in the midst of the room, the smoke whereof goeth out at a hole in the top thereof. An Italian friar coming of old into

Ireland and seeing at Armagh this their diet and the nakedness of the women, is said to have cried out—

"*Civitas Armachana, civitas vana,
Carnes crudæ, mulieres nudæ.*"

"Vain Armagh city, I did thee pity,
Thy meat's rawness and women's nakedness.

I trust no man expects among these gallants any beds, much less feather beds and sheets, who, like the Nomades removing their dwellings according to the commodity of pastures for their cows, sleep under the canopy of heaven, or in a poor house of clay, or in a cabin made of the boughs of trees and covered with turf, for such are the dwellings of the very lords among them. And in such places they make a fire in the midst of the room, and round about it they sleep upon the ground, without straw or other thing under them, lying all in a circle about the fire, with their feet towards it. And their bodies being naked, they cover their heads and upper parts with their mantles, which they first make very wet, steeping them in water of purpose; for they find that when their bodies have once warmed the wet mantles, the smoke of them keeps their bodies in temperate heat all the night following. And this manner of lodging not only the mere Irish lords and their followers use, but even some of the English-Irish lords and their followers when, after the old but tyrannical and prohibited manner vulgarly called coshering, they go, as it were, on progress, to live upon their tenants till they have consumed all the victuals that the poor men have or can get. To conclude, not only in lodging passengers not at all or most rudely, but even in their inhospitality towards them, these wild Irish are not much unlike to wild beasts, in whose caves a beast passing that way might perhaps find meat, but not without danger to be ill entertained, perhaps devoured, of his insatiable host.

APPENDIX.

I.

THE GERALDINES.

THE first Gerald of the Fitzgeralds was grandson to Walter Fitzother, who appears in Domesday Book as lord of manors in Surrey, Hampshire, Berkshire, Middlesex, and Buckinghamshire. That Gerald married Nesta, daughter of Rhys, King of South Wales. They had a son, Maurice Fitzgerald, who died in 1176. The same Nesta had a son by Stephen, Constable of Cardigan, and he was Robert Fitzstephen, half-brother to Maurice Fitzgerald. She had a son also by King Henry I., who was named Meilyr Fitzhenry. These three sons of Nesta went to Ireland together in 1169, where Dermod, King of Leinster, who had been seeking help in South Wales against those who had turned him out of his kingdom, promised that Maurice Fitzgerald and Robert Fitzstephen should have Wexford and the two adjoining cantreds given to them for their services. The King of Leinster obtained also letters patent from Henry II. saying, " Whosoever within our jurisdiction will aid and help him, our trusty subject, for the recovery of his land, let him be assured of our favour and license in that behalf." Dermod M'Murrough, seeking further, found Richard de Clare, Earl of Pembroke, surnamed Strongbow, ready to help him. In Strongbow's invasion of Ireland, Raymond Fitzgerald was the foremost leader of the English force. He married Strongbow's sister, who had been at first denied to him, but when he retired in dudgeon into Wales disaster followed, and want of his aid caused his recall, with full assent to his wishes. After the death of Strongbow, Raymond Fitzgerald ruled over the English in Ireland till the coming of William Fitzaldhelm, who set himself to despoil the Geraldines. But Raymond died master of Cork about the year 1182. Henry the Second had given him the middle cantred of Ophelan, Offaly, which is the district about Naas in Kildare. His son Gerald Fitzgerald, who had fought by his side, succeeded to his estates, and was known also as Lord of Offaly, which barony he held of the Earl of Pembroke. He was dead in 1204. His successor was a second Maurice, known also as Lord of Offaly, who became Justiciar of Ireland in 1232, an active defender of the King of England's interests. He died in 1258, and the barony passed to the son of his eldest son, who had died before his father. That grandson, another Maurice, was drowned in 1268, when crossing between England and Ireland. He left an infant, Gerald Fitzmaurice, for whom the barony was held against Irish attacks. The succession of Fitzgeralds now becomes confused. Along one line of Geraldines we come to John Fitzthomas, sixth Lord Offaly and first Earl of Kildare. A younger son of the Maurice Fitzgerald who fought by the side of Strongbow and founded the great family of the Geraldines was a Thomas Fitzmaurice, who had a son John Fitzthomas, killed at the battle of Callan in 1261, together with his son Maurice Fitzjohn, who had a son Thomas Fitzmaurice, Justice of Ireland in 1295. The son of the last-named Thomas was the Maurice Fitzthomas or Fitzgerald who married, in 1312, the daughter of Richard de Burgh, the second Earl of Ulster, who levied private war against Arnold le Poer for calling him a rhymer, and who in 1329, as a leader of the English colony, was created Earl of Desmond, with a grant to him of the County Palatine of Kerry.

THE GERALDINES.

That first Earl of Desmond came into conflict with the authority of England when Edward III. set on foot a policy that gave advantage to the English born in England over the English born in Ireland. His estates were forfeited, but, on his submission, afterwards restored to him, and in 1355 he was appointed Viceroy in Ireland. The first Earl of Desmond was the first prominent upholder of the claims of the descendants of those who first came over with Strongbow to be independent chiefs in Ireland. He died in 1356 while he still held office as Viceroy. Two sons of his, Maurice and John, became the second and third Earls of Desmond. The fourth Earl, Gerald Fitzgerald, was the son of the first Earl by his second wife. In 1367 he succeeded Lionel Duke of Clarence as Justiciar of Ireland. He went far in the adoption of Irish customs, was well versed in the Irish language and history, wrote verse, and made war with nobody for calling him Gerald the Poet. He died in 1398, but the Munster peasantry, who thought him a magician, said that he had only gone under the water of Lough Air near Limerick, whence he came up every seven years to pay a visit to his castle. His son John, the fifth Earl of Desmond, was drowned soon after his father's death, leaving a son Thomas, the sixth Earl, who was supplanted by his uncle James, third son of Gerald. James was seventh Earl, and his son Thomas Fitzgerald eighth. Thomas Fitzgerald, who succeeded in 1462 to the earldom, was in 1463 made Deputy to George Duke of Clarence, the Lord-Lieutenant of Ireland. He was executed at Drogheda in 1468, upon a charge urged against him by John Tiptoft, Earl of Worcester, who superseded him in his office. He was accused of fosterage and alliance with the Irish, giving the Irish horses, harness, and arms, and supporting them against the faithful subjects of the King. Four of his sons became, in succession, ninth, tenth, eleventh, and twelfth Earls of Desmond. James Fitzmaurice Fitzgerald, grandson of Thomas, was the thirteenth Earl, but his succession was disputed, and he was waylaid and killed by Sir Maurice of Desmond, a brother of the James Fitzmaurice who succeeded him as fourteenth Earl. A son of that Sir Maurice was the James Fitzmaurice Fitzgerald who was known as the Arch-Traitor in Elizabeth's reign. It was he who went to the Pope and planned an invasion of Ireland, came with the Pope's nuncio, Dr. Sanders, and landed in 1577 a few troops in the Fort del Ore in Smerwick Bay, where they were joined in a few days by two galleys with a hundred soldiers. James Fitzmaurice then sought in vain to bring his cousin, the Earl of Desmond, into the rebellion, and presently afterwards he was killed in a skirmish when on his way to pay a vow at the Monastery of the Holy Cross in Tipperary. His brother's son, Gerald Fitzgerald, who became in 1558 fifteenth Earl of Desmond, survived until 1583. He carried on an old family feud with the Butlers, but Sir Henry Sidney reported of him that "his light and loose dealing (whereunto he runneth many times rashly) proceedeth rather of imperfection of judgment than of malicious intendment against your Majesty." Dr. Sanders, however, sought to move the Earl of Desmond, who hesitated, and so fell under suspicion. On the 1st of November 1579 he was proclaimed a traitor.

Then he was driven into action and sacked Youghal, but his fortresses were captured in March and April 1580. In the year of the action of Lord Grey of Wilton at the Fort del Ore, Thomas Butler, the tenth Earl of Ormond, inheritor of the old feud between the Butlers and Fitzgeralds, and whose own territories his rival Desmond had once invaded, was made military governor of Munster, "to banish and vanquish those cankered Desmonds." He carried into Kerry fire and sword. In July 1580 he reported with satisfaction that within three months he had killed forty-six captains, eight hundred 'notorious traitors and malefactors,' and four thousand other persons. A price was set upon the Earl of Desmond's head. On the 15th of June 1581 he was surprised near Castlemange, and fled to the woods in his shirt. Driven to bay, he made head again, and escaped capture until November 1582, when he was taken by five soldiers, one of whom cut off his head to be sent into England. An Act of Parliament in 1586 declared his estate forfeited to the Crown. His elder son, James Fitzgerald, who after his birth in 1570 had Queen Elizabeth for godmother, had been brought to England by his mother in 1579, when she separated herself from her husband's fortunes. He was kept for sixteen years a prisoner in the Tower, where he was well educated. In 1600, when Tyrone's rebellion was at its height and the Geraldines added force to it, the unfortunate young man, who was of weak health, was carried to Ireland—very sea-sick on the way—with a patent of Earldom provisionally restored to him, and an allowance of £500 a ye r to show himself among his father's people as the true Earl and to win back their allegiance. He came back, and died soon afterwards, in November 1601.

II.

THE O'NEILLS.

THE family of the O'Neills was purely Irish. Camden speaks of a Neill the Great who was in Ulster about the year 431, before the coming of St. Patrick. About the year 1318, when the Scots tried to conquer Ireland, there was a Donald O'Neill, who, in letters to the Pope, called himself King of Ulster and true heir of all Ireland. After the time of our Civil Wars of the Roses, Henry, the son of Owen O'Neill, married a daughter of a Geraldine, who was Earl of Kildare. Their son, Con the Great, married another Geraldine, his mother's niece, and thought all titles, Prince, Duke, Earl, or Marquis, lower than the title of O'Neill.

In the year 1542, when Henry VIII. assumed the name of King of Ireland, the O'Neill of Ulster was a son of Con the Great, another Con O'Neill, surnamed Baccagh the Lame. He was among those who accepted Henry as their King, and was made Earl of Tyr-Owen or Tyrone. He had a reputed son, Matthew, called by the Irish Fardoragh, whose real father was said to be a smith at Dundalk. King Henry VIII. gave to Matthew O'Neill the title of Baron Dungannon. His Majesty suppressed 370 religious houses in Ireland, and usually attached their lands and revenues to the possessions of his new Irish peers. But although the religious houses of Ulster were formally given and granted to the King of England, under shelter of the O'Neills their inmates were left undisturbed until the reign of James I. Nevertheless, Con O'Neill, as Earl of Tyrone and liegeman of the King of England, lost favour with the northern Irish. He had a son Shane, who struck for independence, raised war in which Matthew O'Neill, Baron Dungannon, was killed, and Shane succeeded his father as the head of the O'Neills. Matthew left at his death an infant son, Aodh or Hugh O'Neill. An Act of the Irish Parliament in the 33rd year of Henry VIII. had made it a capital offence for an Earl of Tyrone to take the title of O'Neill.

Shane O'Neill took the title, and supported his supremacy by war with neighbours who disputed it, O'Reilly of Cavan, the O'Donnells of Tyrconnel, and M'Guire of Fermanagh. When Elizabeth became Queen, attempt was made to bring Shane O'Neill into some reasonable allegiance. Sir Henry Sidney reasoned with him, and was told that Con Baccagh had by the Irish laws no power of surrender; he had only a life-interest in his rank. Matthew was a bastard, and by the law of tanistry Shane was now chieftain for his life and only for his life. There was nothing that he had power to surrender except by the consent of his country. Afterwards Shane O'Neill went boldly to Elizabeth in London, with unkempt hair and followers in saffron shirts carrying battle-axes. He told the Queen that he was only following the laws of his country. The Queen, for the time, accepted him as an ally rather than as a subject, and he went home commissioned to make war upon the Scots of Dalriada, which he was most willing to do. But in the meantime Queen Elizabeth was pursuing her endeavour to make Ireland Protestant, and though the Act of Uniformity could only be enforced within the English Pale, she established clergy beyond the Pale and made a young Cambridge scholar, Adam Loftus, Archbishop of Armagh at the age of twenty-eight, with the Deanery of St. Patrick to be held while his Archbishopric was "in name and title only to be esteemed, without worldly emolument." English troops being then sent to occupy the cathedral of Armagh, Shane O'Neill burnt church and town. At last Shane O'Neill was killed by the

Scots in the year 1567, and his head was sent pickled in a pipkin to the Lord Deputy in Dublin. He was condemned after death as traitor by a Parliament in Dublin, and his lands were confiscated.

In Ulster, Tirlogh Lynnogh O'Neill, a grandson of Con the Great, was made chief in the place of Shane. The English Government hoped to educate into friendly allegiance young Aodh or Hugh O'Neill, son of the bastard Matthew. Tirlogh Lynnogh O'Neill was an old man who kept peace with Queen Elizabeth and all his neighbours except the Scots, among whom he found and killed Shane's murderer. Ulster was quiet and unmolested. Its Catholicism was left untouched. Hugh O'Neill accepted quietly his English training, and when he went to Ireland lived in peace at Dungannon without questioning the chieftain's rights settled in Tirlogh Lynnogh O'Neill. That was the state of things in Ulster during the first years of Spenser's residence in Ireland. In 1584 Hugh O'Neill joined Sir John Perrot, the Lord Deputy, in attack on the Scots in Claneboy and Tyr-Owen. The Scots were reduced, and Sir John Perrot, believing that he had secured the submission of the north, divided the country west of the Bann into seven new counties, Armagh, Monaghan, Tyrone, Coleraine, Donegal, Fermanagh, and Cavan. In London in 1587 Hugh O'Neill flattered Elizabeth, and won from her at last the restoration of his lands and title, with reservation of a piece of ground on the Blackwater for building of an English fortress. He went back to Dungannon. The Earl of Tyrone kept in the Queen's name six companies of troops on foot, taught them use of arms, then changed them for new men of his own, whom he also drilled. He imported lead, and it was said that he was casting bullets. In the end of 1588 Sir John Perrot was recalled, and Sir William Fitzwilliams sent as Lord Deputy into Ireland, Sir John Norreys being then Lord President of Munster, and Sir Richard Bingham Governor of Connaught. The course of events from this time may be passed over until, after many dissemblings, oppositions, and submissions, Hugh O'Neill found himself at the head of a strong northern league, and on the 14th of August 1598 defeated the English troops at Blackwater. Charles Blount, then a man of five-and-thirty, who on his elder brother's death in 1594 had become eighth Lord Mountjoy, had shown intellectual vigour and an appetite for war. He would have been sent to Ireland as Lord Deputy when Essex went, and failed. He followed Essex in February 1600, and found all Ireland outside Dublin in the rebels' hands. In December 1601 Tyrone marched, with the largest Irish army ever known, to relieve four thousand Spaniards in Kinsala, whom Mountjoy was besieging. Tyrone's army was defeated; the Spaniards surrendered and left the country. Mountjoy followed up his victory. In 1602 new forces came from England. Lord Mountjoy in the north and Sir George Carew in the south were masters of the country, and Tyrone was reduced to the offer of unconditional submission on the 22nd of December 1602. It was six days after the Queen's death, as we have seen already, that Mountjoy received Tyrone in state in Dublin; and when he left Ireland at the end of May, not to return again, he took O'Neill with him that he might make personal submission to King James.

The full story of Mountjoy's successes in the north is told by Fynes Moryson, his Secretary, in that "History of Ireland from the Year 1599 to the Year 1603," to which he added the "Description of Ireland." It was first published as a separate work in two volumes at Dublin in 1735, but it had been included in the folio, published in 1617, of Fynes Moryson's "Itinerary, containing his Ten Yeeres Travel through Germany, Bohmerland, Switzerland, Netherland, Denmark, Poland, Italy, Turkey, France, England, Scotland, and Ireland; in three Parts."

The full story of Sir George Carew's successes in the south is told in "*Pacata Hibernia*, Ireland appeased and reduced: or an

Historie of the late Warres of Ireland, especially within the Province of Mounster under the Government of Sir George Carew, Knight, then Lord President of that Province, and afterwards Lord Carew of Clopton, and Earl of Totnes, &c." This was published four years after the death of Carew, in 1633, in two volumes, including seventeen maps and plans. It was dedicated by Sir Thomas Stafford, its editor, to Charles the First. Sir Thomas Stafford had served under Carew in Munster, and was supposed to be his illegitimate son. Carew had antiquarian tastes, and his interest in Irish affairs caused him to leave notes and documents from which Sir Thomas Stafford shaped the *Pacata Hibernia*, which covered, like Fynes Moryson's History, the period from 1599 to 1602.

III.

CHARLES BLOUNT, LORD MOUNTJOY.

Described by Fynes Moryson in his "History of Ireland from 1599 to 1603."

ERE I take my pencil in hand to figure this noble lord's person, I must acknowledge my weakness such as I cannot fully apprehend his complete worthiness, and therefore desire that those of greater judgment to discern the same will impute all defects to the unskilfulness of the workman, and that with others to whom his lordship was less known my rude pen may not derogate anything from his due praise. Again, give me leave to remember that which I received from his mouth, that in his childhood, when his parents would have his picture, he chose to be drawn with a trowel in his hand, and this motto, *Ad rædificandum antiquam domum*, To Rebuild the Ancient House. For this noble and ancient barony was decayed, not so much by his progenitors' prodigality, as his father's obstinate addiction to the study and practice of alchemy, by which he so long laboured to increase his revenues, till he had almost fully consumed them. Now to the purpose, let us observe how he fulfilled this ominous presage, in rebuilding that noble House, till by his untimely death the same was fatally eclipsed again.

He was of stature tall, and of very comely proportion, his skin fair, with little hair on his body, which hair was of colour blackish, or inclining to black, and thin on his head, where he wore it short, except a lock under his left ear which he nourished the time of this war, and being woven up, hid it in his neck under his ruff. The crown of his head was in his latter days something bald, as the forepart naturally curled. He only used the barber for his head, for the hair on his chin growing slowly, and that on his cheeks and throat, he used almost daily to cut it with his scissors, keeping it so low with his own hand that it could scarce be discerned, as likewise himself kept the hair of his upper lip something short, only suffering that under his nether lip to grow at length and full; yet some two or three years before his death he nourished a sharp and short piquedevant on his chin. His forehead was broad and high; his eyes great, black, and lovely; his nose something low and short, and a little blunt in the end; his chin round; his cheeks full, round, and ruddy; his countenance cheerful, and as amiable as ever I beheld of any man; only some two years before his death, upon discontentment, his face grew thin, his ruddy colour failed, growing somewhat swarthy, and his countenance was sad and dejected. His arms were long, and of proportionable bigness; his hands long and white; his fingers great in the end, and his legs somewhat little, which he gartered ever above the knee, wearing the garter of St. George's Order under the left knee, except when he was booted, and so wore not that garter, but a blue ribbon instead thereof above his knee, and hanging over his boot.

The description of his apparel may be thought a needless curiosity, yet I must add some few words thereof, because, having promised the lively portraiture of his body as well as his mind, the same cannot otherwise be so lively represented to the imagination; besides that by his clothes some disabilities of his body to undertake this hard war may be conjectured, and especially the temper of his mind may be lively shadowed, since the wise man hath taught us that the apparel in some sort shows the man. His apparel in court and cities was commonly of white or black taffatas or satins, and he wore two, yea, sometimes three, pairs of silk stockings, with black silk grogram clocks, guarded, and ruffs

LORD MOUNTJOY.

of comely depth and thickness, never wearing any falling band; black beaver hats with plain black bands; a taffata quilted waistcoat in summer, a scarlet waistcoat, and sometimes both, in winter. But in the country, and specially keeping the field in Ireland (yea, sometimes in the cities) he wore jerkins and round hose, for he never wore other fashion than round, with laced panes of russet cloth, and cloaks of the same cloth, lined with velvet, and white beaver hats with plain bands. And besides his ordinary stockings of silk, he wore under boots another pair of woollen or worsted, with a pair of high linen boot-hose; yea, three waistcoats in cold weather, and a thick ruff, besides a russet scarf about his neck thrice folded under it, so as I never observed any of his age or strength to keep his body so warm. He was very comely in all his apparel, but the robes of St. George's Order became him extraordinarily well.

For his diet, he used to fare plentifully and of the best, and as his means increased, so his table was better served, so that in his latter time no lord in England might compare with him in that kind of bounty. Before these wars he used to have nourishing breakfasts, as panadas and broths; but in the time of the war he used commonly to break his fast with a dry crust of bread, and in the spring-time with butter and sage, with a cup of stale beer, wherewith in winter he would have sugar and nutmeg mixed. He fed plentifully both at dinner and supper, having the choicest and most nourishing meats with the best wines, which he drunk plentifully, but never in great excess; and in his latter years (especially in the time of the war, as well when his night sleeps were broken as at other times upon full diet) he used to sleep in the afternoons, and that long, upon his bed. He took tobacco abundantly and of the best, which I think preserved him from sickness, especially in Ireland, where the foggy air of the bogs and waterish fowl, plenty of fish, and generally all meats, with the common sort always unsalted and green roasted, do most prejudice the health.

For he was very seldom sick, only he was troubled with the headache, which duly and constantly, like an ague, for many years till his death, took him once every three months and vehemently held him some three days; and himself in good part attributed as well the reducing of this pain to these certain and distant times as the ease he found therein to the virtue of this herb. He was very neat, loving cleanliness both in apparel and diet, and was so modest in the necessities of nature as myself being at all hours but time of sleep admitted into his chamber, and I think his most familiar friends, never saw him use any liberty therein out of the privilege of his private chamber, except perhaps in Irish journeys where he had no withdrawing room.

The tender using of his body, and his dainty fare before the wars, gave Tyrone occasion, upon hearing of his coming over, to jest at him, as if all occasions of doing service would be past ere he could be made ready and have his breakfast. But by woful experience he found this jesting to be the laughter of Solomon's fool. His behaviour was courtly, grave, and exceeding comely, especially in actions of solemn pomps. In his nature he loved private retiredness, with good fare and some few choice friends. He delighted in study, in gardens, an house richly furnished and delectable for rooms of retreat, in riding on a pad to take the air, in playing at shuffle-board or at cards, in reading play-books for recreation, and especially in fishing and fish-ponds, seldom using any other exercises, and using these rightly as pastimes only for a short and convenient time, and with great variety and change from one to the other. He was undoubtedly valiant and wise. He much affected glory and honour, and had a great desire to raise his House, being also frugal in gathering and saving, which in his latter days declined to vice, rather in greedy gathering than in restraining his former bounties of expense. So that howsoever his retiredness did alienate his mind from all action, yet his desire of honour and hope of reward and advancement by the wars,—

yea, of returning to this retiredness after the wars ended,—made him hotly embrace the forced course of the war; to which he was so fitted by his wisdom, valour, and frugality, that in short time he became a captain no less wise, wary, and deliberate in counsel than cheerful and bold in execution, and more covetous in issuing the public treasure than frugal in spending his own revenues.

Touching his affecting honour and glory, I may not omit that his most familiar friends must needs observe the discourses of his Irish actions to have been extraordinarily pleasing to him; so that, howsoever he was not prone to hold discourses with ladies, yet I have observed him more willingly drawn to those of this nature, with which the Irish ladies entertained him, than into any other. And as he had that commendable, yea, necessary, ability of a good captain, not only to fight and manage the war well abroad, but to write and set forth his actions to the full at home, so I have seldom observed any omission of like narrations in him, whereof he used to dilate the more weighty seriously, and to mention the smallest, at least by way of jest.

. . . Of a layman he was the best divine I ever heard argue, especially for disputing against the papists out of the Fathers, Schoolmen, and above all out of the written Word, whereof some chapters were each night read to him, besides his never-intermitted prayers at morning and night. . . . He never used swearing, but rather hated it, which I have often seen him control at his table with a frowning brow, and an angry cast of his black eye.

www.ingramcontent.com/pod-product-compliance
Lightning Source LLC
Chambersburg PA
CBHW020534300426
44111CB00008B/664